THE CRITICAL PRAGMATISM OF ALAIN LOCKE

THE CRITICAL PRAGMATISM OF ALAIN LOCKE

*A Reader on Value Theory, Aesthetics, Community,
Culture, Race, and Education*

Edited by Leonard Harris

ROWMAN & LITTLEFIELD PUBLISHERS, INC.
Lanham • Boulder • New York • Oxford

ROWMAN & LITTLEFIELD PUBLISHERS, INC.

Published in the United States of America
by Rowman & Littlefield Publishers, Inc.
4720 Boston Way, Lanham, Maryland 20706

12 Hid's Copse Road
Cumnor Hill, Oxford OX2 9JJ, England

British Library Cataloguing in Publication Information Available

Library of Congress Cataloging-in-Publication Data

The critical pragmatism of Alain Locke : a reader on value theory,
aesthetics, community, culture, race, and education / edited by
Leonard Harris.
    p. cm.
    Includes bibliographical references and index.
    ISBN 0–8476–8807–0 (cloth : alk. paper). — ISBN 0-8476-8808-9
(pbk. : alk. paper)
    1. Afro-Americans—Intellectual life. 2. Afro-American
aesthetics. 3. Afro-Americans—Race identity. 4. Afro-Americans—
Education. 5. Pluralism (Social sciences)—United States.
6. Locke, Alain LeRoy, 1886–1954—Philosophy. 7. Values.
8. Pragmatism. I. Harris, Leonard., 1948– .
E185.6.C925 1999
305.896073—dc21   98–47886
                                                                    CIP

Printed in the United States of America

For Eugene Harris Sr. and Agnes Chappell Harris,
on behalf of their children, who carry on in their memory:
Eugene Jr., Geraldine, Marlene, Agnes, and I.

For people who carried me when I thought
I was walking but was lying still;
who, when I fell, caught me so that I never hit the ground;
who, when I read it wrong, provided the best interpretation:
L. Nawatu Harris, Jarrard L. Harris,
Jamila R. Harris Grant, Joyce Cotton, Kube Jones,
Diane Gibson, Lucius Outlaw, William McBride,
Judith M. Green, J. Everett Green, Caroline Johnson,
Vernon Williams, and my spirit guardian, Linda Lucas.

For future owners of the world we help create:
Jaliyah R. and Jade R. Grant.

Contents

PART III. COMMUNITY AND CULTURE

PART IV. EDIFICATION AND EDUCATION

PART V. PARADOXES, DILEMMAS, AND CRITIQUES

PART VI. POSTSCRIPT

Preface

Alain Locke was a pragmatist. However, "pragmatism" is an inadequate name for Locke's philosophy. It fails to capture the radical implications of Locke's approach within pragmatism: the critical temper embedded in his works, the central role of power and empowerment of the oppressed, and the concept of broad democracy that Locke employed. The school of thought that Locke can be accredited with initiating is what I describe as *critical pragmatism.*

Locke, in concert with other original developers of pragmatism, such as John Dewey, William James, and Jane Addams, rejected popular fundamentalist metaphysics, epistemology, and aesthetics. Pragmatism is noted for denying that philosophies grounded on metaphysical, epistemic, or aesthetic foundations are capable of providing substantive answers to pressing questions. Simultaneously, pragmatism is not noted for providing substantive direction or sustained commitment. This is arguably what Cornel West alludes to in *The American Evasion of Philosophy.* However, Locke, unique among pragmatists, insisted on the role of power in human affairs. Rather than romantic hopes for conflict resolution through dialogue, without providing for the role of desires, interests, and preferences, Locke works through conflict resolutions intended to foreground and respect diversity. Locke does not simply decry the misguided tendency to treat general categories—for example, the tendency to treat races, classes, or nations as objective entities with stable essences whereby each individual invidiously represents a kind—he also faces the challenge to identify moral imperatives and provide a model of representation. Locke confronted the most divisive social reality of his time—race—and offered an approach to representation and collective identity that sought to avoid Afro-kitsch as well as inauthentic color-blindness. In addition, Locke held a balanced aesthetic view of the beautiful as form and instrument, including the use of the aesthetic as advocacy. American democracy for Locke was hardly a finished social experiment, especially since it excluded most of the population from participation. However, democracy, if practiced throughout the world, offered for Locke the possibility of socially warranted change. This possibility was especially hopeful if tolerance, reciprocity, and diversity informed democratic sensibilities and values.

A general theory of value would describe preferences and traits endemic to human nature. It would also explain the vicissitudes of evaluations that rely on shifting preferences and traits. One reason that a general theory has eluded scholars is that the object of such a theory—values—is at best a term with multiple meanings and at worst a ubiquitous reference for all forms of emotion. Locke recognized that a general theory of value was more a wish than a likely reality. The most one could expect is a revisable list of general human preferences and traits. In the context of this fallibilism, Locke provides a rich critical pragmatism, one that refigures our approach to valuation but maintains hope for democratic values open to diversity.

Locke's critical pragmatism favors a visceral ontology; social entities are anabsolute. That is, ontological or general categories are fundamentally shifting entities. There are peoples, for example, and not biologically determined social groups with inalterable traits. The ontology of race in Locke's approach is arguably a heuristic or strategic ontology rather than one that grants an essence to ethnic, racial, religious, or national groups. There are reasoned debates about the effectiveness of social identities as a source of empowerment of the oppressed, but viable multicultural plurality of open identities was Locke's goal. The "critical" terminology I draw from the critical theory tradition.

Critical theory, whether post-Marxist, legal, race, or gender theory, is characterized by suspicion of an established philosophy. The critical theories of Jürgen Habermas and Herbert Marcuse, for example, offer a critique of classical Marxism. Such post-Marxist critical theorists question the certitude of Marx's epistemological methods and the cohesion and salience of Marx's ontological class categories. Critical race theorists believe that race is embedded in numerous categories, such as concepts of property and individual rights. Thus, for such authors, one target is traditional race relation theories that define societies in terms of fairly well defined racial categories that "relate" in healthy or unhealthy fashions. Critical race theorists find categories of race to be historically constructed and constantly in transition; that is, there are no stable racial ontological categories for such authors. However, critical race theorists hold that law, like all forms of language, is a servant of numerous interpretations, always informed by subjective and socialized values. Critical theorists share a suspicion of universal principles, epistemological methods as guides to certain truth, objective criteria, stable ontological categories, and practices that rely on presumed impartial actors or interpretations.

Critical theories are noted for a set of dismal failures: they rarely offer substantive alternatives that differ sufficiently from the criticized social order to provide definitive choices between unpleasant alternatives or offer moral imperatives. Post-Marxist critical theorists, for example, almost all remain socialist and have not offered justifications for social actions sufficient to motivate any worldwide significant social movements. Critical race theorists often maintain faith that civil law can provide just results. Their hope that racial categories will dissipate is rarely accompanied by the hope that private property, class distinctions, and forms of status rankings will dissipate. If a critical race theorist is pessimistic about the dissipation of racial categories, he or she is thereby left without a vision of a radically different future. In addition, the condemnation of theories and practices that treat abstractions and ontological categories as if they were real rather than heuristic categories, valuable for a given, temporal purpose, renders critical theory often bereft of resources for providing direction. Controversial cases, social dilemmas, and actual conflicts require substantive decisions. Deconstructing or revealing the subjective character of legal decisions, for example, does not thereby tell us what decisions we should make.

Locke's critical pragmatism arguably avoids the pitfalls of critical theory, anticipates its tremendous contribution to human liberation, finds a middle ground between objectivism and subjectivism, and offers an alternative to the limitations of classical pragmatism. This anthology introduces unique individual interpretations of Locke and critical reflections on his philosophy. Each author, in the spirit of Locke's critical temper, offers his or her own contribution to extremely difficult issues. Collectively, I believe they provide the basis for a Lockean critical pragmatism.

Critical Pragmatism and Value Theory

Nancy Fraser argues that Locke offers us "another pragmatism." The importance of this claim lies in providing those who propose a revival of pragmatism with several pragmatisms from which to choose. Fraser proposes that Locke's pragmatism differs from that of John Dewey, George Herbert Mead, Jane Addams, and W. I. Thomas in that his pragmatism is grounded in a critical theory of society, specifically the history and political economy of racism. Linking race with culture and political economy, Locke is able to escape the charge of idealism brought against classical pragmatists by giving sufficient weight to the "hard facts" of power and domination in social life.

Fraser's interpretation of the five lectures that make up Locke's *Race Contacts and Interracial Relations* allows us to position Locke in the pragmatist pantheon. On Fraser's account, we can read Locke's cultural nationalism as a strategically essentialist one. He rests his cultural politics on a social-theoretical substructure in which power and political economy are central. Locke's critical theory of race proposes a three-tiered analysis of the concept of race that encompasses political economy and culture. With this three-tiered analysis, Locke is able to lay the groundwork for his new "social conception of race." By linking cultural issues directly to the problem of inequality, Locke stresses the centrality of power in the regulation of group differences in the United States. This emphasis on power is to be contrasted with the mainstream traditional pragmatism that neglects power.

The final concern is the debate about multiculturalism. The debate, centering on the delinking of cultural differences from questions of power and political economy, highlights the weaknesses of mainstream pragmatist discussions of cultural pluralism. Locke avoids this by proposing an alternative multiculturalism that integrates a nonessentialist cultural politics with an egalitarian social politics. Fraser shows that while Locke's alternative pragmatism is not without its own inadequacies and political naïveté, he does offer us a pragmatism that recognizes the possible need for a dominated group to adopt a pragmatic cultural identity as a guard against, and a solution for, oppression.

Astrid Franke, in "Struggling with Stereotypes: The Problems of Representing a Collective Identity," addresses the problems confronted by Locke, who, when trying to destroy one set of stereotypes, finds himself creating another. Diversification in collective identities, for example, is always contrary to the stability of collective identities; however, recognizing that there is diversity within collective groups is crucial for a healthy identity. Simultaneously, Locke appeals to folk images, images undermined by class divisions and modernity.

Franke considers the import for Locke's approach to representation by his appeal to different images. Locke applauds the urban reality of Harlem, for example, as well as the melting-pot image of integration. Franke inquires how, and whether, it is possible to represent African Americans and retain respect for individuality or avoid establishing a frozen identity. In addition, Franke reviews Locke's conception of the aesthetic and the way it overcomes the dualism of individual versus social representations. Franke considers the strategies Locke uses to overcome problems associated with debunking illegitimate stereotypes while invariably creating others. Locke, on Franke's account, avoids simplistic antistereotypes, although the vagueness and oscillation of some of his concepts can tend to create just another stereotype; yet the dynamism of his approach to representation makes possible a continuous search for new consensus and a sense of self-worth, always negotiating new images.

In "Values and Language: Toward a Theory of Translation for Alain Locke," Sally J. Scholz argues that Locke's theory of value provides us with a Lockean linguistics that meets the requirements set out for a feminist linguistics. Scholz compares Locke's views with Quine's pragmatic approach to translatability. The chapter is ordered in three sections: the first sets out Quine's indeterminacy of translation; the second discusses Locke's conception of values and how it can be mapped onto Quine's translation theory; and the final section lists the requirements for a feminist linguistics as given by Andrea Nye. Scholz explains how Lockean linguistics is able to meet Nye's requirements. Scholz says that by challenging the notion of "pure knowledge" and "absolute truth," Locke has also challenged the notion that there is a determinate or correct translation that preserves meaning and truth from a sentence to its translation. For Locke, values are a function both of structure and of the subject's attitude. His theory of meaning for this reason is compatible with a Quinean notion of stimulus meaning. Scholz concludes that given Locke's functional view of values, indeterminacy of translation can be seen as a manifestation of unity in cultural diversity, as well as transvaluation.

Drawing from Locke's view of value, Scholz argues that her derivative Lockean theory of languages grounded in his cultural relativism is able to account for the interpretation of incommensurable languages. Translation takes on the role of relaying specific cultural or subjective commitments. In the final section, she explains how this works in the development of a feminist linguistics. By analyzing requirements for such a linguistics, Scholz shows that Locke, through his work in value theory, has provided future generations of feminist linguists with a model from which to work.

Mark Helbling's "African Art and the Harlem Renaissance" argues that Franz Boas, Melville Herskovits, Alfred Stieglitz, Paul Guillaume, Roger Fry, and Albert C. Barnes—names not always associated with the Harlem Renaissance—were important contributors to that communal project. One way to see these important links is to consider Locke's approach to the relationship of African and African American art. Helbling argues that we should move beyond the view that Locke, and the Harlem Renaissance generally, only fostered a sort of stereotypical Afro-kitsch. Locke offers important distinctions between classical and modernist concerns, as well as the concerns and techniques of African and African American artists. He anticipates criticism of aesthetic essentialism made by Cornel West, Henry Louis Gates, and Anthony Appiah. In concert with Houston Baker, George Hutchinson, and others, Helbling focuses on the context of modernization, Locke's criticism of all absolutisms, and the distinctions Locke made in developing his approach to African art.

"Alain Locke's Multicultural Philosophy of Value," by Judith M. Green, describes the intellectual tension within feminist, postmodernist, and Africana philosophers who long for "unity amid diversity" and yet are skeptical of the possibility of its occurrence. She argues that Alain Locke's philosophy of value "offers important elements of both the theoretical and practical guidance needed to transform current global patterns of violent ethnic value strife into peaceful multicultural collaboration amid differences." Such elements are cross-cultural norms of tolerance and reciprocity. The explication of these elements is expanded with discourse on the principles of cultural equivalence, cultural reciprocity, and limited cultural convertibility. Green maintains that by understanding that unity does not require uniformity, it is clear that unity is fully compatible with diversity and that "the quest for unity so understood need not lead to oppression of the less powerful and repress interchanges within or between cultures, as some feminist and Africana critics have feared."

Aesthetics

The fallibility of reasoning methods is endemic to pragmatic sensibilities. Locke offers an aesthetic dimension, not based on a model of emotive essentialism, classical puritanism, or natural science.

Richard Shusterman's "Pragmatist Aesthetics: Roots and Radicalism" establishes that combining advocatory theory with detailed practical criticism is the best method of pragmatist aesthetics. Shusterman reviews the major contributory features of pragmatic aesthetics and their development and design by Locke. Pragmatic aesthetics emphasizes the importance of time, place, and situation. Locke, however, on Shusterman's interpretation, brings out the importance of unity through diversity and exemplifies a pragmatic balance of form and instrumentality.

Shusterman covers Locke's value theory and the way that theory lends itself to a strategy for handling the heuristics of representation, including racial representation. Locke's approach risks a form of overgeneralized racial essentialism yet presages a defensible form of advocacy of racial representation under conditions of duress. A critical facet of pragmatic aesthetics is the creation of respect for different cultural traditions. A crucial factor in improving social attitudes of self-deprecation as well as social disdain for a group is to increase respect for the social and cultural traditions that produce the artworks in question; and here the pragmatic style of aesthetic advocacy can play a major role. If value, as Locke argues, is essentially experiential and affective, a way to gain a deep respect for a cultural tradition is through a deep, affective experience of representative works rather than a stereotypical or cursory association. The advocacy feature of art is subject to continual revaluation and appreciation and is an important feature that Locke brings to, and creates within, the pragmatist tradition.

Jane Duran and Earl L. Stewart's "Alain Locke, Essentialism, and the Notion of a Black Aesthetic" covers Locke's aesthetic essentialism. Aesthetic essentialism is the view that "properties of the artistic works of a given cultural or racial group are essentially, or universally, related to members of that group." Locke's advocacy approach entailed this view, and Duran and Stewart provide a rich assessment of its strengths and weaknesses. Anthony Appiah's, Paulin Hountondji's, and Tommy Lott's critical views of essentialist conceptions of Black or African experiences, philosophy, and art are considered for their contributions to an appreciation of the limitations of essentialist approaches. Claudia Mills's critical perception of the view that "individuals representing the experiences [which would form the basis of a philosophy] of group A should (generally or even always) be members of group A" is a cautionary consideration when considering the possibility of delineating the requirements and conditions of a Black aesthetic. Locke's views of authenticity, expressionism, and formalism are addressed, with particular attention to Tommy Lott's rejection of the possibility of a Black aesthetic. Rather than a broad and sweeping aesthetic essentialism, Duran and Stewart take account of the advocacy role of Locke's approach in its context and offer a provocative refiguring of a limited version of aesthetic essentialism focused on historical continuities and music.

Richard Keaveny's "Aesthetics and the Issue of Identity" considers the ideas of W. E. B. Du Bois and Locke regarding the pursuit of the aesthetic as an essential quality of the pursuit of a collective identity. The tension between the aesthetic, as a quality to be appreciated for its own sake, and the pursuit of collective identity was a deeply divisive issue. The two authors differed in their assessments of which of those pursuits should be primary. As a social scientist and a historian, Du Bois viewed the struggle of the African American minority in America as an event-based linear struggle toward the acceptance of African American equality. In contrast, as a philosopher, Locke envisions the struggle of the African American as a dialectical struggle posing the African and the American cultures on either end of a spectrum and producing the African American culture in the synthesis. Locke rejects absolutism, dogmatism, and universalism. Thus, on Keaveny's account, Locke believes that "the common man . . . sets up personal, private and group norms as standards and principles, and rightly or wrongly hypostatizes them as universals for all conditions, all times and all men." Locke believes in the constant evolution of culture and rejects the view that African America culture was arrested as a result of slavery and prejudice. Locke, in contrast to Du Bois, on Keaveny's account, argues in favor of art for art's sake, while recognizing that art performs numerous social functions. Locke favors the free reign of expression. Keaveny skillfully evaluates the polemical struggle over the role of art.

Rudolph V. Vanterpool's "Open-Textured Aesthetic Boundaries" argues persuasively against aesthetic essentialism and in favor of a transcendent aesthetics that appreciates the historic contributions of W. E. B. Du Bois and Alain Locke. Locke's tendency to glorify the "ancestral arts of Africa helped black artists to concentrate on dynamic racial subject matter in their works"; however, to the extent that racial essentialism is a by-product of these glorifications, it needs to be supplanted by a more liberating *race-transcending* aesthetic. For Vanterpool, "artmaking is predicated on the assumption that the core aesthetic categories are socially constructed and are not universal absolutes." Art has penetrable cultural boundaries.

The paradigm of race transcendence significantly demystifies the symbols of race identity. Echoing Cornel West, who warns against racial reasoning that contends that there "is a black essence that all black people share" and the view "that there is one black perspective to which all black people should adhere," Vanterpool favors a complex approach to multiple identities. Multi-faceted experiences of otherness reveal as much as they conceal, Vanterpool argues. Moreover, "oppositional discourse on *otherness* serves constructive ends." Vanterpool offers a way of escaping the confines of modernist categories while yet addressing the needs of multi-identities, unique communities, and oppositional discourse.

Community and Culture

The conflict between communitarians and liberals is a conflict between those who differ on the relative importance of inherited bonds between persons and individual rights. Pragmatists normally believe that such conflicts can be resolved by dialogue rather than by reference to a prefigured theory of either community or individual rights. The role of culture in the debate, however, has often been ignored. Locke foregrounds the significance of culture in considering the import of democracy, community, race, ethnicity, and cultural conflict.

Greg Moses's "Two Lockes, Two Keys: Tolerance and Reciprocity in a Culture of Democracy" argues that the philosophy of Alain Locke calls attention to the reciprocal imperatives of democracy and invites deeper commitments to progressive reform. By placing emphasis upon collective forms of society as found in groups, cultures, and "psychological tribes," Locke encourages pluralistic paths to peace and power, substituting an ethic of reciprocity wherever the will to power would prevail. Locke proposes that once "our varied absolutes are revealed as largely the rationalization of our preferred values," and once we realize that their impulse stems "more from the will to power than the will to know," we see clearly that such conflicts cannot be explained or reconciled by resort to a common, rational plane; then we can try to arrange the field of conflict in such a way that reasoned desires of each side proliferate. In this manner we do not discount the "emotional and functional incommensurability of values in conflict"; rather, "we realize their complementary character in human experience."

Locke's concept of value pluralism involves two important corollaries: the principle of tolerance and the principle of reciprocity. His notion of tolerance, on Moses's account, draws upon the work of John Locke, but whereas John Locke's epistemology emphasized the experience of individual judgment as individual choice, Locke calls attention to the ways that we cultivate attitudes as socialized norms. And whereas John Locke encouraged tolerant dialogue as a means to improve our individual judgment-making process, Locke encourages intergroup reciprocity as a way to enhance our normative cultural process of attitudinal socialization. No doubt the old conception of tolerance is helpful to Locke, but he seeks especially to avoid forms of tolerance in the liberal tradition that are little more than "attitudes of condescension" that mask an underlying will to power. Thus Locke's principle of democratic reciprocity, for Moses, is meant to raise human encounter to a plateau of mutual engagement and interaction.

Charles Molesworth's "Alain Locke and Walt Whitman" explores the similarities between Walt Whitman and Locke with respect to their views about national identity within a democracy. Molesworth describes how Locke's essay "The American Temperament" combines elements of political analysis, social psychology, historicizing sensibility, and an aesthetic imagination to try to represent the national character. This echoes Whitman's work *Democratic Vistas*. According to Molesworth, Locke shares Whitman's commitments to the alignment between the artistic self and the national character that is at the heart of Whitman's project.

Molesworth proposes that Locke aligns the aesthetic and national dimensions in a dual facet of art: art must serve as a means of personal expression and group experience. While Whitman undoubtedly commits himself to democracy, embracing all forms of American art with hope, Locke's egalitarian democracy is tempered by his personal experiences abroad with national differences, his experience with the internal contradictions present in American democracy, and his elitist training and preferences for "high culture." Locke asserts that a group's identity is known only by the group's relations with other groups, offering a definition of identity, both public and individual, grounded in difference. This is where the author believes Locke and Whitman diverge.

Verner D. Mitchell's "Alain Locke: Philosophical 'Midwife' of the Harlem Renaissance" considers Locke's history narrowly, in African American circles. As the new century was coming into full swing, Locke was by any objective yardstick among the nation's most well trained intellectuals. But even with his impressive academic pedigree, Locke would have been hard pressed to land a job at any of America's white universities. He accepted an instructor position at Howard University in 1912. There he founded the department of philosophy in 1918 and served as its chair for the next thirty-five years. Throughout his career, Locke wrote on topics ranging from philosophy and political science to literature, art, and music. Locke played a leading role in the artistic movement of the Harlem Renaissance, encouraging and nurturing the great outpouring of fiction, social discourse, visual art, dance, and poetry that flourished when Harlem "was in vogue." Yet for Locke there were paradoxes and incongruities. Like Du Bois, he believed that talented Black artists should function as "the advance-guard of the African peoples" to rehabilitate "the race in world esteem." His conservative aesthetic views eventually clashed with the artistic tastes of the younger generation. Mitchell explores the conflict between the world of elitism and the desire to represent folk culture.

Clevis Headley, in "Alain Locke: A Sociocultural Conception of Race," addresses Locke's approach to race as a social construction, drawing on that side of Locke's works that attempts to defend African American culture. Headley rejects the view that "talk about race sustains racism." On some accounts, race is a semantically invalid concept that warrants immediate removal from our thinking. All racialist thinking, on this account, is misleading to the extent that this thinking embraces the notion of race. Alain Locke's conception of race provides an interpretation, according to Headley, that transcends this analytic approach. Locke seeks an alternative conceptual space for the concept of race that precludes declaring race hopelessly meaningless even if it is impossible to provide a plausible scientific or anthropological definition of race. Locke aggressively distances the concept of race from biological entanglement; instead of viewing race as semantically destined to find a home in biology, he cultivates a conception of race nourished by highly suggestive cultural insights. To this extent, he focuses particularly "on the political [and cultural] implications of human beings in concrete historical and social contexts." His lesson is that despite the marvelous analytical skills we competently employ to question the concept of race, issues of empowerment remain. Locke acknowledges the frustrations associated with attempts to provide criteria for the definition. Race, according to Locke, is a collective construction. It is a conceptual artifact burdened with discharging various social and cultural tasks; the semantic character of race and its instrumental and social malfunctions are distinct.

Kenneth W. Stikkers, in "Instrumental Relativism and Cultivated Pluralism," argues that African American philosophy generally and Locke in particular have not abandoned the search for a common world in deference to the quietism of relativism. Stikkers argues that African American philosophy, analogous to feminist philosophy, is a legitimate quest. The political agenda of concern with human liberation and the ending of oppression in the works of such authors as Broadus Butler, Angela Davis, and Du Bois, Stikkers contends, should deeply influence philosophizing. Locke, on Stikkers's account, "teaches" Dewey numerous nuances of a defensible conception of democracy. Stikkers notes several features of Locke's philosophy that benefit his interpretation, despite the unfortunate use of the term "relativism," which tends to be understood in absolutist terms. Stikkers provides a unique interpretation of Locke that focuses on the role of Josiah Royce's concept of loyalty.

Edification and Education

Conceptions of epistemology, especially as they relate to education, often proffer a single method by which we can gain knowledge. However, Locke's approach to edification and education is predicated on an appreciation of cultural differentiation. Thus, no single method is recommended for education. Rather, edification is informed by differentiation. There is no algorithm for truth or edification, but there are preferred approaches and attitudes.

"Adult Education and Democratic Values," by Talmadge C. Guy, links Locke's work on democracy with his work on education to provide a revealing picture of the rarely discussed efforts of African American educators and activists to build an adult education movement and meet the educational needs of African American adults. This essay provides Locke's rationale and model for African American adult education, covering the period of the late 1930s and early 1940s during which interest grew in the nascent African American adult education movement. Guy draws on discussions at a series of conferences on adult education and the Negro held from 1938 to 1941 along with the publication of syllabi on African American issues and a national program of adult education. In a 1938 keynote speech before the First Conference on Adult Education and the Negro at Hampton Institute in Virginia, Locke offered a definitive approach. The caste condition of African Americans was difficult to justify in a society alleging to hold democratic values; moreover, the use of cultural pluralism as a surreptitious justification for segregation was difficult to maintain. Locke's attention to the peculiar problems of the American democracy and race meant the rethinking of democracy and cultural pluralist principles. In addition to presenting Locke's approach to adult education as a method to help resolve racial conflict, Guy takes account of the tension between education as an elitist enterprise and popular edification.

LaVerne Gyant, in "Alain Locke and His Contributions to Black Studies," argues persuasively for considering Locke's contribution to education in a broad field of scholars who have shaped the theoretical foundations of Black studies. Locke has been noted for his contribution to adult education and the Harlem Renaissance and, on occasion, for his contribution to multicultural education. However, Gyant focuses on the import of Locke's arguments and historical contributions in establishing a warrant for, and an incentive to undertake, the study of the culture and history of African Americans. Locke's Herculean labors occurred during a period when African American culture and history were often the object of derision. Gyant explores the positive roles that Black studies have played in contributing to the alteration of self-deprecating consciousness and demeaning cultural roles. Gyant compares the content of Locke's work to important subjects and themes that various authors believe enliven Black studies programs. By linking Locke's works to various trends in Black studies, Gyant establishes that Locke's works have played positive roles in a broad array of approaches, including those of thinkers who are often at odds. In this fashion, Gyant explores numerous variables that shape debates about the role of African American culture and history.

Rudolph A. Cain's "Andragogy and the Education of African American Adults" presents the work of Alain Locke in the context of adult education. Such education, which Cain conceptually categorizes as *andragogy,* "presupposes a set of assumptions about how adults learn, as opposed to pedagogy, which focuses on how youth learn." Cain contends that Locke was an andragogue in the sense that he recognized that adult education required alternative instructional methods and materials other than those used in conventional pedagogy. Cain notes three reasons given by Locke to support the need for adult education: (1) youth education alone is insufficient to sustain one in adulthood; (2) recurrent education is necessary to keep pace with changing world conditions; and (3) the demands of an increasingly technological society require new strategies for living. Moreover, the needs and learning styles of adults differ from those of young learners. Locke's approach takes this into account. Cain argues in favor of Locke's approach to teaching adults and advocates the implementation of audio and visual aids, particularly in the education of African Americans. He begins by presenting an explication of andragogy, via Malcolm Knowles, and builds upon this concept with Locke's writings to argue for an African-centered approach to African American adult education.

Blanche Radford Curry's "Alain Locke: A Paradigm for Transformative Education" acknowledges the need expressed by Locke in 1950 to " reform the abstract, neutral, and contentless critical thinking that was the paradigm for reasoning methodologies and logical techniques." Curry shares Locke's desire to negotiate the channel between the philosophical and the educational in the quest to address common objectives of knowledge. For this task Locke calls for a "New Organon in Education." Curry analyzes Locke's work as a paradigm for a transformative model of education. She notes the emphasis that Locke placed on the conjunction of values and education, arguing that values provide an initial point of contact between thought and actual living. Identifying Locke's methodological approach to a transformative model of education as "critical relativism," Curry proceeds by maintaining that critical relativism provides a systematic program of value analysis in response to rigid value conceptions and dogmatism in that it allows for successful multicultural education.

Paradoxes, Dilemmas, and Critiques

Segun Gbadegesin's "Values, Imperatives, and the Imperative of Democratic Values" raises numerous paradoxes and dilemmas regarding Locke's value theory, a theory that influences all of Locke's work. This chapter evaluates the major categories and distinctions explicitly and implicitly entailed by Locke's value theory. In addition, Locke's defense of functionalism is substantially reviewed. Gbadegesin queries in what sense Locke may be committed to some version of absolutism or foundationalism and whether Locke has a way of avoiding Protagorean relativism (absolute relativism and subjectivism) as well as uniformitarianism and scientific objectivism. In addition, Gbadegesin takes account of Locke's views on education, culture, and democracy to consider the import of his revealing analysis. Gbadegesin confronts difficult issues, such as value conflicts between militarism and democracy, in the context of whether Locke's value pluralism offers a defensible approach. Gbadegesin's cutting-edge critique of Locke forces a continued rethinking of major distinctions.

"Meaning in an Epistemic System," by Stephen Lester Thompson, is a critical approach to Locke's linguistic theory and relativist inclinations. Thompson begins by pointing out that there is no consensus among Locke scholars with regard to meaning. Thompson defines his project as showing why some accounts that have been offered, particularly those of Ernest Mason and Leonard Harris, are unpromising. Both, for Thompson, fall under the category of deconstructivist.

Thompson gives his own account of what Locke takes to be the semantic gap, from which the facts about meaning can be inferred. After this account, according to Thompson, the problems with the deconstructivist notion of meaning are discernible. Thompson suggests that Locke begins by determining the presence of the semantic gap that shows that meaning has both a loose and a tight relationship to what we know and what we value. The semantic gap is ineliminable in a normative sense. In seeking an epistemological justification for his relativism, Locke distinguishes between the symbol and the value, questioning the dangerous identification of the two. Moreover, according to

Locke, we should remain a bit suspicious of the symbols used to stand for values.

Having stated what he feels can be rightfully said about Locke's concept of the semantic gap, Thompson moves on to his criticism of Mason's and Harris's approaches to Locke. He takes both to be treating meaning and interpretation in Locke's relativism with a deconstructive qualification. The criticism that Thompson offers against Locke's account of meaning is that it is too strongly negative. He suggests that Lockeans ought to take Locke's commitment to, and optimism about, objective, systematic science seriously enough to try to reconcile it with his suspicion of absolutes.

Paul Weithman's "Alain Locke, Critical Relativism, and Multicultural Education" is a provocative counterpoint to Locke's view of education as a carrier of multiculturalism. Weithman criticizes Locke's critical relativism on the grounds that it is a self-defeating concept; that is, the culture out of which the concept comes is presumed to have an underlying sense of correctness. Weithman argues that critical relativism provides little security against validating the culture of the slaveholding South. Cultural reciprocity is therefore a dubious concept. Weithman contends that critical relativism is not necessary for multiculturalism to flourish. He further claims that while Locke advocates only a kind of "aesthetic multiculturalism," multicultural education can and should assume diverse forms for different purposes. He argues for the introduction of a multiculturalism that stresses education in economics, sociology, and philosophy, as well as literature, art, and poetry.

Postscript

Beth J. Singer's "Alain Locke Remembered" offers a unique window into Locke the person, as a teacher, as a scholar, as a human being within this all too fragile world where we too often ignore that philosophers are persons. Singer takes us on a journey through more than the life of the mind—the life of timeless moments of contact. It is fitting that we begin with Locke the high theorist and end with Locke the person: the person who lived the theory with all its fullness, fallibility, paradoxes, and fruitful guidance.

Acknowledgments

The pioneering work of Houston Baker and the late Arna Bontemps—courageously reevaluating Locke and the Harlem Renaissance when it was fashionable to disdain the sheroes and heroes of modernity—contributions to Locke's history by Esme Bhan and Jeffrey Stewart, and the theoretically rich work of the late Ernest Mason are the pillars upon which much of this anthology stands.

I am grateful to JoEllen P. ElBashir, Daphne Thompson, Dorothy Washington, and Carol Black, who provided invaluable help and friendship throughout this project.

And I would like to thank the folks of the Alain L. Locke Society and the Philosophy Born of Struggle Association, especially J. Everett Green, Zia Green, James Williams, Judith M. Green, Blanche Radford Curry, and Beth J. Singer, for being there on the front line with love.

I am also appreciative of the support provided by the Department of Philosophy, Addis Ababa University, especially Girma Taye, and by the Fulbright Scholarship program.

The Philosophy Born of Struggle Conference IV, held 16–17 October 1997 at the New School for Social Research included a session sponsored by the Alain L. Locke Society. The chapters by Blanche Radford Curry, Nancy Fraser, Judith M. Green, and Beth J. Singer were originally presented at that conference. The Jerrico Project, under the auspices of William Hardy, Tennessee State University, maintains the videotapes of the Philosophy Born of Struggle conferences, which have been held annually since 1994 under the management of J. Everett Green. The chapters by Kenneth W. Stikkers and Segun Gbadegesin were originally presented at the World Congress of Philosophy, Boston University, 15 October 1998. The chapter by Sally J. Scholz was originally prepared as a paper in a graduate course taught in 1996 by the editor, Identity and Difference, and was later revised by Dr. Sally J. Scholz. The contribution by Jane Duran and Earl L. Stewart was originally presented, in November 1995, at the American Society for Aesthetics. Paul Weithman's chapter was originally written as a commentary on Blanche Radford Curry's essay "Alain Locke: A Provocative Analysis of Multicultural Education" for the Alain Locke Society session at the American Philosophical Association on 30 December 1996. The remaining chapters were submitted for this volume at the request of the editor.

Chapter 1, by Nancy Fraser, was published in *The Revival of Pragmatism: New Essays on Social Tought, Law, and Culture,* edited by Morris Dickstein (Durham, N.C.: Duke University Press, 1998), pp. 157–75, and is reprinted by permission of the author and Duke University Press. Chapter 17 was published in *Alain LeRoy Locke: Race, Culture, and the Education of African American Adults,* by Rudolph A. Cain (Rodopi, Amsterdam–Atlanta, GA, 1999), and is reprinted with the kind permission of Rodopi.

PART I

CRITICAL PRAGMATISM AND VALUE THEORY

1

Another Pragmatism: Alain Locke, Critical "Race" Theory, and the Politics of Culture

Nancy Fraser

In *The American Evasion of Philosophy,* Cornel West offers an unusually broad view of the pragmatist tradition. Far from restricting himself to the usual trinity of Peirce, James, and Dewey, West includes the life and thought of W. E. B. Du Bois.[1] In thus expanding the pragmatist canon to encompass a major body of critical reflection on "race" and racism in America, West also poses a challenge to anyone contemplating a revival of pragmatism today. We are challenged to cast a net wide enough to catch not only the concerns of Stanley Fish, Hilary Putnam, and Richard Rorty but also what Du Bois famously called "the problem of the color line," a problem certain to outlast the twentieth century and a crucial test for the pragmatist enterprise of using social intelligence to guide social practice.

In this chapter, I intend to take up Cornel West's challenge. I am going to discuss a recently rediscovered work by another African American theorist of "race" and racism who was trained in philosophy at Harvard under Josiah Royce and William James early in this century and who also deserves a place in the pragmatist pantheon. Alain Locke is remembered today primarily as an aesthetician. To be sure, he was the leading theorist of the Harlem Renaissance; the creator of "the New Negro"; the editor of the 1925 volume of that name, which anthologized Langston Hughes, Zora Neale Hurston, and Countee Cullen; and a prominent early exponent of the idea of a distinctive, syncretistic African American culture. But the work I shall discuss reveals a forgotten side of Locke. This Alain Locke is not only a theorist of culture and a proponent of black cultural nationalism; he is also a critical theorist of society, specifically of the history and political economy of racism. Even more important, he is a thinker who is grappling precisely with the tangled relations between culture, political economy, and "race" in ways that remain highly relevant today.

To introduce this relatively unknown Locke, I shall propose a reading of his

1916 lectures, "Race Contacts and Interracial Relations." Focusing on his account of the concept of "race" in this early, youthful work, I seek to illuminate four overlapping sets of concerns. The first is the interpretation and assessment of Locke's mature cultural nationalism. Much writing on the Harlem Renaissance assumes that he was naive in emphasizing black cultural production as opposed to economic interests and political struggle.[2] Yet the 1916 lectures reveal that his cultural politics rested on a social theoretical substructure in which power and political economy were central. Seen in this light, I shall argue, Locke was no simpleminded cultural nationalist but a sophisticated "strategic essentialist."[3]

My second concern is Locke's place in the broader field of critical theorizing about "race." The key debates in this field have often turned on the relative weight of political economy and culture in the construction of "race." The economistic side, best exemplified by the West Indian American Marxist sociologist Oliver Cromwell Cox, holds that "race" is a mystification of class, a superstructural ideological effect of the capitalist-imperialist organization of exploitation.[4] The culturalist side, exemplified in its essentialist form by the early W. E. B. Du Bois and in its more recent antiessentialist form by Kwame Anthony Appiah, holds that "race" is a cultural classification, corresponding for Du Bois to actual historical forms of human differentiation, corresponding for Appiah to nothing at all.[5] What is chiefly at stake in these debates is the remedy for racism: for the economistic side, the key to overcoming racism is economic transformation or redistribution; for the culturalist side, in contrast, it is cultural recognition or, more recently, deconstruction.[6] Yet Locke's 1916 lectures cast the issue in a different light. Proposing a novel, three-tiered analysis of the concept of "race," he was seeking to encompass both political economy and culture. The result should have been to expose the economism/ culturalism opposition as a false antithesis and to show that overcoming racism requires redistribution, recognition, and deconstruction. In fact, however, as we shall see, Locke did not himself draw that conclusion. Rather, he effectively endorsed Booker T. Washington's postponement of politics by proposing a "culture first" strategy. I hope to show, nevertheless, that Locke's early three-tiered account of the category of "race" constitutes an important contribution to critical "race" theorizing, one whose implications have still not been appreciated.

My third concern is the assessment of pragmatist social thought. Many commentators have noted the overly integrative and idealist character of the social thought of the classical pragmatists. Their many important insights notwithstanding, John Dewey, George Herbert Mead, Jane Addams, and W. I. Thomas are widely seen as having failed to give adequate weight to the "hard facts" of power and domination in social life.[7] Assuming the inevitable unfolding of an increasingly integrated world civilization, and emphasizing culture at the expense of political economy, they tended at times to posit imaginary, holistic "solutions" to difficult, sometimes irreconcilable, social conflicts. Yet Locke's 1916 lectures provide a glimpse of another pragmatism. Because he was theorizing about "race" and racism, he linked cultural issues directly to the problem of inequality; and he stressed the centrality of power to the regulation of group differences in the United States. Thus, in contrast to the mainstream pragmatists of the World War I period, Locke pioneered an approach to social theory that took domination seriously. He himself, however, did not consistently hew to this approach; he sometimes overestimated the integrative tendencies of modern societies, especially when assessing the prospects for Negro "assimilation" in the United States. I shall suggest, nevertheless, that his 1916 lectures contain the seeds of a version of pragmatist social thought that can escape the charge of idealism.

The fourth and final context for my reading of Locke is today's debates about multiculturalism. These debates tend at times to recapitulate the weaknesses of mainstream pragmatist discussions of "cultural pluralism" in the 1920s. Divorcing the question of cultural differences from questions of power and political economy, influential multiculturalists such as Charles Taylor implicitly treat ethnicity as the privileged model of social differentiation, as if group differences were simply cultural variations.[8] They tend accordingly to hypostatize culture, to neglect domination and group interaction, and to decouple the politics of recognition from the politics of redistribution.[9] Locke's 1916 lectures, in contrast, suggest the possibility of another approach. Grounding his understanding of group differences in an account of the history of domination and of international political economy, Locke developed a nonessentializing, syncretistic conception of culture that foregrounded group interaction. Implicit in Locke's approach, moreover, although by no means fully developed, is the prospect of an alternative multiculturalism that would integrate a nonessentialist cultural politics with an egalitarian social politics. Or so I shall suggest in what follows.

The Background of the 1916 Lectures

Race Contacts and Interracial Relations began as a series of five lectures that Locke delivered at Howard University in March and April of 1916. The lectures remained unpublished and were presumed lost until the transcriptions were discovered in the Howard archives in 1982. Edited and introduced by Jeffrey C. Stewart, the text of the lectures was published in 1992 by Howard University Press.[10]

At the time of the lectures Locke was thirty years old. He had not yet begun his Harvard Ph.D. work, but he had already completed his B.A. there in philosophy and English. He had also studied at Oxford, where he was the first African American Rhodes scholar (and the last until the 1960s!), and at the University of Berlin. As a Harvard undergraduate, Locke worked mainly with George Herbert Palmer and Josiah Royce. His exposure to William James, in contrast, was at this stage only indirect, via Horace Kallen, then a graduate student and Locke's teaching assistant in Greek philosophy. Locke and Kallen formed a close intellectual friendship, which continued when both men went to Oxford. According to Kallen, it was discussions with Locke in 1907 and 1908 about the significance of "racial differences" that gave rise to the expression "cultural pluralism," an expression that Kallen is credited with originating. It was at Oxford that Locke first encountered both fierce, visceral racism and an internationalist framework for interpreting it. Constrained by racist practices of exclusion to fraternize primarily with colonial students of color, he was exposed to anticolonialist and socialist critiques of imperialism. Later, at Berlin, he studied the social-interactionist sociology of Georg Simmel and the historical economics of Gustav Schmoller. Back in London for the Universal Race Congress of 1911, he appears to have heard Franz Boas's lecture "The Instability of Race Types." Refuting reigning anthropological views of fixed racial natures, Boas argued that civilizations progressed via cultural exchanges. Locke's 1916 lectures drew on these views and drew out their implications for the American Negro's struggle against racism. Before returning to the States, Locke traveled in Eastern Europe, observing ethnic antagonisms and the emergence of new nationalities. These he would treat in his lectures as products not of volkisch essences but of social interaction, historical economics, and cultural and political activism.[11]

Here, then, was the remarkable combination of intellectual influences that Locke brought back to the United States: a Roycean tendency to cast what appeared as differences in kind as differences in degree; a Jamesian view of an open pluriverse of human possibilities; a conception of cultural pluralism that served primarily to contest the "Americanization" of U.S. immigrants but that could be extended to the struggle against racism; a Boasian critique of racial essentialism; a nonessentialist understanding of nationalism; and a critical perspective on international imperialism. It was from these materials that Locke forged a distinctive synthesis in his Howard University lectures.

The immediate context provided two powerful impetuses to his thinking. The first was the steeply declining situation of African Americans since the 1890s. Disfranchisement, lynchings, debt peonage, and the imposition of Jim Crow laws in the South and in the federal government had mocked the hopes raised by Reconstruction. To justify segregation, meanwhile, a surge of racialist thinking pervaded intellectual life, including the universities. Locke's aim in the lectures was to rebut such thinking in hopes of reopening some space for "racial progress." The second critical impetus was World War I. An early and militant opponent of the war, Locke analyzed it as "an imperialist race war" in which the European powers fought over the spoils of colonialism, that is, for title to exploit peoples of color. But, in his eyes, the war nevertheless served to demystify imperialism's principal rationale. Showing themselves to be the true barbarians, the European belligerents could no longer credibly claim to be the bearers of a civilizing mission; their racialist ideology could now be delegitimated. "Race war" abroad and rampant racialism at home thus spurred Locke to rethink the question of "race."

Rethinking Race: A Three-Tiered Analysis

The aim of "Race Contacts and Interracial Relations" is at once simple and highly ambitious: to interrogate the concept of race from the ground up.[12] Noting that the term 'race' has not one meaning but many, Locke proposes to clarify the subject by distinguishing three principal levels of meaning and proceeding systematically to analyze them. Beginning with what he calls "the theoretical and scientific conceptions of race," he goes on to examine "the practical and political conceptions of race" and finally "the social conception of race." The point of the exercise is evaluative. Locke seeks through "scientific scrutiny of the various meanings . . . to discriminate among them and to perpetuate [only] those meanings—those concepts—which are promising and really sound" (*Race Contacts and Interracial Relations* [RCIR],1).

The result is an original analysis of race as a concept with three distinct tiers. The first, "theoretical" tier comprises biological and physical interpretations of race. The second, "practical" tier comprehends a political-economic interpretation of race as a construct of imperialist domination. The third, "social" tier encompasses modern forms of solidarity that could in principle be decoupled from domination. After distinguishing these tiers analytically, Locke subjects each of them to a distinctive mode of analysis: the theoretical conception is demystified, the practical conception is genealogized, and the social conception is reconstructed. Each conception, too, he evaluates for its promise and soundness, distinguishing those that can be "redeemed" and should be revised from those that cannot and must be dropped. Finally, the three levels of Locke's analysis are connected in an overarching argument. When the first, biological tier is shown to be beyond redemption, he is led to the second, political-economic tier in order to explain where the first tier originates and why it has enjoyed credibility. Likewise, when his political-economic critique establishes the practical basis of the concept of race in domination, Locke is led in turn to the third, social tier in order to determine whether and how a new understanding of race could serve the Negro's struggle *against* domination—without, however, resurrecting the retrogressive racialism that he has just so painstakingly demystified and without jeopardizing the larger solidarities he deems appropriate to a modern civilization. While each tier of Locke's analysis is impressive taken singly, the three taken together are a tour de force.

In what follows I want to explicate Locke's argument in some detail. Along the way, I shall pay special attention to what I take to be the key critical strands of his thought: his "strategic essentialism," his attempt to encompass both culture and political economy in the analysis of "race," his insistence on facing up to "the fact of domination," and his effort to envision a critical multiculturalism.

"Theoretical Race": A Demystification

Locke's first lecture, entitled "The Theoretical and Scientific Conceptions of Race," undertakes to explicate and evaluate the physical/biological meanings of the term. It is chiefly an exercise in demystification. Sketching a conceptual history of racialist theorizing from Gobineau to Boas, Locke exposes the epistemological deficiencies of pseudoscience. In the process, he anticipates virtually every argument recently made by the critics of *The Bell Curve*.[13]

Racialist thought conflates the descriptive enterprise of classifying human groups with the normative project of distinguishing "superior" from "inferior" groups. Casting racial inequalities as effects of prior racial differences, it inverts the proper order of causation and assumes what it claims to prove. More generally, these "theoretical conceptions of race" mistake what are actually sociocultural factors for biological and anthropological factors; they neglect the great variation within human groups while exaggerating variation among them. In addition, these theories maintain a false "fetish" of group purity. In fact, says Locke, soi-disant racial groups "have neither purity of blood nor purity of type. They are the products of countless interminglings [and] infinite crossings of types" (RCIR, 10). Finally, and most important, racialist theory neglects history. Appealing to static, fixed racial types, it misses the dynamic development of human culture and even human biology, a curious anachronism in the age of Darwin. Marshaling Boasian arguments, then, Locke concludes that "there are no static factors of race at all. Even the anthropological factors are variable. . . . [R]ace inequalities must have an historical explanation" (RCIR, 10). "Any true history of race must be . . . sociological" (RCIR, 11). Mingled with these Boasian arguments are some distinctively pragmatist strands. Although biological race is "an ethnic fiction," Locke insists that it is not as a result simply nonexistent but has practical uses and effects. Overall the effects have been pernicious. Nevertheless, some advantages must accrue to a group that "considers itself an ethnic unit." Thus, Locke clearly distinguishes the plausible pragmatist claim that a group may need in some circumstances and for some purposes to consider itself "an ethnic unit" from the untenable pseudoscientific view that the group is in fact such a unit. Considered in this light, the question whether African Americans should "conserve the Negro race" takes on a different valence than it had in Du Bois's influential 1896 essay "The Conservation of Races."

It is in the spirit of pragmatism, too, that Locke asks whether a genuinely scientific biological theory of race is possible and/or desirable. On both counts, his answer is no. Racialist theories, like all theories, develop in relation to "men's practical ideas about human society." When these practical ideas change, so too must the idea of race. Racialist theory emerged in a period of initial, relatively sparse "contacts" between widely divergent groups. In that context, it served the practical needs of dominant groups, providing a "brief for the prevailing civilization." But this context is now giving way. The present tendency is toward a "world civilization" in which all "social cultures" will be bound up with one another and none will be insulated from the rest. In this new context of vastly increased "race contacts," there will not necessarily emerge a "single type of social culture," and practical needs for human classification may well persist. But the kind of classification needed will change. Static, purity-obsessed, biological conceptions will have to give way to dynamic, interactive, sociological ones. Only insofar as it is transformed in this manner will the concept of race survive.

Locke's first lecture, then, elaborated a Boasian critique of "the theoretical and scientific conceptions of race," inflected with a pragmatist spin. The crucial point was not simply that "race relations" are not physically determined but also that they are not definitively fixed. Essentially historical and dynamic, the product of social interaction, race relations can be changed by deliberate human action. "Variability," he states in a later lecture, "provides a margin of social control, and establishes . . . the moral responsibility of society in these matters" (RCIR, 54).

"Practical Race": A Political-Economic Genealogy

Having disposed in his first lecture of physical race, Locke turns in his second to "the political and practical conception of race." The move is quintessentially pragmatist. Descending from the biological theory of racialism to the social practice that underlies it, Locke shifts the analysis from the "modern race creed" to the "modern race practice." That practice he designates as "imperialism." "Imperialism," he says, is "the practical aspect of what one might call 'race practice' as distinguished from race theory" (RCIR, 24). Or, as we might say today, racialism is the theory, imperialism is the practice.

The approach in this lecture is genealogical. Locke argues that the idea of race is a creature of the practices of power. Following the pragmatist heuristic that ideas have roots in social practice, he inverts the prevailing racialist view that a preexisting condition of white superiority is the basis for white supremacy. On the contrary, he claims, political supremacy spawns the idea of superiority.

> The conception of 'inferior' races or 'backward' races and of 'advanced' races or 'superior' races largely comes from the political fortunes and political capacities of peoples. [T]he people who have not been successful in acquiring dominance . . . will be called the inferior people. . . . The ruling people not only dominate the group practically but control the . . . class distinctions . . . justifying their success in terms of . . . innate forms. . . . It behooves us then to keep our distinctions in their proper places and . . . to assume humbly that such notions as 'superiority' refer only to the political fortunes of a group and not to any intrinsic or inherent qualities with respect to social culture. (RCIR, 22–23)

Racial categorization, then, is the offspring of domination. The domination in question is imperialism, moreover, which Locke defines as "the practices of dominant or ruling groups." This is of course a broad definition that encompasses both ancient and modern, nonracialist and racialist systems of domination. For a genealogy of race, however, Locke must specify the narrower historical conditions that gave rise to a distinctively modern, racialist form of imperialism. The crucial factor, he claims, is an international economic system of competitive commerce. In this system, which has included both slavery and colonialism, European nation-states vie with one another for domination over non-Western peoples. Seeking markets for their manufactures, imperial powers aim to implant their mode of life in the colonies and to uproot indigenous cultural forms. They rationalize these commercial imperatives, with the aid of Christian missionaries, by proclaiming their own civilization to be the only true civilization and by deprecating the cultural capacities of colonized peoples. Thus, commercial imperialism spawns racialist theory and a "practical culture" of alleged Anglo-Saxon superiority. Locke invokes his own painful experiences at the "Imperial Training School"—that is, Oxford University—to illustrate the character of that culture.

By late-twentieth-century standards, of course, Locke's account of modern imperialism is rudimentary. Elaborated chiefly in terms of competition for Third World markets, it says little about the extraction of primary resources or the exploitation of labor power. Nevertheless, he clearly distinguishes the non-racialist and at times relatively tolerant character of ancient tribute-collecting empires from modern color-based commercial imperialism, which depreciates and even destroys indigenous cultures. More important than its precise content, moreover, is the role Locke's account of imperialism plays in his overall argument. Introducing an international dimension to the practical genealogy of race, imperialism supplies the "broader" context Locke insists is needed to understand racial practice in the United States (RCIR, 35).

Having established his international frame, Locke turns in his third and fourth lectures to U.S. intranational "race relations." His account begins implausibly with the denial that the United States is an imperial power—a curious lapse of critical judgment in 1916. Nevertheless, he goes on to argue, imperialist culture pervades the society and infects its internal racial order. Institutionalized in Jim Crow, the practical feeling of Anglo-Saxon superiority imperils the social standing not only of colonial subjects but also of freed people of color living as minorities in predominantly Anglo-Saxon countries.

To explain the specific racial dynamics of the United States, Locke constructs a synthetic account that combines economics, historical sociology, and social psychology. A democratic (white-settler) society, the country has no fixed caste hierarchy (among whites) and relatively fluid class lines. Social mobility and economic uncertainty generate status anxiety, hence a longing for fixed divisions and boundaries, a longing that Jim Crow arrangements seem to satisfy. Elites exploit these anxieties, which are rooted not only in economics but also in social conditions and social psychology. Racial antagonism waxes and wanes with shifts in economic conditions, status anxiety, and the deliberate fomenting of racism by elites.

His gaffe about U.S. imperialism notwithstanding, then, Locke's account of intranational racial antagonisms is sophisticated. Anticipating recent conceptions of "Herrenvolk democracy," it avoids the twin reductions of economism and culturalism. Thus, it points beyond the standard oppositions in critical "race" theory to a pragmatic conception of race that can encompass both culture and political economy.

All told, then, the second tier of Locke's analysis roots the idea of race in the practices of white-supremacist domination, both international imperialism and intranational Jim Crow. Race in this "political" sense is a practical reality, to be sure, but Locke maintains that its existence is historically contingent. Speculating that racial domination may no longer be functional for modern economic life, he considers the future of political race to be "doubtful." His goal, in any case, is to put an end to race in the practical sense of domination. It follows from the logic of his argument, moreover, that this requires dismantling modern imperialism, although Locke himself fails to draw that conclusion.[14]

"Social Race": A Reconstruction

Having demystified biological race and delegitimated political race, Locke arrives at the question, what remains of the idea of race? What, if anything, is left, in other words, after we have refuted the theoretical conception intellectually and dismantled the political conception practically, presumably by abolishing imperialism? Today, perhaps, the most plausible answer is "nothing." But that reply is rejected by Locke. He contends that something potentially useful and pragmatically defensible remains, namely, "the social conception of race."

The social conception of race constitutes the third tier of Locke's analysis and the subject of his fifth and final lecture, titled "Racial Progress and Race Adjustment." Here he argues, on pragmatic grounds, that the idea of race ought not to be eradicated. Instead, it should be "revised" and "redeemed." A properly reformulated social conception of race could serve a salutary function, helping to resolve racial antagonisms and to advance the progress of civilization.

How can this be? How can a category that has produced such baleful effects in the past now be expected to have positive uses? To make his case, Locke retrieves a "very old" aspect of the idea of race, namely, the sense of group belonging and solidarity. This, he maintains, will never entirely disappear, as it is necessary to human society. He wagers, however, that this sense of race can now be dissociated from both the false biological sense and the unjust political sense. Thus, he claims to have discovered the kernel of a pragmatically defensible—"social"—conception of race that should be reconstructed and preserved.

So far, however, the social conception of race remains abstract. Fleshing it out involves elaborating a modern sense of group belonging and solidarity, one that does not feed imperial domination, segregation, or "reactionary nationalism." What sort of modern solidarity can redeem the social conception of race?

Locke's response is formulated at two levels. One pertains to the general developmental tendencies of modern societies, while the other concerns the specific situation of subordinated groups within them, especially American Negroes.

Social Race as Modern "Civilization Type." On the first level, the key question for Locke is, what is the appropriate unit of solidarity in a modern society? His answer hinges on the general tendency of such societies to produce a single "standard of living," not in the sense of economic equality but in the sense of shared practices and modes of life consistent with participation in a competitive economy and other common core institutions. (In this, modern societies differ from feudal societies and ancient imperial systems, which encompassed several distinct standards of living.) Consequently, modern societies also tend to produce a single "civilization type," an ideal-typical sort of person, which members come roughly to approximate by virtue of participating in a common social structure and institutional framework. Civilization type, according to Locke, is the proper overarching unit of solidarity in modern societies. Those who conform to type must be admitted as full citizens and partners. What precisely this entails Locke unfortunately does not say, although he explicitly denies that conformity to civilization type requires either homogeneity of customs and belief or religious and artistic conformity. These latter sorts of homogeneity and conformity he associates with a very different idea, mentioned earlier, that he refers to as "social culture."

Locke's effort to redeem the idea of race as a defensible form of modern social solidarity turns largely on the contrast between civilization type and social culture. The distinction, alas, is not directly explained in *Race Contacts and Interracial Relations,* but its essence can be read between the lines. More restricted than a civilization type, a social structure in Locke's usage comprehends a substantive nexus of concrete life forms, including ethical horizons and interpretive traditions. Civilization type, in contrast, comprehends the more abstract, formal structures that subtend such life forms in a modern pluralist society. Thus, a single modern civilization type can encompass a plurality of social cultures. To invoke a language not available to Locke, members of different ethnicities, subcultures, "communities of value," and religious confessions can all participate in the same civilization type. Or, as theorists of multiculturalism might put it today, whereas a social culture is an ethnos with an ethical or cultural identity, a civilization type is a demos with a political identity.

Conformity to civilization type, then, does not require the homogenization of social cultures. For Locke, moreover, the essential point is this: A civilization type has nothing whatever to do with blood. Unlike an ethnic type, it encompasses those qualities required for integration into the principal institutions of a modern society. Hence, the former Berlin student uses the term "civilization," as opposed to "culture" or "Volk."

With the idea of civilization type, Locke claims to have found an adequate basis for modern sociability and thus a redeemed social conception of race. "The only kind of race that is left to believe in and to be applied to modern problems is what we call the idea of social race [defined] as a conception of civilization type. This seems to be the only thoroughly rational meaning of race. . . . [T]his is to be the race concept of the future" (RCIR, 88).

Where does this leave the American Negro? According to Locke, conformity to civilization type is both a necessary and sufficient condition for full membership in a modern nation-state. It is necessary in that modern forms of economic and social integration require it. It is sufficient in that a nation has no right to require more. Thus, for their part, Negroes must conform to the emerging American civilization type. But then for *their* part, white Americans must accept Negroes as full members. In general, then, Locke's notion of civilization type functions in part to argue that American nationality cannot be based on race or ethnicity. "If a nation should be expanded and incorporate other . . . elements, the same kind of [social] race type would be shared by people who . . . biologically have no connection, proving that a rational cult of a nation will never make the mistake of basing national type and civilization type upon a [biological] racial division" (RCIR, 86).

It is in the looming shadow of Jim Crow that Locke insists on the necessarily "assimilative" tendencies of modern societies. There is no way to prevent Negro assimilation, he claims, however much segregationists try. Assimilation is the inevitable outcome of interaction, and segregation cannot eliminate interaction. Thus, dominant groups do not control assimilation. But assimilation is not a one-way street. The civilization type that emerges under modern social conditions cannot be identified with traits specific to any single constituent subgroup. On the contrary, it is in part a composite result of interaction among subgroups. It incorporates traits previously associated with various groups and in so doing transforms all the parties. Thus, the Negro has contributed, and will continue to contribute, to the making of the American civilization type, hence to the evolving social culture of Anglo-America.

Historically, of course, Locke was wildly overoptimistic, greatly underestimating the capacity of segregation to marginalize Black America and prevent its assimilation, while also failing to contemplate the possibility that such assimilation as did occur might spawn a vacuous, lowest-common-denominator mass culture. We should note, however, that he was not only making (bad) historical predictions but also elaborating an ideal. To this point, Locke's ideal resonates with Israel Zangwill's vision of America as a "melting pot," to which Locke refers with approval. Because he is theorizing with a view to the situation of the Negro under Jim Crow, and hence with a view to the question of power, Locke appreciates the emancipatory dimension of this ideal. Unlike Randolph Bourne and Horace Kallen, for example, he does not conflate it with "Americanization" in the sense of the forced Anglo-Saxonization of European immigrants.[15]

One may question whether Locke can consistently endorse both the melting-pot vision and the view of a modern civilization type as comprehending a plurality of social cultures. To find the answer, one must recall that he does not end his discussion of social race here. Rather, he goes on to propose a second redemptive conception tailored specifically to the situation of American Negroes.

"Secondary Race Consciousness." This second conception of social race Locke calls "secondary race consciousness." He commends it to American Negroes on pragmatic grounds. Anticipating the spirit of Hannah Arendt's dictum that "when one is attacked as a Jew, one must defend oneself as a Jew," Locke argues that

> while social assimilation is in progress there seems to be necessary some . . . counter-doctrine [of] racial solidarity and culture. The stimulation of a secondary race-consciousness within a [dominated] group . . . is necessary for . . . practical reasons. The group needs . . . to get a right conception of itself, and it can only do that through stimulation of pride in itself . . . Race pride or secondary race consciousness [is] the social equivalent to self-respect in the individual moral life. (RCIR, 96–97)

Secondary race consciousness for the Negro is thus a matter of self-defense and self-respect. In addition, it will serve to stimulate the sort of "collective activity" that will hasten Negro assimilation to the emerging civilization type and therefore admission to full membership in American society. Thus, Locke claims that secondary race pride and "loyalty to the joint or common civilization type" are not mutually antithetical. On the contrary, the first serves as a means for realizing the second. In what only appears to be a paradox, then, "we will find it necessary to recreate the race type . . . only for the purpose ultimately to merge it with the general civilization type" (RCIR, 97). Thus, Locke proposes Negro "race pride" as a pragmatic transitional strategy for realizing the long-term goal of assimilation. Inflecting Du Bois's term "conservation" with an antiracialist, antiessentialist, pragmatic spirit, he suggests a program of *Negro "social* conservation," which does not rely on a "doctrine of race integrity" (RCIR, 98, my emphasis). Whereas Du Bois's argument for "conserving the Negro race" was premised on an essentialist racialist ontology, Locke's argument turns on political pragmatics. He was, in Gayatri Spivak's terms, a "strategic essentialist" *avant la lettre.*[16]

How, then, is secondary race consciousness created? The chief avenue, according to Locke, is via cultural production. Negroes should cultivate a self-conscious relation to their distinctive social culture, which is a syncretistic blend of African and Anglo-American elements. This requires recovering what is valuable in African traditions, from which Negroes have been cut off as a result of slavery. It also involves giving expression to African American traditions in public cultural forms, such as literature, music, and painting, where they can be recognized by the larger society. Locke recommends that American Negroes follow the example of the Poles and the Irish in Europe and pursue an intranational variant of cultural nationalism. In those cases, he says, a "racial sense" has inspired great movements in arts and letters, which have redeemed the false meanings of race. Negroes should therefore pursue "culture-citizenship" both to forge solidarity among themselves and to win respect from Anglo-America. By making their own distinctive contribution to the emerging joint civilization, as opposed to merely imitating the dominant culture, they will eventually win full citizenship.

Here, at last, we begin to recognize the future Alain Locke of the Harlem Renaissance. But that Alain Locke now looks somewhat different. The New Negro project appears to be a bid for culture-citizenship as a step on the way to political and economic citizenship. Locke's mature cultural nationalism thus appears as a strategy aimed at overcoming a form of racial domination that he understood as ultimately economic and political. Its roots lie in a sophisticated pragmatist understanding of race conjoined with an anti-imperialist political analysis.

The strategy is, of course, paradoxical. In these lectures, as we have seen, Locke traced the roots of race and racism to imperialism, to political domination based in historical economics. Why, then, does he propose to redeem the idea of race and overcome racism through the creation of Negro literature and art? Why propose a cultural remedy for a political-economic harm? Why cultural production instead of political struggle?

The answer surely lies in part in the bleakness of 1916. At that moment the prospects were dim indeed for Negro civil and political rights, not to mention the social and economic rights that the mass of sharecroppers would have needed to make civil and political rights meaningful. In addition, Locke's squeamishness about political struggle betrays some remnants of the influence of Booker T. Washington, from whose patronage he had earlier benefited. He ends the Howard lectures by acknowledging that his culture-citizenship strategy appears to "fall in line" with the dominant segregationist agenda, even as he maintains, nevertheless, that it is the necessary "forerunner . . . of that kind of recognition [we] are ultimately striving for, namely, recognition of an economic, civic, and social sort" (RCIR, 99–100).

Here, of course, history again proved Locke wrong. The extraordinary flowering of Black cultural production he envisioned and promoted did not serve to win civil and political rights. Only mass political struggle, directly confronting the racist state, could do that. Notwithstanding the theoretical sophistication of Locke's pragmatist antiessentialism, then, it was not he, but the Hegelian racialist-essentialist Du Bois, who understood this.

Locke concluded his 1916 lectures by returning to his first conception of social race, defined as civilization type. This, he proclaims, is the goal of "race progress and race adjustment": the creation of a novel, composite civilization type. This finally redeems the idea of race. "Whatever theory or practice moves toward [this end] is sound," the pragmatist adds; "whatever opposes and retards it false" (RCIR, 100).

Another Pragmatism

Pragmatism undoubtedly lay at the core of Locke's 1916 vision. It was central to the overall plan and argument of his Howard University lectures and is at the root of several of his best insights. It was through pragmatism that Locke first came to reject racialist essentialism and to embrace Franz Boas's alternative. Yet it was also as a result of his pragmatism that he was not content to stop there but went on to seek out the roots of racialist theory in racist-imperialist social practice. Likewise, it was as a pragmatist that Locke contemplated the future of the concept of race and the uses of a successor concept. Seeking a form of social integration appropriate to a modern civilization, he envisioned a social conception of race as civilization type utterly divorced from ethnicity and blood. Yet it was also as a pragmatist, finally, that Locke found civilization type by itself insufficient. He realized that a dominated group such as American Negroes required a secondary race consciousness in order to struggle for liberation and inclusion. Pragmatism, in short, was the key to his "strategic essentialism."

If many of Locke's insights derive from his pragmatism, his lectures present a strand of pragmatist thought that differs importantly from the mainstream of the movement. Like Kallen, Bourne, and Dewey, Locke was concerned with the regulation of group difference in twentieth-century America. Unlike them, however, he did not understand the problem as one of harmoniously orchestrating the cultural differences of immigrant groups, a view largely irrelevant to Negroes and to the struggle against racism. Rather, Locke understood difference in the light of power, domination, and political economy. Thus, unlike the pragmatist mainstream, he grasped that a dominated group might need to forge a cultural identity as a weapon of struggle against oppression. Locke represents, in sum, another pragmatism.

Locke's pragmatism also has an ironic side, however, one that those seeking to revive pragmatism today would do well to contemplate. The theoretically sophisticated antiessentialist, antiracialist Locke was considerably less astute with respect to politics than the Hegelian racialist-essentialist (and soon-to-be-Marxist) Du Bois. Locke's philosophical pragmatism was apparently no guarantee of political savvy.

Locke's 1916 lectures did not in fact influence his mainstream pragmatist contemporaries—at least not so far as we now know. Nevertheless, they might still prove instructive for us today. They provide a point of contrast that highlights some of the limits of the mainstream tradition of classical pragmatist social thought: its neglect of power, its emphasis on culture at the expense of political economy, and its tendency to posit imaginary holistic "solutions" to difficult, sometimes irreconcilable, conflicts. These limits were perhaps less clear in 1916 because pragmatism was then part of a broad-based movement for democratization in social, economic, and political life, as well as in intellectual spheres. Today, however, the situation is more ambiguous. Some revivals of pragmatism seem actually to celebrate the decline of the democratizing movements of our day, while others apparently hope that appeals to the spirit of Dewey can help rekindle such movements, even as the Progressive-era legacy is being dismantled before our eyes. In this context it is salutary to read the youthful Alain Locke. His 1916 lectures give us a sense of those aspects of pragmatism that are genuinely worth reviving.

At the same time, Locke's lectures also supply some more specific critical insights into contemporary conflicts over cultural identity and multiculturalism. His distinction between civilization type and social culture, although by no means adequately developed, anticipates promising recent efforts to distinguish political solidarity and citizenship, on the one hand, from ethical solidarity and ethnicity, on the other.[17] Equally important, Locke's conception of secondary race consciousness introduces the hard fact of domination squarely into discussions that too often rely on the euphemistic idioms of "difference" and "pluralism." He thereby exposes the false symmetry of approaches that assume that all groups and individuals stand in essentially the same relation to the problem of recognition of difference. Locke reminds us, rather, that systematically dominated social groups have pragmatic political needs for solidarity that differ from the needs of others. In the case of African Americans, such domination continues to encompass both cultural misrecognition and political-economic maldistribution. Thus, Locke's attempt to connect the struggle for recognition with a struggle for redistribution remains relevant to this day.

What, finally, can we learn from this "other pragmatism" of the unknown Alain Locke? The most important lesson for those proposing to revive pragmatism today is this: There is not one pragmatism, but several. We had better know which of them we want to revive.

Notes

1. Cornel West, *The American Evasion of Philosophy* (Madison: University of Wisconsin Press, 1989).

2. See, e.g., Nathan Irvin Huggins, *Harlem Renaissance* (Oxford: Oxford University Press, 1971).

3. I borrow this expression from Gayatri Spivak. See Gayatri Spivak with Ellen Rooney, "In a Word," *differences* 1, no. 2 (Summer 1989).

4. Oliver Cromwell Cox, *Caste, Class, and Race* (New York: Monthly Review Press, 1970). For a recent version of this position, see Barbara Fields, "Ideology and Race in American History," in *Region, Race, and Reconstruction: Essays in Honor of C. Vann Woodward,* ed. J. M. Kousser and J. M. McPherson (Oxford: Oxford University Press, 1982).

5. W. E. B. Du Bois, "The Conservation of Races," American Negro Academy Occasional Papers no. 2, 1897. Reprinted in *W. E. B. Du Bois Speaks: Speeches and Addresses, 1890–1919,* ed. Philip S. Foner (New York: Pathfinder Press, 1970). Kwame Anthony Appiah, *In My Father's House: Africa in the Philosophy of Culture* (Oxford: Oxford University Press, 1992).

6. For a fuller account of these various tendencies, see Nancy Fraser, "From Redistribution to Recognition? Dilemmas of Justice in a 'Postsocialist' Age," *New Left Review* 212 (July/August 1995): 68–93; reprinted in Nancy Fraser, *Justice Interruptus: Critical Reflections on the 'Postsocialist' Condition* (London: Routledge, 1997).

7. For an interesting reflection on this question, see Robert Westbrook's discussion of Dewey's early socialism in Robert B. Westbrook, *John Dewey and American Democracy* (Ithaca: Cornell University Press, 1991).

8. Charles Taylor, "The Politics of Recognition," in *Multiculturalism: Examining the Politics of Recognition,* ed. Amy Gutmann (Princeton: Princeton University Press, 1994). See also Iris Marion Young, *Justice and the Politics of Difference* (Princeton: Princeton University Press, 1990). For a critique of Taylor's implicit privileging of the ethnic model, see Linda Nicholson, "To Be or Not to Be: Charles Taylor and the Politics of Recognition," *Constellations* 3, no. 1 (April 1996): 1–16.

9. See Fraser, "From Redistribution to Recognition?"

10. Alain Locke, *Race Contacts and Interracial Relations,* ed. Jeffrey C. Stewart (Washington, D.C.: Howard University Press, 1992). Hereafter cited as RCIR. All references are to this edition.

11. Stewart, introduction to RCIR.

12. Heretofore I placed the term "race" in scare quotes in accord with current critical "race" theory usage and my own philosophical-political commitments. It is unlikely, however, that Locke would have used scare quotes, given the conventions in force in 1916. Accordingly, I shall follow Jeffrey Stewart's practice of omitting scare quotes when explicating the argument of Locke's lectures. Following standard practice in contemporary philosophical writing, I shall use single quotes when the word 'race' is mentioned, as opposed to used. For a discussion of the use of scare quotes, see Henry Louis Gates Jr., ed., *"Race," Writing, and Difference* (Chicago: University of Chicago Press, 1986).

13. Richard J. Herrnstein and Charles Murray, *The Bell Curve: Intelligence and Class Structure in American Life* (New York: Free Press, 1994).

14. This is another point at which Locke shrinks from drawing out the full implications of his argument. Instead of calling for the dismantling of imperialism, he seems at points to assume it is destined to persist.

15. See Horace M. Kallen, "Democracy and the Melting Pot," in *Culture and Democracy in the United States: Studies in the Group Psychology of the American*

Peoples (New York: Boni & Liveright, 1924); and Randolph S. Bourne, "Trans-National America," in *The Radical Will: Randolph Bourne, Selected Writings, 1911–1918,* ed. Olaf Hansen (New York: Urizen, 1977). For a thoughtful discussion, see Wemer Sollors, *Beyond Ethnicity: Consent and Descent in American Culture* (Oxford: Oxford University Press, 1986).

16.   Spivak with Rooney, "In a Word."

17.   See, e.g., Jürgen Habermas, "Struggles for Recognition in the Democratic Constitutional State," in *Multiculturalism: Examining the Politics of Recognition,* ed. Amy Gutmann (Princeton: Princeton University Press, 1994).

2

Struggling with Stereotypes: The Problems of Representing a Collective Identity

Astrid Franke

The New Negro, presented by Alain Locke as a new public image of black Americans in 1925, has subsequently suffered harsh criticism. Though meant to replace the Old Negro who "had long become more of a myth than a man," the New Negro itself has been called a "fictitious Negro," who "became merely a new stereotype," a depoliticized image, and not even new.[1] The charges underline that to proclaim a collective identity and to represent it by a type is an extremely precarious endeavor: while it might enhance the coherence of a group, capturing diverse individuals in one representation, it is also necessarily reductive. In this chapter I want to show that not only is this insight one of our own contemporary struggles with stereotypes and role models but that awareness of it is a central aspect of Locke's essays in *The New Negro*. Moreover, Locke's particular attempt to denounce one set of collective representations as stereotypes and yet to proclaim a new one is embedded in a sophisticated argument whose relevance transcends the context of the Harlem Renaissance.

It is well worth noting that three years before the publication of *The New Negro,* Walter Lippmann had explicitly described one of the ambivalences of stereotypes with regard to individual and collective identity. In his *Public Opinion* (1922), he argued that stereotypes, as collective categories shared with a larger community and handed down by tradition, connect the individual to the social body. They are thus part, even a "defense," of a shared history and identity.[2] What can be regarded as defense, however, can also be a viable tool for propaganda and discrimination. Hence, denouncing and demystifying stereotypes are vital to fight racism and defamation and to defend human dignity and individuality. Indeed, it is at this moment of explicit dissent in social representation that public opinion and stereotypes are seen as such; as Lippmann noted, "a great deal of confusion arises when people decline to classify themselves as we have classified them."[3]

It is hardly surprising that some of the earliest attempts to conceptualize stereotypes but also to work with or against them should have been made by members of minority groups. During the preceding decades, black writers and intellectuals had already put Lippmann's insights into practice without necessarily using the term "stereotype." Being sensitive to the effects of cultural domination and sharing the assumption that the realm of culture is an important battleground in the fight for black emancipation, many black writers and critics had directed their attention to the psychosocial realm of "popular opinion" and representation in and through art.[4]

Perhaps this emphasis on art happened at the expense of political and economic issues. When Walter White, one of the key figures and "entrepreneurs" of the Harlem Renaissance, "boasted that he has persuaded Paul Robeson to forsake law for the concert stage, as he also had encouraged the singing career of Julius Bledsoe, a Columbia medical student, and the writing career of Rudolph Fisher, a Harlem physician," there is something fascinating but also touchingly trusting about this immense faith in the power of art to transform race relations.[5] However, what is at stake here is not primarily the political effectiveness of their strategy. Rather, it is the underlying strong belief in the power of altered representations to change a social and economic reality that led to an explicit attack on stereotypes, combined with the organized attempt to publicize a new self-representation—in fact, the struggle against stereotypes is part of the raison d'être of the Harlem Renaissance. Thus the Harlem Renaissance was not just a great creative outburst in the stimulating atmosphere of the 1920s but actually a highly self-conscious modern artistic movement.

Much like today, the struggle against stereotypes as outmoded and offending forms of representation partly consisted in revealing their repetitive nature in literature. By pointing out where artists drew on the plantation and minstrelsy tradition in depicting black characters, critics not only deplored dehumanizing characterizations but also their aesthetic deficiency with regard to a realist aesthetic. For realism usually represents its protagonists as "characters"—complex human beings, capable of development, learning through experience, and interacting with the social world around them. With few exceptions, blacks were not represented in this mode but were reduced to simple figures, characterized and widely recognized by a few redundant features—stereotypes.

A second line of argument added that the social reality of many blacks had changed as they had migrated to the cities. Of course, a majority of blacks still lived in the rural South, but by pointing to a growing black urban population, critics could emphasize the diminishing mimetic validity—if there ever was one—of stereotypes rooted in plantation culture. Thus, Benjamin Brawley claimed in 1916 that the "day of Uncle Remus as well as of Uncle Tom is over."[6] But if these old representations are, or should be, superseded, how then should "the Negro" be portrayed? In the course of a general discussion about literary representation, a number of articles in *Opportunity* and *Crisis* dealt with this issue around 1925.[7] It was in this context that Alain Locke launched his project, *The New Negro*.

Echoing Brawley, Locke denounces stereotypes of "aunties," "uncles," "mammies," "Uncle Tom," and "Sambo" (*The New Negro* [NN], 5) by pointing to the changed social situation of black Americans due to northern migration and increasing urbanization. Carefully avoiding moral judgment, Locke emphasizes the inadequacy of old stereotypes to capture blacks as a homogeneous group: "with the Negro rapidly in process of class differentiation, if it ever was warrantable to regard and treat the Negro *en masse* it is becoming with every day less possible, more unjust and more ridiculous" (NN, 6). Diversification seems to undermine any kind of collective representation—but this is not the conclusion Locke is aiming at. Rather, he proclaims the Negro as another public image, indeed, as an "often radical type" (NN, 8). In contrast to earlier images, this one is announced as a self-portrait arising from self-expression in art, yet it is supposed to fulfill the same desire for essential and comprehensive knowledge that earlier stereotypes offered: "Whoever wishes to see the Negro in his essential traits, in the full perspective of his achievement and possibilities, must seek the enlightenment of that self-portraiture which the present developments of Negro culture are offering" (NN, xxv).

So why should someone who is obviously aware of the dangers and abuses of stereotypes still proclaim a new essentializing image?[8] To make his case, Locke draws on the role of stereotypes in establishing a sense of group belonging and solidarity, a common consciousness underlying an imagined community—Harlem. Presenting Harlem as "the largest Negro community in the world," "the laboratory of a great race-welding," and a "race capital," Locke evokes the familiar metaphor of the melting pot. However, unlike Zangwill, Kallen, or Bourne, Locke applies it to intraracial rather than interracial processes. This allows a central passage of his essay to move from a diversification of "Negro life" to the shaping of a community:

Here in Manhattan is not merely the largest Negro community in the world, but the first concentration in history of so many diverse elements of Negro life. It has attracted the African, the West Indian, the Negro American; has brought together the Negro of the North and the Negro of the South; the man from the city and the man from the town and village; the peasant, the student, the business man, the professional man, artist, poet, musician, adventurer and worker, preacher and criminal, exploiter and social outcast. Each group has come with its own separate motives and for its own special ends, but their greatest experience has been the finding of one another. Proscription and prejudice have thrown these dissimilar elements into a common area of contact and interaction. Within this area, race sympathy and unity have determined a further fusing of sentiment and experience. So what began in terms of segregation becomes more and more, as its elements mix and react, the laboratory of a great race-welding. Hitherto, it must be admitted that American Negroes have been a race more in name than in fact, or to be exact more in sentiment than in experience. The chief bond between them has been that of a common condition rather than a common consciousness; a problem in common rather than a life in common. In Harlem, Negro life is seizing upon its first chances for group expression and self-determination. It is—or promises at least to be—a race capital. (NN, 6)

While diversification debunks old stereotypes as illegitimate reductions, it also undermines any claim of a collective representation, yielding this important cultural gesture to others. The familiar images of the melting pot and the city as an experimental space allow Locke to create unity out of diversity and announce the welding of a new race, bound by a common consciousness and a common life, to be represented by the New Negro. Encapsulated in this representative type is the vital link between the individual and the community, for it can turn the self-expression of individuals into the expression of a collective experience; it combines "group expression" and "self-determination" and thus the artistic and the political. Insisting on individual expression and "the freedom and neutrality of art as an analogy for the freedom of his race," Locke can actually overcome the dichotomy between art and propaganda that is often seen as structuring the debate between him and Du Bois.[9] As cultural emancipation includes and goes beyond the political, these two realms of human activity are no longer separated and questions of ethics and aesthetics do not oppose each other anymore. And yet, the last two sentences of the long passage also indicate that this synthesis is somewhat unstable. They demonstrate how Locke's language welds together present and future, the artistic and the political, the self and the group in an argument that hovers between representing the New Negro as something that exists already and prophesying a collective identity that still has to be realized. How this precarious construction is possible is the subject of his essay "Negro Youth Speaks." In this essay, whose title merges the individual youth with the group in the choice of a noun that can be used as both singular and plural, Locke argues that the assumed link between the black individual and the group is a natural outcome of blacks' experience as an oppressed group. The experience of Negro youth can therefore be both "unique" and "common":

Primarily, of course, it is youth that speaks in the voice of Negro youth, but the overtones are distinctive; Negro youth speaks out of a unique experience and with a particular representativeness. All classes of a people under social pressure are permeated with a common experience; they are emotionally welded as others cannot be. (NN, 47)

Again, Locke is extremely careful and subtle in his wording. Certainly, black youth in the 1920s experienced intensified racism and segregation; "social pressure" seems to be a rather mild and vague expression, for who, including even the "dominant minority" of Anglo-Saxons, did not claim to be under social pressure at the time?[10] And yet, a euphemism is perhaps a small price to pay for "particular representativeness": it is precisely because the experience is phrased in broad terms that a marginalized group can claim to voice a "common experience" transcending the limits of the group. This allows Locke to intertwine the Harlem Renaissance with a national American movement of cultural emancipation, but it also raises the question of what the coherence and solidarity of a group as diverse as Locke has previously described it should be based upon. In his review of *The New Negro* the white writer and critic Carl Van Vechten, who was enthusiastic about the anthology as a whole, was yet skeptical about any claim for a general intellectual attitude of the new literary figures, maintaining that "the New Negro does very little group thinking."[11] As we shall see, this seemingly marginal remark in his review is central to Van Vechten's own involvement in the Harlem Renaissance, as he had reasons to support a much more individualistic concept of art. For Van Vechten understood well that the more unified the community appeared to be and the more this unity was based on the particular experience of slavery and racism, the less it was possible for white writers to identify with it as a national movement. Moreover, to found a black collective identity more explicitly on a traumatic historical experience unique to blacks, as Locke could have done, holds both an empowering and a constraining side for black artists as well: to be perceived as artists whose creative source lies in slavery and oppression might give their art a particular significance and depth, but it could also lead to limiting expectations that individual black artists hope to escape.

These, of course, are the two sides of any collective identity: it sets a group apart and gives it a particular profile—after all, many artists deliberately join groups with a specific image and program—and yet, setting a group apart makes it vulnerable to discrimination and may prevent its members from being seen as individuals. Moreover, an accepted model of identity may easily turn into a frozen, trivialized form and, as such, a constraining trap that can be used for polemic purposes. So how can this simultaneous individual and collective identity of the New Negro be prevented from being as limiting as the old stereotypes? This might be a question of the sheer quantity of details attributed to characterize the type, as a stereotype is often marked by a "poverty of its constituents."[12] However, the more details are given and the more the type is thus individualized, the smaller is its chance to be accepted as "representative," as a basis for a collective identity. A second way to prevent the New Negro from being perceived as stereotype is to make it historically specific and to deny all ties with older images. This explains the strong emphasis on newness, a claim that, as Gates and others have pointed out, was not entirely justified. The major strategy, however, is to see the New Negro as an artist and to postulate a particular aesthetic identity. It implies intense self-expression and speaking from experience rather than "moralism and guarded idealizations" (NN, 50). It is individually variable and open to historical change just as individual experience is. And yet, it can be representative, because the self-expression of the black artist and the quality of black art arises out of black life itself. For the misery and hardship of blacks' experience have given their lives an inherent aesthetic quality, as Locke continues in "Negro Youth Speaks":

> With them, even ordinary living has epic depth and lyric intensity, and this, their material handicap, is their spiritual advantage. So in a day when art has run to classes, cliques and coteries, and life lacks more and more a vital common background, the Negro artist, out of the depths of his group and personal experience, has to his hand almost the conditions of a classical art. (NN, 47)

Since ordinary black life already possesses the qualities of art, black individual self-expression is not only always already aesthetic but also by implication a group expression, so that "race expression need not be deliberate to be vital" (NN, 47). To produce art, black artists need no longer be self-conscious in representing and interpreting "the Negro" to a white world; they can simply "speak as Negroes" (NN, 48). The emphasis on speech, voice, and song as well as on youth rather than on texts and writing underlines the idea of immediate and direct expression that associates Locke's envisioned black aesthetic with the frequently mentioned "folk" culture and with Romantic concepts such as can be found in Whitman's preface to *Leaves of Grass*. So, what exactly characterizes a black contribution to art, and what is the central "experience" from which black art emerges?

As we have seen before, this experience is not specified any further and while this allows Locke to claim a particular representativeness of the modern black artist, it again draws attention to the fact that Locke is not interested in raising the issue of slavery as a clear example of a specific historical experience. In fact, as Locke's contribution to the anthology's section "The Negro Digs Up His Past" demonstrates, the past is also conceived of in aesthetic terms. Since the New Negro is an artist, his history is the history of art and his inheritance the "legacy of the ancestral arts" (NN, 254). Nor does "experience" pertain to the social conditions under which blacks were living at the time, whether in rural areas or in cities like New York where segregation continued. Rather, Locke looks to the future, and he describes black life continuously in terms of metamorphosis, change, and the emergence of something new. Rapid movement is its most salient feature, as blacks are involved in a "flight not only from countryside to city, but from medieval America to modern" (NN, 6). The frequent use of the progressive form as well as the use of tenses hovering between present and future (between "it is" and "promises at least to be") emphasize black life in transition. One of the most condensed expressions of this notion is the sentence, "In the very process of being transplanted, the Negro is becoming transformed" (NN, 6). Because of such formulations, it is difficult to decide whether the New Negro already exists and is represented in the anthology or whether his image is one the anthology hopes to create. This is not a logical weakness, though, for Locke's emphasis is on transformation, not the foundation of a concept. Accordingly, the New Negro is a project and a projection, not a new fixed image. Locke knows that it is only the acknowledged social contingency of any proclaimed collective identity that can save the new type from the rigidity and redundancy so characteristic of the stereotype. Similarly, the "new aesthetic" and "philosophy of life" (NN, 49) underlying new representations of blacks in literature and art cannot proclaim fixed principles but serve primarily to "break through the stereotypes to a new style, a distinctive fresh technique, and some sort of characteristic idiom" (NN, 267). Yet, it is difficult to see how an identity in process can serve the positive purpose of providing a sense of group belonging or how an aesthetic based on changing experience can lead to a "characteristic idiom." In his sketch of the New Negro as a modern black American artist, Locke thus carefully maneuvers between providing us with a black aesthetic and evading various entrapping positions that threaten to freeze the new representation into just another stereotype. Taking up some key terms of Locke's essays, these potential traps might be marked as 'modernism,' 'Africa,' and 'Folk.'

The claim of white modernists to "re-name the things seen" or to "Make It New" is obviously also one the anthology can adopt.[13] It can inscribe itself into the modernist project, first, because the emphasis on defamiliarization of old modes of perception through art is also its own; and, second, because it can intertwine the issue of a new representation with a cultural awakening, a national renewal through a new aesthetic. Yet, both these aspects become problematic, even conflicting, when put in the service of black cultural emancipation; therefore Locke is not merely adopting a modernist aesthetic but also transforming it. Let us trace in more detail this transformational process in the course of his argument.

In Locke's assumption of an inherently aesthetic life in which individual expression is always simultaneously group expression, the distinctions between artist, subject, and audience are overcome. Therefore "Harlem" not only assumes mythical qualities for the New Negro as a place for emancipation and self-determination but is also an artist's utopia—a place where the artist is embedded and embraced by a community and yet not restrained by it, where the artist's self-expression is not only expressing a common—that is communal— experience but also helps to shape that experience, where, consequently, the aesthetic and the sociopolitical are one. As I have pointed out before, this allows Locke to overcome the stifling dichotomy between art and propaganda, it pro- jects a new black identity rooted in art, and finally it offers America the fulfill- ment of an old, though constantly renewed, Romantic vision.

A paradigmatic expression of that vision is Whitman's preface to *Leaves of Grass* with its announcement of an "American poet" who is a common man who is representative, as the "United States themselves are essentially the greatest poem."[14] More important at the beginning of this century, however, were the many attempts at national self-criticism and redefinition current among white writers and intellectuals. Rebelling against the genteel literary tradition and even sharing a certain "anglophobia," the New York avant-garde movement sometimes called the Little Renaissance might serve as an example here.[15] The literary and social critics Van Wyck Brooks, Randolph Bourne, Waldo Frank, James Oppenheim, Paul Rosenfeld, and Herbert Croly "rallied around the need to create a new indigenous culture."[16] Believing, like the black intellectuals of the Harlem Renaissance, that a community of artists could improve society and culture, they argued for a collective artistic endeavor aris- ing from individual expression. In many respects, Locke's text echoes their "cultural nationalism" as it is expressed, for instance, in *The Seven Arts* mani- festo, published in November 1916:

> It is our faith and the faith of many, that we are living in the first days of a renascent period, a time which means for America the coming of that national self-consciousness which is the beginning of greatness. In all such epochs the arts cease to be private matters; they become not only the expression of the national life but a means to its enhancement.
>
> Our arts shown [*sic*] signs of this change. It is the aim of *The Seven Arts* to become a channel for the flow of these new tendencies: an expression of our American arts which shall be fundamentally an expression of our American life. What we ask of the writer is simply self-expression without regard to current magazine standards. We should prefer that portion of his work that is done through a joyous necessity of the writer himself. . . .
>
> In short, *The Seven Arts* is not a magazine for artists, but an expression of artists for the community.[17]

Within a few lines, this manifesto contains a number of topics that we also find in Locke's texts, such as the notion of transition and change and the emphasis on expression, particularly self-expression. Most important, there is the connection between the personal and the national, mediated by the artist embedded in, and vital to, a community.

It is this link that Locke applies in a particular way to the Harlem Renaissance. As blacks are seeking "something like a spiritual emancipation" (NN, 4), they are part of a national endeavor, similarly searching for its own voice: "America seeking a new spiritual expansion and artistic maturity, trying to found an American literature, a national art, and national music implies a Negro-American culture seeking the same satisfactions and objectives" (NN, xxvi). This is why "Negro Youth" can speak out of a unique experience and yet achieve a particular representativeness as his voice transcends not only the distinction between the individual and the group but also that between the "race" and the nation. Locke's suggestion that African American culture partake in a general American emancipatory movement is not just absorbing the cultural criticism of its time; it also makes it possible to overcome another major dichotomy that has paralyzed the intellectual debates at least since Du Bois's *Souls of Black Folk* (1903): that between being black and being American. The concept of a black and ultimately American modernism helps to heal the split of Du Bois's "double-consciousness" and also to counter a split of the black movement through black nationalism and separatism.[18] In fact, Locke mentions black and white separatism as a threat to American democracy, arguing that the full integration of blacks into American life is a fulfillment of American ideals: "the choice is not between one way for the Negro and another way for the rest, but between American institutions frustrated on the one hand and American ideals progressively fulfilled and realized on the other" (NN, 12). Finally, then, the new black art is not just offering another version of modernism. It will improve modernism since it reconciles the originality and uniqueness of individual expression with a genuine relevance to a community, the solidarity of a particular group with the unity of a nation, the artistic and the political, and it thus avoids the self-absorbed fragmentation into "classes, cliques and coteries" of contemporary art (NN, 47).

And yet there is another reason for Locke to associate the new black art with modernism, one that is not entirely inimical to rather elitist concepts of black art. While Locke emphasizes the embeddedness of the artist in his community, he is also careful to avoid the image of the "primitive" artist, for blacks had long been associated with popular art and entertainment. Minstrel shows, for instance, associated blacks with an exaggerated theatricality of dance, music, and verbal play. Local-color fiction depicted them as queer but lovable uncles and mammies who were sentimental singers and cunning storytellers. To avoid these art forms reminiscent of southern life, Locke is careful to mention aspects of technique and craftsmanship. It is important

> to evolve from the racial substance something technically distinctive, something that as an idiom of style may become a contribution to the general resources of art. In flavor of language, flow of phrase, accent of rhythm in prose, verse and music, color and tone of imagery, idiom and timbre of emotion and symbolism, it is the ambition and promise of Negro artists to make a distinctive contribution. (NN, 51)

Locke identifies the new art—and the "ancestral arts" it may draw upon—with formal and stylistic features, not primarily with its subject matter. While he has previously stressed the relevance of a transformed modernist art for a community, he now regards art forms that are clearly embedded in social practices through the eyes of a modernist. In this perspective, folk art and African art, rather than being inspiring examples of art involved in the daily lives of people, are offered as a source of experimental innovation.

This, I believe, is a deliberate and creative misunderstanding of African art or folk art, for it allows the anthology to defamiliarize the Old Negro by associating him with new and unfamiliar African artworks. This strategy exoticizes familiar blackness and revalues it as aesthetically desirable. Yet, as the generic titles of the illustrations (such as "Young Negro" [46], "The Poet" [128], "The Spirit of Africa" [228], or "Blues Singer" [227]), the mythology invoked by African masks and statues, and Barnes's programmatic claim that the "Negro is a poet by birth" suggest, art and Africa as major constituents of a new identity can easily be as simplistic and reductive as old stereotypes.[19] With the benefit of hindsight, we can see how this new image may easily follow "the three golden rules of stereotyping: the poverty of its constituents, redundancy, and homogeneity."[20] Clearly, a continent and one human endeavor, however creative, cannot comprise the complexity of human experience and are thus reductive. Redundancy is a danger since theatrical performance, music, and dance have also been associated with older stereotypes of blacks, such as the entertaining minstrel characters. Homogeneity reigns as Africa and its descendants seem already to be aesthetically pleasing; and as the concepts thus seem identical they do not leave room for tensions and contradictions.

In addition, the combination of art and Africa fascinated European and increasingly also American intellectual circles at the beginning of this century as highly appreciated 'Primitivism.' As Michael North has pointed out, European and a growing number of American modern artists often defined themselves against what they perceived as the sterile, white, genteel culture by imagining themselves as "racial outsiders."[21] Thus, the deviation from standard English, the new liberty in depicting sexuality and the emphasis on the body, the psychological, and the grotesque were all associated with "blackness," "primitivism," or a certain exoticism. T. S. Eliot's *Sweeney Agonistes,* Eugene O'Neill's *Emperor Jones,* or Gertrude Stein's "Melanctha" may serve as examples here. All these works urge us to overcome conventional modes of perception and reading, but part of their effort to create a reading experience of unsettling defamiliarization is to evoke the familiar images of blacks with roots in traditional racist discourse and use it in the context of formal and stylistic innovation. A crucial question in the context of *The New Negro* is whether formal complexity and the processes of defamiliarization can transform the social meanings of the stereotypes evoked.

This was particularly doubtful in America since the "exoticism" of black skin is somewhat difficult to maintain in a country with a large black population that has been living there for centuries. More than their counterparts in Europe, American artists faced the possibility that their new representations of blacks could just be subsumed under old stereotypes with a long, potentially racist, tradition. And even if modern art could change the way blacks were perceived, whatever change in the representation of blacks could be achieved would be effective only if it reached a wide audience—something that clearly was not likely for many modernist texts. Another drawback of the emphasis on Africa is that while it defamiliarizes familiar blackness and revalues it as aesthetically desirable, it also renders it less "American." The further removed the source of creativity and the kind of art seem to be, however, the less likely it is that the art will be accepted as a new national art. And only by being accepted as American could the New Negro hope to counter old stereotypes branding him as entirely different, excluding him yet again from mainstream American culture.

A complementary strategy is therefore to reimport the potentially exotic and claim that this source of creativity is already part of an indigenous national culture, in what Locke repeatedly calls "folk culture." While European artists look elsewhere for new and unfamiliar modes of representation, America has the sources of renewal in its own country, in forms of art associated with black life in rural areas: "Here for the enrichment of American and modern art, among our contemporaries, in a people who still have the ancient key, are some of the things we thought culture had forever lost" (NN, 52). To appreciate folk culture may lead to a new evaluation of "dialect," "racial idiom of imagery," "a musical folk-lilt and a glamorous sensuous ecstasy," "peasant irony," "folk clarity and naiveté," and the "terseness and emotional raciness of Uncle Remus" (NN, 51) as contributions to a new modern American art. As before, Locke stresses formal features of folk art and thus their potential to stimulate innovation. Yet, it might also just recall Uncle Tom, Uncle Remus, Mammy, Sambo, and a number of other ridiculed characters associated with plantation life—and here we are back at the beginning of the argument.

It no longer comes as a surprise that Locke does not offer a clear aesthetic concept to capture black art. Like the New Negro itself, Locke's argument is characterized by movement, reconciliation of opposites, and continuous maneuvering between entrapping stereotypes. Following the moves of his thoughts illuminates not only the intricacies of the argument but also conflicting positions within a cultural matrix. As a result of the particular situation of artists in America, the representation of the New Negro faces a peculiar dilemma: it can be too familiar or else not familiar enough. Being too familiar, it might easily be subsumed under older images. Defamiliarized, it threatens to be either elitist and thus not powerful enough for a renewal on a national scale, or else another exotic stereotype.

On a more theoretical level, this problem sheds light on certain aspects of modern art that proved difficult to adopt for an artistic movement so deeply embedded in the social and material conditions of life—that of the artist as well as that of the envisioned audience. This is obviously the case when it comes to questions of public appeal of a work of art that a writer like Stein, for instance, could afford to ignore. A new representation meant to change the public image of a group needs to be somewhat popular and thus implicated in market mechanisms. Moreover, as phrases like "Make It New" or "rename the things seen" already reveal, white modernists' emphasis on renewal is accompanied by a certain indifference towards the object of renewal.[22] Again, this is a stance that is not attractive, and perhaps not even possible, for Locke or indeed any black artist at the time. It is not just any representation that is to be renewed but a demeaning one that had concrete social and political roots. Needless to say, the result of the transformation was likewise important, for it proclaimed improved social and cultural conditions of black people in America. Thus the New Negro is and must be both "new" and "Negro," and Locke's essays are marked by his continuous attempts to forge these terms into an empowering cultural tool without resorting to mere formalism or an essentializing image.

While Locke is thus struggling with stereotypes, white critics themselves modified old stereotypes to use blacks as marking different positions in a cultural controversy over aesthetic values. In the context of this debate, Americans had repeatedly voiced a need for "fire," "color," and "expression" and expected this need to be satisfied by black artists. Carl Van Doren, for instance, claimed that "what American literature decidedly needs at the moment is color, music, gusto, the free expression of gay or desperate moods. If the Negroes are not in a position to contribute these items, I do not know what

Americans are."[23] This praise of black art as a welcome alternative to the presumed sterility and conformity of white American cultural life by white critics was obviously a mixed blessing for black artists and critics. While it could lead to a democratic redefinition of American culture that would include formerly ignored artists and their work, it could also simply reaffirm white superiority when it opposed intellect and industry to the supposed black gift for emotion and entertainment. Moreover, it meant that while black artists and critics were searching for a new kind of representation, there was already one provided for them. And yet this "new" representation was dangerously close to one with a long tradition within racist imagery: the uninhibited, spontaneous, emotional, and expressive Negro. That he existed not only outside the anthology but could actually invade it can be seen in the beginning of Albert C. Barnes's essay "Negro Art and America." In fact, we can appreciate the subtlety of Locke's style and the thoughtful choice of words all the more when we compare it to Barnes's well-meant and yet limiting and condescending characterization of "the Negroes' individual traits":

> The most important element to be considered is the psychological complexion of the Negro as he inherited it from his primitive ancestors and which he maintains to this day. The outstanding characteristics are his tremendous emotional endowment, his luxuriant and free imagination and a truly great power of individual expression. He has in superlative measure that fire and light which, coming from within, bathes his whole world, colors his images and impels him to expression. The Negro is a poet by birth.[24]

What happens between Locke's essay and Barnes's is a swift mutation of Locke's New Negro into an expressive "primitive" whose psychological make-up can be summarized in a few words and who offers precisely what Van Doren asked for.

As Locke did not establish a fixed image, there is always the potential to modify the New Negro further. In fact, his transformation of entertaining minstrel characters into appreciated black modern artists can also be reversed. This is exactly what happens in Carl Van Vechten's best-seller *Nigger Heaven*. The book, which appeared in 1926 and was said to popularize a new stereotype, puts forward an argument that seems strikingly similar to Locke's and yet involves entirely different ideas about the relation between an individual artist and a community. The text begins with a highly entertaining prologue centering on the Scarlet Creeper, a figure based on the minstrel stereotype of the urban Zip Coon. The novel then surveys the disparate lifestyles of black people in Harlem, including those of highly educated intellectuals—the New Negroes. While this emphasis on diversity undermines the presumed representativeness of the initial stereotype, it also subverts that of the New Negro. In another step, the novel modifies the minstrel stereotype to reintroduce race as an aesthetic category: black people, such as the Scarlet Creeper and his female equivalent, are artists, not because they consciously create art but because they live it. Encapsulated in the stereotype of the urban primitive, black life in Harlem is marked by theatricality, beauty, sensuousness, color, and expressivity. This may still remind one of Locke's concept, but while Locke took pains to reconcile individual self-expression with the relevance of art to a black community, Van Vechten celebrates blackness as unconstrained individuality, a cultivated hedonism marked by its disregard for conventional morality and the claims of society. This allows Van Vechten quite an unexpected twist within Locke's pragmatist idea of art as "living beauty."[25] If life in Harlem is inherently aesthetic, to create art oneself, one need only immerse oneself in it and write about that experience. If, furthermore, a black experience and expression is highly individualistic and thus separated from a black community and history, then there is no reason that a white man cannot be a "black" writer. Through its careful manipulation of stereotypes, *Nigger Heaven* conceptualizes blackness as an aesthetic term that allows the white Van Vechten to fashion himself as a black artist. It is difficult to assess how much damage Van Vechten's best-seller may have done to the Harlem Renaissance, but the novel raises an important issue that Locke seems to avoid but—in contrast to white modernism—could not afford to ignore: popularity. When it comes to the power of an image to shape people's conception of each other and themselves, popularity is certainly an aspect that should not be ignored. For what keeps a stereotype alive is its ongoing attraction despite all opposition and despite all changes in the world it pretends to represent. To replace a stereotype, a new representation must be accepted, not necessarily as more representative in the sense of having greater mimetic validity, but primarily as more attractive, emotionally appealing, and more widely disseminated—that is, more popular.

It is here, I think, that Locke's concept reaches its limits. Having overcome so many stifling oppositions, he would now have to develop a kind of popular aesthetic—an idea of valued art whose creators would likewise be appreciated, but which is also powerful enough to counter representations that have long been part of popular culture, entertaining the masses. In that light, Locke's frequent recourse to "folk" when describing the specific black contribution to modernism can be regarded as a way to avoid talking about the urban masses he started out with. Indeed, "folk," as his phrases and the illustrations suggest, seems to have more to do with a rural, perhaps mythical, past than with the contemporary urban black working class in Harlem.

To be sure, as other contributions to the anthology and Locke's own later work on jazz suggest, folk art might well develop into urban popular entertainment.[26] In a fascinating ongoing dialectic between original creation, commercialization, and renewed claims for authenticity, jazz might have provided Locke with an example of a "distinctive contribution" (NN, 51) of black artists to American "national" culture. However, his emphasis in the anthology is a different one. Writing on spirituals and sculpture, Locke focuses on the possibility of folk art feeding into modernist "high" art. The idea is clearly inspired by European developments in the arts, by composers like Dvořák and Stravinsky and painters and sculptors like Matisse, Picasso, and Modigliani. Thus, however, Locke is avoiding the field of popular culture where most of the stereotypes he wants to combat reside.

If he had developed a popular aesthetics, he would have had to face the difficult question of how one could prevent a representation from being fixed, despite the fact that its specific historical context has long been superseded, when this representation becomes part of popular entertainment. To signal that this process had taken place is exactly what the term "stereotype" was used to denote at the beginning of the anthology. In the context of the Harlem Renaissance, however, this transformation carried an immense social and political significance, for, in all probability, it signaled the moment when blacks lost control yet again over their self-representation.

Still, Locke's essays are marked by an intense awareness of the potential as well as the dangers of representing a collective identity. He resists the temptation to suggest merely a counterimage, an antistereotype that would, by mere negation, always evoke the original stereotype and become just as limiting. Rather, his goal is constant transformation and changeability. He suggests the New Negro as a new racial and even national consensus of what black people may stand for and yet, through his vagueness and oscillation between the specific and the common, leaves this representation open to future modifications. This is both his weakness and his strength. It is a weakness because, as the contours of the New Negro are necessarily vague, the concept is extremely vulnerable to the danger of being turned into just another stereotype. But Locke's strategy also has its strength because by developing a dynamic concept he is able to avoid the pitfalls of stereotypes. More important, however, voicing dissent from current forms of representation, he instigates the quest for "new" representations as a continuous search for a new consensus. Thus Locke not only conjures up the New Negro but also shows his relevance. For the more the value of representations to a people's sense of self-worth and identity is discussed, the more valuable these representations become and the more important it becomes to negotiate them continuously. If we look at the intense debates about representation of blacks in American culture today, it is clear that this aspect of Locke's prophecy has certainly been fulfilled.

Notes

1. Alain Locke, "The New Negro," in *The New Negro: Voices of the Harlem Renaissance,* ed. Alain Locke (New York: Atheneum, 1992), 3–16. The other texts I focus upon are Locke's foreword, xxv; and his essays "Negro Youth Speaks," 47–53; "The Negro Spirituals," 199–213; and "The Legacy of the Past," 254–67. All page numbers in my text refer to this edition.

The critique of the New Negro comes from George Chester Morse, "The Fictitious Negro," *Outlook and Independent* 15, no. 2 (1929): 684–79; and Warrington Hudlin, "The Renaissance Re-examined," in *The Harlem Renaissance Remembered,* ed. Arna Bontemps (New York: Dodd, Mead, 1972), 275. Henry L. Gates Jr. argues that Locke only "transformed the militancy associated with the trope and translated this into an apolitical movement of the arts." Gates, "The Trope of a New Negro and the Reconstruction of the Image of the Black," *The New American Studies: Essays from* Representations, ed. Philip Fisher (Berkeley and Los Angeles: University of California Press, 1991), 337. For another discussion of the many earlier attempts to proclaim a "New Negro ," see also Eric Sundquist, *To Wake the Nations: Race in the Making of American Literature* (Cambridge: Harvard University Press, Belknap Press, 1993), 334–37.

2. Walter Lippmann, *Public Opinion* (New York: Free Press, 1965), 64.

3. Lippmann, *Public Opinion,* 97.

4. In this vein, Du Bois writes: "[I]t has long been the consensus among the wise, that the great gift of the Negro to the world is going to be a gift to Art. This is quite contrary to popular opinion, to whom the Negro means labor, sweat of brow, the bent back and bloated eye, the beast and burden bearer." Du Bois is not only arguing here that, assuming art to be the epitome of civilization, the artistic contribution of a people can surely prove its worth; he is also hoping that the image of blacks in "popular opinion" can be changed when they are associated with art. W. E. B. Du Bois, "Can the Negro Serve the Drama?" in *Writings by W. E. B. Du Bois in Periodicals Edited by Others,* ed. Herbert Aptheker (Millwood, N. Y.: Kraus-Thomson, 1982), 2: 210–11. The fallacy of the first step of this argument, as Henry L. Gates Jr. has pointed out, is that it accepts the premise that black people have to prove their humanity in the first place. Henry L. Gates Jr., "Writing, 'Race,' and the Difference It Makes," in *"Race," Writing, and Difference* (Chicago: University of Chicago Press, 1986), 13.

5. David L. Lewis, "Parallels and Divergences: Assimilationist Strategies of Afro-American and Jewish Elites from 1910 to the Early 1930s," in *Bridges and Boundaries. African Americans and American Jews,* ed. Jack Salzman (New York: George Braziller and The Jewish Museum, 1992), 29.

6. Benjamin Brawley, "The Negro in American Fiction," *The Dial,* 11 May 1916. Reprinted in Benjamin Brawley, *The Negro in Literature and Art in the United States,* 3d ed. (New York: Duffield, 1929). See also Seymour L. Gross, "Stereotype to Archetype: The Negro in American Literary Criticism," in *Images of the Negro in American Literature,* ed. Seymour L. Gross and John E. Hardy (Chicago: University of Chicago Press, 1966).

7. See, e.g., Wilfis Richardson, "Characters," *Opportunity,* June 1925, 183; "On

Writing about Negroes," *Opportunity,* August 1925, 227; "The Negro in Art: How Shall He Be Portrayed," *Crisis* 31, no. 3 (1926): 219–20, and 31, no. 4 (1926): 278–80. More than half a century later, altered sensitivities required a different choice of words, but the question remained the same: Henry L. Gates Jr., "The Black Person in Art: How Should S/he Be Portrayed?" part 1, *Black American Literature Forum,* 21, no. 1 (1987): 3–24; part 2, *Black American Literature Forum,* 22, no. 2 (1987): 317–32. Gates attributes the original question to Du Bois, who was the main editor of *Crisis.* Leon D. Coleman claims, however, that the question was actually put forward by Carl Van Vechten as part of his public relations campaign for *Nigger Heaven.* Coleman writes: "He constructed a questionnaire which was sent to a number of Negro and white writers. Along with the questions went a covering letter which was signed by Jessie Fauset of the *Crisis* but which was actually composed by Van Vechten. The questionnaire was printed in the March 1926 issue of *Crisis* and contained seven questions dealing with the depiction of the Negro in art." Leon D. Coleman, *The Contribution of Carl Van Vechten to the Negro Renaissance, 1920–1930* (Ann Arbor: University of Michigan Press, 1969), 165.

8. A similar question is asked by Nancy Fraser with regard to Locke's use of the concept of "race" as it emerges from Locke's "Race Contacts and Interracial Relations." See her essay in this volume, chap. 1.

9. Michael North, "The Literary Criticism of the Harlem Renaissance," in *History of Literary Criticism* (New York: Columbia University Press, forthcoming), 7:10–12.

10. Heinz Ickstadt, "Transnational Democracy and Anglo-Saxondom: Fears and Visions of a Dominant Minority in the 1920s," in *Ethnic Cultures in the 1920s in North America,* ed. Wolfgang Binder (Frankfurt am Main: Peter Lang, 1993), 1–16.

11. Carl Van Vechten, "Uncle Tom's Mansion," *New York Herald Tribune Books,* 20 December 1925, reprinted in Bruce Kellner, ed., *"Keep A-Inchin' Along": Selected Writings of Carl Van Vechten about Black Art and Letters* (Westport, Conn.: Greenwood Press, 1979), 59.

12. Ruth Amossy, "Stereotypes and Representation in Fiction," *Poetics Today* 5, no. 4 (1984): 695.

13. Ezra Pound, *Make It New* (London: Faber & Faber, 1934). William Carlos Williams, *In the American Grain* (New York: New Directions, 1956), v.

14. Walt Whitman, *Leaves of Grass: The First (1855) Edition* (New York: Penguin Books, 1986), 5.

15. North, " Literary Criticism," 10.

16. Arthur F. Wertheim, *The New York Little Renaissance: Iconoclasm, Modernism, and Nationalism in American Culture, 1908–1917* (New York: New York University Press, 1976), xii.

17. Both the term "cultural nationalism" and the manifesto are quoted from Wertheim, *New York Little Renaissance,* 178.

18. North, " Literary Criticism," 10–12.

19. Albert C. Barnes, "Negro Art and America," in *The New Negro,* 19.

20. Amossy, "Stereotypes and Representation," 395.

21. Michael North, preface to *The Dialect of Modernism: Race, Language, and Twentieth-Century Literature* (New York: Oxford University Press, 1994).

22. This implied aesthetic assumption is explicated by Victor Shkiovsky's claim, "Art is a way of experiencing the artfulness of an object; the object is not important." Victor Shkiovsky, "Art as Technique," in *Modern Criticism and Theory: A Reader,* ed. David Lodge (London: Longman, 1988), 20.

23. Carl Van Doren, "The Younger Generation of Negro Writers," *Opportunity,* May 1924, 144–45.

24. Barnes, "Negro Art and America," 19.

25. Richard Shusterman, *Pragmatist Aesthetics: Living Beauty, Rethinking Art* (Oxford: Blackwell, 1992).

26. See, e.g., J. A. Rogers, "Jazz at Home," in *The New Negro,* 216–24; and Alain Locke, *The Negro and His Music* (New York: Arno Press, 1969), chaps. 8–13.

3

Values and Language: Toward a Theory of Translation for Alain Locke

Sally J. Scholz

Alain Locke's conception of values lends itself, though not explicitly, to a philosophy of language. Specifically, it offers a theory of translation not unlike that of Willard Van Orman Quine. Locke's conception of values, including functionalism and cultural/contextual relativism, provides the content for a theory of translation that allows for cross-cultural communication of belief without requiring sameness of objective meaning for an utterance in one language and its translation into another. The framework has been developed by Quine in *Word and Object*.

Quine takes a pragmatist approach to translatability in his theory of radical translation. The indeterminacy of translation focuses not on the preservation of objective meaning between a sentence and its translation, according to Quine, but rather on the practical purposes of translation and the social nature of language. In what follows I briefly present Quine's notion of indeterminacy of translation and then argue that Locke's conception of values makes for a comparable theory of translation.

In the first section of this chapter I discuss Quine's notion of radical translation. I then move on to a discussion of Alain Locke's conception of values, mapping what Locke has to say about value onto Quine's radical translation, and then point out the primary area in which a Lockean theory of translation would diverge from that of Quine. Finally, in the last section I briefly show how Locke's linguistics (as I present it, as Locke himself does not offer a linguistic theory) answers Andrea Nye's demand for a feminist linguistics.

Quine's Indeterminacy of Translation

Willard Van Orman Quine's theory of radical translation stresses the social aspect of language. That is, according to Quine, "the correct use of language generally . . . is inculcated in the individual by training on the part of society."[1] Quine uses the following analogy to illustrate social groupings of language given subjective diversity: "Different persons growing up in the same language are like different bushes trimmed and trained to take the shape of identical elephants. The anatomical details of twigs and branches will fulfill the elephantine form differently from bush to bush, but the overall outward results are alike."[2] This social context of language makes possible only indeterminate translations from one natural language to another. In *Word and Object* Quine presents his indeterminacy of translation thesis:

> Manuals for translating one language into another can be set up in divergent ways, all compatible with the totality of speech dispositions, yet incompatible with one another. In countless places they will diverge in giving, as their respective translations of a sentence of the one language, sentences of the other language which stand to each other in no plausible sort of equivalence however loose.[3]

In other words, for any two natural languages, say, L and M, there are an indefinite number of possibilities for translating a sentence of L into M. For example, sentence s of L may be translated into p of M or q of M depending on the translation manual used. According to the indeterminacy of translation thesis, then, p and q of M are incompatible translations each based on a different system of translation or translation manual, and there is no objective way to determine a definitive translation.[4] Consider also Michael Dummett's description of the indeterminacy of translation thesis, which clearly indicates the combination of the underdetermination thesis and the thesis of essential accessibility to facts. This thesis states that

> certain criteria of correct translation [exist] whose application can be determined by observation of the linguistic behaviour of the speakers of the language, but that, within the limits imposed by these criteria, many different translation schemes may be possible between which there is no objective criterion which will select any one as alone correct.[5]

Translation manuals are formulated through a linguistic experiment in which the linguist (the translator) observes a native speaker, for example, and notes certain linguistic responses to stimuli. The linguist then formulates hypotheses about what certain utterances mean and tests these hypotheses through carefully calculated questions, marking the native speaker's assent and dissent. This does not mean that any sort of "correct" translation manual will result. On the contrary, it is precisely the point of Quine's indeterminacy thesis to claim that a "correct" or "true" translation is not determinable.

The linguist, in developing and testing the hypotheses in an attempt to translate the native language, makes certain practical assumptions. That is, the linguist assumes that the native speaker "perceives things in more or less the way he (the linguist) does, that the native is not a logical idiot, that the native shares pretty much the same general background beliefs, etc."[6] Note that "background beliefs" here does not mean cultural agreement of belief systems. Rather, it is referring to the metatheory that language is used, for example, to name objects of reference. In order to allow for even indeterminate translation, a "uniformity that unites us in communication and belief" must be assumed.[7]

Quine's indeterminacy of translation thesis combines two theses: the *thesis of the underdetermination of translation* and the *thesis of the essential accessibility of facts*.[8] The underdetermination thesis says that "[f]or any social group there will be more than one system of triads of meaning, belief and action (based on different translation manuals) all of which render the group's behaviour intelligible."[9] The linguist's evidence leaves the precise system of "meaning, belief and action" underdetermined. Or to put the underdetermination thesis another way, "there will be more than one translation manual which fits equally well the behavior" of a certain linguistic community.[10]

The thesis of the essential accessibility of facts has to do with the empirical content/verification of facts. In other words, the closer a sentence is connected with empirical stimulation, the more it is subject to be affected by experience/verification. This becomes clearer in discussing meaning according to Quine.

Perhaps the most important aspect of a theory of translation is the role of meaning and truth in translating from one language to another. As Quine says, "meaning, supposedly, is what a sentence shares with its translation."[11] Meaning in an objective, definitive sense gets set aside in the indeterminacy of translation thesis. That is, meaning also is indeterminate. Quine's famous "Gavagai" example illustrates this. Briefly, it amounts to the fact

> that stimulus meaning as defined falls short in various ways of one's intuitive demands on 'meaning' as undefined, and that sameness of stimulus meaning is too strict a relation to expect between a native occasion sentence and its translation—even in so benign a case as 'Gavagai' and 'Rabbit.' Yet stimulus meaning, by whatever name, may be properly looked upon still as the objective reality that the linguist has to probe when he undertakes radical translation.[12]

Quine's indeterminacy of translation argues for a theory of meaning in the tradition of Frege in that meaning is not a function of the word but of the sentence. It is not solely a function of the structure of the sentence. For translation this means that there can be no single correct translation based on syntax or grammar conjoined with a literal translation of terms. Quine replaces traditional theories of objective meaning with his notion of stimulus meaning, which he calls "the class of all the stimulations."[13] That is, "a stimulus meaning is the stimulus meaning *modulo n* seconds [that is, maximum stimulation duration allowed] of sentence S for speaker *a* at time *t*."[14] For radical translation, stimulus meaning is the "objective reality that the linguist has to probe." That is, it is the uniformity of impressions that are shared by the native and the linguist, even though they may organize those impressions differently. The linguist translates, however, "not by identity of stimulus meanings, but by the significant approximation of stimulus meanings."[15] Translation cannot be by identity of stimulus meanings because the linguist has no way of knowing whether or not the native perceives and organizes stimuli in the same manner as the linguist.

In unpacking this notion of stimulus meaning, Quine contends that occasion sentences, whose stimulus meanings tend to coincide for various speakers, may be called observational. The model of language suggested by Quine is comparable to a web. Observational sentences are at the outer edges of the web and thus connected closely with experience. The inner sentences are more determined by the relations to other sentences.[16] All, however, are dependent to some degree on each other. Observationality, then, is the "degree of constancy of stimulus meaning from speaker to speaker."[17] This is important for translation because the greater the degree of observationality, the better the possibility of translation according to stimulus meaning. Conversely, intersubjective variability of stimulus meaning, according to Quine, makes a sentence low on observationality. In this case, for example, a low observational or unobservational occasion sentence, stimulus meaning is "a product of two factors, a fairly standard set of sentence-to-sentence connections and a random personal history; hence, the largely random character of the stimulus meaning from speaker to speaker."[18] Thus, even with a high degree of observationality, the translation of the native sentence will be indeterminate.

Now that I have briefly discussed some of the main aspects of Quine's indeterminacy of translation thesis, I turn to Alain Locke's understanding of values where we can find, I will show, notions that are compatible with Quine's theory of translation.

Alain Locke's Conception of Values and Translation

I began my discussion of Quine by indicating that language is socially inculcated. Similarly, we can infer from Locke's views of culture as the fusion of values that language is socially instilled. Locke says that "in the large majority of cases the culture is only to be explained as the resultant of the meeting and reciprocal influence of several culture strains."[19] If language also can be explained as the meeting of "several culture strains," then a Lockean theory of language learning would certainly resemble Quine's indeterminacy of translation thesis. In addition, Locke states that all philosophies are subject to place and time and that the categories by which we organize our world are socially instilled.[20] Hence, a philosophy of language for Locke would be subject to situational elements, and language itself subject to social "training."

As a philosopher of language, Locke would certainly be averse to any attempt to derive a formal language theory of translation. Rather, any Lockean theory of translation must arise from a particular historical context. As Locke writes, "All philosophies . . . are in ultimate derivation philosophies of life and not of abstract, disembodied 'objective' reality; products of time, place and situation, and thus systems of timed history rather than timeless eternity."[21] Locke's notion of value and the challenge he issues against "traditional" notions of knowledge and truth provide a link to language and thus also offer insight into what a theory of translation might look like for Locke.

From what Locke argues in "A Functional View of Value Ultimates," we can infer that he would hold an indeterminate theory of translation (and also theory of meaning). In his critique of the value realist, Locke says

> From the functionalist's point of view the basic error lies in regarding the formal value as the cause of the valuation or as an essence of the value object rather than the system of value of the mode of valuing, which is sometimes the symbol, sometimes its rationale, but in practise an implementation of the value as apprehended.[22]

That is, the value realist is mistaken in formalizing values and fixing content. Instead, Locke turns his attention to how values function. So too with translation. To explicate: the possibility of a determinate translation is rejected as unable to account for practical instances of communication that cannot be explained in a formal model. Rather, translation focuses on what is apprehended between, for example, the native and the linguist. This apprehension is conditioned by situation, and thus a variety of incompatible but equally "correct" translations could be made, with no objective criteria to determine a single definitive translation. This also is implicit in what Locke says about values: "All values are disputable. They involve a relation to a valuer whose valuation need not be correct, and need not be accepted."[23] Hence, a Lockean theory of translation would entail the indeterminacy of translation.

To put the matter somewhat differently, a theory of translation for Locke would be interested in a translation in which the understanding of a cultural belief, for example, is communicated from one natural language culture to another. Cultural agreement, though, is not presupposed, because that would indicate that there is some "absolute" truth that various cultures would discover in translating their belief statements. Rather, as Locke says, "we shall probably have to content ourselves with agreement of the common-denominator type and with 'unity in diversity' discovered in the search for unities of a functional rather than a content character, and therefore of a pragmatic rather than an ideological sort."[24] By challenging the notions of "pure knowledge" and "absolute truth" Locke has also, in effect, challenged the notion that there is a determinate or correct translation that preserves meaning and truth from a sentence to its translation. The recognition that valuations are present in the process of assessing facts is part of the pragmatist's challenge of so-called absolute truth: "Facts, being the objects of truths, must all imply values, and it must be vain to search for any existence which is wholly free from valuation."[25] So in terms of philosophy of language, a Lockean theory of translation ought to be a functional theory that allows for conveyance of approximate meaning from one language to another.

The above quotation illustrates that Locke's translation theory would include assumptions similar to the practical assumptions Quine's linguist makes about the native speaker. That is, from Locke's discussion of "common denominator" we can infer that in translation a person could assume some sort of "uniformity that unites us in communication and belief."[26]

Recall that for Quine certain sentences that were low observational or unobservational relied on relations with other sentences, while observational sentences relied for their meaning on the relation to other sentences and to experience (that is, stimulus meaning can serve as meaning for observational sentences). A similar thesis can be found in Locke's conception of values. Locke says that value is embodied in human institutions:

> [V]alue cannot be denied existence in any world that can exist for man, and this in several senses. (1) They are operative in and on human minds, and find expression in human acts and *embodiment in human institutions; (2) they can occur in, and relative to, any universe of diction, however fanciful;* (3) hence also in ideals and fictions, both of which are sometimes said to be incapable of real existence, and cited as objections to the connection of values with existence.[27] (my emphasis)

And "Values appear to be positive and negative. As they express the attitude of a subject to an object, they indicate the acceptance or rejection, pursuit or avoidance, of the former, the attractiveness or repulsiveness of the latter."[28]

Here Locke's notion of value and his understanding of "the character of value-generals as system norms" in "A Functional View of Value Ultimates" carve a place for a theory of translation that allows for, and even requires, various "translation manuals," each of which may be said to be conditioned by the behavior of the linguistic community and the situational implementation. Additionally, that values are a function both of structure and of the subject's attitude shows that a theory of meaning for Locke is compatible with a Quinean notion of stimulus meaning.

Truth, for Locke, may include a person's attitude toward something, or the satisfaction of a feeling. Locke presents a cultural and contextual relativism that challenges the "fictive quality of knowledge." In other words, "Knowledge begins not with observed data, but with the set of norms or standards we use for sorting, classifying, measuring, assessing, and ranking data, as well as norms for making linguistic reports about our observations."[29] Thus we can infer that meaning and truth would also be a result both of the way in which we categorize/organize the world and of empirical verification:

> Hence the testing of a value-postulate always, in a sense, presupposes its truth, though not in any sense that makes this presupposition alone a sufficient reason for regarding it as absolutely true; still it is better to get a postulated value confirmed by experience than to accept the mere recognition of value as an adequate guarantee of its existence.[30]

Not unlike Quine, Locke critiques theories of meaning that are "limited to the field of truth and knowledge."[31] Indeed, both Quine and Locke stress empirical aspects of meaning and challenge traditional notions of objective, "absolute" truth and "pure" knowledge. The truth of a proposition, for example, is not merely its correspondence with a fact in the world, even if that fact were known free from any sort of valuation (which Locke claims is not the case). Rather, Locke's conception of value stresses the affective dimension of truth as well. Indeed, all facts are valuations, and all judgments involve the attitude and feeling of the subject.

> It follows (1) that a certain subjectivity, or, better, a relation to personality, is inherent in all values; (2) that value arises out of the mind's practical attitude, when it reacts upon stimulation, and that for a purely theoretic or contemplative view no values would exist; (3) that values are something super-added upon the other qualities of objects by the mind, in order to express their relation to its purpose and acts, and do not inhere in objects *per se.*[32]

Finally, consider what Locke has to say about the functional value of fact in human existence. Locke accounts for the modification of fact according to the state of knowledge. That is, the "recognition of fact . . . is always relative to the existing state of knowledge, and may be modified as knowledge grows."[33] Knowledge, however, as was seen above, involves the subject's attitudinal disposition and feeling mode.

Locke's linguistics carries a conception of truth that requires undergoing constant reevaluation and focuses on the feeling and attitudinal dimension of the subject: "All values are disputable. They involve a relation to a valuer whose valuation need not be correct, and need not be accepted."[34] And later, "valuations necessarily vary according to the changes in the organic needs which condition them."[35] Notice how closely this resembles what I referred to earlier (in the discussion of Quine and observationality) as the web. As for Quine, meaning (in translation) would, in part, be a function of the sentence's dependence upon other sentences as well as stimulus verification, Locke's "web" would be subject to constant transvaluation as the subject's attitude affects meaning.

One of the most striking incompatibilities between Quine and Locke (or where Quine and Locke diverge) is also that aspect of a Lockean linguistics that allows me to choose Locke over Quine in responding to Andrea Nye's criteria for a feminist linguistics. The main difference, as I see it, has to do with how each views indeterminacy. Given Locke's functional view of values, we can infer that the indeterminacy of translation is a positive aspect of communication in that it illustrates one of the ways in which we organize the world and relate with one another. Indeterminacy of translation is a manifestation of unity in cultural diversity as well as transvaluation. The unity is that translation is possible for practical purposes. The cultural diversity is manifest in the variety of translations that result from subjective attitudinal responses to empirical stimuli.

The role of feelings in Locke's conception of values further cements his divergence from Quine. Locke contends that "values are rooted in attitudes, not in reality, and pertain to ourselves, not to the world."[36] From this we can presume that Locke's indeterminacy stems from, and is integral to, the subject's attitude toward the function of translation. Indeterminate translations serve different implementation purposes and thus illustrate how "a transformation of the attitude effects a change of type in the value situation."[37] Translation not only is an effect of varying languages but also involves varying valuations among speakers and communities.

This diverges from Quine in that Quine's linguistics is a pragmatic account of translation. His view of indeterminacy stems from socially inculcated manners of organizing the world. Meaning is a function of stimulation and the interdependent structure of sentences, but there does not appear to be any place in Quine for attitude affecting meaning in translation. Additionally, moral values themselves have a greater extent of cross-cultural objectivity than language. According to Quine,

> Moral values may be expected to vary less radically than language from one society to another, even when the societies are isolated. True, there are societies whose bans and licenses boggle our sheltered imaginations. But we can expect a common core, since the most basic problems of societies are bound to run to type. Morality touches the common lot of mankind.[38]

Language does not have this "common core," with the exception of what was stated above regarding the practical assumptions the linguist makes in formulating a translation manual. Thus, for Quine, indeterminacy is rooted in reality (reality being social norms of belief and meaning). But, apart from personal history, there is little the subject adds to meaning. Both Locke and Quine hold that translation is possible, but they differ in their views of the subject's role in translatability.

Quine draws a boundary between values and language (science). Though it is the case that language is socially inculcated, it is not the case that schemes have political relevance. Lynn Hankinson Nelson argues convincingly that Quine contends that "Advocacy, involvement, and engagement are standardly taken to impair or preclude objectivity."[39] A Lockean account of translation, in contrast, considers the plurality of human beings engaging in speech acts. Language is not just a communal phenomenon, it is also intersubjective. Individual attitudes have no place in Quine's theory of translation. Indeed, from "the practical assumptions" the linguist makes in formulating a translation manual, it is evident that certain "background beliefs" need to be shared by the linguist and the native speaker. As Donald Davidson remarks, "Since knowledge of beliefs comes only with the ability to interpret words, the only possibility at the start is to assume general agreement on beliefs."[40]

The crucial aspect of this distinction for reading Locke, as opposed to Quine, as a precursor of feminist linguistics is the incorporation of subject and communal attitudes, social-political commitments, and norms. While both the Quinean and the Lockean theories of translation account for cross-cultural communication that achieves some level of applicable understanding, only the Lockean theory, grounded in cultural relativism, accounts for interpretation of incommensurable languages. That is, translation takes on the additional task of relaying specific cultural (or subjective) commitments. And, as Richard Bernstein notes, a translation theory grounded in incommensurability rather than an objective, universal framework for all languages need not result in a sort of crude relativism. Rather, such a theory recognizes pluralistic traditions as well as the ethical responsibility to try to understand, interpret, and communicate among, incommensurable languages. As Bernstein says:

> We can never escape the real practical possibility that we may fail to understand 'alien' traditions [and languages] and the ways in which they are incommensurable with the traditions to which we belong. But the response to the threat of this practical failure—which can sometimes be tragic—should be an ethical one, i.e., to assume the responsibility to listen carefully, to use our linguistic, emotional, and cognitive imagination to grasp what is being expressed and said in 'alien' traditions.[41]

Alain Locke as a Feminist Linguist

In this final section I first present the criteria for a feminist linguistics as articulated by Andrea Nye and then show how Locke's conception of values informs just such a linguistics.

In her essay "The Voice of the Serpent: French Feminism and Philosophy of Language," Andrea Nye suggests four things that a feminist linguistics would do. The first is that "such a linguistics would have to focus on the language we all speak to each other."[42] Feminist linguistics would focus on language as communication that establishes relations and not language as an objective, formal study.

Next, a feminist linguistics must "accommodate the fact that we are sometimes 'imprisoned' in ways of thinking and speaking that are alien and not of our making."[43] That is, objects of our desire "are constantly reworked by us, in each conversation between communicating speakers" (243). Communication is not an attempt to convey a private self, as a private self cannot be understood by others. Rather, language is used to speak what others can understand. Language serves as a means of establishing a relationship with those around us.

Third, Nye asserts that a feminist linguistics "must not remove itself from the political power of language" (244). That is, language is the substance of political action when it is "seen as the constantly reworked shape of desires whose reworking constitutes our mutual power over each other—especially the power to understand each other" (244).

Finally, "a feminist linguistics would have to be focused on changing usage and not 'timeless' structures. Language cannot be studied outside its social, economic, familial context. It cannot be separated from the historically situated desires and motivations that give it meaning" (245). In addition, Nye indicates that feeling modes of the speaker are included in particular utterances: "No pretension to the status of an objective metalanguage can elevate any meaningful account of language beyond intention and passion. Even a theory of language must admit to the intentions that make it understandable" (245).

As has already been stated, Locke can be read as offering a model of translation that focuses on approximate cultural understanding to the point that communication is possible without requiring the preservation of objective meaning between the sentence and the translation. Hence his philosophy of language focuses on communication as establishing relations, as Nye's criterion requires. Additionally, like Nye's feminist linguistics, Locke's linguistics would definitely not be a study of formal language but would be the product of "time, place and situation."

Nye's second criterion for a feminist linguistics stipulates that transvaluation takes place and language can only communicate valuation on certain levels. That is, the speaker's belief can only be indeterminately translated /understood by the hearer. Her qualification that objects of our desires are "constantly reworked by us" helps make Locke's theory of language and meaning fit the feminist linguistics where Quine's fails. That is, Locke's inclusion of the subject's attitude allows for the reworking of valuation in each conversational implementation that Nye requires.

Nye's third criterion for a feminist linguistics requires the recognition of the political power of language. Indeed, from Locke's notion of how value preferences have tended to become rationalized into absolutes and from his discussion of transvaluation, we can infer that a Lockean theory of language would emphasize "the constantly reworked shape of desires."[44] According to her criterion, then, Locke's linguistics, presented above, recognizes the political content of language.

Finally, Nye suggests that a feminist linguistics is context dependent; that is, it "cannot be separated from the historically situated desires and motivations that give it meaning." As we have seen, all philosophies, and most certainly a philosophy of language, are, according to Locke, "systems of timed history"—in other words, context dependent. Thus the theory of linguistics proposed for Alain Locke via his conception of values meets the criteria that Andrea Nye suggests for a feminist linguistics. Fortunately, Alain Locke has provided future generations of feminist linguists with a model from which to work.

Notes

1. Willard Van Orman Quine, *Word and Object* (Cambridge: MIT Press, 1960), 5.
2. Quine, *Word and Object,* 8.

3. Quine, *Word and Object*, 27.

4. Ian Hacking, "Language, Truth, and Reason," in *Rationality and Relativism*, ed. Martin Hollis and Steven Lukes (Cambridge: MIT Press, 1989), 58.

5. Michael Dummett, *Truth and Other Enigmas* (Cambridge: Harvard University Press, 1978), 385.

6. William G. Lycan, *Logical Form in Natural Language* (Cambridge: MIT Press, 1986), 221.

7. Quine, *Word and Object*, 8.

8. W. Newton-Smith, "Relativism and the Possibility of Interpretation,"in *Rationality and Relativism*, ed. Martin Hollis and Steven Lukes (Cambridge: MIT Press, 1989), 116. Dummett calls the *thesis of the essential accessibility of facts* the *inextricability thesis*. Dummett, *Truth and Other Enigmas*, 409.

9. Newton-Smith, "Relativism and Interpretation," 116.

10. Newton-Smith, "Relativism and Interpretation," 116.

11. Quine, *Word and Object*, 32.

12. Quine, *Word and Object*, 39.

13. Quine, *Word and Object*, 32.

14. Quine, *Word and Object*, 33.

15. Quine,*Word and Object*, 39–40.

16. This is clearly discussed in Simon Evnine's *Donald Davidson* (Stanford, Calif.: Stanford University Press, 1991).

17. Quine, *Word and Object*, 43.

18. Quine, *Word and Object*, 45.

19. Alain Locke, "The Concept of Race as Applied to Social Culture," in *The Philosophy of Alain Locke: Harlem Renaissance and Beyond,* ed. Leonard Harris (Philadelphia: Temple University Press, 1989), 195. Hereafter cited as "Locke" followed by the name of the particular essay and page.

20. See Locke. "Concept of Race as Applied to Social Values."

21. Locke, "Values and Imperatives," 34.

22. Locke, "A Functional View of Value Ultimates," 86.

23. Locke, "Value," 117.

24. Locke, "Cultural Relativism and Ideological Peace," 75.

25. Locke, "Value," 118.

26. Quine, *Word and Object*, 8.

27. Locke, "Value," 120. My emphasis.

28. Locke, "Value," 117.

29. D. Mason, "Deconstruction in the Philosophy of Alain Locke," *Transactions of the Charles S. Peirce Society* 34, no. 1 (Winter 1988): 94.

30. Locke, "Value," 121.

31. Mason, "Deconstruction," 97.

32. Locke, "Value," 111.

33. Locke, "Value," 119.

34. Locke, "Value," 117. See also 123.

35. Locke, "Value," 124.

36. Locke, "Values and Imperatives," 46.

37. Locke, "Values and Imperatives," 40.

38. Quine, "On the Nature of Moral Values," in *Theories and Things* (Cambridge: Harvard University Press, 1981), 62, quoted in Lynn Hankinson Nelson, *Who Knows: From Quine to a Feminist Empiricism* (Philadelphia: Temple University Press, 1990), 132.

39. Nelson, *Who Knows,* 33.

40. Donald Davidson, "On the Very Idea of a Conceptual Scheme," in *Inquiries into Truth and Interpretation* (New York: Oxford University Press, 1984), 196.

41. Richard Bernstein, "Incommensurability and Otherness Revisited," in *The New Constellation: Ethical-Political Horizons of Modernity/Postmodernity* (Cambridge: MIT Press, 1991), 65–66.

42. Andrea Nye, "The Voice of the Serpent: French Feminism and Philosophy of Language," in *Women, Knowledge, and Reality: Explorations in Feminist Philosophy,* ed. Ann Garry and Marilyn Pearsall (Boston: Unwin Hyman, 1989), 243. For another perspective of feminist linguistics, see in the same volume Janice Moulton, "The Myth of the Neutral 'Man.'"

43. Nye, "Voice of the Serpent," 243.

44. See Locke, "Values and Imperatives," 31–50; and "Values," 109–26.

4

African Art and the Harlem Renaissance: Alain Locke, Melville Herskovits, Roger Fry, and Albert C. Barnes

Mark Helbling

The New Negro both documents, and is meant to be a document for, the "dramatic flowering of a new race-spirit" taking place on American soil. Although Harlem is understood to be the "mainspring," the "laboratory," the "capital" of this "fresh spiritual and cultural focusing," Harlem's roots go deep into "the racy peasant undersoil of the race life." Historically and geographically, the lines of racial consciousness run North and South. At the same time, Harlem also intersects with other lines of awareness that link with Africa and the dispersion of African peoples into the frontiers of the New World. In Locke's striking phrase, Harlem is the "home of the Negro's Zionism," drawing upon, as well as expressing the full diversity of, "Negro life" (the African, the West Indian, and the Negro American). Not only are black Americans conscious of acting as "the advance guard of the African peoples in their contact with Twentieth Century civilization," but also this awareness is, in turn, an "effort to recapture contact with the scattered peoples of African derivation." Thus, *The New Negro* is meant to symbolize, to celebrate, and to further this dramatic shift in racial consciousness.

Locke was not the first black American to link Africa and America both historically and imaginatively. W. E. B. Du Bois's book *The Negro* (1915) was a major effort to establish the cultural importance of Africa and its significance for black Americans. And Du Bois's work takes its place alongside that of the many, often anonymous, others in the nineteenth century who evoked Africa in song, sermon, political tract, novel, and historical essay. But *The New Negro* seeks to fuse past and present on the level of image and imagination. Whereas Jean Toomer suggests that the Dixie Pike "has grown from a goat path in Africa," Langston Hughes writes of the Negro soul that "has grown deep like rivers"—the Euphrates, the Congo, and the Nile. And river and path open, as well, upon Bruce Nugent's "Sahdji," Arthur Schomburg's "The Negro Digs Up His Past," Locke's "Legacy of the Ancestral Arts," trickster stories, Baoule and

Bushongo masks, the drawings and decorative designs of Aaron Douglas, and Du Bois's "The Negro Mind Reaches Out." In its several parts and as a whole, *The New Negro* represents "a fresh spiritual and cultural focusing."

In recent years, several students of the Harlem Renaissance have taken note of Locke's ambitious claims and have offered their own understanding of what was and was not achieved. Harold Cruse, for example, in *The Crisis of the Negro Intellectual,* sees the "black intelligentsia" of the 1920s not as an "advance-guard of the African peoples" but as a generation of intellectuals seduced by white attention and the chimera of radicalism voiced by the Communist Party. As a consequence, Cruse argues, the clarifications that should have been made were never achieved, and subsequent generations have paid the price.[1] Likewise, Nathan Huggins argues in *Harlem Renaissance* that, compelling as it was to identify with Mother Africa, the ultimate results of this identification were ambiguous. Ambiguity, however, was not only in the results per se but also in the search itself. For it is Huggins's claim that Americans—black and white—are provincials "forced through condition and education to look elsewhere for the springs of civilization and culture." As a consequence, Huggins writes, "black men yearned, as American provincials, to find meaning and identity in Africa; their frustration was a measure of their Americanization."[2] Although their analysis differs, both of these critics look back to the 1920s as a time when Africa's imagined importance for black Americans served only to reveal the limits and frustration of the imaginations involved.

Until recently various elements of Cruse's and Huggins's critical concerns have framed subsequent interpretations of the Harlem Renaissance. Houston Baker, however, radically challenged the general emphasis on limits and limitations and, in so doing, offered a very different reading of the importance and accomplishments of these earlier figures. As Baker emphatically states in *Modernism and the Harlem Renaissance,* "I disagree entirely with the general problematic I have just suggested, a problematic that judges the Harlem 1920s a 'failure.' In my discussion I offer what is perhaps a sui generis definition of *modern Afro-American sound* as a function of a specifically Afro-American discursive practice."[3] As Baker's title suggests, his revision of the Harlem Renaissance turns on the conceptual term "modernism"—that, he argues, has prejudiced understanding and ensured misunderstanding ever since.[4] Better to begin with Booker T. Washington's speech at the Negro exhibit of the Atlanta Cotton States and International Exposition (18 September 1895) than Virginia Woolf's calendrical musing that "in or about December, 1910 human character changed."[5] Better to root Afro-American modernism in the trickster language of Washington than the "collaged allusiveness of T. S. Eliot's *The Waste Land* and Joyce's *Ulysses,* the cubist reveries of Picasso, the imagism of Pound, or the subversive politics of surrealists."[6]

Although Baker doesn't pursue the issue, implicit in his critique of modernism as a frame of reference is the allied term "primitivism" that has long served to link the two concepts with each other and with Africa as well.[7] Listen, for example, to Meyer Schapiro's ecstatic salute to the Armory Show that brought modern art to New York City in 1913:

> In this love of the primitive as a stronger, purer humanity, the moderns built upon a novel taste of the nineteenth century. But now for the first time the intensity and simplicity of primitive color and drawing were emulated seriously. . . . [T]ogether with this simplicity and intensity, which seemed to revive a primitive layer of the self . . . the painters admitted to their canvases . . . uncensored fancies and associations of thought akin to the world of dreams; and in this double primitivism of the poetic image and the style they joined hands with the moralists, philosophers, and medical psychologists who were exploring hidden regions and resources of human nature in a critical, reforming spirit. The artists' search for a more intense expression corresponded to new values of forthrightness, simplicity, and openness to a joyous vitality in everyday life.[8]

William Rubin's two-volume *Primitivism in Twentieth-Century Art: Affinity of the Tribal and the Modern* (1984) is but one of many recent efforts to document as well as celebrate the "twin phenomena" of the modern and the primitive.[9]

In the critical literature on the Harlem Renaissance, however, this connection has been central to the ambivalence that has been voiced by various critics. Huggins, for example, linked his comments on Africa and African American provincialism with what he called "the Negro intellectual's fascination with primitivism."[10] Likewise, Robert Bone argued in *Down Home* that in one way or another the writers of the Harlem Renaissance had been victims of this "racist caricature"; "some black authors embraced the new stereotype, others tried to fend it off, or adapt it to their own ends, but all succumbed in one way or another to its seductive power."[11] For Baker, these critical judgments, however well intended, were essentially self-defeating. Taking his cue from Michel Foucault's *Madness and Civilization*—"if you are in a madhouse, then you must be mad"—Baker abandoned altogether the categories that had "dominate[d] the analytical discourse of Afro-Americans."

Freed from the tyranny of this conceptual mistake, it was now possible, Baker argued, to see that Africa and things African had resonance within a field of discourse distinctly and importantly African American. Countee Cullen might write, "One three centuries removed / From the scenes his fathers loved / Spicy grove and banyan tree, / What is Africa to me?" but the significance of his statement was not its problematic blend of images, its imaginative limits, but the fact that Cullen, along with others of his generation, subverted as well as displaced prevailing assumption as to what black Americans thought, felt, and were capable of expressing.[12] At the same time, Baker took note of the African masks and statues from Bushongo, Sudan-Niger, the Ivory Coast, Dahomey, and the Congo that graced the pages of *The New Negro*. They serve, he suggests, as "ancestral and culturally specific leitmotivs." Thus, it was clear to Baker, at least, that Locke's inclusion of these "ancestral arts" contributed importantly to *The New Negro*'s meaning—"a broadening and enlargement of the field of traditional Afro-American discursive possibilities." Africa was not antithetical to one's sense of *patria* but an element of consciousness within a field of awareness whose boundaries only then were in the process of being formed.[13]

More recently, George Hutchinson also argues in *The Harlem Renaissance in Black and White* that modernism is key to a conceptual understanding of the Harlem Renaissance and key, as well, to the intellectual and institutional dynamics that mark these years: "To enter the history of American modernism by way of an interracial perspective, I believe, can offer a new vision of the period."[14] No less than Baker, Hutchinson was unhappy with previous interpretations that employed "high" modernism in one way or another as if it were a relevant concern:

> Indeed, it is still the case that discussions of modernism and the Harlem Renaissance often pit black writers against white writers like Eliot, Pound, and Stein, who inhabited a very different space (literally) in the modernist landscape, while ignoring or giving little careful attention to the forms of uncanonical 'native' (white) modernism with which the African American renaissance was intimately related.[15]

As Hutchinson's comment suggests, he was also critical of Baker. However, Hutchinson, no less than Baker, strongly qualified previous claims that primitivism was central to black and white conceptions of African American identity:

> The point I am suggesting here is that the dominant view of the approach of the New Negro—and their white friends—to African identity simply does not square with the documentary evidence. It recognizes only one side of a complex dialectical relation and ignores the real significance of Boasian anthropology, pragmatism, literary realism, and historicism to the New Negro movement—all of which exerted a powerful and salutary counterpressure to the exploitation of 'primitive and exotic' projections of the white racial psyche.[16]

For both men, the concern for Africa and African art was important emotionally and symbolically, a key element in the "notion of a renaissance as a recovery of 'classical heritage heretofore overlooked or ignored.'"[17]

Although Baker's and Hutchinson's emphasis contrasts in important ways with other interpretations, their work adds little to our understanding of how Locke came to assemble these forms, the specific aesthetic and cultural meaning they were meant to have, and the particular dilemmas he tried to resolve in giving to Africa a visible presence in *The New Negro*. At the same time, these modernist figures cannot easily be dismissed or set aside. Their presence was significant, and no one was more aware of their presence and their significance than Locke himself. In his essay "The Legacy of the Ancestral Arts," Locke called attention to almost every major painter and sculptor in Germany and France to respond to African art in the beginning decades of the twentieth century. And beyond the works of Picasso, Matisse, Marc, Modigliani, Epstein, and Lipschitz, Locke's thoughts also included the poets Guillaume Apollinaire and Blaise Cendrars as well as critics and collectors Paul Guillaume and Roger Fry. Locke's point is that (1) "there would be little hope of an influence of African art upon the western African descendants if there were not at present a growing influence of African art upon European art in general"[18] and (2) that "African sculpture has been for contemporary European painting and sculpture . . . a mine of fresh *motifs*." As a consequence, shouldn't there be, he proposes, no less an influence "upon the blood descendants, bound to it by a sense of direct cultural kinship?"

To answer Locke's challenge, to pursue the aesthetic and cultural considerations that he brings to bear, it is necessary to trace the vein of riches he himself first opened. In so doing, it will become clear, as well, that names not usually associated with the "prospects of [this] rich yield"—Franz Boas, Melville Herskovits, Alfred Stieglitz, Albert C. Barnes, Paul Guillaume, and Roger Fry—were also important contributors to the *communal* project known as *The New Negro*.[19]

Locke's essay "The Legacy of the Ancestral Arts" is the revision of an earlier article "A Note on African Art" that first appeared in *Opportunity* (May 1924), a special issue on African art that also included Barnes's "Temple" and Guillaume's "African Art at the Barnes Foundation." Not only does Locke's essay "A Note on African Art" provide a perspective on the second essay, its elaboration, and its shift in emphasis, but it also suggests a theoretical framework for the evaluation of African art.

Locke begins this essay with the emphatic claim that "The significance of African art is incontestable; at this stage it needs no apologia."[20] In fact, given the range of fantasy and misinformation with which African art has been burdened, Locke suggests that "Its chief need is to be allowed to speak for itself, to be studied and interpreted rather than to be praised or exploited."[21] What he offers, as a consequence, is a brief historical sketch to help trace the altered perception of things African from "dumb, dusty trophies of imperialism" to objects of art. What seems most significant to Locke, however, is that African art has both an aesthetic and a cultural meaning:

> What it is as a thing of beauty ranges it with the absolute standards of art and makes it a pure art form capable of universal appreciation and comparison; what it is as an expression of African life and thought makes it an equally precious cultural document, perhaps the ultimate key for the interpretation of the African mind.[22]

Ideally, these two considerations, the universality of a pure art form and the formal particularity of African expressions, would be related. But for the present, they represented two important but as yet separate understandings.

Locke's thoughts were partly an act of clarification, an effort to sort out present concerns from past assumptions and misconceptions. Beyond this, he also looked forward to "the construction of a new broadly comparative and scientific aesthetics" to help answer such basic questions as the origin and function of art. For this reason, he singled out the work of Emile Torday and J. A. Joyce on the Bushongo and A. A. Goldenweiser's *Early Civilization* (1922) as especially promising ethnographic "lines of interpretation."[23] At the same time, he anticipated that the comparative study of such "culture elements as art, folklore and language" would eventually provide "the most reliable clues and tests for African values" as well as the sense of a cultural past for black Americans as they "struggle for a racial idiom of expression" all their own.

Although Locke singled out Goldenweiser and his work *Early Civilization* as a hopeful beginning for comparative study, it was Melville Herskovits, not Goldenweiser, who most nearly fulfilled this role. Whereas Goldenweiser did most of his work among the native peoples of North America, as did Boas and almost all of his students, it was Herskovits, soon to be a close friend and colleague of Locke, who would devote his life to the study of African culture and its spread into the Western Hemisphere.[24] More important, however, than attempting to distinguish the particular impact of any one individual on Locke's understanding of African art were the broad lines of analysis that students and colleagues of Boas all shared with their common mentor. In his praise for *Early Civilization,* for example, Locke called attention to Goldenweiser's "rejection of the evolutionary formula which would make all African art originate from crude representationalism" and his emphasis on abstract principles of design and aesthetic form as "determinants of its stylistic technique and conventions." These concerns and this emphasis, however, were rooted in Boas's groundbreaking work, *The Mind of Primitive Man,* which appeared in 1911.

In his revolt against the evolutionary racial science of the nineteenth century (what George Stocking calls "the critique of racial formalism"), Boas challenged the fundamental presumption, "a lack of originality," that supposedly distinguished Europeans from non-Europeans and justified the world's peoples being ranked in stages of ascending superiority. In so doing, Boas offered an alternative formalism in which the "rational forms" evident in the cultural objects of non-Europeans (basketry, carvings, architecture, pottery, metalwork, and spinning) revealed both technical skill and the play of individual imaginations. To be creative, quite simply, was intrinsically a human phenomenon and "the evaluation of actions from [an] ethical and aesthetic viewpoint" something "peculiar" to mankind as a species. However, more than universality was being argued here. For Boas's emphasis on a shared "aesthetic impulse" was cast within an intellectual framework that stressed diversity and the plurality of standards necessary to evaluate the success and meaning of a people's aesthetic achievements. Art, like culture, had its own intrinsic integrity. As a consequence, the problematics of history, not the uniformities of science, were best suited to help reveal their shared integrity. Herein was the matrix of ideas that Boas would develop more fully in his later work *Primitive Art* (1929).

Primitive Art is built on the premises that "in one way or another esthetic pleasure is felt by all members of mankind" and that "no matter how diverse the ideals of beauty may be, the general character of the enjoyment of beauty is of the same order everywhere."[25] Beauty, however, is knowable only by its form, and form, in turn, is directly related to technique, the technical skills and traditions carried within a people's cultural experience. Thus, in making form ("fundamental forms," "fixity of form," and "fixity of design") and not content the essential critical consideration, Boas argued for both the universality of human consciousness and the diversity of human expression.[26] In isolating the formal properties of art, however, Boas introduced a tension into his argument that he, as well as Locke, would struggle to resolve. For in validating the arts of other peoples, and with form the theoretical centerpiece, the relationship between art and culture became increasingly strained.

The immediate problem Boas sought to address, how best to contextualize or arrange the available artifactual evidence, was central to his lifelong challenge to nineteenth-century evolutionary anthropology. In his earlier disputes with the principal authorities of the Smithsonian, for example, Boas argued with John Wesley Powell and Otis T. Mason for displays that grouped objects so as to suggest the "whole way of life" of a particular people. "Life-groups," not man in the abstract, were Boas's intellectual focus. But no matter how they were grouped, once objects were removed from their original context, their meaning became increasingly unclear. As George Stocking notes, "Removed . . . from their original contexts in space and time, and recontextualized in others that may or may not seek to recreate them, the meaning of the material forms preserved in a museum must always be acutely problematic."[27] Although Stocking was speaking more generally of the museum movement in anthropology, his comments are no less appropriate for judging Boas's efforts in *Primitive Art* to provide a context for the art he presented.

Boas introduces *Primitive Art* with the comment that "our object is . . . an attempt to determine the dynamic conditions under which art styles grow up."[28] He immediately notes, however, that the historical record is woefully inadequate to accomplish this goal: "the specific historical problem requires much fuller material than what we now possess. There are very few parts of the world in which we can trace, by archaeological or comparative geographical study, the growth of art styles."[29] As a consequence, Boas's effort to contextualize form(s) so as to suggest its meaning, the meaning to those who authored it, is severely compromised. To help fill this gap in space and time, he inserted into his text a carefully detailed, descriptive analysis of the style of the decorative art of the Coast Indians of the Pacific Northwest. His analysis, anchored in the continuity of "fixed formal elements found in this art," is meant to show that "this art style can be fully understood only as an integral part of the structure of Northwest coast culture."[30] But the leaves of this book, much like the ethnographic exhibits Boas battled to change, do not echo with the voices of those whose work we try to understand. Instead, the interpretive logic of Franz Boas fills the void left by history and research. Since, as he recognized, this strategy might not be entirely satisfactory, we the readers are asked to draw upon our own thoughts and feelings. It is presumed that, thus encouraged, we can now see not only ourselves in others but also others within ourselves.

Context was one challenge. Art or artifact was another. In his concluding remarks, Boas asks, "Do they [primitive peoples] possess the same keenness of esthetic appreciation that is found at least in part of our population?"[31] By now, given the detail and documentation of his work, the question is clearly rhetorical. The answer is yes. But the question has other implications. In making form central to the question posed, has Boas now undercut the problem of context from another direction? As Marianna Torgovnick writes:

> The tension between the designations "art" and "functional object" permeates the politics of art theory and museum exhibitions when they pertain to primitive societies. In turn, that tension forms part of this century's most characteristic intellectual debates between contextual and formal approaches, between differentiating via historical and cultural backgrounds and universalizing via the study of deep structures and continuing forms.[32]

Although the tensions Torgovnick refers to are rooted in a deeper and more general intellectual tradition than Boas's immediate concern for primitive art, they serve to frame his thinking. Perhaps, as James Clifford suggests, "the separation of ethnography and art has not been watertight."[33] But, as Clifford concludes, "generally speaking, the ethnographic museum and the art museum have developed fundamentally different modes of classification."[34]

Boas's remarks made in 1929 have no direct bearing on the ideas Locke put forth in "A Note on African Art." However, Locke was a careful student of *The Mind of Primitive Man*. And, as Herskovits's class notes from 1922 and 1923 reveal, these ideas were first introduced in Boas's teaching at Columbia and became part of the intellectual heritage his students took with them as they embarked on their own scholarly careers.[35] At the same time, a major strand of the friendship that developed between Locke and Herskovits was their shared interest in Africa and African culture. Six months after they first met in January 1924 and prior to teaching with Locke at Howard University, Herskovits made an extensive tour of the principal European anthropological and African ethnological collections.[36] One year later, he outlined to the National Research Council his hopes to trace the cultural roots of African Americans:

> I wish to continue my work on the Negro in Africa as well as in this country, on both the physical make-up of the African peoples in the region from which the ancestors of the American Negroes have come, and the cultural background which characterized those ancestors. . . . Although I have felt that the behavior of the American Negro is, in the main, quite like that of the Whites in this country, I must confess that there is a possibility of their being something of a differing temperamental base which has not been studied.[37]

Herskovits proposed returning to "the great African collections of the major European ethnological museums."[38] Later, with the help of Boas and Elsie Clews Parsons, he would do research in Surinam, West Africa (Dahomey, Nigeria, and the Gold Coast), and the Caribbean (Trinidad, Haiti). Throughout these years, Herskovits kept in touch with Locke. In 1931 he wrote:

> I am forwarding to you . . . something that you asked me for when I saw you before we left on our field trip. It comes from Nigeria and is a figure that is used by twins. When one of a pair of twins dies the other will always carry one figure such as this about with him and anything that happens to the living twin must also happen to the effigy or the spirit of the dead one will come to take away that of his brother or sister thus causing the death of the remaining one of the pair. . . . This was made by the grandfather of the present woodcarver, who also does beautiful things, and comes from the city of Abeokuta in Nigeria. Incidentally, don't let anyone talk to you about the extinction of African wood-carving or any other form of West African culturization. The cultures over there are very vital and are thoroughly integrated and resistant to European influences.[39]

Locke was delighted with the gift: "it is doubly precious for itself, and as a gift from you." "I don't suppose," he added, "it can affect me, except aesthetically."[40]

Important as the anthropological concerns of Boas and Herskovits were, the tensions Boas confronted in relating the part to the whole were compounded by Locke's effort to bridge the gap between Africa and America. At the same time, given the understanding that African art was "pure form," the gap Locke sought to bridge between Africa and America included that between "culture meaning" and "aesthetic meaning." Perhaps it was not yet possible to place African art within a meaningful historical or cultural framework.[41] As a consequence, one could only speculate as to what a particular carving or casting meant to its anonymous creator or to those by whom it was meant to be used. Aesthetically, however, as the embodiment of elemental form and as a catalyst for the European imagination, African art was at least knowable.

> It follows that this art must first be evaluated as a pure form of art and in terms of the marked influences upon modern art which it has already exerted, and then that it must be finally interpreted historically to explain its cultural meaning and derivation. What the cubists and post-expressionists have seen in it intuitively must be reinterpreted in scientific terms, for we realize now that the study of exotic art holds for us a serious and important message in aesthetics.[42]

The place to begin, then, was to pay close attention to its influence upon contemporary French art. For, Locke claimed, in contrast to the English and the Germans, the French had been most sensitive to the aesthetic values of African art, language, and music.[43] To help chart the way aesthetically, Locke singled out Paul Guillaume and Roger Fry as having provided the most "authentic interpretations."

In 1933 Fry was awarded the prestigious Slade Professorship of Fine Arts at Cambridge University. Although many thought the recognition unconscionably late, it did acknowledge Fry's long reign (perhaps along with Clive Bell) as the preeminent art historian and critic in English intellectual life. In Stephen Spender's estimation, at least, Fry was "the most constructive and creative influence on England between the two wars." In 1910 Fry organized the first postimpressionist exhibition, "Manet and the Post-Impressionists," and two years later followed this succès d'estime with a second postimpressionist exhibition. Thus, under Fry's continuing inspiration and goading, France in general and artists all but unknown in England—Cézanne, van Gogh, Gaugin, Vlaminck, Derain, and Picasso—soon became the center of a new consciousness called modern. At the same time, beginning with his essay "The Art of the Bushmen" (1910), Fry initiated a line of argument that linked the arts of non-

Western peoples with the cultural ferment he sought to inspire. In his important volume of essays *Vision and Design* (1920), Fry combined such diverse essays as "Negro Sculpture," "Ancient American Art," "The Ottoman and the Whatnot," "The Munich Exhibition of Mohammedan Art," and "The Art of the Bushmen" with essays on Paul Cézanne, Renoir, and the French postimpressionists.

In an important sense, Fry was a midwife in his own right, seeking to free his contemporaries from the "comfortable mental furniture" of the Greco-Roman tradition and the emphasis on content (or subject matter) as the essence of artistic accomplishment. To do this, he initiated a new vocabulary and a new sensibility to accompany and explain the art he challenged others to accept. What distinguished Fry's theoretical efforts to define "the re-establishment of purely aesthetic criterion in place of the criterion of conformity to appearance" was form ("significant form")—the essential parts (line, mass, space, light and shade, color, and the inclination of the eye of the plane) that constituted the separate but related parts of the total configuration.[44] As Beverly Twitchell suggests, "Though manifesting some diversity and incorporating shifts over a period of many years, Roger Fry's formalism was a broad but consistent feature unifying his massive work."[45] Here, then, was a voice to be heeded, one that contributed significantly to the profound changes taking place in "aesthetic sensibility" and the linking of this sensibility with a challenge as clear as it was astonishing: "The artist of to-day has therefore to some extent a choice before him of whether he will think form like the early artists of European races or merely see it like the Bushman."[46]

In "A Note on African Art" and then in *The New Negro,* Locke quoted directly from Fry's essay "Negro Sculpture." Most important, Locke claimed, Fry established the terms in which one could understand the historic and aesthetic importance of African art: "Some of these things are great sculpture—greater, I think, than anything we produced even in the Middle Ages."[47] What made this sculpture so great was "its complete plastic freedom." In contrast with Western notions of plasticity, burdened with concerns for representation, these "African artists really can see form in three dimensions."[48] As a result, these forms were not "mere echoes of actual figures" but possessed an "inner life of their own." Not only did Locke utilize Fry to provide his approach to perspective, but the question of perspective itself was no less important for Locke. As he pointedly remarked, "the problems raised by African art are now recognized at the very core of art theory and art history."[49] Thus, in the context of Fry's response to modern art and the problems Fry sought to resolve, Locke understood African art to be an imaginative awakening to the prevailing limitations of his and his people's cultural identity. However, within the configuration of modernism itself, which was defined by Fry as vision and design, there was a complex inner tension that rendered problematic the connections that Locke sought to achieve.

As Marianna Torgovnick has forcefully argued, Fry clearly had little to offer regarding the cultural meaning of the sculpture he praised so highly:[50]

> Quite strikingly, Fry makes no attempt to distinguish between different parts and different peoples in Africa. Hundreds of distinctions must be made; Fry makes only two—Bushman and 'Negro'—the breadth of the second category creating an overlap. More important, Fry shows no recognition that the objects discussed as museum pieces were often functional items, and sometimes sacred objects, in the daily life or special rituals of a people. . . . But even if we grant the validity of sometimes giving aesthetic considerations priority over ethnographic ones, the latter do not lose all relevance. Fry's discussion of African objects is analogous to a discussion of medieval chalices and reliquaries that proceeds without reference to Christianity or to the organization of the medieval church, indeed which neither knows nor cares that such things existed.[51]

But Locke did not seek this in Fry, nor did he comment on Fry's failure to integrate these "significant forms" into a cultural setting. Perhaps Locke was disappointed. More likely he did not expect this from someone like Fry. Instead, Fry offered something theoretically important, the possibility of conceptualizing art in such a way as to answer some of the questions that Locke had already explored philosophically and psychologically. Integration would be the work of others, individuals like Locke himself.

Locke wanted, as he writes in "A Note on African Art," a "scientific aesthetics," and Fry, in his effort to identify the "specifically aesthetic emotion by means of which the necessity of relations is apprehended," had drawn important analogies between art and science.[52] The two men, in effect, shared a desire to link the aesthetic with elemental states of emotion and to translate this emotion into a synthesis that was more than the sum of its parts. How to proceed, however, was not entirely clear. Form was the key. At a certain level, Fry argued, form and content became inextricably fused. But the translation of "the chaotic and accidental conjunction of forms and colours" into "the whole mosaic of vision" would prove to be elusive.

Fry never completely accepted Clive Bell's contention that "significant form" was some elemental quality entirely independent of time and space. What Fry called "the emotional elements of design" also included the artist's intentions and the observer's responses.[53] But, as Fry's biographers have noted, Fry was never fully able to pinpoint the meaning of form or its relationship to the meaning of the structured whole.[54] In 1914 he wrote, "is it not the fusion of this something with form that makes the difference between the finest pattern-making and a real design?"[55] Six years later, in the "Retrospect" to *Vision and Design,* he simply referred to "this vague adumbration of the nature of significant form."[56] Now, rather than slide into "the depths of mysticism," he preferred to leave the problem "on the edge of that gulf."[57] But the challenge remained, to be taken up by Albert C. Barnes. In his hand, the dilemmas Fry faced would be passed directly to Locke.

Highly opinionated and abrasive, Barnes dedicated his life to collecting and teaching art. In 1922, having amassed the largest private collection of modern art (Matisse, Monet, Picasso, Cézanne, Renoir, and Degas) and African art in the world, he established the Barnes Foundation in Merion, Pennsylvania.[58] Although Barnes's valuable collection of paintings has recently been made available for public viewing, he remains for most Americans an obscure and mysterious figure.[59] In December 1923 Barnes and Locke met in Paris. In the following month Barnes sought Locke's assistance for an article, "Contribution to the Study of Negro Art in America," to be published in *Ex Libris,* the journal of the American Library in Paris.[60] Three months later, Barnes informed Locke that his article would also appear in Paul Guillaume's *Les Arts à Paris* and hoped that if Locke thought "Contribution" had any merit, he would send it to an American journal so as to reach "the most sympathetic and intelligent attention."[61] One week later, Locke invited Barnes, who was now in Pennsylvania, to meet with several friends in New York City.[62] Thus began a friendship of uncertain complexity that would include, as well, Barnes's close and often strained involvement with several of the most prominent figures of the Harlem Renaissance.

Through Locke, Barnes was introduced to Walter White and Charles S. Johnson, who would both marvel at his formidable energy and quickly tire of his explosive temper and heavy-handed sense of self-importance. Upon their first meeting, White immediately asked for Barnes's assistance with an article, "If White Had Been Black," which he felt exceeded his own specific knowledge.[63] Barnes advised him that what he had written was "trash and shouldn't be published" and virtually overwhelmed him with a slashing critique of all whom White had used to make his argument:

[Stuart] Culin nice guy but a mental cripple, a hopeless doddering old ignoramus in anything which relates to art. [Carl] Einstein is a mental giant and a connoisseur compare[d] to him—that doesn't detract anything of truth of statement from my public assertion the other night that Einstein is a colossal bluff. De Zayas is in somewhat the same class as Einstein with dullness substituted for Einstein's Clive Bell–like counterfeit thinking in smooth, slick language.[64]

According to Barnes, the only individual of stature was Roger Fry: "let the sole reference to Negro plastic art be what Roger Fry has written." All the rest,

Barnes advised, were "the literary equivalents of prostitution."[65]

With Johnson, there was less acrimony. As editor of *Opportunity,* Johnson was in a position to be of use to Barnes and was generally receptive to Barnes's ideas.[66] In March, while abusing White both to his face and to others, Barnes asked Johnson if he would be interested in publishing his article on Guillaume, "The Temple," and coupled this inquiry with a prospectus for a future issue of *Opportunity* to be devoted to African art and the special role he and Guillaume had played in giving recognition to Africa's rich cultural heritage:

> 1. Paul Guillaume is potentially the most influential white friend the Negro has today. . . . [T]hat debt should be acknowledged.
> 2. The Barnes Foundation has ready a crack between the eyes for the so-called authorities in antique art. It consists in showing the masterpieces of Negro sculpture side by side with finer pieces of ancient Greek and Egyptian sculpture than can be found in the Metropolitan Museum of Art. It may be left to us to apply scientific method to make known that Negro art is in just that highest class of creations.
> 3. Nobody competent has ever studied Negro art according to the modern conceptions of the psychology of aesthetics utilized according to the scientific method.[67]

Johnson was especially eager to pursue Barnes's idea and promised that "this suggestion of yours should bear fruit and you may depend upon me to push it to the limit."[68] In May *Opportunity* offered a special issue on African art. The cover, provided by the Barnes Foundation, was a reproduction of a ceremonial mask from the Ivory Coast, and the lead editorial was a very complimentary introduction to Barnes and the work he was doing.[69] In addition to the article by Barnes and Guillaume's "African Art at the Barnes Foundation," Locke's "Note on African Art" comprised the content of this special issue.

Although Johnson had expressed interest in Barnes's "Contributions to the Study of Negro Art," he used "The Temple," Barnes's special tribute to the electricity of French intellectual life and Paul Guillaume's early and influential appreciation of African art. Now, however, Locke wanted "Contributions" (retitled "Negro Art and America") for the special Harlem issue of *Survey Graphic,* and this was soon followed by Locke's use of the same article in *The New Negro.* In fact, Locke had been reluctant to use Barnes's article in *The New Negro.* He would have liked to have Carl Van Vechten, the novelist and friend of almost every black cultural figure in the 1920s, write an article on the Negro in American art, but Van Vechten was committed to writing an article for *Vanity Fair* and pleaded lack of time. As a consequence, Locke had to settle for what he called the "kindly but vague assertions" of Dr. Barnes. Although Locke did not fully explain to Van Vechten his dissatisfaction with

Barnes, it seems clear that Barnes had offered little to help resolve some of the questions Locke had raised in "A Note on African Art."

Barnes's essay is an uneven blend of historical and cultural analysis. His generalizations, however, are grouped and somewhat unified by the sharp distinction he makes between the cultural and historical experience of whites and blacks: "That there should have developed a distinctively Negro art in America was natural and inevitable. A primitive race, transported into an Anglo-Saxon environment and held in subjection to that fundamentally alien influence, was bound to undergo the soul stirring experiences which always find their expression in great art."[70] In these terms, Barnes spoke forcefully of what "the cultured white race owes to the soul-expressions of its black brother" and singled out "the renascence of Negro art" not only as something of great beauty but also "as characteristically Negro as are the primitive African sculptures."[71] Barnes, however, no less than Fry, sent mixed messages. In this essay, Africa is little more than a timeless and placeless expanse of energy, its primary significance being its contrast to the aimless and devitalized ways of modern life. And in "Negro Art, Past and Present," an essay that appeared one year later in *Opportunity*, Barnes celebrates the achievements of black Americans, a people "torn from their native environment and from their carefree, irresponsible life."[72] Clearly, Barnes was of marginal help to Locke in his effort to provide a cultural context for the art he so greatly valued.

Barnes, like Fry, was essentially uninterested in the historical complexities of Africa and the myriad cultural distinctions that distinguished peoples who lived on the African continent from one another. In fact, the concern for this kind of detail in various ethnographic museums of the world was understood to be a problem that had to be overcome.[73] For this reason Barnes praised Guillaume as one who "had rescued the obscure ancient Negro art from its mere ethnological significance."[74] What mattered was art, not artifact, and as art these objects were understood to have a formal significance independent of their social and material context. Thus, Barnes notes that "ancient Negro sculpture" reveals in "the Negro race" an "entirely unsuspected wealth of plastic endowments" and "an ability to arrange forms in varied, rhythmic, harmonious, moving designs which do not suffer by comparison with the most distinguished classic achievements of any of the other races."[75] Barnes's response to African art, sustained in great part by Fry's critical authority, was itself an extension of the more general modernist concerns that Fry articulated in *Vision and Design, Transformations* (1926), and *Cézanne: A Study of His Development* (1927). Thus, Barnes's own work, *The Art of Painting* (1925), as well as *The Art of Cézanne, The Art of Matisse*, and *The Art of Renoir*, bears, in Beverly Twitchell's words, Fry's "distinctive imprint."[76]

Barnes lacked Fry's sophistication and Fry's awareness that theoretically formalism remained an ongoing intellectual and aesthetic challenge. For Barnes, in contrast, art was simply a self-contained dynamic of intrinsically meaningful elements (color, light, line, and space). And he applied his formula as if it were a stamp. As a result, his books are "lengthy, leaden, and often redundant."[77] In his own mind, at least, Barnes saw himself as "stripping [art] of the emotional bunk with which the longhaired phonies and that fading class of egoists, the art patrons, have encumbered it."[78] As he confided to Locke, he thought of himself as one of the few white friends of black Americans, a friend constantly beleaguered by misinformed and racist others.[79] From the point of view of Walter White and Charles S. Johnson, however, Barnes's presence was decidedly a mixed blessing. As for Locke, Barnes's "Negro Art in America" was acceptable only by default. He wanted "something more suggestive and concrete." Unable to find a suitable alternative, Locke offered his own interpretation of the past, "The Legacy of the Ancestral Arts," both to supplement and to extend Barnes's inadequate sketch.[80]

Much of "Legacy" is a rewording of material brought forward from his *Opportunity* article "A Note on African Art." Now, however, Locke's intention is to explore more directly the implications that African art might have for the social and cultural identity of black Americans. At the very least, Barnes, Guillaume, and Fry had helped to make African art visible as a vital and invaluable cultural heritage. But beyond the importance of this recognition, there remained for black Americans an inner psychic landscape to be explored and revealed—"hints of a new technique, enlightening and interpretative revelations of the mysterious substrata of feeling under our characteristically intense emotionality."[81] But again the conundrum: Blacks no less than the "average European Westerner" seemed to confront an enigma, strange forms from the void of time and distance. As Locke expressed it, "Except then in his remarkable carry-over of the rhythmic gift, there is little evidence of any direct connection of the American Negro with his ancestral arts."[82] What, then, to make of these compelling, yet alien, objects?

One answer Locke offered was to turn the alienation and incomprehension of the viewer into the very significance of what was observed. Thus, Locke argued that the inability to make sense of these unfamiliar objects was the result of a cultural conditioning that had imprisoned both whites and blacks within a limited range of increasingly meaningless forms and sterile conventions. Blacks, however, had been the more insidiously circumscribed in that the prevailing conventions had promoted little self-recognition beyond "caricature and genre study." Thus, African art functioned as a revelation through which to achieve new forms of self-expression and self-awareness. Such an answer, however, did little more than reword the problem that Locke had intended to answer.

More promising was his definition of African art as the expression of a folk temperament and a folk tradition. Now, more directly and inwardly racial, Locke here assumed an emotional bond between peoples of African origin, a bond foreign to those whose cultural roots traced back to Europe. And yet, Locke immediately confronted an impasse of even greater complexity than the limbo of past neglect he initially addressed:

> The characteristic African art expressions are rigid, controlled, disciplined, abstract, heavily conventionalized; those of Afraamericans—free, exuberant, emotional, sentimental and human. Only by the misinterpretation of the African spirit, can one claim any emotional kinship between them—for the spirit of African expression, by and large, is disciplined, sophisticated, laconic and fatalistic. The emotional temper of the American Negro is exactly the opposite.[83]

Black Americans were Americans, a people separated from their geographic and cultural origins and molded within the "peculiar experience [of] America and the emotional upheaval of its trials and ordeals." If, then, one could not expect from "the arts of the forefathers" either "cultural inspiration" or "technical innovations," perhaps it was possible to learn "the lesson of discipline of style, of technical control pushed to the limits of technical mastery."[84] However, whether such abstraction led to a "racial art" or rendered such an idea problematic remained to be seen.

Although Locke sought to improve upon Barnes's contribution to *Survey Graphic*, his argument was not strikingly different. The two defined and accounted for the creative vitality of black Americans in a similar way. Both celebrated the "pure plasticity" of African art and its impact on the intellectual and artistic imagination of Europeans. If Locke was more concerned than Barnes to relate the formal aesthetic properties of African art to an underlying racial and emotional temperament, his success advanced little beyond Barnes's declared intent to restrict himself to the "psychology of aesthetics."[85] Locke's dilemma lay in trying to discover in African art the very meaning(s) his aesthetic understanding and his critical vocabulary seemed to deny. At the conclusion of "Legacy," Locke was cautious yet hopeful that he had singled out a minimal basis upon which to proceed: "The African spirit is at its best in abstract decorative forms. Design, and to a lesser degree, color, are its original fortes." But Locke himself was not fully satisfied with this minimal answer.

Aware that a synthesis of the aesthetic and the cultural significance of African art remained to be achieved, Locke eagerly responded one year later to Carter G. Woodson's suggestion that he propose a plan of study of African art for possible funding by the Association for the Study of Negro Life and History. Locke indicated that what he proposed would be a study of "African art as an Expression (or index) of African culture." And he submitted a bibliography of readings as well as a list of the principal collections of African art that would constitute the initial research needed.[86] Upon receipt of Locke's proposal, Woodson consulted with Boas as to the potential value of such a study:

> Dr. Alain Leroy Locke, the author of a recent book entitled *The New Negro*, has suggested that the Association make him an allowance for the study of African art. His study will be partly research and partly interpretation. He has outlined it as the memorandum herewith enclosed will show. Kindly inform me frankly whether you feel that this study properly comes within the purview of what we planned to do in Anthropology or whether we can justly use our Anthropology fund to finance a study of this sort. I feel that such a work as Prof. Locke would produce should be very informing. I am in doubt, however, as to whether he can produce anything original on this side of the Atlantic and the fund will not be sufficient to finance him in Europe. I shall be governed by whatever you and Prof. Hooton may have to say.[87]

Boas, although he knew Locke personally and admired his work, regretted that he was unable to endorse his plan.[88] In a follow-up letter to a second inquiry from Woodson, Boas expressed doubt that Locke had sufficient "ethnological knowledge . . . to carry through a plan of this kind."[89] As a consequence, Locke's proposal was rejected, and the research he hoped to do was set aside.

For the remainder of the decade and into the next, Locke played a role similar to the one he discussed in "A Note on African Art," championing African art and its potential to help configure the cultural identity of black Americans. In "To Certain of Our Phillistines" (*Opportunity*, May 1925), "Art Lessons from the Congo" (*Survey Graphic*, February 1927), "A Collection of Congo Art" (*The Arts*, February 1927), "Beauty Instead of Ashes (*Nation*, April 1928), and "The American Negro as Artist" (*American Magazine of Art*, September 1931), Locke kept his audience informed as to the impact African art had had and continued to have on Europe's "leading modernists"—Picasso, Modigliani, Matisse, Epstein, Lipschitz, and Brancusi. And he coupled this ongoing instruction with the recognition of young black sculptors and painters ("the younger modernists") who had "begun to reflect African influences" in their work.[90] However, by the middle of the next decade, Locke's emphasis had shifted dramatically.

"African Art Classic Style" is Locke's response to the exhibition of African art organized by James Sweeney for the Museum of Modern Art in 1935. Locke was extremely impressed, stating that of the seven major exhibitions since Alfred Stieglitz first showed African art at Gallery 291 in 1914, this was clearly "the definitive exhibition of African classics." Not only did Sweeney draw from seventy-two European and American collections (the

Barnes Foundation being a conspicuous oversight), but also, and most important, he provided "a master lesson in the classic idioms of at least fourteen of the great regional art styles of the African continent."[91] Although Locke still associated "classic" with the "art object" itself, his emphasis now was on context (fourteen regional styles) and the historical "phase" when this art came to fruition.

African art, Locke now argued, was "best understood directly, and in terms of its own historical development." To look at Africa through modernist eyes was, in effect, to see African art "through a glass darkly." Not only were analogies with the classic art of Greece and Rome misleading, but also it was a distortion to see this art in terms of "its correlation with modern art or its admitted influence upon modern art."[92] To do so was to dilute its strength and simplicity. Locke even accepted Sweeney's suggestions that (1) "the new appreciation of African art" and the "Negro plastic tradition" and (2) "the working out of the new aesthetic in European art" were "coincidental rather than cause and effect."[93] Nowhere in this essay does Locke encourage his reader to see Africa as a mirror. Nowhere does form hold promise for an African American identity. Africa expresses Africa, and we, together with Locke, stand on the margins—"Apart from texture and feel," Locke notes, "I fancy there can be little appreciation of it [African art] in anything approaching native terms."[94] Differences, not similarities, are what one must now learn, and learn to accept. The Museum of Modern Art, Locke concludes, has rendered a great service, for what we now learn is that African art is "really too great for imitation or superficial transcription."

Ernest Mason and Leonard Harris have addressed Locke's cultural and aesthetic concerns and in so doing provide a complement to the general argument that Houston Baker made in *Modernism and the Harlem Renaissance*. In "Black Art and the Configurations of Experience: The Philosophy of the Black Aesthetic," Mason links the etymological sense of the term "aesthetic" ("perceptible by the senses") together with Locke's understanding of experience as "form-quality." In so doing, the boundaries of experience are understood to be extremely elastic, and the province of the "aesthetic attitude" is neither provincial nor limited to the formal properties of art: "perceptual recognition is, as Locke tells us, the act of experiencing figures (objects, events, situations, persons) not in isolation but contextualized with a reciprocating movement of perception, conception and valuation."[95] Thus, Mason argues, Locke provided an important theoretical foundation for a black aesthetic, one that included "the experiences and perceptions that black people [had] of themselves and others."[96] And Harris, in "Identity: Alain Locke's Atavism," also argues that much of what Locke wrote was an effort to broaden the political and cultural identity of black Americans, "weapons in the theoretical battles of the day."[97]

In particular, to counter the critical views of Nathan Huggins and Harold Cruse, Harris understands Locke's intellectual concerns to be a serious effort to shift attention away from essentialist ("atavistic") explanations of cultural identity to cultural and historical forms of explanation. It is in the context of this argument, then, that Harris pays special attention to Locke's need to confront "the anthropological status of black people as humans" and his interest in Africa and African art.

Both points of view situate Locke within the mainstream of concerns that black intellectuals addressed in the 1920s. Importantly, Mason and Harris relate these concerns to Locke's intellectual and theoretical imagination. What we don't see, however, is what Locke shared with others, most notably Franz Boas and Melville Herskovits, Roger Fry, Paul Guillaume, and Albert C. Barnes.[98] To paraphrase Mason, the "experience" Locke sought to configure included a range of critical opinion that linked New York with London and Paris.[99] At the same time, this shared understanding posed problems for Locke that he was unable to resolve. Leonard Harris is quite right to emphasize that context and contingency, not "innate temperaments and quintessential cultural traits," distinguish Locke's philosophic and cultural discourse. But Locke shared with others the "essential" understanding that African art was form. However, as Jean Laude has argued, such appreciation was highly selective and, uniquely modern and gave to African art an abstract significance it rarely possessed for those who created it.[100] As a consequence, providing a context for these "rigid, controlled, disciplined, abstract, heavily conventionalized" figures proved difficult. No less difficult was the effort to construct an "emotional kinship." Ultimately, Locke had to question the adequacy of the intellectual resources he had drawn upon. No less problematic were the emotional qualities of form that Locke derived from epistemology as well as experience.

At a 1996 showing of African art objects at the Guggenheim, "Africa: The Art of a Continent," considerations that Locke struggled to resolve sixty to seventy years earlier continued to challenge informed opinion. Most notably, Cornel West, Kwame Anthony Appiah, and Henry Louis Gates Jr. all addressed the Western response to things African (Africa itself) so as to free the present from this limited and limiting intellectual heritage. West, for example, declared:

Gone are the old intellectual frameworks predicated on crude white supremacy and subtle Eurocenticism. The once popular categories of "barbarism," "primitivism," and "exoticism" have been cast by the academic wayside. The homogeneous definitions and monolithic formulations of "African art" have been shattered. The Whiggish historiographical paradigms of cultural "evolution" and political "modernization" have been discarded.[101]

Appiah offered an even more fundamental challenge, addressing his reader as well as the exhibition itself:

> So we might as well face up to the obvious problem: neither *African* nor *art*— the two animating principles of this exhibition—played a role as ideas in the creation of the objects in this spectacular show.[102]

In their critique of the Western response to African art, neither West nor Appiah made any effort to establish a particular need or concern that African Americans might have in the exhibition's brilliant presence. For both men, the exhibition simply challenged "our prevailing views of reality," and, as Appiah suggested, these magnificent pieces "should be a potent reminder of the humanity you share with the men and women that made them."

Gates, too, critiqued "the court of judgment that is Western art," focusing on the European modernists for whom African art was so important and whose response to this art so deeply shaped future understanding.[103] Although Gates is no less intent than West and Appiah to insist on the intrinsic beauty of African art, he is more explicitly concerned with the interpretive response of African Americans.[104] In this context, he calls attention to Locke's essay "The Legacy of the Ancestral Arts," which appeared in *The New Negro*:

> Locke's solution to this quandary . . . is as curious as Picasso's waffling about influences upon him: by imitating the European modernists who so clearly have been influenced by African art . . . African Americans will become African by being modern.[105]

However, if Locke's attitude toward African art and, by extension, the attitudes of other African Americans are to be addressed, his ideas must be given a fuller reading. Clearly, there is an argument to be made that the ambivalence that individuals such as Picasso felt toward Africans—"this assembly of degenerate and feeble-minded posterity"—contributed to the ambivalence that African Americans also felt regarding the beauty of African art. But this was a consideration that Locke himself had already voiced (though not directed at Picasso per se) in his ambivalence toward the writing of Albert C. Barnes and in his efforts to encourage an awakened black consciousness. At the same time, Locke did not argue that "African Americans will become African by becoming modern. His thinking was more complex than that. In fact, he came to understand that modernism was not so much a universal that subsumed the particular but itself a particular understanding or conception no less partial than the diversity it was thought to transcend.

It is unfortunate that the only reference to Locke that appears in the entire volume on the Guggenheim exhibit suggests that, at best, his efforts only fostered a kind of "Afro-kitsch." Ironically, Locke's struggle to make sense of African art anticipates many of the same critical considerations later made by West, Appiah, and Gates in their response to "Africa: The Art of a Continent." Although he draws upon the critical opinions of James Sweeney and other non-African sources in his essay "African Art Classic Style" (1935), Locke, as we have seen, distinguishes African and modernist concerns as well as the concerns of Africans and African Americans. Above all, he concludes (sounding very much like these later commentators): "It [this exhibit] presents African art as really too great for imitation or superficial transcription. Its result must surely be to engender respect for the native insight and amazement for the native technique."[106] It is time that Locke's pioneering interests be placed no only in his own time but also in ours.

Notes

1. Harold Cruse, *The Crisis of the Negro Intellectual* (New York: William Morris, 1967), 21–22.
2. Nathan Huggins, *Harlem Renaissance* (New York: Oxford University Press, 1971), 83.
3. Houston Baker Jr., *Modernism and the Harlem Renaissance* (Chicago: University of Chicago Press, 1987), xiv.
4. "I would suggest that judgments on Afro-American 'modernity' and the 'Harlem Renaissance' that begin with notions of British, Anglo-American, and Irish 'modernism' as 'successful' objects, projects, and processes to be emulated by Afro-Americans are misguided. It seems to me that Africans and Afro-Americans—through conscious and unconscious designs of various Western 'modernisms'—have little in common with Joycean or Eliotic projects. Further, it seems to me that the very *histories* that are assumed in the chronologies of British, Anglo-American, and Irish modernisms are radically opposed to any adequate and accurate account of the history of Afro-American modernism, especially the *discursive* history of such modernism." Baker, *Modernism and Harlem Renaissance,* xv–xvi.
5. Virginia Woolf, "Modern Fiction," in *The Common Reader,* ed. Andrew McNeillie (New York: Harcourt Brace Jovanovich, 1984).
6. Baker, *Modernism and Harlem Renaissance,* xiii.
7. It is interesting to note that Woolf dated the shift in human character to the response to the first postimpressionist exhibition in England, "Manet and the Post-Impressionists," organized by Roger Fry. And in the same year, Fry had published his essay "The Art of the Bushman" in the journal *Atheneum.* See also Roger Fry, "Bushman Paintings," Burlington Magazine for Connoisseurs 16 (October 1909–March 1910): 334.
8. Meyer Schapiro, "Rebellion in Art," in *America in Crisis,* ed. Daniel Aaron (New York: Alfred Knopf, 1952), 214–15.

9. Other important books in this celebratory tradition are Robert Goldwater, *Primitivism in Modern Painting* (New York: Harper Brothers, 1938; repr. Cambridge: Harvard University Press, Belknap Press, 1986); Carl Einstein, *Negerplastik* (Leipzig: Verlag der Weissen Bucher, 1915); and Marius de Zayas, *African Negro Art: Its Influence on Modern Art* (New York: Modern Gallery, 1916); Thomas Munro, "Primitive Negro Sculpture," *Opportunity* 4, no. 41 (May 1926): 150–52; and Paul Guillaume, *Primitive Negro Sculpture* (New York: Harcourt, Brace, 1926).

10. Huggins, *Harlem Renaissance,* 187.

11. Robert Bone, *Down Home* (New York: G. P. Putnam's Sons, 1975), 125. Beyond the immediate focus of this ambivalence there has flowered an immense literature that has critically addressed a larger ambivalence—Western conceptions of "others" and the political and social consequences of these conceptions. Marianna Torgovnick *Gone Primitive: Savage Intellects, Modern Lives* (Chicago: University of Chicago Press, 1990); Adam Kuper, *The Invention of Primitive Society* (London: Routledge, 1988); and Susan Hiller, *The Myth of Primitivism* (New York: Routledge, 1991) are but three recent studies that have sought "to reevaluate basic Western conceptions from the viewpoint of systems of thought outside or aslant from those in the West." Torgovnick, *Gone Primitive,* 83. See also Michael North, *The Dialect of Modernism: Race, Language, and Twentieth-Century Literature* (New York: Oxford University Press, 1994).

12. As Baker writes, "Certainly Countee Cullen, for example, served a national need in a time of forced institution building and national projection. He gained white American recognition for 'Negro poetry' at a moment when there was little encouraging recognition in the United States for *anything* Negro. And Cullen gained such recognition by means of a mastery of form pleasing *to Afro-Americans* as well as Anglo Americans." Baker, *Modernism and Harlem Renaissance,* 86.

13. Although Arnold Rampersad addresses the Harlem Renaissance from a different perspective than Baker and with a specific focus on the imagination and poetry of Langston Hughes, he also addresses the "question of modernism" and suggests that "Hughes's place in it needs to be seen in the context not merely of Harlem but of international cultural change in the twentieth century." Arnold Rampersad, "Langston Hughes and Approaches to Modernism," in *The Harlem Renaissance: Revaluations* (New York: Garland, 1989), 67.

14. George Hutchinson, *The Harlem Renaissance in Black and White* (Cambridge: Harvard University Press, 1995), 31.

15. Hutchinson, *Harlem Renaissance in Black and White,* 14.

16. Hutchinson, *Harlem Renaissance in Black and White,* 185.

17. Hutchinson, *Harlem Renaissance in Black and White,* 428.

18. Alain Locke, "The Legacy of the Ancestral Arts," in *The New Negro* (New York: Atheneum, 1992), 255–56.

19. See also Marlgorzata Irek, "From Berlin to Harlem: Felix von Luschan, Alain Locke, and the New Negro," in *The Black Columbiad,* ed. Werner Sollors and Maria Diedrich (Cambridge: Harvard University Press, 1994), 174–84. Hutchinson has given extended attention to Locke's relationship with Barnes and John Dewey, Dewey and Barnes's close relationship, and their common interest in African art and the "aesthetics

of experience." Hutchinson's comments on Dewey help to clarify Locke's intellectual focus. And, as Hutchinson writes, "It was in dialogue with Guillaume and Barnes that Locke developed his chief orientation to African art." Hutchinson, *Harlem Renaissance in Black and White*, 427. However, Locke did not, as Hutchinson claims, borrow Barnes's views of African art "wholesale."

20. Alain Locke, "A Note on African Art," in *The Critical Temper of Alain Locke: A Selection of His Essays on Art and Culture* (New York: Garland, 1983), 131.

21. Locke, "Note on African Art," 131.

22. Locke, "Note on African Art," 131.

23. As Locke writes: "It is most encouraging therefore to see an emancipated type of scientific treatment appearing, with Torday and Joyce's historical interpretation of art in terms of its corresponding culture values, and in Goldenweiser's rejection of the evolutionary formula which would make all African art originate from crude representationalism, that is to say, naive and non-aesthetic realism. For Goldenweiser, primitive art has in it both the decorative and the realistic motives, and often as not it is the abstract principles of design and aesthetic form which are the determinants of its stylistic technique and conventions." Locke, "Note on African Art," 133.

24. In "Feeling Universality and Thinking Particularistically: Alain Locke, Franz Boas, Melville Herskovits, and the Harlem Renaissance," (in *Prospects* 19 [1994]: 289–314), I detail Herskovits's relationship with Locke and his becoming a colleague at Howard University.

25. Franz Boas, *Primitive Art* (New York: Dover, 1955), 9.

26. In addressing the question of style, whether the "purely decorative" or the "idea of representation," Boas concludes: "In every case . . . the formal element that characterizes the style is older than the particular type of representation. This does not signify that early representations do not occur, it means that the method of representation was always controlled by formal elements of distinctive origin." Boas, *Primitive Art*, 354.

27. George Stocking, *Objects and Others: Essays on Museums and Material Culture*, vol. 3 of *History of Anthropology* (Madison: University of Wisconsin Press, 1985), 4. See also in the same volume Elizabeth Williams, "Art and Artifact at the Trocadero: Ars Americana and the Primitivist Revolution," 146–66; Ira Jacknis, "Franz Boas and Exhibits: On the Limitations of the Museum Method of Anthropology," 75–111; and Edwin L. Wade, "The Ethnic Art Market in the American Southwest, 1880–1980," 167–91.

28. Boas, *Primitive Art*, 7.

29. Boas, *Primitive Art*, 280.

30. Boas, *Primitive Art*, 356.

31. Boas, *Primitive Art*, 356.

32. Torgovnick, *Gone Primitive*, 81.

33. James Clifford, "Objects and Selves: An Afterword," in *Objects and Others: Essays on Museums and Material Culture*, ed. George Stocking (Madison: University of Wisconsin Press, 1985), 242. John Dewey's comment in *Art as Experience* ([New York: Capricorn Books, 1958], 48–49), remains pertinent: "Suppose, for the sake of illustration, that a finely wrought, one whose texture and proportions are highly pleas-

ing in perception, has been believed to be a product of some primitive people. Then there is discovered evidence that proves it to be an accidental product. As an external thing, it is now precisely what it was before. Yet at once it ceases to be a work of art and becomes a natural 'curiosity.' It now belongs in a museum of natural history, not on a museum of art. And the extraordinary thing is that the difference that is thus made is not one of just intellectual classification. A difference is made in appreciative perception and in a direct way."

34. Clifford, "Objects and Selves," 242.

35. These are Herskovits's class notes taken 17 January 1923: "Thus in the case of representative and interpretive art we must see that the psychological attitude toward the two on the part of the artist is different—in the case of the latter there is the lively aesthetic-technological feeling, while in the case of representation the motive is very different—merely as a reminder or play or what not. The aesthetic motive is absent and the artist only has representation in view. When the artist gets virtuosity in technique the representation takes on an aesthetic element. This virtuosity can be highly developed in technical processes—basketry in California, tying in Polynesia, or trades (iron-working, weaving, pottery-making) in Africa—and technical excellence has an aesthetic value—e.g., a basket made with a regularity of stitch we call beautiful. Also, there is the tendency of the virtuoso to make his own task difficult. As soon as specialization occurs and the worker plays with his technique, pattern and design are bound to appear—as twilling in basketry. Similarly with the handling of planks with edges, geometrical patterns result from the playing with technique. Similarly with African ironwork.

"Thus, in art there are two unrelated sources of development—representative art, which may or may not have aesthetic value, and geometrical or conventional design, which develops from the play with technique. These may affect each other reciprocally but to arrange designs in series from representative to geometric art is a naive disregarding of the psychological background of art." Melville Herskovits Papers, Northwestern University Archives.

Importantly, Boas argues for the universality of the creative impulse. Herskovits and Locke, however, would both make efforts to give "the psychological background of art" a cultural meaning.

36. In his report to the Board of Fellowships in the Biological Sciences, National Research Council, Herskovits detailed his travels: England, France, Germany, Belgium, the Netherlands, Denmark, Sweden, and Italy (28 February 1925). Melville Herskovits Papers, Northwestern University Archives.

37. Melville Herskovits to Edith L. Elliot, 21 January 1926, National Research Council, p. 2. Melville Herskovits Papers, Northwestern University Archives.

38. "A study of such a problem as wood-carving of these people, an outstanding characteristic of their cultures, of their designs, or of some other cultural trait would at the same time give us an idea toward connecting the culture of the African with whatever vestiges of it might be observable in the American Negroes, and give me the most excellent possible preparation for the African field work I hope later to do. The problem of the West African wood-carving is of particular significance in the light of my

particular problem, since it is in the realm of the artistic products manifested in this country particularly through the Negro spiritual that any innate connection with the African temperament might most easily be seen." Herskovits to Elliot, 21 January 1926.

39. Herskovits concludes: "I hope you will be getting out here [Evanston] this winter as I should like nothing better than to show you some of the things that I brought back from this trip. My bush-Negro specimens are also out where they can at least be looked at and I would like you to see those, too." Melville Herskovits to Alain Locke, 29 October 1931, Melville Herskovits Papers, Northwestern University Archives.

40. Alain Locke to Melville Herskovits, 30 November 1931, Melville Herskovits Papers, Northwestern University Archives.

41. At least, Locke drew upon Guillaume Apollinaire's comments in *Apropos de l'art des noirs—1917* to make this point: "In the present condition of anthropology, one cannot without unwarranted temerity advance definite and final assertions, either from the point of view of archeology or that of aesthetics, concerning these African images that have aroused enthusiastic appreciation from their admirers in spite of a lack of definite information as to their origin and use and as to their definite authorship." Locke, "Note on African Art," 131.

42. Locke, "Note on African Art," 131.

43. As Locke writes, "Roughly speaking, one may say that the French have been pioneers in the appreciation of the aesthetic values of African languages, their poetry, idiom and rhythm." Locke, "Note on African Art," 134–35.

44. Although the term "significant form" is generally attributed to Clive Bell in his work *Art* (New York: Frederick Stokes, 1915), the inspiration and its more complex elaboration are understood to be Fry's. See Frances Spalding, *Roger Fry: Art and Life* (Berkeley and Los Angeles: University of California Press, 1980).

45. Beverly H. Twitchell, *Cézanne and Formalism in Bloomsbury* (Ann Arbor: University of Michigan Research Press, 1987), 78.

46. Roger Fry, "The Art of the Bushmen," in *Vision and Design* (New York: Meridian Books, 1966), 97.

47. Locke, "Note on African Art," 132.

48. Locke, "Note on African Art," 133.

49. Locke, "Note on African Art," 132.

50. Torgovnick, "The Politics of Roger Fry's *Vision and Design*," in *Gone Primitive*, 85–104.

51. Torgovnick, *Gone Primitive*, 97.

52. Fry writes, e.g.: "None the less, perhaps, the highest pleasure in art is identical with the highest pleasure in scientific theory. The emotion which accompanies the clear recognition of unity in a complex seems to be so similar in art and in science that it is difficult not to suppose that they are psychologically the same. It is, as it were, the final stage of both processes. This unity-emotion in science supervenes upon a process of pure mechanical reasoning; in art it supervenes upon a process of which emotion has all along been an essential concomitant." Fry, "Art and Science," 83.

53. "It may be that in the complete apprehension of art there occurs more than one

kind of feeling. There is generally a basis of purely physiological pleasure, as in seeing pure colours or hearing pure sounds; then there is the specifically aesthetic emotion by means of which the necessity of relations is apprehended, and which corresponds in science to the purely logical process; and finally there is the unity-emotion, which may not improbably be of an identical kind in both art and science." Fry, "Art and Science," 83.

54. See Frances Spalding, "Significant Form," in *Roger Fry: Art and Life,* 153–73.

55. Spalding, "Significant Form," 165.

56. Roger Fry, "Retrospect," in *Vision and Design* (New York: Meridian Books, 1966), 302.

57. Fry, "Retrospect," 302.

58. See Bruce Kellner, ed., *The Harlem Renaissance: A Historical Dictionary for the Era* (Westport, Conn.: Greenwood Press, 1984), 24–25.

59. In 1996 the Barnes collection made its first appearance outside the carefully guarded walls of Barnes's private estate. As reported in the *International Herald Tribune* (22 October 1996): "It was the first time the Haus der Kunst had ever stayed open all night. Then again, it was also the first time a museum show in Munich had drawn more than 400,000 people. . . . The exhibition, "From Cezanne to Matisse: Great French Paintings from the Barnes Foundation," was on the last day of its last stop on a two-and-a-half-year international tour. . . . Barnes had amassed about 800 paintings and 200 sculptures, including some 170 Renoirs, 55 Cezannes and 20 Picassos, which he liked to display in crowded, quirky arrangements that included Gothic hardware, African sculpture, furniture and porcelains. . . . the mystery of seeing these hidden treasures, major masterpieces by major artists that would never [be] shown outside Pennsylvania again, gave it serious news value."

60. "Thanks for your letter and your kind promise to send me the data requested. I want to glean only a summary of what the best-known Negro artists have done, not to worship them but to show their relation to what the ordinary, unknown, Negro lives every day in spiritual things. . . . I am interested in Negro art which is too commonly unrecognized or overlooked." Albert C. Barnes to Alain Locke, 8 February 1924, Howard University.

61. Gentler and more talented, Guillaume served as the foreign secretary for the Barnes Foundation. In his own right, he was an early collector of African art and a great admirer and friend of modernist painters who appeared at his doorstep and in the pages of his journal, *Les Arts à Paris.*

62. Although eager to make the trip, Barnes was not sure it would be safe. The following letter to Locke reveals Barnes's raw and overbearing personality: "At present if I went to New York I would run the risk of being arrested for criminal libel because of my public reprisals of the dirty trick the *Dial* pulled on Buermeyer in the March issue. Craven is just a propagandist for some ignorant, academic painters who announced their intention to 'wipe up the ring with me.' Thayer knows that, but is sore at me for what Paul Guillaume can tell you I did last summer to him and his then managing editor when I balked their project to do other dirty tricks on two people, one of whom was the honest Paul Guillaume. . . . the Craven article is a mixture of lies and innuendos,

while the statements of objective facts about paintings are sheer moonshine, and the cheapest bluffs." Albert C. Barnes to Alain Locke, 11 March 1924, Howard University.

63. Walter White to Albert C. Barnes, 24 March 1924, Howard University.

64. Albert C. Barnes to Walter White, 25 March 1924, Howard University.

65. Unsure what to make of Barnes's tirades, White forwarded his correspondence with Barnes to Locke, asking Locke to read the letters and "advise me what is the matter with your friend in Philadelphia." Walter White to Alain Locke, 12 April 1924, Manuscript Division, Library of Congress. Barnes, in the meantime, had been confiding to Locke that White's article was "ridiculous," that White was a "light-weight," and that his "manuscript has revealed a cheapness which I hardly suspected. . . . the whole mess is a sloppy offensive mess." Albert C. Barnes to Alain Locke, 25 March 1924, Howard University.

66. As did White, however, Johnson found Barnes to be difficult to take. In a letter to Locke, Johnson confided his feelings: "No, I did not attend the Philadelphia meeting and for several good reasons—one of them the folder which Dr. Barnes had published and distributed. I couldn't face Philadelphia after that. I like his enthusiasm and his extraordinary energy, and without doubt he has given a tremendous impetus to interest in *Opportunity*, but the personal exaggerations are absolutely devastating." Charles S. Johnson to Alain Locke, 16 May 1924, Howard University.

67. Albert C. Barnes to Charles S. Johnson, 22 March 1924, Howard University.

68. Charles S. Johnson to Albert C. Barnes, 26 March 1924, Howard University.

69. As Locke wrote: "Those who know Dr. Albert C. Barnes treat him as a valuable secret. In the heart of Philadelphia he has in successful operation one of the most astounding experiments in human relations in industry yet tried; in his home in Merion, Montgomery County, Pennsylvania, he has the most complete and valuable collection of modern art in this country, and one of the best in the world. He was the first and is distinctly the last word in Primitive African Art and his pieces, the rarest of their kind— exquisite, exotic, distinctive,—once casually valued at fifty thousand dollars, are becoming invaluable. This is primitive art, and there are limits to discovery. And there are yet Philadelphians who ask 'Who is Dr. Barnes?' And there are 'sophisticates' who sense the forcible entry of the primitive African motif into modern art, who take their wisdom from Clive Bell's clever vagaries and de Zayas' outlandish speculations. It is perhaps pardonable if this ritual of silence is broken, if only for a moment, on one who has known the native art of Negroes longer and who still knows it better than any one in the United States, and who ranks close to Paul Guillaume as one of the foremost authorities on it in the world." Alain Locke, "Dr. Barnes," *Opportunity*, May 1924, 133.

70. Albert C. Barnes, "Negro Art and America," *Survey Graphic*, March 1925, 668.

71. Barnes, "Negro Art and America," 668.

72. Albert C. Barnes, "Negro Art, Past and Present," *Opportunity*, 5 May 1926, 149.

73. See Williams, "Art and Artifact," 146–66.

74. Albert C. Barnes, "The Temple," *Opportunity*, May 1924, 139.

75. Barnes, "Negro Art, Past and Present," 168.

76. As Twitchell writes: "Barnes imitated Fry's objective aspirations in both formal analysis and explanation of techniques, as in his notion of taking an 'experimental atti-

tude.' When he analyzed works, Barnes discussed their 'components' and 'distinctive organization,' which united as 'plastic form.' Indeed, Barnes so condensed and simplified the views of Fry and Bell that he concluded that style, form, and expression were identical and inseparable from the artist's life and temperament." Twitchell, *Cézanne and Formalism*, 195.

77. In discussing Picasso's response to African sculpture, e.g., Barnes writes: "About 1909 the sculptural influence began to be paramount, and naturalistic rendering gave place almost completely to the rendering of abstract forms. In his still-lifes of this period several objects are often placed so close together that the whole group functions as a single mass. His former suave, curved lines have become sharp and heavy, and the objects outlined are angular and blocklike. The pinks, blues and yellows of his earlier work have changed into a somber combination of slate, drab green, and dull brownish red. These new shapes and colors are the distinctive mark of Picasso's form at that period and constituted the point of departure for cubism." Albert C. Barnes, *The Art of Painting* (New York: Harcourt, Brace, 1925), 390. For a more appreciative view of Barnes and his response to modern and African art, see Mark Meigs, "The Barnes Foundation and the Philadelphia Museum of Art: Bifurcated Loci of Cultural Memory," in Annales: Lieux de Mémoire aux Etats-Unis no. 18 (Chambéry: Université de Savoie, 1995), 37–64.

78. Carl McCardle, "The Terrible Tempered Barnes," *Saturday Evening Post*, 21 March 1942, 93.

79. Albert C. Barnes to Alain Locke, 7 May 1924, Howard University.

80. Clearly, George Hutchinson has overstated the case when he claims that "Barnes [was] the person upon whom Locke and *Opportunity* relied as their house expert on African aesthetics and its relation to European modernism . . . and [that] he borrowed his views of African art wholesale from the irascible manufacturer. Hutchinson, *Harlem Renaissance in Black and White*, 45.

81. In a letter to Walter White, Locke confirmed his own concern for "race temperament" in telling of a conversation he had with Paul Guillaume: "There is every indication, here and abroad, of increasing interest in the artistic possibilities of our race material and of our race temperament. Discussing the vogue of African Art in Paris and elsewhere on the Continent, M. Paul Guillaume told me that in his judgment merely the surface values had been exploited up to the present, and that in his view final interpretation and development of its possibilities could only conceivably come from within the race group." Alain Locke to Walter White, c. 1924, Manuscript Division, Library of Congress.

82. Alain Locke, "The Legacy of the Ancestral Arts," in *The New Negro* (New York: Atheneum, 1992), 254.

83. Locke, "Ancestral Arts," 254.

84. Locke, "Ancestral Arts," 256.

85. Barnes also envisioned something more than an exclusively formal analysis. As Locke quotes Barnes: "Negro art is so big, so loaded with possibilities for a transfer of its value to other spheres where Negro life must be raised to higher levels, that it should be handled with the utmost care by everybody. . . . It involves intellectual, ethical,

social, psychological, aesthetic values of inseparable interactions." Alain Locke, "Research for Primitive Art," *Opportunity*, June 1924, 165.

86. "My plan would be to undertake directly a study of AFRICAN ART AS AN EXPRESSION or INDEX of AFRICAN CULTUREsc, but in reading through the quite voluminous literature . . . to take notes and citations covering the broader field of the cultural values of the African civilizations in so far as social customs or social philosophy reflected in folk-lore, religious or social beliefs, or institutional practice might give clues to these values. Especially in the field of art symbols and their closely related religious conceptions, I believe we have the only available clues left to the moot question of the antiquity and indigenous character of certain supposedly African contributions to early civilization." The collections Locke listed were Brussels, London, the Pitt-Rivers private museum, Berlin Institute of Ethnology, Hamburg, Dresden, Frankfurt am Main, British Museum, Barnes Foundation Collection, University of Pennsylvania Museum, Ward Collection (Smithsonian), and the Blondiau Collection of Bushongo and Congo Art, which formed the Harlem Museum of African Art installed in 1927 in the Harlem Library on 135th Street. Alain Locke to Carter G. Woodson, 16 November 1926, American Philosophical Society.

87. Woodson went on to say: "I am taking it for granted that you know Prof. Locke is a well educated man of unusual ability. He is a Doctor of Philosophy of Harvard University. He studied at Oxford and in Germany. He can use both French and German in his researches. His advanced work in school, however, was in Philosophy rather than in History or in Anthropology. For some time he has been making a study of the background of the Negro in Africa. He has a keen appreciation of African art. My impression of him, however, is that he is a literary man rather than a research student willing to do drudgery." Carter G. Woodson to Franz Boas, 16 November 1926, American Philosophical Society.

88. Franz Boas to Carter G. Woodson, 18 November 1926, American Philosophical Society.

89. Franz Boas to Carter G. Woodson, 22 November 1926, American Philosophical Society.

90. Those Locke called "the younger modernists" included Archibald Motley, Lillian Dorsey, William H. Johnson, Hale Woodruff, Richmond Barthe, Sargent Johnson, James Lesesne Wells, and Aaron Douglas. This recognition was coupled with Locke's continuing encouragement to black Americans to see in Africa the locus of a new aesthetic and a new consciousness: "However, the constructive lessons of African art are among the soundest and most needed of art creeds today. They offset with equal force the banalities of sterile, imitative classicism and the empty superficialities of literal realism. They emphasize intellectually significant form, abstract design, formal simplicity, restrained dignity, and the unsentimental approach to the emotions. And more important still, since Africa's art creed is beauty in use, they call for an art vitally rooted in the crafts, uncontaminated with the blight of the machine, and soundly integrated with life." Alain Locke, "The American Negro as Artist," *American Magazine of Art* 23 (September 1931): 210–20.

91. Alain Locke, "African Art: Classic Style," *American Magazine of Art* 28, no. 5 (May 1935): 271.

92. Locke, "African Art: Classic Style," 271.

93. Locke, "African Art: Classic Style," 271–72.

94. Locke, "African Art: Classic Style," 271–72.

95. Ernest D. Mason, "Black Art and the Configurations of Experience: The Philosophy of the Black Aesthetic," *College Language Association* 27 (9 September 1983): 3.

96. Mason, "Configurations of Experience," 2.

97. Leonard Harris, "Identity: Alain Locke's Atavism," *Transactions of the Charles S. Peirce Society* 26, no. 1 (Winter 1988): 70.

98. Hutchinson has helped to clarify Locke's intellectual focus by giving extended attention to Locke's relationship with John Dewey and Albert C. Barnes, Dewey and Barnes's close relationship, and their common interest in African art and the "aesthetics of experience." However, Locke, as we have seen, had severe misgivings about Barnes and did not borrow, as Hutchinson claims, "his views of African art wholesale from the irascible manufacturer." Also, Hutchinson gives no attention to the formalist concerns of Roger Fry and his importance for both Barnes and Locke and too little attention to the significance of form in Franz Boas's discussion of culture and aesthetics. Hutchinson, *Harlem Renaissance in Black and White,* 42–50, 62–77.

99. In reply to a critique of *The New Negro,* Locke wrote to the literary editor of the *New York Sun,* "Now as to details, Mr. Seligmann balks both at camels of obviousness and gnats of particularities. When I say 'of one colored writer,' who happens to be Rudolph Fisher, that he combines the 'terseness and emotional raciness of Uncle Remus with the art of Maupassant and O. Henry,' it ought to be obvious that I mean to say he combines the naive and the sophisticated arts of narrative,—and I think he does. If, again, I include in a list of American music influenced by Negro idioms French works that on good authority of Darius Milhaud in *The Living Age,* June, 1925, were direct experimental limitations [imitations] by the French modernists of music they heard played by Negro musicians at the Casino de Paris and elsewhere, it ought to be obvious that I am not 'slipping,' but trailing—and a pretty obvious track. Coming to the other end of the scale with Mr. Seligmann, I don't see how it was particularly incumbent upon me to mention the Stieglitz exhibition as the first exhibit of African sculpture in America, when I didn't mention any. Had I, I would have cited the de Zayas exhibition of 1916, of which the pamphlet catalogue is listed in my bibliography. As to the contention that this or any other American exhibit was the 'first exhibition in the world to relate that (African) sculpture to modern French and American painting, sculpture and other modes of expression,' Mr. Seligmann has made a statement more foolish and unsupported than any he accuses me of making: page Picasso, of if not in the lobby, M. Paul Gullaume [*sic*]!"

100. As Laude writes: "Each African statue has a religious or, in the broad sense, a social purpose. It is an instrument or tool that has at the outset no emotional or aesthetic intent. Very few arts are so unconcerned as African art about the effect produced on viewers. Even the Bini bronze heads and statues, long thought of as products of secular art, were arranged on altars. Some Tellem, Dogon, and Bambara statuettes are covered

over with a sacrificial coating of dried blood or millet gruel or with adventitious elements such as cloth, nails, or shells, which blur or mask the sculpted forms." Jean Laude, *The Arts of Black Africa,* trans. Jean Decock (Berkeley and Los Angeles: University of California Press, 1971), 195–96.

101. Cornel West, introduction to *Africa: The Art of a Continent* (New York: Guggenheim Museum Publishers, 1996), 1.

102. Kwame Anthony Appiah, "Why Africa? Why Art?" in *Africa: Art of a Continent* (New York: Guggenheim Museum Publishers, 1996), 6.

103. Gates wondered "whether or not without black African art, modernism, as it assumed its various forms in European and American art, literature and music and dance in the first three decades of the twentieth century would possibly have existed as well." Gates, *Africa: Art of a Continent,* 6.

104. As Gates concludes: "And if the resurrection of African art, in the court of judgment that is Western art, came about as a result of its modernist variations, this exhibition is testament to the fact, if there need be one, that African art at the end of the century needs no such mediation. It articulates its own sublimity most eloquently. For centuries, it has articulated its own silent sublimity most eloquently." *Africa: Art of a Continent,* 25.

105. Gates, *Africa: Art of a Continent,* 25.

106. Locke, "African Art: Classic Style," 151.

5

Alain Locke's Multicultural Philosophy of Value: A Transformative Guide for the Twenty-First Century

Judith M. Green

In these last years of the twentieth century, intellectuals share both a longing and a fear with many other people who are concerned about practical affairs: a longing for the experience of a cooperative world community characterized by peace, justice, and democracy; and a fear that we must choose between unity so understood and the diverse group identities and values that tell us who we are and where we come from. In the early years of a century already grown old from violence and dislocation, the American philosopher John Dewey expressed a dream of "the Great Community" that many people share today.[1] Though Dewey's dream recognized the importance both of sustaining roots in a local community and of a resurgent, power-wielding greater public brought into self-conscious existence by communication employing shared cultural ideas and symbols, it did not include a mechanism for overcoming the deep ethnic divides within and between many nations, including his own. Philosophers from diverse theoretical backgrounds, including feminists, postmodernists, and Africana philosophers, have expressed skepticism about whether such "unity amidst diversity" is possible and desirable, and even if so, how it can be achieved in a world so divided by the lingering impacts of historical patterns of oppression and well-founded intergroup distrust.[2] Yet few embrace separatisms, perhaps realizing that there is no place to go where one group can safely get away from all the others and live a flourishing, self-sustaining life. Likewise, political and economic leaders, as well as concerned citizens of all nations, realize that we live in an increasingly interconnected world in which our future will be either "chaos or community," in the prophetic phrase of Martin Luther King Jr.;[3] either we will find ways to get along based on mutual respect and mutual benefit, or the interethnic warfare in Bosnia, Rwanda, and Northern Ireland will be only a foreshadowing of the global violence to come. The answer to Rodney King's tearful question to the world after the terrifying explosion of interethnic violence in central Los Angeles, "Can't we all just get along?" seems likely to be "No—not unless we can learn to talk with each other respectfully and work out mutually satisfying resolutions to our current problems that arise from our heritage of intergroup anger, distrust, injustice, and fear." Both theoretical and practical obstacles must be overcome if this sometimes dim hope of democratic community life is to be realized in the twenty-first century. We need the guidance of an insightful and useful philosophy of cultural and political transformation and effective ways to put it into practice. Because it is historically located, culturally specific, broadly humane, and productive of practical transformative strategies and insights, Alain Locke's philosophy of value offers important elements of both the theoretical and the practical guidance we need for transforming current global patterns of violent ethnic value strife into peaceful multicultural collaboration amid differences, the basis for a future democratic world community.

As Locke argues, much of our current interethnic violence springs from the reality that people are motivated by conflicting, universalized, yet constantly changing personal and group-shared value imperatives of feeling, in relation to which Kantian absolute and universal value imperatives of reason would have little relevance, even if they were theoretically well founded. Writing in the years between and following the world wars, Locke assumes the decisiveness of earlier pragmatist critiques of the Kantian theoretical framework instead of offering a comprehensive critique of his own.[4] However, Locke's criticisms of value absolutism focus on two subjects: the philosophical mistake of categorizing values as products of universal reason instead of group-influenced personal feelings, and the commonalities of wrongheadedness among the real and varied value absolutisms that drive the conflicts that have violently divided the world in the twentieth century. Cultural differences about values are real and significant, Locke argues, and there is no reasonable prospect that these differences will go away—nor would cultural uniformity be more desirable, even if it were achievable. Leonard Harris has suggested that, in Locke's view, "cultural diversity was inherently desirable" and "a multitude of ways of valuing is characteristic of our being and not a temporal phase of human history" (17).

Our ways of valuing, Locke argues, are feeling-modes that reflect both personal disposition and the influence of the group norms operative within the actual cultural context in which we grow up, develop our personal identities and group loyalties, and live our lives. These value feelings assert themselves as interpretive guides and imperatives that shape our reactions to situations, though we can revise them somewhat on the basis of reasoned judgment and the evidence of experience. However, because people tend to make the mistake of regarding their own particular individual and group value imperatives as timeless and universal categorical imperatives for all human beings as such, the problem of conflicting categorical imperatives repeatedly arises, made more urgent by competing group loyalties and the will to power.

As Locke insightfully points out, these value conflicts cannot be avoided or resolved by ignoring or disparaging the importance of differing personal and group values, which are fundamental aspects of our experience of reality and give us both interpretive and practical guidance. Rejecting a dualistic division of fact and value, as well as the priority accorded to fact by many twentieth-century theorists and advocates of science, Locke argues that facts and values are inextricably interconnected (47). Instead of trying to persuade people that their values are unreal or unimportant, he suggests, we need to find ways to teach people to hold their values less dogmatically and to bring their differing value systems into productive dialogue with each other.

Therefore, Locke wisely argues, we need to learn to understand the historically located experiences and culturally specific values of various, differing peoples through new culture-specific scholarship and, on that basis, to discover the commonalities within human experience that make certain basic values broadly humane. Locke variably calls the philosophical framework he believed was necessary and useful for guiding this scholarly project "cultural pluralism," "cultural relativism," "value relativism," and "critical relativism," but under each of these labels he rejected the assumption of radical cultural discontinuities in valuation and the belief that it would be disrespectful to comment on other societies' values that so often characterizes what is now commonly called "cultural relativism." Rather, Locke believed that a cross-disciplinary "anthropology in the broadest sense" (72) would reveal the specific and differing functional value adaptations that various peoples have made to their own environmental, historical, and geopolitical context, as well as a set of "functional constants" that underlie and potentially can interconnect differing cultural value frameworks (55). When a pluralistic understanding of cultural value differences is combined with recognition of cross-cultural value commonalities, Locke predicts, a well-founded theory of "unity in diversity" among value systems will become possible (53). Moreover, Locke argues, the functional character of values makes it possible to evaluate pragmatically the relative insightfulness and usefulness of specifically contextualized cultural values and to make progress in our understanding of broadly humane values like human dignity, democracy, freedom, equality, group loyalty, and self-respect.

The keys to transforming value rivalry and conflict between groups into peaceful and democratic multicultural collaboration amid recognized and appreciated differences, Locke insightfully suggests, are cross-cultural norms of tolerance and reciprocity based on a culturally pluralistic understanding of the historical and functional character of groups' various differing values. Such tolerance and reciprocity makes sense, however, only in relation to nondogmatic formulations of cultural value systems; these norms of cultural pluralism are incompatible with, and should not be applied to, fundamentalisms of any variety.

> More important . . . than what this view contributes toward a realistic under-standing of values, are the clues it offers for a more practical and consistent way of holding and advocating them. It is here that a basic connection between pluralism and intellectual democracy becomes evident. In the pluralistic frame of reference value dogmatism is outlawed. A consistent application of this invalidation would sever the trunk nerves of bigotry or arbitrary orthodoxy all along the line, applying to religious, ideological and cultural as well as to political and social values. Value profession or adherence on that basis would need to be critical and selective and tentative (in the sense that science is tentative) and revisionist in procedure rather than dogmatic, final and en bloc. One can visualize the difference by saying that with any articles of faith, each article would need independent scrutiny and justification and would stand, fall or be revised, be accepted, rejected or qualified accordingly. Fundamentalism of the "all or none" or "this goes with it" varieties could neither be demanded, expected nor tolerated. Value assertion would thus be a tolerant assertion of preference, not an intolerant insistence on agreement or finality. Value disciplines would take on the tentative and revisionist procedure of natural science. (57)

One cross-culturally basic humane value to which Locke appeals in explaining and justifying this exclusion of fundamentalisms from the range of tolerance and reciprocity is Royce's "loyalty to loyalty," understood as valuing the importance of value-feelings and respecting a people's loyalty to their own culture's particular value system so long as it is framed in such a way as to respect others' differing specific values as well as the broadly humane values that scholarship and practical experience suggest they do or should share (49–50). In a fuller discussion of the implications of the restricted, pluralistic version of cultural relativism that he advocated, Locke expanded his discussion of tolerance and reciprocity to include three "working principles" to which he believed this perspective gives rise:

1. The principle of *cultural equivalence,* under which we would more wisely press the search for functional similarities in our analyses and comparisons of human cultures, thus offsetting our traditional and excessive emphasis upon cultural difference. Such functional equivalences, which we might term *culture cognates* or *culture correlates,* discovered underneath deceptive but superficial institutional divergence, would provide objective but soundly neutral common denominators for intercultural understanding and cooperation.

2. The principle of *cultural reciprocity,* which, by a general recognition of the reciprocal character of all contacts between cultures and of the fact that all modern cultures are highly composite, would invalidate the lump estimating of cultures in terms of generalized, en bloc assumptions of superiority and inferiority, substituting scientific, point-by-point comparisons with their correspondingly limited, specific, and objectively verifiable superiorities or inferiorities.

3. The principle of *limited cultural convertibility,* that is, since culture elements, though widely interchangeable, are so separable—the institutional forms from their values and the values from their institutional forms—the organic selectivity and assimilative capacity of a borrowing culture becomes a limiting criterion for cultural exchange. Conversely, pressure acculturation and the mass transplanting of culture, the stock procedure of groups with traditions of culture "superiority" and dominance, are counterindicated as against both the interests of cultural efficiency and the natural trends of cultural selectivity (73).

Some of the important contributions that Locke's three concepts can offer to our contemporary controversies about the possibilities and prerequisites of "unity in diversity" are expressed in his comments that not all cultural differences are equally deep and important, that all modern cultures are highly composite rather than pure and distinct, and that there are limits to the desirable scope of cross-cultural interchange of values and their institutional forms that we must respect in equitable cross-cultural collaborations. Cross-cultural unity does not require uniformity, Locke argues: "it is a fluid and functional unity rather than a fixed and irrevocable one, and its vital norms are equivalence and reciprocity rather than identity or complete agreement" (71). Understood in this way, rather than as Derrida and other postmodernist critics have analyzed the concept, unity is fully compatible with diversity, and the quest for unity so understood need not lead to oppression of the less powerful and repress difference in interchanges within or between cultures, as some feminist and Africana critics have feared.

Rather, guided by Locke's critical relativism in cross-cultural conversation and negotiation, we can recognize the functional value commonalities amid our acknowledged and valued diversity and then employ both aspects of this recognition to direct democratic decision making and collaborative action. Locke projects that there will be stepwise stages of development in the practical capacity of differing groups to engage in cross-difference conversation, negotiation, and collaboration with each other.

Relativism, with no arbitrary specifications of unity, no imperious demand for universality, nevertheless enjoins a beneficent neutrality between divergent positions, and, in the case of the contacts of cultures, would in due course promote, step by step, from an initial stage of cultural tolerance, mutual respect, reciprocal exchange, some specific communities of agreement and, finally, with sufficient mutual understanding and confidence, commonality of purpose and action. (71)

His suggestions about how to employ this process in developing cross-cultural relationships into a deep and lasting peace following the cultural value clashes that led to and sanctioned the violent brutality of World War II have relevance for us today, as we seek ways to end specific ethnic conflicts and to achieve the full, cooperative meaning of democracy.

A reasonable democratic peace (like no other peace before it) must integrate victors and vanquished alike, and justly. With no shadow of cultural superiority, it must respectfully protect the cultural values and institutional forms and traditions of a vast congeries of peoples and races—European, Asiatic, African, American, Australasian. Somehow cultural pluralism may yield a touchstone for such thinking. Direct participational representation of all considerable groups must be provided for, although how imperialism is to concede this is almost beyond immediate imagining. That most absolutistic of all our secular concepts, the autonomous, sacrosanct character of national sovereignty, must surely be modified and voluntarily abridged. Daring reciprocities will have to be worked out if the basic traditional democratic freedoms are ever to be transposed to world practice, not to mention the complicated reconstruction of economic life which consistent reciprocity will demand in this field. One suspects that the practical exigencies of world reconstruction will force many of these issues to solution from the practical side, leaving us intellectuals to rationalize the changes *ex post facto*. Out of the crisis may yet come the forced extension of democratic values and mechanisms in ways that we have not had courage to think of since the days of democracy's early eighteenth century conception, when it was naively, but perhaps very correctly assumed that to have validity at all democracy must have world vogue. (62–63)

Locke suggests here that a cease-fire enforced by military might is not the same as peace, which can only be developed by transforming the conflicting value systems that led to conflicts from absolutisms and fundamentalisms into pluralistically held value loyalties. The best way to bring this about is by stages, starting with bringing together on just terms the representatives of all the conflicting groups who recognize that they have an interest in peace, even though some (perhaps most) of them will still understand their loyalty to their own culture's values in absolutist and perhaps fundamentalist terms. Because differing groups are so closely interconnected and so mutually influential in our modern world of complex cultures and global interchange, representatives will already have some awareness of each other's cultures, but they may not understand each other's historically rooted perspectives. Thus, the first thing they must do is to talk to each other as tolerantly as they can in order to learn about the other's experience and concerns, to discover their functional commonalities, and to learn a deeper respect for each other as individuals and as group representatives. On this basis, specifically appropriate reciprocal exchanges can be arranged, which, if well handled by all involved, may lead to recognition of some areas of agreement, some well-founded trust, and the willingness to undertake some collaborative projects for their groups' mutual benefit. Of course, individuals and groups who persist in their absolutisms and fundamentalisms will be impediments to this process, but Locke expects that these stances will have difficulty enduring in the face of the scholarly evidence and the lived experience of just interaction with others who embody both group value differences and humane value commonalities (70). As an Irish constable in Tipperary said about an underground program of covert, retreat-style weekend meetings that he was operating with his priest-brother in Belfast, in which they brought together in a safe and secret place Catholics and Protestants who had never really talked with a member of the other, "enemy" group, "At least they learn that the other is not the devil with horns." Such strategies as Locke proposed and the Irish brothers employ might also bear fruit in seeking peace in Bosnia, Rwanda, and south central Los Angeles.

The practical role of intellectuals in promoting peace has two aspects, in Locke's view: scholarship and teaching. On the one hand, scholars of "anthropology in the broadest sense" need to learn enough about varying specific cultures to understand their unique functional adaptations to the conditions of their lived experience and, through that process, to discover the humane value commonalities that may become the basis of democratic cross-cultural bridges: "The intellectual core of the problems of the peace, should it be in our control and leadership, will be the discovery of the necessary common denominators and the basic equivalences involved in a democratic world order or democracy on a world scale" (62).

The importance of this responsibility does not imply that intellectuals themselves have already learned to think pluralistically; we must overcome our own absolutisms, fundamentalisms, and suspicions of the prospect of unity in diversity if we are to fulfill our responsibility within the peace process.

What intellectuals can do for the extension of the democratic way of life is to discipline our thinking critically into some sort of realistic worldmindedness. Broadening our cultural values and tempering our orthodoxies is of infinitely more service to enlarged democracy than direct praise and advocacy of democracy itself. For until broadened by relativism and reconstructed accordingly, our current democratic traditions and practice are not ready for world-wide application. Considerable political and cultural dogmatism, in the form of culture bias, nation worship, and racism, still stands in the way and must first be invalidated and abandoned. In sum if we refuse to orient ourselves courageously and intelligently to a universe of peoples and cultures, and continue to base our prime values on fractional segments of nation, race, sect, or particular types of institutional culture, there is indeed little or no hope for a stable world order of any kind—democratic or otherwise. Even when the segment is itself a democratic order, its expansion to world proportions will not necessarily create a world democracy. The democratic mind needs clarifying for the better guidance of the democratic will. (63)

Unless we develop this kind of realistic world-mindedness ourselves, we cannot contribute the scholarship that will allow us the insight to understand cultural differences and to discover the cross-cultural humane commonalities on which we can reconstruct a vision of the processes, institutions, and values of democratic community life appropriate for our time. If we can develop Locke's kind of culturally pluralistic perspective and bring it to our value research and theorizing, our scholarship may be able to influence constructively some of the practical peacemakers who need to come together around the table in the next twenty years. And if this kind of culturally pluralistic perspective and the scholarly research to which it gives rise can direct our teaching as well, we can hope to influence the way future generations hold their own group-value loyalties and understand others.

Thus, one of the important transformative objectives Locke prescribes that we need to undertake now to achieve this kind of peaceful, multicultural collaborative future is transformation of the curricula of our schools, colleges, and universities into broad cross-cultural encounters guided by what he calls critical relativism. Not just extension, revision, or inclusion of new curricular elements, but educational transformation is needed: "A more fundamental methodological change both in ways of teaching and in ways of thinking is necessary, if we are to achieve the objectives of reorientation and integration so obviously required and so ardently sought" (266). We need to teach students to evaluate critically the information they learn about the world's cultures, including their own, and their history of interaction, instead of simply adding more non-Western information to the standard curriculum and perhaps promoting the simplistic form of cultural relativism that is "too polite" to comment about others' values and too intellectually insecure to take a normative stance, even about the broadly humane values that pluralistic scholarship reveals.

Let us suppose, for example, that we have extended the study of history of man and his cultures from the conventional Western hemispheric to a global range and setting, have we automatically exorcised parochial thinking and corrected traditional culture bias? As I see it, not necessarily. It is surely a patent fallacy to assume that a change in the scope of thinking will change the way of thinking. To convert parochial thinking into global thinking involves meeting head on their issues of conflict, realistically accounting for their differences by tracing the history of their development, and out of a process-logic of this development, bravely to take a normative stand. (268)

The alternative Locke proposes is

to discover a way of projecting into the study of social fact a normative dimension objective enough to be scientifically commensurable. Though difficult, such a development is methodologically feasible. It could stem from a broadly comparative and critical study of values and their historical and cultural backgrounds. By so regarding civilizations and cultures as objective institutionalizations of their associated values, beliefs, and ideologies, a realistic basis can be developed not only for a scientific comparison of cultures but for an objective critique of the values and ideologies themselves. Study and training in such analyses and interpretations should develop in students a capacity for thinking objectively but critically about situations and problems involving social and cultural values. (270)

In contrast with the curricular guidance of either a traditional ethnocentrism of the kind that William Bennett and Allan Bloom have advocated in recent years or the kind of uncritical cultural relativism that their opponents have too often posed as its only alternative, Locke's critical relativism would (1) interpret values realistically in relation to backgrounds; (2) interpret values as "functional adaptations" to particular backgrounds, evaluating them pragmatically in terms of their "functional sufficiency and insufficiency"; (3) "claim . . . no validity for values beyond this relativistic framework"; (4) assess ideologies as "adjunct rationalization[s] of values and value interests"; (5) "trace value development and change as a dynamic process"; and (6) substitute this "realistic value dynamics" for "traditional value analytics, with its unrealistic symbols and overgeneralized concepts" (273–74). Though its aspects and implications need further development before we can use it to guide an insightful and democratically useful multicultural transformation of our curricula, Locke's critical relativism suggests the middle path so many teachers of ethics have been seeking between a universalized rational value absolutism that is dangerously blind to cultural differences, on the one hand, and skeptically limited forms of individualist and cultural relativisms that are dangerously antinormative, and thus useless as weapons against absolutist and fundamentalist embodiments of the will to power, on the other.

Thus, Alain Locke's pluralistic value theory offers theoretical and practical guidance that we need now as we long and work for democratic world peace in the twenty-first century, a peace in which the lived experience of community includes the recognition of valued cultural differences. Locke's insights, grounded in his own lived experience as an African American philosopher who helped shape both the Harlem Renaissance and the post-world-war peace process, offer us good transformative guidance today.

Notes

1. John Dewey, *The Public and Its Problems* (New York: Henry Holt, 1927). See also Judith M. Green, "The Diverse Community or the Unoppressive City: Which Ideal for a Transformative Politics of Difference?" (paper presented at the Central Division Meeting of the American Philosophical Association, Kansas City, Missouri, April 1994; forthcoming in *Journal of Social Philosophy*); and Iris Marion Young, "The Ideal of Community and the Politics of Difference," in *Feminism/Postmodernism,* ed. Linda J. Nicholson (New York: Routledge, 1990).

2. For a good summary and example of such skeptical concerns combining feminist, postmodernist, and cross-cultural elements, see Young, "Ideal of Community." For a critical reply, see Green, "Diverse Community."

3. Martin Luther King Jr., *Where Do We Go from Here: Chaos or Community?* (New York: Harper & Row, 1967).

4. Leonard Harris, ed., *The Philosophy of Alain Locke: Harlem Renaissance and Beyond* (Philadelphia: Temple University Press, 1989). Harris has provided an invaluable resource to scholars and activists in the transformative project of creating multicultural democracy by making so many of Locke's papers widely available and offering insightful interpretive guidance in this edited collection. All page citations of Locke's essays in this chapter refer to the Harris edition of his works.

PART II

AESTHETICS

6

Pragmatist Aesthetics: Roots and Radicalism

Richard Shusterman

In the pragmatic tradition of Emerson, James, and Dewey, Alain Locke affirms philosophy as an expression of the individual's personality, an intellectual response to the problems one faces in the project of living.[1] "All philosophies, it seems to me, are in ultimate derivation philosophies of life and not of abstract, disembodied 'objective' reality; products of time, place, and situation, and thus systems of timed history rather than timeless eternity." Recognizing that even one's most impersonal philosophical efforts "may merely be the lineaments of a personality," Locke confessed, "I project my personal history into its inevitable rationalization as cultural pluralism and value relativism" (H 17, 34–35).

Such philosophical honesty of critical self-reflection is exemplary. It inspires one to preface any philosophical commentary on Locke by a similar confession of personal history with regard to him—in my case, with great embarrassment. Though Locke's work should have long ago been known to me, though it could have been preciously useful to my study of pragmatism and hip-hop culture, it was only after the publication of my *Pragmatist Aesthetics* in 1992 that his name began to be mentioned to me as someone I should certainly read.[2] My joy in discovering him was as deep as my shame for having overlooked him.

Building on Dewey's familiar theories to develop my pragmatist aesthetics and defense of popular art, I had never noticed Locke's, which not only anteceded but probably also (through the mediation of Albert C. Barnes) influenced Dewey's. Locke's aesthetic, moreover, was far more relevant to my special concern with legitimating popular art forms like rap. An appalling irony indicative of how heavily the deck is still stacked against black culture: my very attempt to provide a philosophical legitimization of African American popular art unknowingly reinforced a shameful neglect of African American philosophy.

However innocent my ignorance might seem, it is surely no excuse for a philosopher; and what made my ignorance still more poignant was the bond of shared personal history with Locke: both of us born of ethnic minorities in Philadelphia, both graduates of its Central High School, and both postgraduate students of philosophy in Oxford. Like Locke, I appreciatively pursued nationalistic movements of ethnic pride (though my contribution to Israel was far more meager and military than Locke's gift to the Harlem Renaissance), yet, again like Locke, I share the cosmopolitan wanderer's fear of the narrowing provincialism that ethnic and nationalistic enthusiasms too readily foster.

In 1989, Leonard Harris rightly described Alain Locke's philosophy as "radical pragmatism" (H, 17). Now, belatedly claiming Locke as a prophet of pragmatist aesthetics, I briefly sketch twelve themes that demonstrate this rich direction of his thought.

1. Expressing its Darwinian heritage, pragmatist aesthetics is naturalistic and vitalistic. Though art can rightly be described as spiritual and even divine, pragmatism insists on its deep roots in the natural world, in the elemental desires, needs, and rhythms of the human organism interacting with that world. As Dewey put it in 1934, "Underneath the rhythm of every art and every work of art there lies . . . the basic pattern of relations of the live creature to his environment," so that "naturalism in the broadest and deepest sense of nature is a necessity of all great art."[3]

Almost a decade earlier, Alain Locke's collection *The New Negro* stressed the same need for art to sustain its bond to nature's vital forms and basic energies, even while urging art's development toward ever higher levels of spirituality and culture. Locke could thus hail the Negro artist's special advantage in having a more "vital common background," a closer link to the "instinctive" (NN, 47). If tenor Roland Hayes is a better performer of spirituals than a talented white like David Guion, "it is more than a question of musicianship, it is a question of feeling instinctively qualities put there by instinct" (NN, 207). This is not because of something biological in black genes but because of the Negro's closer link to nature's rhythms, which constitutes part of his "original artistic endowment."[4]

Modern art needs the Negro's vitality, Locke argues, because the vital, natural aesthetic energies of European culture have largely dissipated into "a marked decadence and sterility . . . due to generations of the inbreeding of style and idiom," where art worked merely from its own past models while forgetting nature (NN, 254–59). "Art cannot disdain the gift of . . . a return to nature, not by way of the forced and worn formula of Romanticism, but through the closeness of an imagination that has never broken kinship with nature. Art must accept such gifts, and re-evaluate the giver"—the Negro who has preserved his bond with nature (NN, 52). Nor does this naturalism preclude the highest flights of spirituality, as the Negro spiritual makes clear. Though derived "from the 'shout' and the rhythmic elements of the sensuous dance, in their finished form and basic emotional affect all of these elements were completely sublimated in the sincere intensities of religious seriousness" (NN, 201).

2. As naturalism is not the only end of art, neither is it art's sole formative factor. Pragmatist aesthetics insists on history and its changing social conditions as likewise formative. Even art's most distinctively individual expressions are also the expressive product of communal life in a given historical society. No less than philosophy, artworks are "products of time, place, and situation, and thus systems of timed history rather than timeless eternity." If the Negro spirituals seem classics of "compelling universality" and "immortality," it is because they "have outlived the particular generation and the peculiar conditions that produced them" by expressing something that can be shared by succeeding historical ages (NN, 199). As "each generation . . . will have its own creed," so each will have to create its own art through the changing social conditions and historical formations that structure aesthetic expression (NN, 11).

Today's cultural-studies theorists too often present nature and history as incompatible polarities; but pragmatism, suspicious of such dichotomies, realizes that nature has a history, while history works in and with nature. The closer link to nature that Locke sees as distinguishing the Negro's art is not a purely natural affair but the product of the difference between Negro and European history. Similarly, Locke identifies the Harlem Renaissance flowering of "the New Negro" as the product of historical forces: improved material conditions, relaxing of "the tyranny of social intimidation," "shifting of the Negro population" to the northern cities, and worldwide trends of national ethnic pride ("Europe seething in a dozen centers with emergent nationalities, Palestine full of a renascent Judaism," NN, ix, 4–5), all of which encourage the expression of Negro race-pride as an avant-garde cultural expression.

The particular genius of Harlem is also socially explained as resulting not merely from being "the largest Negro community in the world, but the first concentration in history of so many diverse elements of Negro life." Such concentrated diversity of background, talent, and professional activity provides the most creative interaction for cultural flourishing and thus makes Harlem the New Negro's cultural "race capital" (NN, 6–7).

3. The value of such interactive brewing of diversity reflects another aspect of pragmatist aesthetics: its preference for "the mix" over the aesthetics of

purist segregation or isolation. Such aesthetic preference is evident in Locke's multiculturalist advocacy not simply of "unity in diversity" but of "unity through diversity" (H, 134–35), and it can even be discerned in pragmatism's view of distinctions as flexible tools for changing purposes rather than as marking fixed dichotomies. Thus Dewey insists on the continuity between the different arts, on their mixture of elements, and on the definition of aesthetic experience not by any especially unique "aesthetic" dimension but rather by "a greater inclusiveness" and a closer, more zestful integration of all the different elements of ordinary experience (*Art as Experience* [AE], 259; cf. *Pragmatist Aesthetics* [PA], 12–17).

Locke makes similar points about the continuity and fusion of the different arts (e.g., H, 181–82). Moreover, *The New Negro* invokes the pragmatist aesthetic of mix not only to explain how the concentration of "dissimilar elements into a common area of contact and interaction" has resulted in the aesthetic creativity of Harlem life but also to advocate the great artistic promise of the American Negro as someone who can better mix the "original artistic endowment" of Africa with the "more complex patterns and substance" of American life (NN, 256–57). The musical greatness of Negro spirituals is similarly explained as the product of a perfect mix of "distinctiveness of the melodic, harmonic, and rhythmic elements in this music," where we can "separate or even over-stress" no one element without losing the genre's "finer effects." "It is the fusion, and that only, that is finely characteristic" (NN, 206).

Locke evinces his commitment to an aesthetic of diversified mixing in many more ways than can be mentioned in this short chapter. Let me just mention two especially important examples. First, though *The New Negro* is largely devoted to building "race pride" and insisting on "a racial idiom" for Negro artists (NN, 11, 13, 262), Locke is clearly not an exclusionary racist of the separatist or essentialist type. Viewing race itself as a "composite" product of cultural fusion, he thinks race relations for the American Negro can only be improved through greater contact and interaction (H, 192–95; NN, 8–11). Advocating "free-trade in culture" and "the principle of cultural reciprocity," he insists that "cultural goods, once evolved, are no longer the exclusive property of the race or people that originated them. They belong to all who can use them; and belong most to those who can use them best" (H, 206).

Though Locke advocates a distinctive Negro aesthetic, white artists can be recognized as welcome contributors to its artistic mix, and even sometimes hailed as being useful teachers for Negro artists in the portrayal of Negro subjects. Noting "the fine collaboration of white American artists" (e.g., Eugene O'Neill) in advancing Negro literature (by their "bringing of the materials of Negro life out of the shambles of conventional polemics, cheap romance and journalism" [NN, 49]), Locke further praises European painters, especially the

Belgian Auguste Mambour, for developing a "technique of the Negro subject [that] has reached the dignity and skill of virtuoso treatment and a distinctive style" still well in advance of American Negro artists (NN, 264):

> The work of these European artists should even now be the inspiration and guide-posts of a younger school of American Negro artists. They have too long been the victims of the academy tradition and shared the conventional blindness of the Caucasian eye with respect to the racial material at their disposal.

Locke thus chooses the Negro portraits and designs of German artist Winold Reiss to constitute the illustrations of *The New Negro*—exemplifying yet another aspect of Locke's aesthetic of the mix. Not only a mixture of voices (his and those of the many authors he anthologizes, including white authors like Barnes and Herskovits), *The New Negro* is also a composite of high and popular art forms and an amalgam of artistic genres: essay, fiction, poetry, drama, portraiture, decorative art, photos of African sculpture, even music scores. Sometimes the mix of visual, musical, and literary art can be found within the same article.

4. Pragmatist aesthetics insists on the practical value even of so-called pure art. Respectful of art's formal values, it nonetheless recognizes that art is always more than its well-formed objects; it is a purposive activity and needs to be understood also in terms of its social functions. Locke admirably exemplifies this pragmatist balance of form and instrumentality. Analyzing the formal richness of genres like the spiritual, he urges Negro artists to break out of tired forms and stereotypes through formal invention inspired by the exquisite formalist discipline of African plastic art. But Locke puts at least equal emphasis on the wider practical functions of even "pure art values" (NN, 52).

Foremost among these functions is art's use for "self-expression" and "self-determination" of both the individual and the ethnic group. "And so the social promise of our recent art is as great as the artistic. It has brought with it, first of all, that wholesome, welcome virtue of finding beauty in oneself" (NN, ix, xi, 52). Along with "the motives of self-expression and spiritual development" and "the old and still unfinished task of making material headway," Locke advocates the contribution of Negro artists as the privileged means for the Negro's full social acceptance in American life. "The especially cultural recognition they win should in turn prove the key to the revaluation of the Negro which must precede or accompany any further betterment of race relationships" (NN, 15).

Recognizing that art is a practical, purposive form of activity, Locke criticizes Du Bois for interpreting spirituals by mere mood or emotional theme.

Instead, one must "relate these songs to the folk activities that they motivated" and their specific "type of folk use" in "the communal life" they served (NN, 205). For this reason, although he welcomes the prestige acquired in bringing spirituals to the concert hall, Locke warns that they can be misunderstood when transplanted from their original congregational use and turned into entertainment. "We should always remember that they are essentially congregational, not theatrical, just as they are essentially a choral not a solo form" (NN, 202). In short, Locke applies the pragmatist lesson that art is a practice defined by its uses as well as its experience.

5. For pragmatist aesthetics, art's highest and most general use is the improvement of life. Locke's recognition of art's prime meliorative function should already be clear. By providing the joys of beauty, self-expression, and self-respect through perceiving beauty in oneself; by providing cultural recognition, material rewards, and spiritual development (through art's exacting discipline) for oneself and one's group;[5] and finally by providing also "poetry of sturdy social protest, and fiction of calm, dispassionate social analysis," art can make the Negro's life infinitely better, turning "the brands and wounds of social persecution . . . [into] the proud stigmata of spiritual immunity and moral victory." Moreover, through its critical realism and utopian imagination, art can supply "an emancipating vision to America" as a whole (NN, 52–53).

In advocating art's utility for life, Locke highlights the blending unity of the arts in this service, while expressing the ancient pragmatic idea that "life itself is an art, perhaps the finest of fine arts—because it is the composite blend of them all." Not only the formalized elite fine arts belong in this mix; the "amateur arts of personal expression—conversation and manners . . . are as important as the fine arts; in my judgement, they are their foundation." In the same pragmatist spirit of dissolving dualities, the audience's "refined consumption" of art is brought on par with artistic production as equally crucial for creating the aesthetic mix that makes art and life richest. Only "with the products of the fine arts translating themselves back into personal refinement and cultivated sensibilities, culture realizes itself in the full sense, performs its full educative function and becomes a part of the vital art of living" (H, 181–83).

6. Pragmatist aesthetics controversially views art as ultimately more powerful than science for improving life by unique improvements in the quality of experience. Though respecting science (and its aesthetic dimensions that link it to art), pragmatism warns against scientism's "fanatical cult of fact," insisting instead that human life is lived more in felt experience than in objective facts and that art's experience is typically more rich, vivid, and effectively powerful than that of science (H, 36–37, 53; AE, 33, 90–91; PA, 11–12). The

dominantly experiential and affective quality of value is a crucial point of Locke's technical philosophy. Values are most basically "emotional," formed and sensed "directly through feeling": "The value-mode establishes for itself, directly through feeling, a qualitative category, which, as discriminated by its appropriate feeling-quality, constitutes an emotionally mediated form of experience." Values thus should be understood "primarily in terms of feeling or attitude" not in terms of objective predicates and judgments of impersonal reality; "the feeling-quality, irrespective of content, makes a value of a given kind" (H, 38–40).

The consequences of such affective axiology for cultural politics are manifest in *The New Negro*. While welcoming "objective and scientific appraisal" and recognizing that true social recognition is better served by "the new scientific rather than the old sentimental interest" in Negro life, Locke nonetheless advocates art as the better tool for achieving the Negro's full "cultural recognition" and "revaluation" (NN, 8, 11, 15). Negroes will be more highly valued when we (whites *and* blacks) feel better about them; and powerful artworks by and about Negro life are far more able to render this change of affect than the dry statistics of social science, however important and useful Locke knew them to be.[6]

7. In recognizing art's social potential to express and change attitudes, pragmatist aesthetics advocates a distinctively democratic view of art. Though art is often used for antidemocratic ends, it should be put in the service of democracy. This means renouncing the narrow identification of art with elite fine arts as sharply distinguished from forms of popular culture. If a healthy democracy needs the productive understanding that comes from a free and richly interactive contact between its different groups, a democratic aesthetic needs the same sort of open exchange and mutual recognition between different forms of artistic expression. It cannot tolerate a rigid barrier between the canonized high art of culture sophisticates and the expressive forms favored by more common folk. Deploying its historicism, pragmatist aesthetics notes that today's high art classics themselves derived from popular forms and often were themselves formerly disparaged as mass entertainment.

I make this case at length in *Pragmatist Aesthetics* (chaps. 7–8), but Alain Locke clearly anticipates my efforts and laments that "art has run to classes, cliques and coteries," losing its "vital common background" in shared popular experience (NN, 47). With great economy, he undermines the barrier between classical high art and popular culture by linking Negro spirituals to the complex simplicity of medieval art, by noting "the folk song origins of the very tradition which is classic in European music," and by insisting that popular art like spirituals can be rightly appreciated on both the simpler popular level of "emotional intuition" and the more erudite level of musical "technical values" (NN, 200, 209). Applying pragmatism's aesthetic of the productive mix, Locke advocates not a mere purist preservation of Negro folk music but its integration into new forms of Negro music, including classical orchestral forms, just as he urges that elements of African folk art (e.g., disciplined control, abstract decorative forms, and stylization) have inspired the high art tradition of European visual arts and need to be better integrated into the efforts of contemporary Negro artists (NN, 258–67).[7]

The political motives of Locke's aesthetics are similarly democratic. He brings us the art of "the New Negro" not simply to promote the cultural recognition of his people but also to advance "a new democracy in American culture" (NN, 9), since true democracy cannot tolerate cultural disrespect toward any ethnic group. Pragmatist aesthetics insists that democracy and race must not be used as excuses for accepting lower aesthetic standards to justify "vulgarity" and "sub-mediocrity" in the arts (H, 180; PA, 175–77).[8] But it recognizes that democracy, like art and culture, is best served by open exchange between different ways of thought and diverse ethnic voices. Negro expression therefore must be fully integrated as a well-respected, interactive part of American culture.

> Democracy itself is obstructed and stagnated to the extent that any of its channels are closed. Indeed they cannot be selectively closed. So the choice is not between one way for the Negro and another for the rest, but between American institutions frustrated on the one hand and American ideals progressively fulfilled and realized on the other. (NN, 12)

Locke again makes it clear that the advocacy of race pride and a racial idiom for Negro art is not to serve an exclusionary racist separatism: "The racialism of the Negro is no limitation or reservation with respect to American life; it is only a constructive effort to build the obstructions in the stream of his progress into an efficient dam of social energy and power." And "this forced attempt to build his Americanism on race values" cannot succeed "except through the fullest sharing of American culture and institutions" (NN, 12). In short, far from being a Negro purism or essentialism, Locke's policy is rather a proudly mixed African American culture that can contribute more fully to the flowering manifold of American civilization.

8. Locke's complex handling of this issue of race exemplifies his pragmatist recognition that concepts are practical tools whose use depends on context. An intensely careful student of the difficulties of defining race, Locke recognized it as one of the "most inevitable but at the same time most unsatisfactory con-

cepts" (H, 188). Disguised as a biological, scientifically objective concept for the explanation of culture, race typically functions more as a classificational strategy to privilege certain cultures and social groups over others. But outweighing any critical scientific motive to dismiss race as merely a fictional construction on what is really only a "culture-type" that is best "explained in terms of social and historical causes" (H, 192) looms the pragmatic recognition that race remains a concept of entrenched social, political, and cultural power. If it has been (and will continue to be) wielded to damage populations like the Negroes, race must not be dismissed but must instead be redeployed to rehabilitate its past victims.

Hence Locke's *New Negro* repeatedly touts "race pride," "race genius," and the "race-gift," even though his more technical writings of the same period inveigh against "the fallacy of the block conception of race as applied to the Negro peoples" (NN, 11, 47, 199; H, 169). On the strict scientific or philosophical level, Locke attacks the idea of defining race in terms of blood and genetics, defining it instead as essentially cultural and "in terms of social and historical causes."[9] But this hardly prevents him (in more popular and politically engaged texts like *The New Negro*) from affirming, en bloc, the American Negroes' closer racial link to African culture by being "blood descendants" of African "forefathers," even when their "cultural patterns" are so very different from the African, displaying "a curious reversal of emotional temper and attitude" (NN, 254, 256).

This apparent duality of discourse might seem like pragmatism of shifty opportunism and duplicitous double standards, but it is not. Close reading, however, reveals that the blood link, for Locke, functions not on the biological level but instead as a social symbol of connection that provides special "cultural inspiration" through "a sense of direct cultural kinship" far greater than that of Europeans, who come to African art only "through the channels of an exotic curiosity and interest" (NN, 256). That he can sustain such a subtle philosophical nuance in even his most popular writings, deploying his concepts flexibly (aware of their mutability and ambiguity) but still with careful consistency, demonstrates Locke's stature as a pragmatist philosopher of the highest skill and honesty.

9. Locke's abundant writings in aesthetics do not struggle over formal definitions of art and beauty, nor do they issue in substantive theories of criticism. This would be surprising were he not, as I claim, a distinctly pragmatist aesthetician. For pragmatism, the prime aim of aesthetics is not to supply definitions and objective truths about the arts and their values. It is instead to realize, enhance, and deepen those values in actual experience by improving the arts and our aesthetic appreciation of them.

Proud as he is of the Negro's artistic achievements, Locke aims neither merely to document them through descriptive truth nor to preserve them through fetishizing conservation. The prime goal is rather to improve and develop the Negro's artistic creation and thereby also enrich American aesthetics and the world's. As Locke comments on the spiritual: "We cannot accept the attitude that would merely preserve this music, but must cultivate that which would also develop it. Equally with treasuring and appreciating it as music of the past, we must nurture and welcome its contribution to the music of to-morrow" (NN, 210). It is not hard to see here the germ of that pragmatist aesthetic I praised in rap music: the appropriate sampling of respected old works of African American music to make something excitingly new, something that affirms the value of the tradition's past works by transformatively stripping and recycling their elements to move the tradition in new ways and forms.[10]

Locke's aims of artistic development are not narrowly racial. The goal is "to evolve from the racial substance something technically distinctive, something that as an idiom of style may become a contribution to the general resources of art" (NN, 51). As African sculpture has done this for the plastic arts, similar contributions come from the African American musical styles of blues, jazz, rock, and rap—all of which have been fruitfully adopted by artists of very different ethnicities. As pragmatist aesthetics is less concerned with articulating artistic truths than with improving artistic value and experience, so pragmatism more generally affirms "a pragmatically functional type of philosophy, to serve as a guide to life and living" rather than serving truth for mere truth's sake or for "what Dewey calls 'busy work for a few professionals'" (H, 155).[11]

10. Linked to Locke's pragmatist goal of artistic development is his optimistic faith that such development is eminently possible, already on the wing, and apt to be realized by "a new generation" of young artists and writers, who hold the future's key "not because of years only, but because . . . [they share] a new aesthetic and a new philosophy of life" (NN, 49).

> The Younger Generation comes, bringing its gifts. Youth speaks, and the voice of the New Negro is heard. . . . What stirs inarticulately in the masses is already vocal upon the lips of the talented few, and the future listens, however the present may shut its ears. Here we have Negro youth, with arresting visions and vibrant prophecies, forecasting in the mirror of art what we must see and recognize in the streets of reality tomorrow. (NN, 47)

Here again Locke's views foreshadow the artistic renderings and prophecies of street realities that have kept rap music in the headlines, though unfortunately not the best of it.[12]

I see Locke's upbeat respect for youth as pragmatist, since pragmatism defines itself as essentially forward-looking and optimistic, while its critics chide it as juvenile, especially in its hopes of reforming the world. In the same pragmatist style as Dewey, Alain Locke not only respected the potential and imagination of youth but also consecrated enormous theoretical and practical efforts in reforming education so as to bring out the best of youth's promise and even extend its limits by furthering adult education.[13]

11. If pragmatist aesthetics aims at improving both art and experience through developments inspired by youth's new forms and energies, it will be avidly advocatory rather than dispassionately neutral. Locke's work on the Harlem Renaissance and other African American artistic achievements clearly displays such aesthetics of engagement. But this pragmatically partisan posture, I am often told, is false to philosophy's ideal of disinterested objectivity. The counterarguments I usually offer (e.g., PA, 45) are already implied in Locke's critique of scientism and his view of philosophy as a tool of life.

Philosophy's most important achievements were usually motivated by something more than the merely disinterested goal of truth for truth's sake. Moreover, the rigid philosophical posture of lofty disinterestedness too often disguises the narrow interests of a professionalized philosophical conservatism that is either happy to reinforce the status quo by canonizing it as "objective fact" or is simply too timid to risk dirtying its hands in the messy struggle over the shaping of culture. The fetishism of disinterested neutrality obscures the fact that philosophy's ultimate aim is to benefit human life, not simply to articulate truth.

An engaged pragmatism surely risks errors through its zeal; but they can be corrected in the future and perhaps even partly justified, retrospectively, by their strategic function. As Leonard Harris notes, Alain Locke's particular enthusiasms led him in *The New Negro* to exaggerate the primitivism and emotional spirituality in African and African American culture, as well as the paramount role of Negro cultural elites. But through the writings of Richard Wright and others, Locke later reached a greater recognition of "the mass Negro." He also realized that his own vision of "the New Negro" (in 1925), through which he aimed to displace old negative stereotypes, had simply been a helpful "counter-stereotype" rather than "the whole truth" or essence of the Negro (H, 7, 205–10).

12. If pragmatist aesthetics aims at improving the arts, one effective way to do so is to improve the conditions of their creation and reception, conditions that are not merely material but also social and cultural. A crucial factor in improving such conditions is increased respect for the social and cultural

traditions that produce the artworks in question; and here the pragmatic style of aesthetic advocacy can play a major role. But, dialectically, if value, as Locke argues, is essentially experiential and affective, the only way to gain a deep respect for a cultural tradition is through a deep, affective experience of its representative works.

This is precisely Locke's strategy in *The New Negro* and other critical anthologies of African American art and literature: esteem for the Negro cultural tradition (its achievement *and* potential) will best be gained by putting a contemporary sample of its excellent artistic fruits on display, so that people can truly feel its value in their own aesthetic experience.[14] Moreover, to ensure the best experience of these artworks, Locke typically frames them with careful practical criticism and somewhat theoretical essays that provide useful tools of focus for readers approaching the presented artworks, critical tools that constitute in themselves validating symbols of cultural respect for such art.[15] (Nor should we forget that the selection and structuring of an anthology is itself a work of practical criticism.)

Combining advocatory theory with detailed practical criticism is the best method of pragmatist aesthetics, as I conceive it. Hence the arguments for popular art in *Pragmatist Aesthetics* are bolstered with the presentation and detailed critical study of particular artworks, one of them a text of rap. Though Dewey generated my pragmatism, he disappointed me in this matter of method (and in his conservative aesthetic tastes). Deploring popular art's lack of recognition and failure to receive any validating "literary attention" or "theoretical discussion" to remedy this lack (AE, 191), Dewey makes no real effort to provide such attention through practical criticism.[16] In contrast, Alain Locke's tireless and influential critical efforts make him seem a far more radical and effective pragmatist aesthetician. Regretting my belated knowledge of his work, I now salute it as an inspiring source and paradigm of radical pragmatist aesthetics, whose future will be strengthened by returning to draw on its Lockean roots.

Notes

1. In his essay "Good Reading," Locke notes "the continuous role and function of philosophy as sometimes the guide to life and sometimes merely the trail that shows the paths man's mind has taken." Leonard Harris, ed., *The Philosophy of Alain Locke: Harlem Renaissance and Beyond* (Philadelphia: Temple University Press, 1989), 105. Further references to Locke's essays in Harris's excellent book will appear in parentheses with the abbreviation H. This paper will also cite extensively from Locke's own important collection, *The New Negro: An Interpretation* (New York: Boni, 1925). References to this text will appear with the abbreviation NN.

2. Richard Shusterman, *Pragmatist Aesthetics: Living Beauty, Rethinking Art* (Oxford: Blackwell, 1992); henceforth referred to as PA.

3. John Dewey, *Art as Experience* (1934; repr. Carbondale: Southern Illinois University Press, 1987), 355–56. Future references to this work use the abbreviation AE.

4. Locke's choice of the term "instinct" is unfortunate, suggesting physiological hardwiring of fixed reactions rather than the sort of unreflective, habituated feeling and action that is experienced as natural, since it emerges undeliberatively from our familiar natural-social environment.

5. Locke explicitly insists on African art's "lesson of discipline, . . . of technical control pushed to the limits of technical mastery" as an especially needed inspiration for the contemporary Negro artist (NN, 256).

6. This is witnessed, e.g., by his close study of social science on the issues of race and culture and also his collaboration with the social scientist Melville Herskovits. See Mark Helbling's fine article "Feeling Universality and Thinking Particularistically: Alain Locke, Franz Boas, Melville Herskovits, and the Harlem Renaissance," *Prospects* 19 (1994): 289–314.

7. To advocate the general aesthetic principle of mixing does not, of course, mean accepting the value of all mixtures. Locke himself disapproves of one "hybrid treatment" of spirituals that, in trying to merge them with the dominant high-art concert convention, omits their choral accompaniment to highlight solo artistry (NN, 208). Locke also worries about the dangers of mixing interaction between the lower "unfavorable" levels of the white and black races. Displaying what might seem an imperfectly democratic sentiment (but what may just be a wisely prudent sense of the limits of his time), Locke argues "that the only safeguard for mass relations in the future must be provided in the carefully maintained contacts of the enlightened minorities of both race groups" (NN, 9) . Locke later shows greater respect for "the mass Negro" in "Who and What Is 'Negro'?" published in 1942 (H, 209–28).

8. I therefore define my pragmatist position on popular art as "meliorism," which recognizes popular art's grave flaws and abuses but also its merit and potential. It holds that popular art *should be* improved because it leaves so much to be desired but that it *can be* improved because it often does achieve real merit and serve worthy social goals (PA, 177).

9. "Race operates as tradition, as preferred traits and values, and when these things change culturally speaking ethnic remoulding is taking place. Race . . . is . . . that peculiar selective preference for certain cultural-traits and resistance to certain others which is characteristic of all types and levels of social organization" (H, 195).

10. See PA, 200–235; and Richard Shusterman, "Rap Remix: Pragmatism, Postmodernism, and Other Issues in the House," *Critical Inquiry* 22 (1995): 150–58.

11. The pragmatic idea of philosophy as a life practice and guide for living is, in fact, very ancient, and this practice has often been conceived in aesthetic terms. For a study that links its ancient roots to twentieth-century pragmatism, see Richard Shusterman, *Practicing Philosophy: Pragmatism and the Philosophical Life* (New York: Routledge, 1997).

12. For a critique of the excessive attention to gangsta-rap and an advocacy of the

superior merits of "knowledge-rap" as practiced by hip-hop philosophers like KRS-One, Guru, and M. C. Solaar, see Shusterman, *Practicing Philosophy,* chap. 5.

13.   Locke's efforts in educational reform are usefully documented by Leonard Harris; see H, 5–10, 239–76.

14.   These other anthologies include *Four Negro Poets* (New York: Simon & Schuster, 1927); *Plays of Negro Life: A Source-Book of Native American Drama,* ed. with Montgomery Gregory (New York: Harper, 1927); *The Negro and His Music* and *Negro Art: Past and Present,* both published in Washington, D.C., in 1936 by Associates in Negro Folk Education, as was, in 1940, Locke's *The Negro Art: A Pictorial Record of the Negro Artist and of the Negro Theme in Art.* In discussing Locke's practical criticism, one should also note his frequent yearly reviews of black literature, written for *Opportunity* and later for *Phylon.*

15.   I develop this point about the intrinsic symbolic capital of aesthetic critical discourse in "Rap Remix: Pragmatism, Postmodernism, and Other Issues in the House," in response to the critique of sociologists like Bourdieu who challenge my aesthetic-critical approach to popular arts like rap, urging instead a more strictly scientific sociological approach.

16.   For a more detailed critique of Dewey on this point, see Richard Shusterman, "Popular Art and Education," *Studies in Philosophy and Education* 13 (1995): 203–12. Reprinted in J. Garrisson, ed., *The New Scholarship on Dewey* (Dordrecht: Kluwe Academic, 1995), 35–44.

7

Alain Locke, Essentialism, and the Notion of a Black Aesthetic

Jane Duran and Earl L. Stewart

Alain Locke, as a Black philosopher, is mainly known for his work on the theory of value. But insofar as studies of the Harlem Renaissance are concerned, he is known for his work in aesthetics and as the editor of the pivotal volume of that renaissance, *The New Negro*.[1] This anthology of essays, stories, and poems contains the work of Claude McKay, W. E. B. Du Bois, Zora Neale Hurston, Countee Cullen, and many others and is widely cited as one of the most important works of Black scholarship of the 1920s and 1930s.

In three essays in *The New Negro,* Locke advances a theory of the Black aesthetic that is crucially important for work being done today. His introductory essay covers some ground in explicating the atmosphere surrounding the Harlem Renaissance, but two other essays are especially valuable. In an essay entitled "The Legacy of the Ancestral Arts," Locke argues that American Blacks can and should reclaim some of the aesthetic strength that he sees as springing from African roots, and he argues that reclamation of that artistic strength will lead to more disciplined and formal artistic structures.[2] In a third piece, "The Negro Spirituals," Locke develops the notion that the musical genre of the spiritual is worthy not only because it is an example of Black expression but also because its origins and musical structure place it on a par with European folk music.[3] Somewhat confusingly, however, given the importance that Locke attaches to music, the "Legacy" essay is centered almost entirely on the decorative and visual.

Locke's work is important because of what we might term his aesthetic essentialism. The use of the term "essentialism" in the present context pertains to the claim that properties of the artistic works of a given cultural or racial group are essentially, or universally, related to members of that group. Locke claims in particular that Blacks possess, as a group, decided artistic strengths, and the "Negro Spirituals" essay goes on to make the claim that many of these strengths are musical. Such claims are now highly suspect or dubious in certain circles—the development of contemporary work in Black aesthetics, has, for the most part, eschewed essentialist claims of this sort.[4] In this chapter we shall critically examine Locke's early articulations of this controversial claim.

Part of what is constitutive of this essentialism, according to Locke, is a generalized artistic endowment that Locke attributes to Blacks as a group. In the opening to his essay "The Legacy of the Ancestral Arts" Locke says: "But even with the rude transplanting of slavery, that uprooted the technical elements of his former culture, the American Negro brought over as an emotional inheritance a deep-seated aesthetic endowment."[5] The nature of this aesthetic endowment is never spelled out by Locke as fully as we might like. According to Locke, it manifests itself somewhat differently on the African and American continents. This temperament is something like a native plasticity with which one can work, and it emerges both in the stylized and formulaic masks of the West African coast and in the more fluid products of African American culture, such as music. Locke's essay hints at the fact that reliance on music and the rhythmic arts may have been due to historical circumstances; in this particular piece, Locke focuses largely on the visual arts. Locke suggests that "the sensitive artistic mind of the American Negro, stimulated by a cultural pride and interest, will receive from African art a profound and galvanizing influence."[6] He later goes on to claim that sculpture, painting, and the decorative arts would be expected fields of endeavor for this Black gift,[7] and he quotes Roger Fry on the emphatic and pronounced tendency toward formalism in African art of the West Coast. Locke closes his article by enjoining Negro artists of the period to utilize the formal elements of the African heritage for a breakthrough in the visual arts, something that he claims would aid them in the development of a "racial art."[8]

The essentialism espoused by Locke would not be so striking were it not the case, as contemporary commentators seem strongly to affirm, that pronouncements along these lines are frequently dangerous and misguided.[9] Writing on the related question of an African or African American philosophy, Appiah notes that:

> I also have a reason of my own, a reason that survives the rejection of the romantic racialism of the early Pan-Africanists, for exploring the debate on an African philosophy, a debate pursued with a great deal of vigor and in a climate formed, in part, by the culture to which Du Bois and his peers were so central. That reason is that it seems to me that anyone interested in the question of an African-American philosophy can learn a great deal more from the trajectory of that well-established debate than we could from a more abstract reflection on the relationship between peoples, on the one hand, and philosophies, on the other, in

Europe. . . . Since the debate is so well-established, we can pick and choose, with Minerva's owl, among its more illuminating moments.[10]

In other words, not only essentialist aesthetics but any kind of essentialism with regard to African or African American philosophizing or theorizing as a whole is problematic. There is no single Black "folk" or "Volk." What Appiah reminds us of is the fact that, even with regard to the debate on the existence of "African philosophy," as distinct, for example, from African worldviews and folk beliefs, there is an enormous range of opinion.

One of the crucial areas of the debate is broached in the introduction to Paulin Hountondji's classic *African Philosophy: Myth and Reality,* wherein Abiola Irele notes that *negritude,* or African ethnophilosophy as it has been called, is a "hallowed idea of fidelity to one's profound self, [and] reverence for the accumulated heritage of the past."[11] Irele notes that Hountondji, for example, is a "severe" critic of such an approach, since his position is that an emotional stance toward one's African heritage and worldview cannot properly be said to be a philosophy.[12] Some might hold, for instance, that certain African beliefs about the existence of soul-like entities approach Western concepts of dualism in the Cartesian sense, and others might maintain that such beliefs have so little in common with European positions that they do not merit the same appellation. Appiah is merely articulating a point that has been made again and again; it is not clear what is meant by an African philosophy, or an African American philosophy, and these same sorts of paradoxical tensions tend to arise for any theoretical categorization that has the relevant ethnic rubric in front of it. Since aesthetics is, properly speaking, a subdivision of philosophy, the linear heritage here would seem to be clear. A more flat-footed categorization, such as "African animal," presumably might not be as problematic to sustain. The situation is made still more difficult by a related, but subsidiary, point that seems to imply that if some form of essentialism holds—that is, if it is the case that some aesthetics (or some theorizing) can truly be dubbed constitutive of "African" or "African American" theorizing—then something like the "authenticity thesis" holds.[13] This thesis, according to Claudia Mills, runs along the following lines: "individuals representing the experiences [which would form the basis of a philosophy] of group A should (generally or even always) be members of group A." Applied to the present case, this would mean that, if there is a Black aesthetic, then in general only Blacks can be the articulators of it. Mills argues that maintaining this thesis in a forceful and rigid fashion may actually be detrimental to a given group,[14] by rendering the group's culture and cultural artifacts less accessible to others outside the group and lending a tone of defensiveness to the general posture of the group.

This does indeed seem to be the channel in which Locke's thought ran, and much that can be gleaned from his *New Negro* essays supports this reading, since he is specific about the development of an art that is Black and that is the creation of those whose ancestors came from Africa. But Locke apparently not only held that a Black (or African American) aesthetic could be developed and promoted, but that any Black American aesthetic could benefit from what might be called an African aesthetic. It is the running together of these two notions that makes Alain Locke's work here so peculiarly interesting, for one might be inclined to think that the turn toward things African would move one in a direction stylistically different from things Asian or European. African thought involves conceptual elements taken from worldviews radically different from those of many or most Europeans. And yet the elements of an African aesthetic that Locke actually took the trouble to set out precisely have a great deal more in common with a European aesthetic—especially such an aesthetic as applied to the visual arts—or with strands of aesthetic theory taken from the work of British and European thinkers than one might suspect.

A counterargument that seems to occur naturally within this context is that the mere fact that, as the quotation from Appiah indicates, the notion of an African philosophy seems problematic does not necessarily indicate that there might not be less difficulty with aesthetic notions, even if we think of aesthetics as being a branch of philosophy. One could claim that areas of aesthetics are so much more narrowly defined, and the terminology applicable to them in so much greater general use, that pointing to debates surrounding the notion of African philosophical concepts is not illuminating. But this argument does not hold. If we think of aesthetics in its traditional mode as a branch of philosophy, then we can see that the problems associated with it have generally been cast in terms that are European in origin. Questions with respect to the importance of such key notions as form or aesthetic detachment, for example, are questions that have arisen in the realm of the greater European culture. There are, however, indeed reasons for thinking that work on a philosophical aesthetics that is Black will be conceptually difficult.

Theoretical Difficulties

One might be tempted to inquire what precisely it is about African art—and here Locke was dealing very largely, though not entirely, with the ritual art of groups in West Africa, such as the Yoruba and the people of Dahomey—that Locke finds both beneficial and stimulating for the development of a Black aesthetic. Locke is intrigued by the elements of formality, rigor, and stylization of Western African art.[15] To assist us in coming to grips with Locke's take on these elements, we might remember that Locke was looking largely at ritual objects, especially masks, created according to certain canons by local craftspersons. In fact, the preciseness of Locke's characterization of the differences between African and African American art constitutes some of the theoretical difficulty for him as he attempts to spell out the relevant contrasts. Part of the characterization, again, involves the distinction between that which is more stylized (African) and that which is less so (African American). At least three problematic areas come to the fore in "The Legacy of the Ancestral Arts": conundrums revolving around the contrast just mentioned, that is, between African American and African art; difficulties surrounding the authenticity thesis; and areas of vagueness surrounding the notion of the African. We will examine each of these areas in turn, for Locke's powerful articulation of an artistic legacy is somewhat vitiated by these places of theoretical difficulty.

Some clarification of Locke's position on art in general may help us in coming to grips with these difficulties. Locke's view of art, as adumbrated in this essay, appears to be largely an expressionist one, where we may think of the term "expressionist" as being employed somewhat naively and crudely. Locke was not, in his "Legacy" essay, writing in a standard philosophical vein or for a standard philosophical audience, and the essay is also, of course, a product of its time. The kinds of distinctions that one frequently wants to make between, say, various theoretical points as adumbrated in Collingwood's expressionism are not of much use in coming to grips with Locke's work here—Ingram, for example, has written on the damage done to Collingwood's distinction between art and pseudoart by his identification of art and language, but this kind of technical difficulty is one that we associate with a different sort of task.[16] However, Locke employs the term "express[ing]" at more than one juncture, and in so employing the term he reminds us of Collingwood's original distinction between art and craft and the fact that it might be relevant at this juncture.[17] But expressionism as a doctrine in Collingwood's *Principles* adverts, as indicated above, to a number of points concomitant to it, not all of which are actually useful to Locke; there is the distinction between art and magic in addition to the distinction between art and craft. The problem here is that we might be tempted to leave aside the art/craft distinction as not genuinely relevant to most Third World work[18]—for the simple reason that a great deal of what is produced under Third World conditions will be, in European terms, craft (since it is produced with an end in mind and often for ritual). Thus, although the expressionist thesis, in its barebones delineation, harkens to the fact that art is expression of emotion, it may not, on second glance, be easily applicable to African art. In this sense, although one cannot always and for all cases make the claim that the indigenous Western African art to which

Locke refers is not the expression of some emotion or set of emotions, what immediately strikes the reader is that it is African American art that appears, at first glance, to be more expressive, and expressive in the way that is striking to the viewer or listener. Remembering that a Yoruba or Dogon mask would probably have been created under formalized conditions and would very likely have been made for use in religious ritual, as stated earlier, one is impressed by the fact that African American artworks would more closely fit the billing of works of art rather than works of craft.

This forces Locke back to some other area of theorizing in order to sustain his thesis, and he may well have sensed the difficulty here, since expression as a central thesis is dropped in favor of something approaching Fry's formalism, specifically referred to in Locke's text.[19] Here Locke is on surer ground— because the formal properties of line and geometricity are easily seen in much Western African art — but even in this arena minor problems crop up. In much of his work (such as the "Spirituals" essay), Locke cites music as the preeminent African American art, and yet it is the visual arts—an area in which, as Locke admits, African Americans had not at that time been predominant—that he mentions as paradigmatic in the African tradition.[20] Locke seems to have taken this tack because the examples of African art employed in his piece were in fact examples from the visual arts, and it was aspects of formalism—line, contrast, and so forth—that he cited in the visual arts of Western Africa. (For example, Locke says that "[W]hat the Negro artist of to-day has most to gain from the arts of the forefathers is . . . the lesson of a classic background, the lesson of discipline, of style, of technical control pushed to the limits of technical mastery.")[21] Although Locke does indeed take this stance, it creates a difficulty for him. The chief difficulty is, of course, that he is recommending reliance on African art to Black American artists in an arena in which they were comparatively deficient, at a time when, had he chosen to approach the issue, the contributions of African Americans in music could have been analyzed along similar lines. This historical problem itself creates a conceptual difficulty when we remember that part of the development of an aesthetic for a given area will rely on a sense of continuity for the artwork under examination. The comparative strength of his argument for music, as opposed to the visual arts, will be examined later.

One remaining tangle in Locke's theoretical weave might be thought to be the use of the term "African." As we indicated earlier, even if the region is demarcated as "Western Africa" (a labeling that Locke does not actually make in his essay), the variety of peoples, languages, and objects (both those for ritual purposes and any other that might come to hand) could preclude making sense of the notion of "stylization" or "discipline" when applied to a collection as overwhelmingly diverse as the artwork of Western Africa. What Locke clearly means—at least insofar as the depictions contained in *The New Negro* are concerned—is that objects associated with rituals in Western Africa (again, from the Yoruba or the Dogon) display a discipline and rigidity that Locke would like to see inform African American art. But this brings us to a subsidiary problematic area: it is precisely because these African items are associated with ritual use that there is such stylistic rigidity. In an interesting piece in the *Journal of Aesthetics and Art Criticism*, Larry Shiner has carefully pointed out that the very traits that we ordinarily associate with craft (following Collingwood) are, strangely enough, precisely the traits that we associate with "authentic art" of the Third World.[22] This means that something that is done in Mali right now by someone who is not involved in a ritual but who may be expressing himself/herself (in whatever way) will be perceived by Europeans as probably not a work of art, whereas something that is done instrumentally and to be used in some sort of ceremony—produced formulaically, as it were—will be perceived as a work of art. In other words, the usual use of the art/craft distinction is turned on its head; it is not so much that the distinction is irrelevant as that it can be argued that, with respect to Third World art, the distinction may cut the other way.

Expressionism

In a 1991 piece on Black film entitled "A No-Theory Theory," Tommy Lott argues against an essentialist account of Black cinema.[23] In his compelling and clearly argued piece, Lott not only articulates a stance against such an account for the cinema, but he also provides good reasons for doubting whether any essentialist aesthetics is worth the labor required to construct it. It may prove fruitful to examine Lott's stance, since film is, of course, one of the livelier contemporary arts. Given the difficulties that we have already examined with regard to the authenticity thesis, some of the problematic noticed by Lott is helpful in further elucidating why Locke's view has the weaknesses that it does. Commenting upon the desire of many to view "blaxploitation" films as not genuinely part of some larger project called the "Black cinema," Lott notes:

> It can be quite troublesome for a theory of black cinema that relies too strongly on aesthetics to give an account of the influence of blaxploitation films on subsequent black independent films. . . . To denounce a film, such as *Sweetback*, as exploitative is to suggest that aesthetic criteria provide the highest ground of appeal for deciding definitional questions regarding black cinematic representation, for the charge presupposes that there is some sense in which to produce a

blaxploitation film is to have compromised black aesthetic values. . . . How can we best understand the fact that films which aim to present a more authentic black aesthetic are largely ignored by and unknown to black audiences, while being extremely well-received in elite white film circles?[24]

Here Tommy Lott gets at an old problem whose continued existence is by no means irrelevant to an analysis of Locke's work. Works of art may be designated as "Black" not only while (in some cases) not even being created by Black artists but also while (in other cases) being created by Blacks but failing to demonstrate a great deal of artistic merit or social consciousness. And it may very well be the case that these works are more popular with Black audiences than works of greater artistic merit, greater traceably Black lineage, or greater social awareness. Lott is not one to claim that the blaxploitation films fail to be part of something called "Black cinema" (indeed, Lott insists that he will not give a set of necessary and sufficient conditions for the establishment of such a cinema),[25] nor is he one to insist forcefully that films made by white directors and producers about the Black experience automatically fail to be part of such a cinema.[26] Indeed, the whole point of his piece is that it is futile and foolish to attempt to establish criteria for "Black film."

We can learn from Lott's overview of contemporary Black film theory because his encapsulation of several important points helps us see more clearly the kinds of difficulties that we encounter with Locke's work. In a move analogous to the stances taken by film critics, Black and white alike, who would attempt to claim that a film does not qualify as part of the Black cinema because too many non-Blacks were involved in its production, because it is (cinematically) a poor film, or because it perpetuates what some might view as negative stereotypes, Locke creates what amounts to a set of conditions for African American art and then becomes highly critical of any work that does not meet his criteria. For example, Locke suggests that the American Negro "master the mediums" of "the forefathers," where such mediums include "sculpture, painting and the decorative arts"—the facing page contains an illustration of a stylized mask from "Soudan-Niger."[27] Simultaneously, he recommends that the American Negro end or drop his "timid and apologetic imitativeness."[28] In a sense Locke is on firmer ground, because the time period in which he was writing simply did not allow for the numbers to create as problematic a situation with regard to identity questions as now exists. On at least one score, however, he was on less firm ground. Here the specific difficulty of his expressionist position with regard to aesthetics (a position noted by both Cureau and Barnes as being crucial to his work)[29] created the problem that works of art that he might have deemed inferior to, say, African works were actually more expressive and hence, at least in some sense, more worthy of the title "artwork."

In short, although Locke's problems are not identical to those cited by Lott in his piece on Black films, what Locke shares with the Black film critics is a set of paradoxes inherent in the attempt to employ essentialist criteria for artworks produced by a given group. But Locke must, to some extent, have been aware of these problems. The presence of contributions by Herskovits and other whites in *The New Negro* indicates that Locke instinctively saw a difficulty in defining that which was Black, meaning, of course, that he was implicitly aware of the stance that someone not Black could be in some significant sense an articulator of Black theory.

Locke's Essentialist Aesthetic and Music

It may seem that in delineating these problematic areas for Locke, the situation has been so constructed as to leave no room for a more positive view of Locke's essentialist aesthetic. One area of investigation remains, however: although Locke wrote most of "The Legacy of the Ancestral Arts" with the plastic arts in mind, it is clear, as we have indicated earlier, that the situation with respect to music is different, and it would have been helpful for Locke's argument had he made use of musical concepts. The situation is different precisely because the much greater body of artistic endeavor within the realm of music, as opposed to the visual arts, means that much more confirmatory evidence for African holdovers can be found. Furthermore, the nature of music and musical expression means that within that body, it is easier to be precise about the given artistic construct. In this section we will attempt to articulate some of these differences, render specific a more essentialist stance with respect to the creation of a Black musical aesthetic, and then indicate why it is that this particular art may fall under a different analysis.

Alain Locke's essentialist aesthetic is, in our opinion, more strongly formulated and more supportable when applied to Afro–North American music. There is a greater traceable history with respect to this art, it can be linked to a specific region in Africa, and the spontaneous and improvisational nature of much of the music speaks strongly of emotional expression. However, the proof of such an affirmation must, as a first step, be predicated upon the critical identification—the identification of the technical specifics—of the language of Black American music as it existed during Locke's lifetime and as it continues to exist today. Such identification also helps with the Western African notions of "style" and "discipline." Locke acknowledges the existence of such a language but considers rhythm its only African endowment. Of course, given the limited degree to which Afro–North American music had been theoretically examined at that point, it is understandable that such a generalization could go unchallenged.

The truth is, a number of other African-derived elements also existed in Afro–North American vernacular styles during the Harlem Renaissance that were, and still are, definitive aspects of the language of African American music. These include:

1. specific African-derived vocal devices that not only defined Black notions of vocality but also constituted the aesthetic basis for certain instrumental performing techniques as well—that is, attributes of African vocality

2. specific performance practices that influenced Black notions of texture and timbre—for example, call and response

3. specific scale systems that prodigiously influenced Black American concepts of melody and figured significantly in the modal and functional transmutation of the European harmonic conventions borrowed by Blacks, such as pentatonicism and the blues scale

4. specific attributes that defined how Black performers related to their audiences and to their environment, such as collective participation and functionality, and the textural and dramatic musical elements that evolved from them

5. a specific architectonic principle that strongly influences Black American notions of form and structure—for example, the blues paradigm

These African-derived elements relate grammatically to their European analogues, and to one another, in such a way that, when merged with highly sophisticated African-derived rhythmic processes, they establish quite irrefutably a language distinct from both their African and their European musical sources. In citing the alleged differences between the "African art expressions" and those of the African American, Locke, as we have seen, describes the characteristic elements of the former as "rigid, controlled, disciplined, abstract, heavily conventionalized," in contrast to the latter, which he describes as being "free, exuberant, emotional, sentimental, and human."[30] Yet when one examines theoretically those very elements that make for emotionality in Black music (as one of many African-derived artistic expressions alluded to by Locke), one finds these elements to have at least some of the characteristics of the "controlled, disciplined," and "conventionalized" forms deemed to be African. Thus music, qua art, actually comes closer than the visual arts to accomplishing what Locke had originally wanted. Further, the presence of these demonstrably African elements bolsters Locke's essentialism at least with respect to music, even if it remains paradoxical with respect to other arts, for it provides a more specific framework and offers at least a partial response to the problematic areas.

A set of nonrhythmic elements that we will refer to as attributes of African vocality are principally responsible for the emotionalizing of African American music. They constitute a repertory of devices that includes guttural sounds and related utterances, interpolated vocality, falsetto, blues notes, Afromelismas, lyric improvisation, and vocal rhythmization.

Interestingly, the Black vernacular styles contemporaneous with the Harlem Renaissance—styles that Locke would have preferred to see expressed in a more contemplative and rarefied form—in great measure owe their visceral infectiousness and multicultural attractiveness precisely to the highly organized manner in which the attributes of African vocality were employed in them. For the skillful employment of such devices, we contend, was never random, indiscriminate, or aesthetically incurious. In the hands of trained practitioners they were, in fact, always employed in a measured and calculated manner—the intuitive basis of their employment notwithstanding—and integrated into the fabric of Black musical compositions at points that maximized their emotional impact.

Highly influential in the shaping of African American notions of form, structure, and timbre was the African-derived principle of "call and response"—a performance practice and an antiphonal principle that, in its elemental form, featured the alternation of solo passages with choral passages or choral refrains. We claim that this principle had already established itself as an intrinsic aspect of African American and pre-African American vernacular musicality long before the Civil War; thus both expressive and core African elements are present in this particular African American art. From the Reconstruction era onward, however, its manifestation became more creative and sophisticated.

The opera *Treemonisha,* completed by Scott Joplin in 1911—and oddly not cited in the "Negro Music" section of the bibliography of Locke's *New Negro*— is replete with examples showing the creative employment of call and response. One example is "We're Goin' Around," from section 4 of the opera. In it the workers inspire themselves to work with a ring-play and accompanying song.[31] This part of the opera also exemplifies, in a beautifully dramatic way, both the African-derived attribute of functionality and the interconnected notions of music and dance in Black America—also an African-derived idea.

If only the previously discussed elements were used as a basis for defining a Black American musical language, they would still constitute a language quite distinct from any other existing in America. But, as correctly intimated by Locke, the definitive aspect of the language of Black American music is vested principally in its rhythmical attributes, and the extent to which these attributes—and musical attributes as a whole—can be made precise underscores many of the theses Locke would like to apply to the visual arts, particularly insofar as these theses apply to elements that are actually "African." These attributes help shape a musical drama that is principally defined by the actuation of intricate rhythmical plexuses that balance constant elements with various elements of inconstancy.[32] The inconstant elements are generally heard as dissonant or contentive forces against a concrescent harmonious flow created by the constant elements, or ostinatos. In such a structure, only one affect or emotion is possible unless the plexus is subjected to substantial alterations. Within the context of this single affect, however, various sorts of nuancing are made possible by improvisation or by mildly variegating the constant aspects of the plexus.

Locke would not have understood the technical intricacies of Black music in the way they have been presented here. His understanding of the musical language of his people was somewhat superficial. However, the essentialist admonitions he advocated—however elitistly tempered and expressed—are sound affirmations, to the extent that they can be verified and creatively accommodated by a musical language enchoric to African Americans, and eminently capable of expressing their higher intellectual and spiritual planes, as envisioned by Locke. Thus Locke is freed, at least from the standpoint of music as an artistic endeavor, from part of the range of paradoxes that tend to accompany his analysis of painting and sculpture. Music is an art that has a long Black American history, and it has structural elements to which one can point at any given time in the chronology of African American art. The same cannot be said, unfortunately, of the visual arts.

To review briefly, we were first concerned with Locke's positioning himself as a proponent of things African, rather than African American, in the visual arts, because it was clear that his naive expressionist theory was rather undercut by adherence to the forms of the ritualized Yoruba masks. (To be fair, we noted that Locke spends a great deal of time on formalistic theories of art, like Fry's, once the concept of African formality is introduced in his essay.) But with respect to music, Locke would have been on surer ground, had he taken the trouble to articulate it. For here the specific African forms to which we have alluded both allow Locke the reliance on formal elements that he craved and simultaneously reestablish his expressionism, since it is clear that music is, in general, a more spontaneous process than the construction of ceremonial masks. This is especially true, of course, of a great deal of the music composed in the United States to which Locke could have referred at that time. Music composed for specific purposes might be analogous to the objects constructed for ritual use, but this sort of scenario does not apply to the composition of a great deal of the improvisational African American music of this century.

In addition, and perhaps more important, the salience of the "authenticity thesis" as a major objection to the development of an essentialist aesthetic is diminished to some extent when music is taken as the paradigmatic art, for there has long been a tradition of at least a few persons not of African ancestry performing African-based music.[33]

This particular debate has, indeed, been the subject of much intense theorizing. Writing in the *Journal of Aesthetics and Art Criticism,* Joel Rudinow examines key points in the discussion and concludes:

> In other words, the essence of the blues is a *stance* embodied and articulated in sound and poetry, and what distinguishes authentic from inauthentic blues is essentially what distinguishes that stance from its superficial imitations—from *posturing.* I think that if we wish to avoid ethnocentrism, as we would wish to avoid racism, what we should say is that the authenticity of a blues performance turns not on the ethnicity of the performer but on the degree of mastery of the idiom and the integrity of the performer's use of the idiom in performance.[34]

Thus Rudinow's provisional answer to the rhetorical question "Can White People Sing the Blues?" is yes, always remembering that the idiom and the stance are themselves based on the history of people of African ancestry in the New World.

That this sort of issue comes up again and again in debates about essentialism is underscored by the fact that it occurred in Lott's discussion of Black film. In general, one might be tempted to claim that the more surely one can point to specific elements of structure for a given art, the less relevant the ethnicity of the artist, for specific structural elements, named or alluded to over a long period of time, may be indicative of a documented history. Advertence to specific structural elements, particularly in a historical context, undercuts the notion that the relevant art is not "really" from the group in question. The difficulty for arts other than music—filmmaking for one, as Lott has noted—is that referring to precise structural elements is awkward and, in some cases, almost impossible, particularly without a lengthy chronology, and here we note that the debate tends to move back toward ethnicity of the artist. Finally, the charge of vagueness of the generally unspecific term "African" is again largely, if not entirely, vitiated with respect to music, since there seems to be general agreement on the parts of Africa (Western Africa) from which these elements derived.[35] Any given geographical term may be less than specific, but with respect to music the terms are much more specifiable than they are for the other arts, since a long historical tradition between Senegambia and the New World allows us to be precise, as Rudinow is, for example, when he mentions the Yoruba deity commonly known as Elegba in conjunction with

Robert Johnson's "Crossroads."[36] (Locke's visual examples in "Legacy" cover a broader and less specifiable African range, including at least one object from the Sudan.) Thus music and musical examples could well have proven more fructifying for Locke's work than he allowed them to be.

Summary

We have attempted to outline some problems adhering in Locke's work, and a brief recapitulation of these summarizes the work done here. We began with Mills's analysis of weaknesses in essentialist constructions of group identity. We next examined at least three areas of difficulty specifically pertaining to the development of Locke's Black aesthetic as delineated in "The Legacy of the Ancestral Arts": the authenticity thesis, notions of expressionism in African art as opposed to African American art, and notions of what is constitutive of "African." We then examined some of Lott's work on Black film theory, borrowing the concept of a "no-theory theory." All of these conceptual difficulties were then considered against an analysis of structural components of African American music, in which we briefly examined the construction of the concepts of essentialism and expressionism in light of Locke's suggestions about Black art.

It may appear that we do not find Locke's project valuable. This is far from the case, however. The difficulties inherent in the construction of a Black aesthetic have been there all along, so to speak, but Locke was among the first articulators of such a view. To the extent that the essays contained in *The New Negro* are about something that is both new and Black, those essays, including Locke's, pave the way for the future and lead us from essentially nineteenth-century work to something that we recognize today. The richness of Locke's work can be appreciated only when we see the array of challenging conceptual problems that arise from it.[37]

Notes

1. Alain Locke, ed., *The New Negro* (New York: Macmillan, 1992).
2. Locke, *New Negro,* 254–70.
3. The commentators seem to be in agreement on the importance of a Herder-derived conception of the status of folk art for some of Locke's conceptualizations about aesthetics. See, e.g., Rebecca T. Cureau, "Toward an Aesthetic of Black Folk Expression," in *Alain Locke: Reflections on a Modern Renaissance Man,* ed. Russell J. Linnemann (Baton Rouge: Louisiana State University Press, 1982), 77–90. Locke makes this point himself in the essay "The Negro Spirituals" in *New Negro.*

4. For a full view of the notion, see Tommy Lott, "Du Bois on Race," *Philosophical Forum* 24, nos. 1–3, (Fall-Spring 1992–93).

5. Alain Locke, "The Legacy of the Ancestral Arts," in *New Negro*, 254.

6. Locke, "Legacy," 256.

7. Locke, "Legacy," 256.

8. Locke, "Legacy," 264.

9. See, e.g., the group of essays on African American philosophy in *Philosophical Forum* 24, nos. 1–3, (Fall-Spring 1992–93). Two especially pertinent here are "African American Philosophy?" by Kwarne Anthony Appiah, and "Du Bois on Race," by Tommy Lott.

10. Appiah, "African American Philosophy?" 14.

11. Abiola Irele, introduction to *African Philosophy: Myth and Reality*, by Paulin Hountondji (London: Hutchinson, 1983), 25.

12. Irele, introduction, 12.

13. We owe this and some of the following terminology to Claudia Mills, "Multiculturalism and Cultural Authenticity," *Philosophy and Public Policy* 14. nos. 1–2 (Winter/Spring 1994): 1–5.

14. Mills, "Cultural Authenticity," 2.

15. Locke, "Legacy," *passim.*

16. Peter G. Ingram, "Art, Language, and Community in Collingwood's *Principles of Art*," *Journal of Aesthetics and Art Criticism* 36, no. 3 (Fall 1978): 53–64.

17. R. G. Collingwood, *The Principles of Art* (Oxford: Oxford University Press, 1972). With respect to Locke, one passage in the "Legacy" essay that employs "express" or a cognate is found at the bottom of p. 256 and reads, "the original artistic endowment can be sufficiently augmented to express itself with equal power."

18. Collingwood and his followers employ the distinction in such a way that it pertains almost entirely to European art.

19. Although Locke specifically cites Fry, Bell might be thought to be the most noteworthy proponent of this thesis. See Clive Bell, *Art* (New York: Frederick Stokes, 1913).

20. Locke, "Legacy," 256.

21. Locke, "Legacy," 256.

22. Larry Shiner, "'Primitive Fakes,' 'Tourist Art,' and the Ideology of Authenticity," *Journal of Aesthetics and Art Criticism* 52, no. 2 (Spring 1994): 225–34.

23. Tommy Lott, "A No-Theory Theory of Contemporary Black Cinema," *Black-American Literature Forum* 25, no. 2 (Summer 1991): 221–36.

24. Lott, "No-Theory Theory," 226–28.

25. He makes this point on the first page of his article, and this is, in fact, why he calls his view a "no-theory theory."

26. Lott specifically cites such older classics as "Nothing But a Man" and "Hallelujah."

27. Locke, "Legacy," 256.

28. Locke, "Legacy," 256.

29. See esp. Cureau, "Black Folk Expression."

30. Locke, "Legacy," 254.

31. It is interesting that Locke did not use *Treemonisha* and other works by Scott Joplin to symbolize his ideals of Black art music, for *Treemonisha* was an enchoric work if ever there was one. This is to say that it was a composition that was illustrative of African American musical intellectuality, it was written by an African American, and it was substantially predicated upon a contemporaneous yet indigenous African American vernacular art form, ragtime. In addition, as an operatic statement, it combined Black music with Black dance and drama derived from Black folkloric cultural sources,it employed then-contemporary Black literary idioms in its libretto (dialect poetry), and it addressed thematically issues of great contemporaneous import to rural Blacks—education and the politics of ignorance (ironically, these issues are still relevant today).

32. An African-derived rhythmical plexus may be defined as an intricate network of African-derived rhythmical events or rhythmically-oriented pitch events.

33. See, e.g., Joel Rudinow, "Race, Ethnicity, Expressive Authenticity: Can White People Sing the Blues?" *Journal of Aesthetics and Art Criticism* 52, no. 1 (Winter 1994): 127–34.

34. Rudinow, "Can White People Sing the Blues?" 135.

35. Robert Palmer, *Deep Blues* (New York: Penguin, 1981), 29–31. Palmer is specific about the Senegambia region and its musical importance.

36. Rudinow, "Can White People Sing the Blues?" 134.

37. The authors would like to thank Paul Fisher, UCSB undergraduate and Black studies major, for fruitful discussions of the aesthetics of Alain Locke. There is an interesting parallel aesthetic project to which the reader may want to refer. José Vasconcelos, the renowned Mexican philosopher of the earlier part of this century, attempted to establish an aesthetics of the mestizos, the mixed racial group that constitutes the majority of Mexico's population. He wrote: "[I]t is clear that the mission of the New World is to bring about . . . an 'aesthetic state.'" José Vasconcelos, *La Raza Cósmica* (Los Angeles: Centro de Publicaciones CSULA, 1979), 21–22.

8

Aesthetics and the Issue of Identity

Richard Keaveny

A central issue underlying the Harlem Renaissance was the polemical struggle over the expression of African American identity. As African Americans, the members of the Harlem Renaissance accepted that there existed characteristics common to African Americans that distinguished them from other Americans. They also agreed that these characteristics marginalized African American culture from the dominant American culture. The polemical struggle regarding cultural identity was a debate over which of these characteristics should and should not be exalted as being intrinsically African American within the forum of art.

Within the didactic leadership of the Harlem Renaissance, two men exemplified this polemical struggle: Alain Locke and W. E. B. Du Bois. Both men accepted that there existed definitive differences between the African American and the dominant American cultures that marginalized African Americans. The two men also shared an understanding of what many of those differences were. However, they differed in their assessments of which of those characteristics should be espoused as being reflective of African Americans and which should be purged as the product of negative racial prejudice.

The fundamental difference between Locke and Du Bois in terms of both the Harlem Renaissance and their personal philosophies concerned the acceptable content for African American art. As a social scientist and a historian, Du Bois viewed the struggle of the African American minority in America as an event-based linear struggle toward the acceptance of African American equality. As a consequence, Du Bois insisted that African American art must be a positive representation of African Americans and their contributions to American culture.[1] In contrast, as a philosopher, Locke envisioned the struggle of the African American as a dialectical struggle posing the African and the American cultures on either end of a spectrum and producing the African American culture in the synthesis. He therefore wanted art to be a representation of both

127

the positive and the negative features of African American culture.[2]

Although Locke and Du Bois differed in their views on the nature of the general struggle faced by African Americans as a culture, both men agreed that every African American struggled with feelings of marginality. The term "marginal man" was first used by the sociologist Robert E. Park in his 1928 essay "Human Migration and the Marginal Man."[3] However, although unnamed, the concept predated the Harlem Renaissance.

Du Bois described feelings of alienation as feelings of "two-ness," a term he used to describe the emotions about his dual identity as both Black and American.[4] Du Bois defined his concept of two-ness through a series of questions: "Am I an American or am I a Negro? Can I be both? Or is it my duty to cease to be a Negro as soon as possible and be an American?"[5] In *The Souls of Black Folk* (1903) Du Bois reflected that "one ever feels his two-ness—an American, a Negro; two souls, two thoughts, two unreconciled strivings; two warring ideals in one dark body, whose dogged strength alone keeps it from being torn asunder."[6] It was a soul torn, Du Bois reasoned, as a result of its membership in a cultural group that lacked a positive self-identity.

Locke shared Du Bois's belief that the feelings of two-ness were the result of a poor African American identity. As a philosopher and a self-proclaimed philosophical gadfly, Locke focused his efforts on making "abstract ideas pertinent to practical reality."[7] With this in mind, he wrote in 1935 that "all philosophies," it seemed to him, "[were] in ultimate derivation philosophies of life and not of abstract disembodied 'objective' reality; products of time, place and situation, and thus systems of timed history rather than timeless eternity."[8] Accordingly, his philosophies were an attempt to bridge his beliefs in the philosophical concepts of cultural pluralism and in classical value theory with a practical and contemporary explanation of African American identity.

In the late nineteenth and early twentieth centuries, philosophical arguments were often based on pseudoscientific and anthropological data that held that a racial hierarchy existed among humans. In addition, these philosophies held that cultures were representative of race and that through an analysis of cultures, the pecking order of the races could be determined. Locke adapted a philosophical belief in cultural pluralism and the value theory in part to combat these beliefs.[9]

As a philosopher, Locke rejected absolutism, dogmatism, and universalism. "He applauded [William] James' conception of experience as the continual interaction of cognitive and pragmatic factors."[10] But he disagreed with the commonly accepted notion among late-nineteenth-century and early-twentieth-century philosophers that "ideas were fixed entities or stayed cognitive activity." In contrast, Locke argued that "ideas were understandable relations, and thoughts were always a stream or process."[11]

Locke believed that "the common man . . . sets up personal, private and group norms as standards and principles, and rightly or wrongly hypostatizes them as universals for all conditions, all times and all men,"[12] and that "no philosophical system can hope to differentiate itself from descriptive science or present a functional, interpretative version of human experience."[13] It was imperative that, in designing his or her own normative value system, each individual not assume that "an influential value-set," that of the cultural majority, defined the only possible values.[14]

According to Locke, the social environment was the main contributor to the ways in which people assessed their emotions. He believed that no innate emotion carried any connotations but that all connotations were the result of interpretations that society instilled in the individual. As a result, Locke contended that race and culture were not synonymous. He explained that each individual within a culture revaluated or reassessed his or her emotions with each experience and that with each individual revaluation, a subsequent evolution was undergone by the entire culture. Locke described this process in his value theory; the result, he explained, was an ethnogenesis: the constant evolution of ethnicity or culture.

The notion that individuals assign values to their experiences was not unique to Locke. Indeed, without naming it value theory, Plato discussed the concept in his analysis of the idea of good in book 6 of the *Republic*.[15] However, with the birth of pragmatism, the use of values took on an entirely different meaning. Royce, Locke, and other pragmatists "were glad to recognize the presence of valuations in cognitive processes, as a proof of the fictitious nature of 'pure' thought and 'absolute' truth."[16]

One of Locke's central concerns as a philosopher and as a didactic leader of the Harlem Renaissance was "the ethnogenesis of racial identity and the concepts of experience best suited to account for it."[17] He did not use ethnic identity synonymously with racial identity, "nor did he assume that historical analysis or conceptions of experience relevant to the persistence of legitimacy of ethnic identities were simplistically transferable to race."[18] He believed that race and culture were the product of continual revaluation, and he argued against those who believed that race was a stable classification.[19]

Locke's value theory entails that emotions can be heuristically understood as being experienced on two levels within each individual. The first level of experience is the actual experience of the emotion felt universally by people of all races. The second level of experience is the cognitive interpretation of what that emotion means. Locke insisted that individuals, regardless of race, experience identical emotions on the first, innate, level but are taught socially to interpret these emotions differently on the second, or cultural, level.[20]

To Locke, therefore, each individual was unique only in how he or she interpreted emotions and not in the emotions felt. Because emotions were felt in the same way by people of all cultures, it was in the individual's interpretation of each emotion that cultural biases were created. As a result, the struggle was to teach individuals of all cultures to interpret their emotional experiences without egregious bias. In his early work, Locke viewed artistic expression as the greatest means in this struggle of expressing equality.

As a corollary to his value theory, Locke believed in cultural pluralism. Locke accepted that the world was culturally diverse as a result of the revaluation process. He held that the world was destined to remain culturally diverse but that diversity was not a negative state. Cultural diversity was only negative when the differences between people were interpreted negatively within the second level of emotional experience. If individuals interpreted cultural differences positively, Locke contended, then cultural pluralism would enable each individual to gain self-respect through his or her own unique identity. It would enable each individual to draw strength from the differences between him- or herself and others rather than creating insecurities as a result of them. In this way, the differences between cultures in Locke's philosophical scheme became each individual's strength rather than a handicap.[21]

Du Bois held that there existed continuities within human nature that were of greater import than any cultural differences. For Du Bois, what was important was the fact that all individuals felt similar emotions, regardless of their skin color; too strong an assertion of difference, such as Locke's cultural pluralism, was a sure way to allow the perpetuation of cultural stereotypes and prejudices.

In Locke's view of cultural pluralism, white American culture was synonymous with American culture. As a result, all ethnic minorities' cultural practices that contrasted with "American" culture were suspect by the cultural majority. In order that all cultural practices could be accepted without stigma, Locke insisted that it was essential that cultural differences be understood and not stigmatized.

Locke rejected the idea of an evolutionary formula for evaluating cultures and placing them on a continuum from primitive to sophisticated. He argued that the use of "primitive cultures as the stock arguments and illustrations for societal evolution"[22] leads to "the error of assuming basic common factors and commensurate values."[23] Instead, Locke asserted that all cultures held their own integrity and should not be measured by criteria that do not apply to them.

In contrast, as a result of his belief that all societies evolved linearly throughout history, Du Bois gauged that the Western European civilization was the furthest advanced in its evolution and was, therefore, the measure by which all cultures should be judged. Accordingly, Du Bois defended those African American cultural achievements that represented accomplishments by

Western European standards. He was also concerned that too strong a recognition of difference by African Americans about African American culture could be used by other Americans to justify a belief in African American cultural inferiority. Consequently, Du Bois wanted the African American artist of the Harlem Renaissance to be conscious of what he or she portrayed as characteristically African American and strive to produce works of art that could be compared favorably to art produced by Western European artists.

Importantly, Du Bois's view of the history of the African American culture was, in part, a justification of the potential he believed African American culture held to be a great culture as measured by the standards of Western civilization—a potential, he repeatedly argued, that was stifled in its evolution as a result of feelings of cultural marginality.[24] Locke disagreed that African American culture was a lesser American culture that had been arrested in its evolution as a civilization. He argued that the present state of African American culture was a product of centuries of cultural synthesis and not of retarded linear growth.

Although Locke and Du Bois differed in their conception of the nature of African American difference, they shared the belief that the art and letters of the Harlem Renaissance were a means of expression that could help African Americans regain a positive self-image. However, the two men differed on where they believed the ultimate power of expression within the movement should rest. For Locke, didactic leaders such as himself were merely cultural midwives who helped the artists deliver their messages.[25] Because he believed that culture was a natural synthesis, he also believed that art should be, as much as possible, an unbridled expression of that synthesis: both a reflection of, and a contribution to, ethnogenesis. In contrast, Du Bois believed that the power of direction within the Harlem Renaissance should lie in the hands of African Americans who had both an understanding of the historical processes that had created African American cultural stagnation and a conviction about how to reverse its negative results.

Locke and Du Bois shared the belief that the high culture of the Harlem Renaissance represented more to people of color in the United States than merely the art and letters that the individual artists produced in New York City between the late 1910s and early 1930s. Both men contended that each artist or each work of art was a potential piece of evidence demonstrating that African Americans were equal to other Americans. However, the two men differed in the measure of equality they were using. For Du Bois, the measure was a stable Western standard culture; for Locke, it was cultural difference and synthesis.

The dispute between Locke and Du Bois coincided with the common emotion felt by many African Americans that a New Negro had emerged in the United States. In 1925, the editor of *Survey Graphic* magazine asked Locke to guest edit an issue dedicated to the emergence of these New Negroes. Locke's New Negro issue (1 March 1925) expressed his beliefs about African American culture. It exuded the optimism and expressed the concerns of the "Negro" in 1920s America. It told of the new urban nature of African Americans, it praised African American contributions to music and other forms of popular culture, and it demanded that these accomplishments not go unnoticed.

Through *Survey Graphic* Locke expressed his belief in a "Negro Zionism" that was, he concluded, a representation of the acceptance of the African American synthesized culture.[26] The articles Locke wrote for the magazine were aimed at promoting an acceptance of cultural differences, and he spoke for many of the self-proclaimed New Negro Americans when he concluded that it was then, in 1925, that African Americans were enjoying their "spiritual coming of age," or, in Locke's philosophical terms, were enjoying a period of cultural acceptance.[27]

The New Negro issue of *Survey Graphic* announced and explained the feelings of many, but not all, African Americans. To race leaders such as Du Bois, much of what Locke professed as representing the New Negro was not what they believed should be espoused as representative. Du Bois wrote extensively on the roles that African Americans had played in the formation of the United States. In the years prior to the special issue of *Survey Graphic,* Du Bois had published *The Souls of Black Folk* (1903), *The Negro* (1915), *Darkwater* (1920), and *The Gifts of Black Folk* (1924), as well as numerous articles in both black and white journals expounding his views on the truncated evolution of African American culture as a result of cultural bigotry. Du Bois was also the globally recognized founder of the pan-African movement and one of the most powerful driving forces behind the National Association for the Advancement of Colored People (NAACP). But Du Bois's most important influence came through his position as editor of the NAACP's news organ the *Crisis,* which gave him an approximate monthly audience of sixty thousand subscribers and some one hundred thousand readers.[28]

Following the publication of Locke's New Negro issue of *Survey Graphic,* Du Bois's editorials in the *Crisis* grew more vehement in their opposition to Locke's and like-minded thinkers' apparent call for art for art's sake. In the May 1925 issue of the *Crisis,* Du Bois announced a new editorial policy for the magazine in line with his contrary belief in art as propaganda. He said that the editors of, and contributors to, the *Crisis* "shall stress beauty—all beauty, but especially the beauty of Negro life and character; its music, its dancing, its drawing and painting and the new birth of its literature." The magazine would "encourage it in every way . . . keeping the while a high standard of merit and never stooping to cheap flattery and misspent kindness." In subsequent editorials Du Bois reinforced his convictions, claiming in the 31 January 1926 issue that "we [African Americans] want Negro writers to produce beautiful things but we stress the things rather than the beauty." His desire that the emphasis be put on the "things" rather than their "beauty" reflected a consistency not only in his professional criticisms but also in his personal literary works. He wrote in 1926 that whatever talent he had for writing had always been used for propaganda,[29] and in his *Quest of the Silver Fleece* (1911) Du Bois expressed in his introduction a summary of his view on art that characterized his opinions for the next two decades: "He who would tell a tale must look toward three ideals: to tell it well, to tell it beautifully, and to tell the truth. The first is the Gift of God, the second is the vision of Genius, but the third is the reward of honesty."[30]

Indeed, Du Bois's novel *The Quest of the Silver Fleece* was a direct response to Thomas Dixon Jr.'s book *The Leopard's Spots: A Romance of the White Man's Burden* (1902).[31] *The Quest* represented Du Bois's desire to combat racist literature with positive African American literature. The success of novels such as Dixon's *Leopard's Spots* and *The Clansman: A Romance of the Ku Klux Klan* (1905) demonstrated to Du Bois the threat that misused media posed to the advancement of African American culture.[32] This potential danger, according to Du Bois, was only enhanced by calls such as Locke's for an acceptance of cultural plurality. In one of his most succinct attacks on cultural pluralism, Du Bois wrote in the October 1926 issue of the *Crisis* that he did not "care a damn for any art that is not used as propaganda."[33]

Although Locke and Du Bois differed on what assessment of cultural difference they believed was most beneficial to African Americans, they did agree on who they thought was best suited to express African Americans' opinions. Both men agreed that it was necessary for the elite thinkers of the African American culture to gain for African Americans a recognition of equality, either as potential equals, as Du Bois claimed, or, as Locke maintained, equals but different. The two agreed that the "Talented Tenth," a name that Du Bois gave to the roughly top 10 percent of the population who represented the most exceptional intellectual prowess, or the "thinking Negro," in Locke's terms, reflected the most economical way that African Americans could be acknowledged as innately equal to whites.[34] They also agreed that the solution to the problem of negative cultural identity was to ignore, for the moment, the goal of complete recognition of the cultural equality of all African Americans and strive for the recognition of the cultural equality of the African American Talented Tenth. As Locke expressed it, it was "a case of putting the premium upon the capable few, and thus of accelerating the 'levelling up' processes in American society."[35]

To both Locke and Du Bois, the greatest disadvantage any African American faced was not the inequality of condition but the "inequality of comparison" (557) that resulted from the negative cultural stereotypes in the United States. Locke argued that "successful peoples are rated, and rate themselves, in terms of their best." Cultural and national prestige is, Locke argued, "after all, the product of the exceptional few" (557).

Accordingly, Locke argued that "the continuation of the present attitude toward the Negro [was] in fact possible only as long as it [was] possible to take as most representative of the Negro his worst rather than his best" (556). Locke concluded that "the question raised" in regard to African Americans' gaining a recognition of their equality in the United States "can and must be settled in terms of the representation of the exceptional few. For the asserted inferiority of the Negro does not pivot on the average man—black or white—and can not be settled by mass comparisons; as a challenge it must be fought out in terms of the exceptional man" (555). Thus, Locke insisted that if African Americans were to be judged on the promise and accomplishments of their Talented Tenth, then the "cultural recognition of the Negro was imminent" (556).

Locke argued that it was essential that the Talented Tenth be allowed to explore their own uniqueness as African Americans. In order to do this, he argued, it was essential that the artists of the Harlem Renaissance be judged by criteria other than those of Western civilization. Because African Americans were a product of a cultural synthesis, Locke argued that it was imperative that they be judged not in terms of strictly American cultural standards but by standards that took into account their difference.[36]

In contrast, Du Bois argued against the free reign of artistic expression that seemed intrinsic to Locke's New Negro artist. He believed that young African American artists needed a strong and mature hand to help guide their artistic talents, just as great European artists had had. The Harlem Renaissance for Du Bois was too great a tool for helping African Americans gain a recognition of their equality to allow poets to portray elements of the African American community that only maintained the racial stereotypes that had allowed whites to justify their subjugation of blacks in the past. This was especially true when those traits were expressed in artistic forms that suggested that African Americans were incapable of "high" culture.[37]

According to Du Bois, art was propaganda. All art created by African Americans, whether the artist intended it to be or not, was a portrayal of African American culture. As a result, Du Bois contended that, as much as possible, art must be censored to ensure that as propaganda it helped perpetuate only positive African American attributes in order to stimulate acceptance of equality by both black and white Americans.

Equally important was Du Bois's belief that in order for African Americans and African American culture to be accepted as equal in American society, the artists of the Harlem Renaissance must not only adhere to but exceed the accepted moral standards. For Du Bois, the artists of the Harlem Renaissance had a responsibility not only to reflect the uniqueness of being African American but also to show the ways in which African Americans embodied the virtues that America would recognize as proper.[38]

Du Bois argued that anything written by African Americans was inevitably going to be viewed primarily as having been written by an African American; as a result, to demonstrate that African Americans could produce high art, the writing must be pure in content and form. In a published response to a young African American high school student's letter to the editor of the *Crisis,* Du Bois expressed his opinion on the role of the black artist:

> Your work as a Negro lies in two directions. First, to let the world know what there is fine and genuine about the Negro race. And secondly, to see that there is nothing about that race which is worth contempt; your contempt; my contempt; or the contempt of the wide, wide world.[39]

Underlying these criteria was an understanding that the expression of what is "fine and genuine" about African Americans would be given in terms of American high-cultural standards, which were shared equally by black and white elites.

In contrast, central to Locke's belief in the ability of the art of the Harlem Renaissance to free African American culture through an infusion of a sense of African American self-worth was the belief that "art in the best sense is rooted in self-expression and whether naive or sophisticated is self-contained."[40] What he wanted from the artists of the Harlem Renaissance was "a poetry which balanced excellence with social consciousness,"[41] a poetry that drew on the mutual traits shared by all of the African diaspora and that announced "a recognition of spirit"[42] common to all people of color but that drew also on the uniqueness of the African American experience.

Locke accepted that the African American needed "to be known for what he [was], even his faults and shortcomings." He wanted African Americans openly to acknowledge their own and their race's shortcomings rather than continue to accept the African Americans' "craven and precarious survival at the price of seeming to be what [they are] not."[43] Thus, with regard to the question of art or propaganda, Locke differed from Du Bois in his willingness to allow African American artists to draw inspiration from all of African American life and express black life openly.

"In our spiritual growth," Locke announced, "genius and talent must more and more choose the role of free individualistic expression."[44] He objected to the overt call for artistic censorship that was intrinsic to Du Bois's call for art as propaganda, claiming that "it perpetuates the position of group inferiority even in crying out against it."[45] Du Bois's call for art, according to Locke, stifled the ability of African Americans to express their uniqueness. It also appeared to demand that African Americans become "lampblacked Anglo-Saxons" rather than acknowledge their own unique identity.[46]

According to Locke, "the artistic problem of the Young Negro [had] not been so much that of acquiring the outer mastery of form and technique as that of achieving an inner mastery of mood and spirit," of accepting cultural equality as members of a marginal cultural minority.[47] Locke argued that African American artists faced the crisis of struggling not only with the self-doubt faced by all artists but also with the specific self-doubts about cultural equality felt by all African Americans. Locke deemed it necessary for African Americans to come to an acceptance that cultures such as their own could be distinct and equal. He concluded that to force African American artists to draw only on a limited number of positive African American similarities to American culture, as Du Bois demanded, made true expression nearly impossible.

For Locke, all of African American life was a potential source of inspiration for the Harlem Renaissance artist. Locke saw no problem with the African American artist using non-self-effacing slave spirituals, blues, or jazz compositions as inspirations in expressing what African Americans were all about. To Locke the African American poet was an African American, and so too were African American drug dealers, African American lawyers, African American prostitutes, and African American physicians. In this way, Locke asserted that the Harlem Renaissance, as African American high culture, should not be constricted for inspiration by any rules he or any other philanthropist could concoct so long as each artist reflected a positive self-worth.[48]

Locke was foremost a philosopher who attempted to justify African American cultural equality through philosophical discourse and rationale. His cultural pluralism was essentially a philosophical solution to the problem of the pragmatic reality pinpointed by Du Bois's term "two-ness." Also, as a philosopher, Locke viewed the question regarding an individual's reconciliation of cultural marginality as a question that was asked not only by African Americans but also by all members of ethnic minority groups living within a larger, dominant, culture.

In contrast, Du Bois was a sociologist and a historian who combated the emotion of two-ness by minimizing the existence of fundamental differences between cultures. He demanded that the artists of the Harlem Renaissance present as evidence for the equal potential of the African American culture art that could stand alongside great European art. Ironically, however, he wanted the

Talented Tenth to be artistically free while simultaneously sharing his pragmatic desire for cultural censorship.

Through their debate between "art for art's sake" and "art as propaganda," Locke and Du Bois presented both the nature of the struggle for African American identity that existed during the time of the Harlem Renaissance and the two solutions that were in polemical struggle over it. In one respect, however, the two men's views were not very different. Both men agreed on the existence of a Talented Tenth and on the need for that group to acquire positive recognition by the dominant American culture in order for the entire African American culture to receive the same recognition.

Notes

1. Du Bois was not only the most prolific African American intellectual during his lifetime but also the most complicated. Between the time of his first publication while a student at Harvard University during the 1890s and his death, Du Bois often contradicted himself on what he considered to be the criterion of good art. However, during the time of the Harlem Renaissance, Du Bois remained relatively consistent in his published thoughts on African American art. For an analysis of Du Bois's contradictions, see Rayford Logan, *W. E. B. Du Bois: A Profile* (New York: Hill & Wang, 1971).

2. Jeffrey Stewart, ed., *The Critical Temper of Alain Locke: A Collection of His Essays on Art and Culture* (New York: Garland Publishing, 1983); Russell J. Linnemann, *Alain Locke: Reflections of a Modern Renaissance Man* (Baton Rouge: Louisiana State University Press, 1982); Johnny Washington, *Alain Locke and Philosophy: A Quest for Cultural Pluralism* (Westport, Conn.: Greenwood Press, 1986); and Leonard Harris, ed., *The Philosophy of Alain Locke: Harlem Renaissance and Beyond* (Philadelphia: Temple University Press, 1989).

3. Robert E. Park, "Human Migration and the Marginal Man," *American Journal of Sociology* 33 (May 1928): 881–93. For a more in-depth analysis of the concept of the marginal man, see Everett E. Hughes, "Social Change and Status Protest: An Essay on the Marginal Man," *Phylon* 10 (1949); Everett V. Stonequist, *The Marginal Man: A Study in Personality and Culture Conflict* (New York: Russell & Russell, 1961).

4. Du Bois first used the term "two-ness" in "Strivings of the Negro People," *Atlantic Monthly,* August 1897, quoted in Logan, *Du Bois,* ix.

5. Quoted in Logan, *Du Bois,* ix.

6. W. E. B. Du Bois, *The Souls of Black Folk* (Chicago: A. C. McClurg, 1903), 3.

7. Harris, *Philosophy of Alain Locke,* 13. I would like to thank Dr. Harris very much for his correspondence on the subject of Locke's philosophy and his role as a didactic leader in the Harlem Renaissance.

8. Alain Locke, "Values and Imperatives," in *American Philosophy Today and Tomorrow,* ed. Horace M. Kallen and Sidney Hook (New York: L. Furman, 1935), 313.

9. "It is difficult to determine the extent to which Locke influenced the American philosophic tradition generally or a particular American philosopher. We do know

however that there was much philosophic correspondence between Locke and Dewey, between Locke and Kallen, and between Locke and Santayana, among others. Locke regularly visited Santayana in England after Santayana retired from Harvard." Washington, *Alain Locke and Philosophy,* 216.

10. Harris, *Philosophy of Alain Locke,* 12–13. William James was one of the most influential philosophical thinkers during the early part of the twentieth century. He was a leading advocate of pragmatic philosophy and helped popularize this method of thought among his contemporaries. He, along with George Santayana, Josiah Royce, and Horace M. Kallen, was one of Locke's professors at Harvard. For a more complete understanding of the thoughts of William James, see James, *Pragmatism: A New Name for Some Old Ways of Thinking* (New York: Longmans, Green, 1908). For an understanding of what Locke specifically gained and what he rejected from James's thoughts, see Harris, *Philosophy of Alain Locke,* 12–13. For a more comprehensive analysis of how Locke's and George Santayana's philosophies were similar, see Washington, *Alain Locke and Philosophy,* 27.

11. Harris, *Philosophy of Alain Locke,* 13.

12. Locke, "Values and Imperatives," 315.

13. Locke, "Values and Imperatives," 314.

14. Locke. "Values and Imperatives," 317.

15. Harris, *Philosophy of Alain Locke,* 112.

16. Harris, *Philosophy of Alain Locke,* 115. See also Josiah Royce *The Spirit of Modern Philosophy* (New York: Houghton, Mifflin, 1982); Alain Locke, "Pluralism and Ideological Peace," in *Freedom and Experience,* ed. Milton R. Konvitz and Sidney Hook (Ithaca, N.Y.: Cornell University Press, 1947).

17. Harris, *Philosophy of Alain Locke,* 16.

18. Harris, *Philosophy of Alain Locke,* 16.

19. Alain Locke, "The Problem of Race Classification," *Opportunity* 1 (September 1923): 261.

20. Locke, "Values and Imperatives," 321; Ernest D. Mason, "Alain Locke's Philosophy of Value," in *Alain Locke: Reflections of a Modern Renaissance Man,* ed. Russell J. Linnemann (Baton Rouge: Louisiana State University Press, 1982), 6; Washington, *Alain Locke and Philosophy,* 26.

21. Alain Locke, "The Concept of Race as Applied to Social Culture," *Howard Review* 1 (June 1924): 296. In order to prove cultural pluralism, it was important for Locke to show that all individuals were, in fact, equal. Harris, *Philosophy of Alain Locke,* 190–92.

22. Harris, *Philosophy of Alain Locke,* 197.

23. Harris, *Philosophy of Alain Locke,* 196.

24. Du Bois's view of history may be seen as a continuation of nineteenth-century African American intellectual thought. Du Bois's concept of civilizationism reflected that of his mentor Alexander Crummell. Wilson J. Moses summarizes their shared ideology: "The laws [of physical, moral, and economic science] were universal—and hence not the creation of any race or culture. They were discovered, not invented, and hence not the creation of any race or nation. The fact that Europeans were farther along

in the process of civilization did not mean that they had been more intelligent, inventive or creative, merely that they had submitted earlier to the divine and natural law and were now carried along in the current of inevitable progress." Moses, *Alexander Crummell: A Study of Civilization and Discontent* (New York: Oxford University Press, 1989), 7.

25. Locke, "Values and Imperatives," 313.

26. The concept of Negro Zionism was used by Locke in his article "Harlem" to describe the new feelings of black nationalism among African Americans.

27. Alain Locke, "Enter the New Negro," *Survey Graphic* 53, no. 11 (1 March 1925): 634.

28. Herbert Aptheker, introduction to *Dark Princess,* by W. E. B. Du Bois (Millwood, N.J.: Kraus-Thomson, 1974), 5. In this introduction, Aptheker gives an excellent summary of Du Bois's global influence. See also Herbert Aptheker, introduction to *The Correspondence of W. E. B. Du Bois* (Amherst: University of Massachusetts Press, 1973).

29. W. E. B. Du Bois, Opinion, *Crisis* 30 (May 1925): 7; W. E. B. Du Bois, Opinion, *Crisis* 31 (January 1926): 111; W. E. B. Du Bois, Opinion, *Crisis* 32 (October 1926): 33.

30. W. E. B. Du Bois, *The Quest of the Silver Fleece* (Chicago: A. C. McClurg, 1911).

31. Thomas Dixon Jr., *The Leopard's Spots: A Romance of the White Man's Burden* (New York: Doubleday, Page, 1902).

32. Thomas Dixon Jr., *The Clansman: A Romance of the Ku Klux Klan* (New York: Grosset & Dunlap, 1905).

33. Du Bois, Opinion, *Crisis* 32 (October 1926): 33.

34. Locke applauded Du Bois's concept of the Talented Tenth in his article "The Role of the Talented Tenth," *Howard University Review* 18 (December 1918): 12–14.

35. Locke, "The High Cost of Prejudice," *Forum* 78 (December 1927): 557.

36. Harris, *Philosophy of Alain Locke,* 196.

37. Du Bois, Opinion, *Crisis* 32 (October 1926): 33; Du Bois *Quest of the Silver Fleece,* 12.

38. This concept of American standards is part of Du Bois's belief in civilizationism (see note 17). See also Wilson J. Moses, *The Golden Age of Black Nationalism* (Hamden, Conn.: Archon Books, 1978), 15–31.

39. W. E. B. Du Bois, "Postscript," *Crisis* (May 1928): 96–97.

40. Alain Locke, "Art or Propaganda," *Harlem,* November 1928, 12.

41. Stewart, *Critical Temper of Alain Locke,* 33.

42. Alain Locke, "The Art of the Ancestors," *Survey Graphic* 53, no. 11 (1 March 1925): 673.

43. Locke, "Enter the New Negro," 633.

44. Locke, "Art or Propaganda," 12.

45. Locke, "Art or Propaganda," 12.

46. "Lampblacked Anglo-Saxon" was a term coined by George S. Schuyler in his article "The Negro Art Hokum," *Nation.* 122 (16 June 1926): 662.

47. Alain Locke, "Youth Speaks," *Survey Graphic* 53, no. 11 (1 March 1925): 659.

48. Alain Locke, "Propaganda—Or Poetry?" *Race,* Summer 1926, 74; Alain Locke, "Common Clay and Poetry," review of Fine Clothes to the Jew, by Langston Hughes, *Saturday Review of Literature,* 9 April 1927, 33; Locke, "Art or Propaganda," 12.

9

Open-Textured Aesthetic Boundaries: Matters of Art, Race, and Culture

Rudolph V. Vanterpool

Artmaking, as a universal phenomenon, is socially constituted and has characteristically soft or penetrable cultural boundaries. I borrow a characterization suggested by John Ladd that aesthetic concepts are best treated as inexact, fuzzy, or open-textured.[1] Attempts to provide clear-cut definitions for such categories are shortsighted. To speak of aesthetic concepts as open-textured means that they refer to an aggregate of impermanent qualities, grouped together in such a manner that no one quality can fully explain the application of any one concept.[2] Along a similar line of thought, Kwame Anthony Appiah finds that "the art world has denizens whose work is to challenge every definition of art, to push us beyond every boundary, to stand outside and move beyond every attempt to fix art's meaning."[3] I find Ladd's paradigm of open-texturedness quite useful as a means of transcending so-called cultural boundaries in artmaking, particularly in cross-cultural comparisons of art. It makes sense, for example, to speak of African art and art produced in the African diaspora as culturally situated. Such creative productions as expressions of the human will to adorn reveal the potential for art to transcend the narrow confines of race, time, and cultural context.

My discussion of the nature of artmaking is predicated on the assumption that the core aesthetic categories are socially constructed and are not universal absolutes. The principal contentions in this essay are that: (1) it is misleading to classify African art as exclusively functional since African aesthetics is not monolithic; and (2) while W. E. B. Du Bois's concept of double consciousness helps to elucidate important aspects of the black experience in America and while Alain Locke's glorification of the ancestral arts of Africa helped black artists to concentrate on dynamic racial subject matter in their works, racial essentialism as a by-product of these doctrines needs to be supplanted by a more liberating *race-transcending* aesthetic. It is clear that the idea of a dual self or, for that matter, of a multiple self-identity seems to captivate African

American aesthetic discourse beyond anything found in the African's account of aesthetic categories. This is a distinguishing factor that sets up subtle, yet permeable, barriers between the experience with artmaking on the African continent and that of the African diaspora. What I have to say about race transcendence in this chapter, however, is of necessity both sketchy and provisional, given the narrow focus of my discussion. On this latter topic, the intellectual terrain appears to be fertile with opportunities for critical inquiry and informed debate.

Aesthetics in African Contexts

There is a popular belief that African art serves primarily pragmatic social purposes. Of course, there is some merit to the doctrine. But it is overly restrictive as a blanket characterization of the African's creative genius. Indeed, there are purposes beyond strict functionality by means of which to assess African art, whether the specific artistic medium happens to be visual art, sculpture, woodcarving, music, or poetry. Innocent C. Onyewuenyi, among others, is an avid supporter of the functionalistic theory.[4] Functionalists tend to link the meaning of African art with cultural context and use. Related to this account is a further belief that, generally speaking, African aesthetics has a moral-metaphysical basis. According to the functionalist, African art is intended not simply to please the eye (i.e., to express beauty) but also to uphold the society's moral values (i.e., to depict the good). It makes little difference what kind of artistic medium is at work, to functionalists, beauty of appearance is subservient to functional beauty in African arts. That is, a wood carving of a deity has aesthetic beauty to the extent that it is effective in stimulating the community toward the worship of the deity. So, too, in the ritual use of the mask, the mask's beauty is judged by the manner of its manipulation in the accompanying dance movements, normally intended to depict the divine power with which the mask has been imbued.[5] Typically, the artist (as well as the performer as an agent of the community) *designates* through a speech act the ritual purpose of the art-*thing*—that is, its *use*-signification in the communal setting.

Take the typical mask rituals performed everywhere across the African continent. The mask comes closest, perhaps, to the notion of a ritual instrument intended to give expression to the community's beliefs about the gods and its cultural ethos. It is not uncommon for the masks to bear bold motifs representing mythological, legendary, nonhuman beings, frequently of animals associated with founding fathers of the tribe.[6] There are strikingly similar features detected in mask designs outside Africa, ranging from the masked hunters depicted in hunting scenes inscribed on walls in the European caves of so-called Paleolithic man, to the bronze masks of China as early as the Chou dynasty, to the highly complex designs and multicolored masks of the American Indian tribes such as the Hopi, the Zuni, and the Pueblo. Not to be overlooked are the highly stylized wooden masks of the Aztecs in South America, as well as masks found among some aboriginal tribes in Australia where face paintings often take the place of masks.[7]

In a special respect, the mask functions as a concealer (and paradoxically as a revealer) of identities. Both the mask wearer and the community on behalf of whom the mask may be worn become momentarily transformed—sharing in another's identity so as to understand something of one's own identity. Interestingly, this role of masks in altering one's identity has universal parallels. We all, for a variety of reasons, play multiple institutional roles, requiring us to shed one face in favor of another, depending upon its appropriateness to the institutional occasion. We often wear our uniforms as disguises out of which we sometimes step. Even the judge's robe, then, serves as a mask that ritualizes a legal proceeding, adding a tone of seriousness and finality to the event.

Janheinz Jahn helps to clarify this logic of function-designation in his account of the ritual purposes of *muzima* and *muzimu* masks among the Yoruba of Nigeria. Muzima masks represent living persons, and the artist is at liberty to designate profane uses intended mainly to entertain and amuse; by contrast, muzimu masks represent *Muntu*-being (rational life force) and hence serve more profound ritual purposes. According to Jahn:

> Since a muzimu has no body, neither has it any face. . . . The muzimu mask is not, therefore, the *real* face of an 'apparition'; it is an image that goes beyond reality, the negation of the muzima face, and the artist has therefore—in theory—the greatest possible freedom in the creation of the mask, so long as he is able to produce a more than real face, a non-face. The mask becomes the non-face of a *particular* ancestor only through designation.[8]

Clearly, then, the muzimu-masked ritual, with all its ceremonial flair, is meant to enable the community of worshipers to get in closer touch with the unseen realm of Muntu-being. The nonface is unreal, but it does not represent nothingness; it stands for an imagery of existence *in-human-spirit-relation* behind which there is a felt sense of transcendental value-laden realities and meaning constructs. What is particularly characteristic of such performances is the unique function attributed to speech. Through carefully crafted acts of designation or *performative* speech utterances, concrete meanings are given to each ritual performance. Without some definite, instantiating performative utterance, the ritual is practically meaningless. Jahn leaves us with the important insight that the concept of functional beauty associated with ritual objects such as muzima and muzimu masks conveys multiple *meaning*-uses. Basil Davidson is careful to add that while it is true that African art was engaged in for life's sake, art was also created for pleasure's sake.[9] This doctrine of multiplicity of function is reinforced by the repeated use of motifs such as abstraction in artistic creation and openness in ritual performance.

The preoccupation with *abstraction* pervades the very structure of the mask. In the making of the mask, the creator is not simply describing empirical truths. Instead of merely imitating the appearance of natural phenomena, the mask-maker, through an act of *abstract* designation, brings to life, as it were, reality in all its rhythmic proportions and sounds, as "visible projections of what goes on in man's inner life."[10] Often the mask-maker works with idealized forms and shapes that are not mere copies of anything in the real world. What we are talking about here is a power to unify conscious experience at the very level of thought. The technique of abstraction enables the creator of the work to penetrate the mysteries of Being at prereflective levels of awareness.[11] And a vital aspect of the appeal of such art is that what is captured as an imaginative construct remains somewhat elusive; paradoxically, at the bare or essential level, much of Being continues to be incommunicable. Likewise, the unseen faces represented behind the masks are varied and complex. Some masks blend naturalistic and abstract motifs; others are intensely abstract, highly stylized, and sophisticated; some are symbolic of the death experience while others try to represent the very essence of evil, and there are masks that use multiple concentric-ring designs as a means of fusing the natural and invisible realms of existence.[12]

Margaret Thompson Drewal draws attention to an interesting phenomenon of *openness* in Yoruba rituals that enables performers to improvise and the audience participants to entertain concrete, alternate possibilities. Elucidating the meaning of improvisation in ritual performance, Drewal states:

> By improvisation I mean more specifically moment-to-moment maneuvering based on acquired in-body techniques to achieve a particular effect and/or style of performance. . . . Improvisation is transformational, often participatory and competitive, in which case it constitutes a multidimensional process of argumentation. Dancers and drummers, for example, negotiate rhythmically with each other, maintaining a competitive interrelatedness. This is particularly critical because of the close conceptual line between music and dance in Africa.[13]

Through open avenues for improvisation, participants in the ritual play can spontaneously help to construct aesthetic meanings. There is allowance here for accommodating newness in the ritual. Of course, improvisers risk violating time-honored cultural boundaries whenever they experiment with novel elements, but the so-called boundaries are sufficiently fluid to allow the performers to negotiate appropriate levels of improvisation or spontaneous invention.[14] Drewal's concern is to draw attention to elements in Yoruba rituals that allow us to regard such rituals as spiritual journeys in which the participants are not blindly adhering to rigid artistic structures. Instead, the participants become subjectively engaged in monitoring their own transformations through ritual play and improvisation. Adding postmodernist tendencies to the debate, V. Y. Mudimbe notes that there is no such thing as *an* African modernist art, let alone the misleading notion that African art is essentially functional.[15] In fact, even in the so-called primitivistic traditional African art, we find powerful cubist motifs and brilliant rhythmic uses of formal structure that strongly influenced early-twentieth-century artists such as Henri Matisse, Pablo Picasso, and Paul Gauguin. The modern African artist is a child of two traditions who merges and challenges both worlds, deconstructing the memory of history with new creative narratives. The modern ritual of the mask, for instance, is acted out as a complicated marriage of machine-mechanics and the memories of the gods. Mudimbe argues that these art objects, including contemporary visual art and sculpture, do not simply embody commemorative social functions; they also deconstruct silent discourses of colonial experiences and construct new discourses of difference.[16] Appiah's observation that traditions of each mask-making society exhibit recognizably different roles and modes of performance makes a great deal of sense.[17] It would thus be futile to search for one collective, unitary African aesthetic ideal. Without attachment to essentialism, contemporary African artists have greater potential, then, for detachment from a concrete social milieu and can be freer to contemplate universal themes and produce works that are less parochial.

A quite interesting *essentialist* position is espoused by Wole Soyinka.[18] We are not talking here of racial essentialism so characteristic of the Negritude tenets of Leopold Senghor and Aime Cesaire.[19] Racial essentialists maintain that the properties of an artwork of a given racial group express *essential* or special traits belonging to members of the group. Senghor, the poet-philosopher of Negritude, argued that there are distinct patterns of behavior and lifestyles indigenous to the African continent that supply the necessary ingredients for a unique racial art. A special slant on the theme of racialistic essentialism is prevalent among Harlem Renaissance artists who were inspired by Alain Locke to emulate the African ancestral arts. In the second section of the chapter I will have more to say about the proper characterization of Locke's racialism. Instead of looking for unique *black* racial traits in African art, Soyinka selects three deity paradigms to elucidate *universal* meanings of the aesthetic in ritual archetype. Several Yoruba plays are performed among the Yorubas themselves and among transplanted Africans in the Americas, particularly among Afro-Cubans and Brazilians. Three deities feature prominently in the plays: Sango, Obatala, and Ogun. Each deity has a special role to play as intermediary pursuer or explorer of essence-ideals at the edges of which finite human beings live.[20] Sango's essence consists in meting out swift justice. He is, however, not always impartial in his judgments. Obatala's essence is quietude or forbearance, and he is specifically charged with molding human beings into whose forms life is breathed. But he has a weakness for palm wine, a propensity that helps explain instances of flawed human craftsmanship, which are attributable to his drunken states.[21]

Of most far-reaching aesthetic significance is Ogun's attribute.[22] Ogun represents the very essence of creativity and destruction. He is master craftsman and artist, the ultimate expression of cosmic will. Soyinka notes that in Ogun we discover the correlation with the numinous temper of the fourth area of being: the abyss of transition. This is the abyss of nonbeing, the black hole of the cosmos at the crossroads of the outer limits. Ogun, as it were, guides human beings in their journey across the dark void, away from material incompleteness toward transcendental essence-ideals. From across the abyss of emptiness he beckons the artisan, the poet, the musician, and the dancer, inspiring each to master special skills capable of bringing order to chaos. A related way to conceive of this seemingly contradictory motif of dissolution and reintegration by means of which the artist narrows the gulf between himself and the cosmic ordering is to think of secrecy associated with *negative space*.[23] The black hole or dark matter concept carries, of course, purely theoretical meaning in the modern study of gravitational fields. These so-called black holes are extremely dense bodies and are believed to have fields of gravity so intense that nothing can escape their vicinity. Since light can penetrate but not escape their boundaries or horizons, these spaces appear totally black. The suggestion that dark matter exists is alluded to in much of traditional African art. The idea of the black hole space draws attention to ultimate mystery in the universe, to unknown cosmic destinations of no return. Ogun's special attribute both hides and shares knowledge, permitting artists and other participants in the quest for knowledge to explore and be aware of the unknown. In this way, artists often deliberately obstruct, obscure, or withhold knowledge, suggesting that in "seeing," you do not see. In effect, the encounter with cosmic secrecy is a connection with a deeper dimension of seeing the unfathomable dark secrets of life. It is a meeting with the black hole, temporarily traversed by Ogun on his creative odysseys; it represents a journey through unexplored secret paths that few artists dare to enter. As Mary H. Nooter notes, "Implicated in the secret is the possibility of something unknown waiting to be discovered, but the secret is always poised on the threshold of understanding and obscurity, of penetration and prohibition."[24] In a related context, D.

Francine Farr traces "black hole aspects" in various tribal arts of Asia, the Pacific, Australia, Africa, and the Americas. She identifies repeated use of negative space (black hole space) in two- and three-dimensional artifacts of tribal peoples.[25]

Ogun as intermediary quester between the abyss of transition and the visible world permits the artist to be a signifier of ontological secrets. The work of art thereby has the potential to be a discourse on the dialectics of presence and absence. For Soyinka, such is the universal will to create. I share Appiah's view that in evaluating African art it is necessary to look beyond functionalistic considerations such as politics, economics, or even morality. Art is to be judged in ways that go beyond a concern with whether the art object serves such *extrinsic* purposes.[26] We see then that the creative imagination, in Africa as elsewhere, is involved in a subtle conspiracy to add continuity to existential flux and to enlarge our universal and individual consciousness of being.

Double Consciousness, Racial Art, and Race Transcendence

The question whether there is a black aesthetic generally and, more specifically, a distinct African American aesthetic has been extensively debated.[27] The search for an acceptable answer has led both artists and critics nowhere in particular. One thing is clear: in the genre of artworks produced by the African American there is neither unifying theme nor any compelling evidence of a recognizable black essence or black art. So-called *black* art is part of the corpus of *American* art, subject to constant influences from an American cultural context. It is in this latter respect that I find it most profitable to address issues focusing on the relationship of art to race. In a frequently cited passage from *The Souls of Black Folk,* W. E. B. Du Bois reasons:

> After the Egyptian and Indian, the Greek and Roman, the Teuton and Mongolian, the Negro is a sort of seventh son, born with a veil, and gifted with second-sight in this American world,—a world which yields him no true self-consciousness, but only lets him see himself through the revelation of the other world. It is a peculiar sensation, this double-consciousness, this sense of always looking at one's self through the eyes of others, of measuring one's soul by the tape of a world that looks on in amused contempt and pity. One ever feels this two-ness,—an American, a Negro; two souls, two thoughts, two unreconciled strivings; two warring ideals in one dark body, whose dogged strength alone keeps it from being torn asunder.[28]

Du Bois is speaking here of an ambiguous, bipolar understanding of black selfhood. What he is not talking about is a notion of multiple personalities or the idea of an essentially fragmented ego. Neither is he referring to two separate and distinct selves occupying the same body with their own distinct life histories. Rather, to be split into two signifies that to think of oneself as a black American carries two meanings in incommensurate languages.[29] It is as if I, a thinking black person (a so-called *other*), am telling you who I am, but you (the *outsider* construing my authentic essence) are telling me that this is not what I am. We are dealing here with a self-concept that helps explain feelings of inferiority as well as the desire to realize genuine personhood. The double consciousness is in part something imposed from the outside and in part the product of an ambivalent self-constructed image, together constituting the ambiguity and essence of being black in America.

This characteristic of duality, it seems to me, yields outcomes that diverge somewhat from the organicism we so frequently encounter in traditional African aesthetics. Du Bois's notion of the African American multiple Other places the artistic self in a challenging setting, to say the least. African Americans are forced not only to deal with their own identities but also to take just as seriously the domination of the white culture that made them into *objects*, so to speak. Here is a tremendous shift from African artistic expression. While, from the African's perspective, art has multiple motives and ends, the one constant is integration or organic unity. It is a concern with multiple otherness that seems to set African American aesthetics somewhat apart. The idea of double consciousness yields an artistic awareness that seems to embody oppositionality. To Du Bois and Harlem Renaissance artists such as Aaron Douglas, artmaking requires marginalization or oppositionality as a necessary condition. Indeed, the Harlem Renaissance was a critical moment in history that highlighted this antithesis between African heritage and American realities. More than ever the black artist in America could not afford to simply imitate the classicism of African art. While they undoubtedly found formal influences in African art, African American artists had to counterbalance these with the iconoclasm of being Other, of being American, yet outside the mainstream of America.

Du Bois stressed the importance of nurturing racial art as one vehicle for merging this feeling of two-ness, this double self, into a better and more authentic self. However, he never intended to propose a form of racist cultural nationalism in art. Like Wole Soyinka, Du Bois was not promoting the production of art along Negritude lines. For him, racial identity or race spirit is a consciousness in which one takes pride, a positive vehicle for articulating the collective cultural heritage of a people. I find Du Bois's intriguing doubleness imagery used in other, related contexts. Hegel, for example, discusses the "master-slave" relationship as a relationship of lordship and bondage.[30] The slave's experience is complex since the slave is forced to live a dual life—his own and that "life" of himself created in the master's image. While the slave unhappily struggles through life, he does and will develop through the power of the double consciousness. The master is left behind with nowhere to go, living with the illusion of an *independent* autonomous self. In several of Toni Morrison's novels—for example, in *Sula, The Bluest Eye,* and *Tar Baby*—we come across descriptions of the duality, of paradoxical inner struggles at the heart of those forced to confront their double consciousness.[31] Cognizant of Du Bois's portrayal of black bipolarity, the African American philosopher Alain Locke rearticulated the racial ideal in his call for the production of a racial art by black artists in the Americas.

Locke is of course best known for his leadership role in the Harlem Renaissance, a period of reawakening in literature and the arts among African Americans. In a work he edited, *The New Negro,* Locke authored an essay entitled "The Legacy of the Ancestral Arts."[32] There he challenged emerging black artists to become involved in the production of a racial art that looks to the African ancestral arts for inspiration. Locke's call was for a vital artistic expression that uses racial material in ways that would elevate the race in the eyes of the global family. He was fascinated by what he saw as characteristic of African art in general. African art expressions were essentially rigid, controlled, disciplined, abstract, heavily conventionalized, and subtly infused with laconic and fatalistic features. To him, it was not surprising to find representatives of abstract modernist art such as Pablo Picasso, Henri Matisse, and Paul Gauguin seeking connectedness with *primitivistic* elements in African art. While it seems appropriate to classify Locke as a racialistic essentialist in aesthetics, it is incorrect to infer from such a designation that he was advancing a doctrine of genetic racial endowments reminiscent of Negritude.[33] He repeatedly asserts the very opposite, namely, that there are no fixed racial identities.[34] Leonard Harris draws attention to the potential for misconstruing Locke's view of the black artist as a representative of the black community whose artmaking is informed by the rhythms, symbols, and rituals of Africa. Harris grants that Locke tended to exaggerate the aesthetic qualities of the ancestral arts. Noting, however, that Locke's philosophy was not supportive of either nativistic or atavistic racial cultural virtues, Harris points out that "his [Locke's] notion of the New Negro was constituted to alter the nature of public discourse about African people and to re-envision African self-concepts across various social strata."[35] For Locke, our identities are not objectively given or shaped by immutable biologies. Likewise, aesthetic categories, as social constructions, do not reflect eternal absolutes. Consequently, there are no immutable objective properties of beauty and ugliness inseparably tied to racial biologies. Nevertheless, Locke's call for a connectedness with the ancestral arts along with the controversial association of art with racial essence helped pave the way for an artistic discourse of race and cultural differences among African Americans.

Among the work of noted Harlem Renaissance artists, that of Aaron Douglas best exemplifies the use of Du Boisian double consciousness and Lockean aesthetic themes. By Douglas's own admission, Locke influenced his beliefs about the black artist's role in the black community.[36] Douglas is a Harlem Renaissance pathfinder. He uses African art as a source of influence but travels beyond the classical constraints of that art into a modernist expression of an American consciousness that was capable of portraying the African American subject in both oppression and strength. Douglas believed that the artist should take on his work as a vocation of service dedicated to the ideal of the creation of a local and racially representative tradition. On close inspection, the main corpus of Douglas's paintings reflects his exposure to modernist motifs, primitivistic tendencies, and African-inspired cubism. Characteristically, you will notice jagged, broken forms, angular contours of human figures, massive expanses of solid black spaces with shining white backgrounds, all choreographed against subtle yet suggestively bold African settings. Patent and subtle imageries depicting concentric circles allude to a constant interplay of the mundane interlaced with transcendental, mystical detail.[37] A few examples should suffice to illustrate the point.

In a 1927 piece, *The Crucifixion,* Douglas breaks with the Western tradition and depicts a black Jesus strenuously carrying the cross. There are the concentric circles of light, and from the top right-hand corner a bright stream of light pierces the scenery, emanating, as it were, from God above. In *Let My People Go* (also 1927) there is once again the imagery of God intervening in human affairs: a black Moses kneels obediently, engulfed in a ray of divine light, attending to the Word of God. What piques my interest are the large, stylized waves that gracefully curve across the picture and the soldiers' conical head-pieces, resembling the Egyptian crowns common in Egyptian art. *Go Down Death* (1927) depicts death as an angel on horseback coming down to earth like a fast-moving comet in the skies, masterfully suggested by the trail left behind from the horse's foam. The entire drama appears safely encircled by clockwork patterning of cubic lines and circling rays of celestial light. Finally, in the second of a series of panels, *Aspects of Negro Life: From Slavery through Reconstruction* (1934), Douglas's imagery tries to recapture something of the exuberant feelings of the experience of emancipation. The flat silhouette of the reader of the Emancipation Proclamation occupies center stage. Subtle geometrical effects dominate the festive occasion, particularly the interweaving clusters of concentric circles that permeate the happy crowd, penetrating freedom fighters and ordinary folks alike. Douglas's cubist technique is not strictly analytic: it is primitive yet cerebral.

An intriguing set of Douglas's paintings shows his love of knowledge of the arts and the humanities.[38] *Philosophy* is pictured by a single meditating figure who, seated upon ruins of Athenian columns, looks up pensively to the heavens, reflecting perhaps upon the meaning of time, space, and substance. Concentric circles expand into larger and larger proportions as they move from the bottom of the scene upwards. *Drama* is expressed through both comic and tragic themes, softly blending Grecian and Egyptian dramatic effects. Two masks, one symbolic of comedy and the other of tragedy, decorate a standing column; an actress with a mask in hand looks towards the skies for inspiration, while her male counterpart sits as if chained to the earth. The scene is alive with primitivistic and modernistic messages in symbiotic coexistence. Again, concentric circles grow larger and larger as the focus moves toward the heavens. *Music* is symbolized by three musicians—a man playing a stringed instrument, one playing the trumpet, and, at center stage, a female singer looking to the heavens. The overall feeling conveyed seems "jazzy" and rhythmic. The performers, engulfed by concentric circles, participate in the cosmic music of the spheres. *Poetry* depicts a poet cradled in a cosmic sea of jagged and smooth formal structural patterns. The poet stands insecurely on an unsteady piece of revolving earth, trying to get a glimpse, it seems, of the planets in their predetermined orbits. Finally, *Science* depicts a scientist hard at work with his experiments. The scientist finds some stability for his work from a standing Greek column, a seeming reminder of the necessary role of human reason in the intelligent pursuit of knowledge. The scientist is holding a torch that casts its rays upwards, enabling us to get glimpses of expanding worlds beyond our galaxy.

In the artwork of post–Harlem Renaissance novelist-artist Clarence Major, the idea of African American double consciousness is raised to new heights. In his major fictional writings such as *All-Night Visitors* and *My Amputations,* the theme of double consciousness is played out in multifaceted dimensions.[39] While a closer study of these works must await a future discussion,[40] suffice it now to say that Major is able to show that the polarities of being black in America are not exclusively racial in nature. As a black postmodernist artist he pushed the metaphor of doubleness, that is, otherness, to its outer limits by exploring the fragile boundaries of language and imaginative consciousness. What becomes readily apparent is that Major is cognizant of the variety and similarity of questions we each ask about ourselves and that informed answers don't always come neatly packaged in surface-level skin qualities. While Douglas's paintings unmistakably draw attention to racial bipolarities, Clarence Major sought liberation from the narrow confines of race-conscious artistic expression. He managed to create art that could (and should) rise above race while at the same time it is firmly grounded in concrete experiences of the African American. A pattern of self-conscious transformation evolves in his discourse as he engages in the acts of painting and writing. The lines between reality and fantasy seem to get blurred, as do the so-called boundaries between racial realities. The black artist's double vision is really a multiple vision, consisting of a vast array of symbols, ideas, and images that sometimes mesh, at other times overlap, and all too frequently conflict. These sorts of considerations lead Lisa C. Roney to conclude that "Clarence Major's many colors can share one skin and his voices can share one volume, merging with each other into one resonant and touching whole. His double vision has become a genuine gift."[41] With Clarence Major, therefore, aesthetic discourse about race becomes essentially a discourse of multiple otherness aimed at achieving race *transcendence.*

This paradigm of race transcendence significantly demystifies the symbols of race identity. In *Race Matters,* Cornel West's insights pertaining to the decoding of worn-out symbols by means of a more liberating race-transcending prophetic framework have profound implications for the construction not only of race-transcending aesthetic categories but also of gender-transcending ones.[42] This style of discourse is unlike racial reasoning that maintains that there is "a black essence that all black people share" and unlike that of black cultural conservatives who believe that there is "one black perspective to which all black people should adhere."[43] At race- and gender-transcending levels of discussion, the hard questions of personal identity explored in art touch upon multifaceted experiences of otherness that will always conceal as much as they reveal. Such socially constituted aesthetic accounts are less partial, hence more inclusive.

Conclusion

This excursion into multiracial and multicultural terrains shows how artists thematize self-reflective processes in their creation of multifaceted selves and art. While it is tempting in this endeavor to blur differences and magnify similarities, oppositional discourse on otherness serves constructive ends. Acceptance of diversity should be the norm rather than the exception. This much we can extract from our comparative study of African and African American art-making: art histories are not arranged hierarchically. There is no superior standard-bearer. Rather, traditions of art genre develop along parallel lines, yielding pluralities of paradigms of reality and representations of truth. If this account of the relationship between art, race, and culture is warranted, it means that in the West in particular we need to increase our sensitivity to the discourse of difference. From our shared encounters with otherness we may each come to better understand why art is a way of *imaginative* making, a means of breaking through the veil of cosmic secrets in space and time. With Zora Neale Hurston, it may still be possible to see in artmaking something of the sublime, something of the human will to adorn.[44] In less partial and more inclusive modes of thinking about and doing art, it might yet be possible to construct and perhaps reconstruct deconstructed aesthetic landscapes.

Notes

1. My intellectual indebtedness in this paper is broad. John Ladd's article "Conceptual Problems Relating to the Comparative Study of Art" is one example of this indebtedness. I was intrigued in particular by his treatment of aesthetic concepts as open-textured. I saw in this notion a wealth of potential for understanding artmaking as a cross-cultural yet universal phenomenon. Ladd's essay appears in *The Traditional Artist in African Societies,* ed. Warren L. d'Azevedo, (Bloomington: Indiana University Press, 1973), 417–24.

2. Ladd, "Conceptual Problems," 418.

3. From *Africa: The Art of a Continent* (New York: Solomon R. Guggenheim Museum, 1996), 7. The book, organized around an exhibition of African art, comprises works from seven geographical areas of the African continent.

4. Innocent C. Onyewuenyi, "Traditional African Aesthetics: A Philosophical Perspective," *International Philosophical Quarterly* 24 (September 1984): 237–44. Of special note in Onyewuenyi's discussion is his incorporation of John Dewey's pragmatic ideas of art as an expression of experience. He cited Dewey approvingly for the proposition that the full aesthetic dimension of a work of art can be realized only when the *function* of the work in relation to the community is known and appreciated. See also John Dewey, *Art as Experience* (1934; repr. New York: Capricorn Books, 1958).

5. Onyewuenyi, "Traditional African Aesthetics," 239.

6. Ladislas Segy, *Masks of Black Africa* (New York: Dover, 1976), 3. According to Segy, the boldness motif was needed to compensate for the distance between the masked dancer and his audience and to give expression to the spirit beings as forces fantastic in appearance.

7. Segy, *Masks of Black Africa,* 3–4.

8. Janheinz Jahn, *Muntu: African Culture and the Western World,* trans. Marjorie Grene, rev. ed. (New York: Grove Weidenfeld, 1990), 170. This general discussion of the function of masks is treated in chap. 6, "Immutability of Style," 156–84. Additionally, Jahn looks at the relationships between image and form, the function of rhythm, and the new regional art of Africa.

9. Basil Davidson, *The African Genius* (Boston: Little, Brown, 1969), 160–67.

10. Segy, *Masks of Black Africa,* 43.

11. Segy, *Masks of Black Africa,* 43.

12. Segy, *Masks of Black Africa,* 57 ff. Plate 66 depicts a mask from the Ivory Coast

that blends naturalism and abstraction. Both facial and nasal features are elongated, and the hairdo is geometrically symmetrical. The mask itself was believed to be the special abode of ancestor spirits. Plate 68 shows a sophisticated style of zigzag patterning on both sides of the face. Here a human face is pictured with an animal cradled on its head between a pair of protruding horns. Humans and animals can coexist in symbiotic relationship. Plate 140 portrays a characteristically white-faced mask found among the Ibo of Nigeria. Whiteness was symbolic of death. Masked dancers at burial rituals not only were believed to represent the departed but also were to be looked upon as the spirits of the dead themselves. Plate 137, a Nigerian face mask, shows bold, exaggerated, and frightening features. The grotesquely bearded face supposedly represents the spirit of the underworld, the embodiment of ugliness and evil. Plate 165 is a nice example of use of scarification facial marks and concentric-ring designs for the shape of the hair. The concentric patterns allude to the artist's intention to match natural rhythms with the transcendental, otherwise invisible realm of existence. Finally, plate 194 depicts a quite unusual motif. Here we are shown a mask with female features that are curiously Asian in appearance. The face is painted white, and scarification marks appear in bold relief. The high-piled hairdo, of the sort worn by women in the Ogowe River area, highlights preoccupation with meticulous geometrical detail.

13.   Margaret Thompson Drewal, *Yoruba Ritual: Performers, Play, Agency* (Bloomington: Indiana University Press, 1992), 7. Similarly, Robert Farris Thompson notes that the Yoruba notion of the aesthetic is complex and has great depth. The Yoruba art critic makes use of multiple qualitative criteria in assessing artworks. These criteria include abstraction, visibility, shining smoothness, emotional proportion, roundness, delicacy, protrusions, and pleasing angularity, among others. See Robert Farris Thompson, "Yoruba Artistic Criticism," in *The Traditional Artist in African Societies,* 31–58.

14.   Drewal, *Yoruba Ritual,* 7.

15.   See V. Y. Mudimbe, *The Idea of Africa* (Bloomington: Indiana University Press, 1994).

16.   Mudimbe, *Idea of Africa,* 67–68, 164–65. Mudimbe insists that it is misleading to conclude that African art is essentially functional. Instead, African artworks resemble literary texts; they are narrative compositions open to multiple interpretations and use-designations.

17.   *Africa: The Art of a Continent,* 6.

18.   See Wole Soyinka, *Myth, Literature, and the African World* (1976; repr. Cambridge: Cambridge University Press, 1992).

19.   See Norman R. Shapiro, ed. and trans., *Negritude: Black Poetry from Africa and the Caribbean* (New York: October House, 1970). For samples of Negritude poetry by Aime Cesaire and Leopold S. Senghor, see 78–84 and 130–36, respectively.

20.   Soyinka, *Myth, Literature, and African World,* 1.

21.   Soyinka, *Myth, Literature, and African World,* 7–25. As we see, a constant theme associated with the essence of the gods is that they have some act of excess, a character flaw, a propensity toward a weakness. This tragic limitation demystifies somewhat their "purity" of essence, and, as a consequence, they need human beings to help them "perfect' their own natures.

22. Soyinka, *Myth, Literature, and African World,* 25–32.

23. See esp. Mary H. Nooter, "Secrecy: African Art That Conceals and Reveals," *African Arts* 26, no. 1 (January 1993): 55–69. Secrecy is a sort of paradoxical synthesis of revelation and concealment, of meaning and nonmeaning. This ontological human condition is a further revelation of the imperfections of human knowledge over against the profound mysteries of undifferentiated reality. Nooter's article incorporates portions of the preface, introduction, and conclusion from a volume by the same name that accompanied an exhibition of African art at the inauguration of the Museum for African Art in 1973 in New York City.

24. Nooter, "Secrecy," 68.

25. D. Francine Farr, "Black Hole Aesthetics: Provisional Definition with Examples from Aboriginal Asia, the Pacific, Africa, and African America" (paper presented at the annual meeting of the American Society for Aesthetics, College of Charleston, Charleston, South Carolina, 27 October 1994).

26. *Africa: The Art of a Continent,* 7.

27. For a concise, informative assessment of the dispute, see Elsa Honig Fine, *The Afro-American Artist: A Search for Identity* (New York: Holt, Rinehart & Winston, 1973), 280–81.

28. W. E. B. Du Bois, *The Souls of Black Folk* (New York: New American Library, 1969), 45.

29. For a balanced, critical discussion of the meaning of double consciousness, see Ronald A. T. Judy, "The New Black Aesthetic and W. E. B. Du Bois, or Hephaestus Limping," *Massachusetts Review* 35 (Summer 1994): 249–82.

30. G. W. F. Hegel, *The Phenomenology of Mind,* trans. J. B. Baillie (New York: Harper & Row, 1967), 228–40.

31. Toni Morrison, *Sula* (New York: Plume/Penguin, 1982); Toni Morrison, *The Bluest Eye* (New York: Alfred A. Knopf, 1995); and Toni Morrison *Tar Baby* (New York: Plume/Penguin, 1982).

32. Alain Locke, "The Legacy of the Ancestral Arts," in *The New Negro,* ed. Alain Locke (1925; repr. New York: Atheneum, 1968), 254–67.

33. For an interesting critical analysis of the possible connections of racialistic essentialism to Alain Locke's views on aesthetics, see Jane Duran and Earl L. Stewart, "Alain Locke: Essentialism and the Notion of a Black Aesthetic," this volume, chap. 7. The paper was initially presented at the American Society for Aesthetics National Meeting in St. Louis, Missouri, in November 1995.

34. Locke wrote several essays on the intertwining subjects of race and culture. There is a consistent theme that race is not a changeless biological category; instead, the idea of race is closer to a social myth and functions as a useful explanatory tool in the context of sociocultural dynamics. See "The Problem of Race Classification," "The Concept of Race as Applied to Social Culture," and "The Contribution of Race to Culture," in *The Philosophy of Alain Locke: Harlem Renaissance and Beyond,* ed. Leonard Harris (Philadelphia: Temple University Press, 1989), 163–206.

35. Harris, introduction to *Philosophy of Alain Locke,* 7.

36. Amy Helene Kirsche, *Aaron Douglas: Art, Race, and the Harlem Renaissance* (Jackson: University Press of Mississippi, 1995), 16–17.

37. Kirsche, *Aaron Douglas,* 92–112. Here Kirsche provides a lucid interpretation of the composition and stylistic motifs of Douglas's graphic art completed during the peak period of the Harlem Renaissance and the relationship of this art to Locke's *New Negro* and other literature .

38. Kirsche, *Aaron Douglas,* 113.

39. Clarence Major, *All-Night Visitors* (New York: Olympia, 1969); and Clarence Major, *My Amputations* (New York: Fiction Collective, 1986). For interesting discussions of Major's works, see Bernard W. Bell, "Introduction: Clarence Major's Double Consciousness as a Black Postmodernist Artist," *African American Review* 28, no. 1 (1994): 5–9; Lisa C. Roney, "The Double Vision of Clarence Major, Painter and Writer," *African American Review* 28, no. 1 (1994): 65–75; and James W. Coleman, "Clarence Major's *All-Night Visitors*: Calabanic Discourse and Black Male Expression," *African American Review* 28, no. 1 (1994): 95–108.

40. In an essay under construction, "The Double Consciousness Phenomenon: Discourses on Otherness and Ambivalent Self-Knowledge," I am critically examining the concept of double consciousness insofar as it appears as a theme in selected novels. The study has an interdisciplinary focus, bridging philosophy, literature, and art. The theoretical grounding for the research is informed by G. W. F. Hegel's *Phenomenology of Mind* and W. E. B. Du Bois's *Souls of Black Folk.* Arguing that double consciousness is a theme with many variations, I examine its literary use in the novel. My primary sources are Carson McCullers's novel *The Heart Is a Lonely Hunter*; William Faulkner's *Light in August*; Toni Morrison's *Sula, The Bluest Eye,* and *Tar Baby*; and Clarence Major's *All-Night Visitors, Emergency Exit, My Amputations,* and *Such Was the Season.* My principal contention is that the phenomenon of double consciousness is multilayered, yielding a plurality of discourses, multiple visions, and imageries of otherness that frequently transcend race identity or surface-level skin qualities.

41. Roney, "Double Vision of Clarence Major," 74.

42. See Cornel West, *Race Matters* (Boston: Beacon Press, 1993).

43. West, *Race Matters,* 28. In an earlier work, *Prophesy Deliverance: An Afro-American Revolutionary Christianity* (Philadelphia: Westminster, 1982), 74–77, West engages in a fierce criticism of the stereotypical depictions of black lifestyles by Harlem Renaissance writers and artists. He extends his dissatisfaction to the post–Harlem Renaissance Black Arts Movement associated with Addison Gayle and others. For a better understanding of the Black Arts Movement, see Addison Gayle, *The Black Aesthetic* (New York: Doubleday, 1972). The next most representative text on African aesthetics since publication of Gayle's work is Kariamu Welsh-Asante, *The African Aesthetic: Keeper of the Traditions* (Westport, Conn.: Greenwood Press, 1993). Analogous to race-transcending discourse is the potentially gender-transcending feminist account of aesthetic categories reflected in Patricia Hill Collins, *Black Feminist Thought: Knowledge, Consciousness, and the Politics of Empowerment* (New York: Routledge, 1991), 88–89.

44. Zora Neale Hurston, "Characteristics of Negro Expression" (1934) in *The Gender of Modernism,* ed. Bonnie Kime Scott (Bloomington: Indiana University Press, 1990), 176, 178. See also Cheryl A. Wall, "On Freedom and the Will to Adorn: Debating Aesthetics and/as Ideology in African American Literature," in *Aesthetics and Ideology,* ed. George Levine (New Brunswick, N.J.: Rutgers University Press, 1994), 283–303.

PART III

COMMUNITY AND CULTURE

10

Two Lockes, Two Keys: Tolerance and Reciprocity in a Culture of Democracy

Greg Moses

Among reasons for vigorous reappraisal of the philosophy of Alain Locke is the epochal significance of his elegant contribution to a theory of progressive democracy. By emphasizing collective forms of society as found in groups, cultures, and "psychological tribes," Locke encourages pluralistic paths to peace and power, substituting an ethic of reciprocity wherever the will to power would prevail. "As serious-minded Americans," writes Locke, "we must all be thinking gravely and rigorously about the present state of the national culture and mindful of the special and yet unrealized demands of culture in a democratic setting."[1] That the demands of culture in democracy are both special and unrealized awakens us to the warning that fundamentalism and monopoly are, even today, chronic products of American popular culture. Yet Locke seeks "promising enlargements of the common mind and spirit," reminding us in various ways that if we are to be democratic, then we must not forget that "democracy is a *two-way* process and accomplishment" (42; emphasis added).[2] By calling attention to the reciprocal imperative of democracy, Locke invites deeper commitments to progressive reform.

Locke's quest for a two-way culture of democracy begins with a classification of values founded upon "feeling factors" (43). How do we determine what is distinctive about each of the well-known arenas of value, such as the religious, ethical, scientific, and aesthetic? For Locke the answer is to be found in attitudes, not objects. Our own exaltation determines religious value, just as tension identifies what is moral or ethical *for us*. Likewise, acceptance or agreement inscribes what is logical or scientific, while repose or equilibrium tells us when value has entered the realm of the aesthetic (45). For Locke, truth is chiefly to be found in the attitudes we insist on sustaining. According to such a perspective, conflicts of value pertain to contrary modalities of feeling more than to incommensurable qualities between objects themselves.

Locke's approach to value does not reduce the likely preponderance of conflict in human affairs, but it does suggest a new approach to peace. Even the "grand ultimates" of beauty, truth, and goodness are not harmonized once and for all in Locke's accounting; rather they are "doomed to perpetual logical opposition because their basic value attitudes are psychologically incompatible" (45). Our different attitudes "create natural antinomies, irresolvable orders of value; and the only peace a scientific view of value can sanction between them is one based not upon priority and precedence but upon parity and reciprocity" (45). When "our varied absolutes are revealed as largely the rationalization of our preferred values," when their impulse stems "more from the will to power than the will to know," when we see clearly that such conflicts will not be explained or reconciled by resort to a common, rational plane, then Locke suggests that we try to arrange the field of conflict in such a way that the values of *both sides* may proliferate (46). In this manner we do not discount the "emotional and functional incommensurability" of values in conflict; rather, "we realize their complementary character in human experience" (47). If beauty will never be truth, exactly, then who would force us to choose between them? Such antinomies of value are to be reconciled by resort to wider living.

The consequences of Locke's axiology are devastating for materialist accounts of human values and conflicts. Not even "a milieu of scarcity" can determine the kinds of values that will emerge into the world—not until some *attitude* appears, either of selfishness, sacrifice, or care. If the vaunted "lifeboat" of an ethical model were to arrive already loaded with moral imperatives of exclusion, then Locke's method would warn us that some presuppositions about attitudes of selfishness or foreclosure must have been smuggled on board. With Locke's revolution of values, what once masqueraded as bare material conflicts are interrogated to disclose the organized attitudinal presuppositions that thrust the materials into situations of conflict. Locke's preoccupation with progressive democracy may be seen to originate in a value theory that holds attitudes responsible for conflict.

Suspicion falls upon attitudes by which groups seek to monopolize life. Take the perennial conflict between science and religion and treat it as a conflict of attitudes not as an inherent conflict between incommensurable objects. If we cannot usually seek exaltation in the instant of experimental inquiry, then we need not conclude that one attitude or the other must be preferred *every time*. After all, each attitude may have appropriate moments of expression. But this method of mutual proliferation presupposes that a will to democracy can overcome the will to power between competing attitudes and groups. Locke's "value pluralism" thus guides inquiry in a way that seeks to make multiple value modes "coordinate and complementary." With this general rule in mind, Locke proposes "two most important corollaries,—the principles of tolerance and reciprocity" (47).

Alain Locke's first ethical corollary, "tolerance," suggests that he draws upon a liberal tradition, influenced by the work of John Locke. The suggestion gains force when we recount how John Locke's concept of tolerance itself was proposed as a corollary of epistemological investigations that revealed how few of our practical beliefs could be based upon certain knowledge. "For where is the Man, that has uncontestable Evidence of the Truth of all that he holds?"[2] Given the "very slight grounds" upon which we sustain our beliefs, "in this fleeting state of Action and Blindness we are in," John Locke encourages us to maintain *"Peace, and the Common Offices of Humanity, and Friendship, in the diversity of Opinions."*[3] Our judgments are vulnerable, warns the principle of tolerance. We do well not to impose our judgments upon others, because judgments are practical formations shaped from a universe of unexamined beliefs.

In a similar spirit, Alain Locke argues that our norms of value are pervaded by cultural attitudes to such an extent that, for the most part, we tend to proceed with our lives in an ambiance of perpetual prejudgment. Our values are thus best understood as cultural functions that have been developed as complex social-psychological approaches to the problems of group life. Inevitably, we run in psychological tribes. So whereas John Locke's epistemology emphasized the experience of individual judgment as fallible choice, Alain Locke calls attention to the ways that we cultivate attitudes as socialized norms. And whereas John Locke encouraged tolerant dialogue as a means to improve our individual judgment-making process, Alain Locke encourages intergroup reciprocity as a method to enhance our normative cultural process of attitudinal socialization.

In his quest for cultural tolerance, Alain Locke does not settle for the pose of neutrality. Especially in his role as an educator who takes seriously the meaning of crisis, Locke wants a tolerance that can yet find courage for *democratic* reform. If "parochial thinking" is to be transformed into "global thinking," then "issues of conflict" do not just vaporize into a weightless world of difference. Some conflicts are open to a realistic accounting in terms of the "history of their development" such that inquiry discovers an imperative— "bravely to take a normative stand"—that would nurture the spirit of democracy.[4] With the history of racism in mind, for instance, we may trace the kinds of attitudes and differences that have been historically developed, and bravely insist upon reform. "If on the other hand, we keep scholarship's traditional neutrality as to values in the name of impartial objectivity, if we proceed with the old academic balancings of *pros* and *cons,* we are likely to have as an end-product a student, more widely informed, but with the same old mind-sets, perhaps more substantially entrenched in the conceit of knowing more."[5] To propound a version of tolerance that refuses to oppose racism, for example, is to place education in the position of "augmenting" rather than resolving those parts of the "current 'culture crisis'" that are perpetuated through "intellectual defaults and dilemmas."[6] Without exaggerating the certainties of our own evaluations, we may *teach* from an antiracist point of view. The objective of progressive democracy may be cultivated as a normative value, especially in the classroom.

In ways different from John Locke, but sharing a sense that toleration should serve the spirit of democracy, Alain Locke sets out to instruct the "popular thinking" of "English imperialism" in its various European and American forms. A reformed social ethic is needed to democratize collective contacts with "other groups." The principle of reciprocity suggests that group contacts should be conducted in such a way that "basic and objective common denominators" may be discerned with greater perspicacity. No doubt the old principle of tolerance will be helpful, but Alain Locke seeks especially to avoid forms of tolerance in the liberal tradition that are little more than "attitudes of condescension"—that mask an underlying will to power. Thus a more rigorous principle is needed to indicate the kind of reformation that Locke has in mind. If the meaning of culture may be taken in its biological sense of nourishment, then cultural reciprocity strives to epitomize the nourishment of various and contradictory attitudes that human beings usually promulgate whenever peoples meet.

By his transformations of epistemology and ethics, Locke opens up a new mode of democratic theory that is explicitly multicultural. And I think that the value of what Locke has in mind might be concretely illustrated in the example of affirmative action. Or should I say that the theory of democracy implicit in Locke's philosophy might help us discover how the practice of affirmative action might strive for its highest democratic aspirations? After all, the one thing to be said for the practice of affirmative action is that it is so poorly understood. According to the view for which I will argue, there is a version of affirmative action theory that should be applicable so long as democracy is practiced by civilizations that are avowedly "composite"—which is to say, made up of various groups who have determinate histories of intergroup relations. The practice of affirmative action becomes most relevant whenever groups consciously seek to transform the will to power into a spirit of democratic reciprocity. Thus, to the dismay of all who may be weary of the affirmative action question and who look forward to the imminent demise of affirmative action practices, I think a deep reading of Locke would suggest that affirmative action is, and ought to be, here to stay.

Yet, having suggested how affirmative action might be viewed as a perpetual process of multiculturation, disciplined by a democratic ethic of reciprocity in a world of conflict, it will be important to clarify an issue that tends to cloud multicultural terms of debate. To quote Locke: "Cultural conflict, although often associated with cultural differences, does not arise from differences of culture, but from the conflict of group interest."[7] In other words, the more we treat our group conflicts as if they arise from *cultural* difference, the more we mask the difficulties and evade functional solutions toward peace. Difference is such a constant in human experience, when viewed in a fair and rigorous way, that one ought to ask why some differences become the source of so much delight while others provoke conflict. It is the will to power, says Locke, that turns difference into conflict. "Relative status and advantage are, then, the core of the culture conflict situation in all of its varieties, whether the struggle be between groups within a society or between societies as competing units" (123). The will to power, more than the will to homogenize cultural differences—and more even than the "wish to exclude"—drives the engine of so-called culture conflict. For this reason, we should work with clarified terminology, realizing that multiculturalism is neither the root cause of, nor the ultimate cure for, conflict between groups and that no syllabus of comparative culture will be sufficient to resolve the kinds of conflicts that do the most damage in our world today. How to achieve intergroup justice—hopefully with multicultural appreciation—is the more rigorous problem that confronts us, should we dare to name it more precisely. Such a thorough ethics of intergroup appreciation and reciprocity would indeed be quite revolutionary and subversive to "European" attitudes toward life.

Just as John Locke postulated that an intelligent nation would best emerge by means of a tolerant exchange of ideas between individuals, Alain Locke suggests that an intelligent world now requires new levels of reciprocity between groups. Needless to say, this virtue of reciprocity has not been a pervasive characteristic of the march of English-style imperialism. "However, even in this more or less one-sided process, a certain amount of reciprocal influence and interchange has persisted" (7). Thus, Alain Locke begins his systematic quest for a new democratic ethics by affirming that a certain amount of cultural reciprocity is unavoidable. "Modern imperialism has bred, in addition to its half-castes, its hybrid and border-line cultures"(7).[8] And what we take to be essentially Western is often grafted upon Eastern roots. "The hand-loom, for instance, stands in an ancestral relation to the power-loom which hardly justifies the cultural arrogance of the peoples of the power loom stage of culture, as they foist the products of their machine age upon cultures still in the hand-loom stage. The civilizing process was at one time flowing in the other direction. This reciprocity, even if separated by centuries, cannot be overlooked or ignored; indeed it is vital to the complete understanding of both the past and present stages of culture" (31). Furthermore, "It will be a revelation to many readers to learn how far-flung were the trade routes of the ancient world, how deliberate and elaborate the exchanges of culture products were then, and how much the development of our civilization has depended upon the technological and institutional influences of cultures now decadent or vanished" (31). In such observations, the moral force of today's Afrocentric scholarship is prefigured. Western arrogance is asked to acknowledge the heritage upon which it stands. "The foundations of our composite civilization were really laid by the ancient empires, most of them Oriental" (31).

The cultural fundamentalist who wails at the hyphenation of America is asked to understand that "Europeanization and its moving force of economic imperialism are best understood as an interesting and complex variant of the process which has basically underlain all historic culture contacts; a process which has been the primary cause of what we know as 'civilization'" (7). In strictly cultural terms, civilization is a process of hyphenation. It is the lack of hyphens that exposes true barbarism. "Cultures may develop complexity through certain internal development and variation, but by far the main source of cultural growth and development seems always to have been through the forces of external contact" (7). Locke's principle of reciprocity first emerges as a generalized historical law that may be discerned through careful consideration of what has contributed to civilized progress in many an age. Yet if cultural reciprocity cannot be denied in fact, there remains the problematic habit of the process of "Europeanization" that tends to suppress intergroup reciprocity as an ethical principle. Thus, the "colonial-mindedness" of Europe's advance, "is the predominant and now chronic attitude which has stood in the way of much reciprocity of cultural exchange between European and non-European peoples" (88). And the attitude may be attributed in part to a "comprehension of group relations" that is "provincial and intellectually unsound" (93).

Insofar as cultural contacts are concerned, the membranes between human groups are quite porous and absorbent. What might be called white culture, for instance, is in many instances an accumulation of popularized black culture.[9] Or, as the Afrocentric scholars suggest, what is touted as European culture is very often an internalized absorption of African influences.[10] But note that it would not solve the surplus problem that would remain even if all our education affirmed the cultural propositions of Afrocentric scholarship: how to mediate the "relative status and advantages" between existing groups. Appreciation would still beg the question of justice. With these general principles in mind, Locke suggests that progressive change in America would best proceed not by "ironing out the *cultural* divergences of the many national and racial elements in the American population" but by "forcing" these groups "into new situations of mutual stress and common experiences." No longer would we share a "diversity of isolation"; rather, we would have "a more challenging type of situation involving reaction across lines which have been previously divided."[11] The terms of Locke's philosophy provide a worthwhile conceptual framework for the ethics of affirmative action. Instigating and motivating the important work that must be accomplished at the cultural level, Locke insists upon forcing a two-way relationship between groups.

If groups are to live together in a spirit of democracy that eschews the will to power, then a talent for cultural reciprocity can minimize provocations of conflict. Here the challenge begins at the level of appreciation whenever one sees in "other cultures" how modes of value experience retain functional similarities in the face of formal diversity and apparent contradiction. For instance, the forms of the sacred may change, and attention to formal differences may tempt us to infer mutual incompatibility. Thus, missionaries are dispatched and "false idols" smashed. But perhaps the human attitude of the sacred may thrive in a plurality of formal systems. Locke's principle of reciprocity encourages us to follow the dictum of his Harvard mentor, Josiah Royce, to have "loyalty to loyalty" such that the attitude of loyalty is recognized and shared. Likewise, we would be encouraged to have reverence for reverence, even as formal attributes of sacred images change. And once again, we are not far from the liberal ethic of tolerance. "Social reciprocity for value loyalties is but a new name for the old virtue of tolerance, yet it does bring the question of tolerance down from the lofty thin air of idealism and chivalry to the plane of enlightened self-interest and the practical possibilities of effective value sharing."[12] In other words, groups that appear to be divided by culture could minimize their conflicts if they coordinated their functional value norms in such a way that formal differences were not so often taken as provocations. Armed, as it were, with a reciprocal approach to cultural values, enlightened groups might see that their conflicts arise not out of cultural difference but out of nonreciprocal group relations of power. To the extent that democracy is the desired outcome, an ethic of reciprocity will help delegitimate ploys of group domination.

Locke extends democratic theory along two fronts: first, by taking intergroup relations more seriously; and, second, by extending the ethic of reciprocity between cultures and groups. If we study what it means to extend democratic theory along both dimensions, then I think we learn something about the growing pains that characterize the "popular mind" of our day. Especially if we think about the predicament of civil rights, we might see that intergroup reciprocity is the new value struggling to emerge from the tenuous ground of individualized tolerance. For surely *interpersonal tolerance* is not yet to be taken for granted—that is why we now strive to teach it. Yet *intergroup reciprocity* can no longer wait. What is needed is a "new wave" of civil rights theory, defined by a wholehearted pursuit of democracy that extends interpersonal tolerance into the metamorphosis that is needed for intergroup reciprocity to emerge. Thus, a "first-wave" consensus has largely been won that establishes a common value for interpersonal tolerance, which we also call the principle of nondiscrimination. And along with this development comes tentative progress toward multicultural curricula. But affirmative action's attempt to mitigate the will to power in intergroup relations requires new reserves of maturity beyond the limited gains that have been won in behalf of tolerant nondiscrimination or multicultural appreciation. Thus, defenders of affirmative action commonly point out that to the values of nondiscrimination and multiculturalism, which we do not want to abandon, we must add a new principle that leads in the direction of affirmative action.

Perhaps it is not John Locke's fault that his principle of toleration has been so poorly applied by liberal civilizations, but a common-sense version of toleration seems to insist upon constricted boundary limitations. Take, for example, the common emotion each of us has felt in moments when we are tolerated. No doubt we were grateful at the time, but such moments are hardly thrilling. To be tolerated is to be accorded a kind of minimal respect, but tolerance also draws a line: "I have let you come so far," says tolerance, "but I will thank you to come no further." It is this voice of tolerance also that fills the air in our contemporary crisis of civil rights. Common experience thus tells us that reciprocity is something quite different from tolerance. To be treated in a reciprocal fashion is to be engaged, encountered, taken in, but also to receive some kind of invitation in return. With reciprocity we have agreed not just to share space but to intermingle. Tolerance often connotes a one-sided affair, but reciprocity raises us to a plateau of mutual interaction.

A relatively fresh example is illustrated by the observations of Laurence Mordekhai Thomas.[13] For decades, Professor Thomas has enjoyed the *toleration* of his colleagues, but more rarely has he been privileged to experience their *gratitude.* And this feature of experience noted by a black philosopher who ponders his life in a white profession gives us concrete grounding for the motivation that animates the philosophical project of Alain Locke. It is this feature of experience—to have tolerance without reciprocity—that Thomas explores to suggest how the heritage of cultural racism works. By extension we may see how the first phase of civil rights has ensured Thomas a consensual experience of toleration but not reciprocity. Indeed, we have experienced a time when the formal mechanisms of affirmative action have helped to force a certain exchange in intergroup relations that had not previously been experienced. Thus, in a period of desegregation, white institutions have yielded opportunities to black professionals so that a limited reciprocity has undeniably been experienced. But this formalized affirmative action has not been accompanied by any thoroughgoing reform in social ethics that would encourage participants of white racist heritage to move beyond the psychology of tolerance into the larger universe of reciprocity—what Thomas calls "gratitude." Under the kind of value system that needs to emerge, black talent would not merely be tolerated but would be welcomed and reciprocally engaged.

One more thing is missing from affirmative action as we know it. The will to power has not been transformed into a spirit of democracy, and it is simply too charitable to characterize progress to date as integration in a truly reciprocal sense. At the level of group relations, dominance is still the prevailing practice. And this is why Harris asks the provocative question from a Lockean perspective: what is the functional difference between the philosophy profession and the Ku Klux Klan? What Harris seeks is evidence that reciprocity rules, but this he does not find. And so his provocative question exposes the current practice of affirmative action as something that is not ruled by a spirit of democracy seeking reciprocal group relations. Rather, affirmative action may be practiced as just the minimal sort of tolerance experienced by Professor Thomas or the minimalist commitment exposed by Professor Harris—what Martin Luther King Jr. once called the ploy of tokenism.[14]

On two counts, then, the new age of affirmative action so far fails a rigorous Lockean test of reciprocity. First, at the cultural level, white values have not ventured far enough afield to find themselves free from parochial bonds. Not much has been learned through cultural contact, and what has been learned is taken for granted. Second, there has been little genuine effort to effect a new standard of intergroup relations based upon reciprocity rather than domination. Affirmative action currently produces the kind of token integration that insulates white institutions from embarrassment but also discourages any genuine experiments in power sharing.

The value of Locke's reciprocity may be concretely illustrated at the plateau of public policy, where reform would be remarkable and worthwhile. But deeper down we can also indicate that reflections upon reciprocity would open new pores of cooperation, intimacy, and sexuality. Once we begin to reflect on the wider implications of reciprocity, we see what a powerful, subversive force it could be. This is how I take Harris's suggestion that Locke's project is a deep, subterranean deconstruction.[15] If reciprocity is taken seriously as an ethical obligation, our explorations and contacts between groups and individuals are moved to profound new spheres of possibility.

But returning to the realm of public policy, we can see how the lights of reciprocity expose the politics of toleration as a thin ploy of "acceptance" that has been predicated all along upon dominance. Such acceptance has really nothing to offer in return. "At last," says this privileged stance, "I will accept you." But how is this to be distinguished from the egotistical command to "give me more"? In terms that inscribe the American color line, it is a suspicious dialectic indeed that transforms the "extortion" of unpaid labor during slavery into the "exploitation" of skilled labor during emancipation and Jim Crow into the "tokenism" of professional labor during the age of civil rights. The contributions that used to be taken for free or at discount will now be accepted as if it were a privilege to make such offerings in the first place. No one exactly wants to go backward on such a scale, but how proud can anyone be to have come this far? In the broader terms of American culture, a kind of collective voice is heard to say, "We accept your work, your art, your music, your style, your talent, your incredible ability to keep contributing something of value to our everyday lives. So why are you angry still?" But this is liberalism the old-fashioned way, self-absorbed, full of tolerance, with no shred of reciprocity in sight. And it is easy to see how maddening such a world can be, especially when you get the feeling that you are here to "keep the numbers up" and little else. Affirmative action, pursued with the democratic spirit encouraged by Locke, would seek intergroup reciprocity and cultural revaluations. But by what metaphysical alchemy is the will to power transformed into the spirit of democracy? For Locke, the problem continues to reside in organized group attitudes.

Today the "common mind" formulates a frequent complaint, that it is wrong to transform affirmative action from procedural into preferential terms. As I understand the difference, *procedural* affirmative action *does not object* to the participation of diverse groups. Hence, black professionals and women should not be excluded from applicant pools for admissions, hiring, or promotion. But *preferential* affirmative action *makes an effort* to select just such applicants as a positive outcome. In other words, according to the above formulations, it is good to tolerate difference, but it is unethical to prefer it. Or, to move the debate into more Lockean terms, it is good that traditionally white, male groups should show toleration toward other groups, but it would be wrong to seek reciprocity. For procedural tolerance is just the kind of ethic that stands willing to judge without prejudice, while reciprocal preference takes another kind of position altogether. Reciprocal preference seeks to reconstruct organized attitudes and terms of judgment in order to open a civilizing exchange of intergroup nourishment. Idealistic, you say? But I think this is how Locke contributes to a new epoch in democratic ethics. Especially given some awareness that Europeanization has been an especially offensive process of group domination at home, Locke soberly suggests a thoroughgoing reform in the ethics of developing cultural contacts and nourishing intergroup relations.

But the common mind does not often share Locke's appreciation of the extent to which Europeanization has been morally offensive. It is often declared, for instance, that Western traditions are inherently multicultural. Thus, the attempt to establish reciprocity along lines of race, gender, or ethnicity is open to the accusation that such efforts are arbitrary or contrived. As true as it may be that racism, patriarchy, and ethnocentrism are not the only fronts that might deserve attention (homophobia, anti-Semitism, and classism come to mind), it nevertheless seems strange to complain that such categories are morally arbitrary or that Western traditions have already exhausted their multicultural energies. Especially if we seek to systematically replace the will to power with the spirit of democracy, the affirmative action categories are arguably reasonable points of departure. Even the American courts have tended (so far) to agree that the affirmative action groups deserve legal consideration because of determinate findings of fact that such groups have suffered more from the will to power than they have benefited from the spirit of democracy. But perhaps the affirmative action categories could be viewed as morally arbitrary only from a thoroughly Europeanized point of view, self-satisfied that multiculturalism is already an accomplished fact of Western heritage. Locke's principle of reciprocity requires an ethical standpoint that is able to shift perspectives long enough to see how the above categories have not been lived in arbitrary ways. And a general ethic of affirmative action would stand ready to admit new classes into protected status whenever appropriate findings are made.

Consider the popular attitude that only the "best-qualified" applicants should be selected. Here Locke's cultural approach to value norms would assert new demands. For Locke, "best qualified" becomes a cultural norm that must be opened up to functional, rather than formal, equivalents. Without reciprocity, a test score might stand alone as an absolute and final fact. In the hands of Locke's reciprocity, however, the meaning of such formalized facts will vary as contexts, cultures, and value functions change. Thus, the notion of what counts as best qualified is problematized as an ethnocentric construction in need of ethical reform. Behind every test score lies an organization of attitudes. This is one meaning that Locke suggests when he warns that American popular culture is pervaded by a fundamentalist spirit that tends to monopolize value criteria. This is also what he warns against when he cautions that our criteria of superiority should not be co-opted to do supremacist chores.

In fact, the practical force of Locke's approach, as applied to standardized testing, has long been recognized by front-line managers. A steel company executive, speaking in 1967, "argued that it was not always best to select the 'most qualified' job applicants as revealed by standard evaluation techniques." The object of testing, he said, "is to screen people into the system instead of screening them out." Or as a Los Angeles civil servant noted, it is important to get past the screening and measuring devices in order to focus on "what the devices are attempting to measure." Such devices are standardized in contexts that limit their application. The scientific use of such criteria requires that we not allow the form of qualification to impede a functional integration.[16]

We have seen how truth, for Locke, is to be found in the organizing and sustaining of attitudes. By such lights we might ask what kinds of attitudes are organized by the stance that supports preferential affirmative action and what kinds of attitudes are sustained by the stance that does not. Preferential, or reciprocal, affirmative action seeks to organize an attitude that some intergroup relationships are in need of systematic reform and that the initiative for such reform belongs especially—though never exclusively—to those who have been acculturated along European lines. Rather than declare multiculturalism to be the West's accomplishment, this attitude is aware how parochial forms of superiority have too often been used as supremacist tools. To liberate our perceptions of superior value thus involves more than acknowledging and overcoming skin-color prejudice. A thoroughgoing reconstruction is wanted to better nourish intergroup reciprocity.

Discernment that nurtures a proliferation of values in a composite, multicultural world requires an entirely new heuristic for disclosing what superior value is—a method that must revalue attitudes and groups that have been historically discounted, a method that must indeed revalue its own method for counting and discounting formal differences, a method that works to create functional enhancements of intergroup reciprocity. Such a reformation of value inquiry is hindered, if not completely blocked, by the stance that opposes preferential affirmative action. Certainly we approach with suspicion whenever the interpositionist suggests that preferring "other groups" is equivalent to preferring value inferiority. "We already know what value is," says the interpositionist. "Just let that single standard be applied to everyone regardless of who they are." It is the singular voice of value monopoly that knows in advance how to judge the value of other groups across cultural lines. It is the heritage of Europeanization—what Locke called the "parochial" limitation of the "colonial" mind augmented by a will to power. On the other hand, value inquiry may be expanded by the attitude of preferential treatment, first, because it is directed toward groups that in the past have arbitrarily been devalued by cultural fundamentalism and value monopoly; second, because such a stance interrogates the cultural forms and functions of qualifications; and, finally, because preferential affirmative action begins to look for functional equivalents where only formal equivalents were counted in the past. Integration need not entail assimilation, nor should the refusal to assimilate entail an inability to integrate. Deeper investigations into the functions implied by apparent formal conflicts may lead us into surprising, creative transvaluations and subtle shifts of attitude all around.

The late Broadus Butler was fond of arguing that African American struggles in particular had provided historical levers for the advancement of the theory and practice of American democracy.[17] From the abolition of slavery to the equal protection amendment, from the enfranchisement of black males to the Civil Rights Act of 1964, a string of important innovations in democracy has been won from the perspective of black struggle. Even the rights of white males to be protected from "reverse discrimination" were established by the Fourteenth Amendment. At each turn in the black struggle for democracy, new principles enter into a kind of common model for what counts as progressive justice. So I think that affirmative action, when understood as a practical policy that nourishes intergroup reciprocity as a matter of law, brings us again into a new epoch of progressive democracy in America.

From deep within his American experience, Alain Locke nurtured seedlings of unlikely intuitions: values proceed from attitudes; attitudes are often incommensurable; and yet wide ranges of values are needed to nourish life. The root of such intuitions sought grounding in the principle of tolerance, while the stem reached for the light of reciprocity. And tolerance, as we know, had already been harvested by John Locke a couple of centuries before. Thus in the work of Alain Locke we find embedded an implicit concern for what could be cultivated from the old soil of liberalism and what would have to be grafted brand-new. Reciprocity—to shift figures in function and form—would be key to the new Locke, as tolerance had been key to the old.

Notes

1. Leonard Harris, ed., *The Philosophy of Alain Locke: Harlem Renaissance and Beyond* (Philadelphia: Temple University Press, 1989), 236.

2. Alain Locke and Bernard J. Stern, eds., *When Peoples Meet: A Study in Race and Culture Contacts* (New York: Hinds, Hayden & Eldridge, 1946), 660.

3. Locke and Stern, *When Peoples Meet*, 659–60.

4. Harris, *Philosophy of Alain Locke*, 268.

5. Harris, *Philosophy of Alain Locke*, 268.

6. Harris, *Philosophy of Alain Locke*, 268.

7. Locke and Stern, *When Peoples Meet*, 123.

8. See also Gloria Anzaldúa, *Borderlands: The New Mestiza—La Frontera* (San Francisco: Spinsters/Aunt Lute, 1987).

9. Amiri Baraka [Leroi Jones], *Blues People: Negro Music in White America* (New York: Morrow Quill, 1963).

10. Cheikh Anta Diop, *Civilization or Barbarism: Authentic Anthropology*, trans. Yaa-Lengi Meema Ngemi, ed. Harold J. Salemson and Marjolin de Jager (Brooklyn: Lawrence Hill Books, 1991). (au: L. Hill *Books*?)

11. Locke and Stern, *When Peoples Meet*, 687–88.

12. Harris, *Philosophy of Alain Locke*, 48.

13. See Laurence M. Thomas, *Vessels of Evil* (Philadelphia: Temple University Press, 1993).

14. Harris, *Philosophy of Alain Locke,* 279.

15. Harris, *Philosophy of Alain Locke,* 279.

16. See John David Skrentny, *The Ironies of Affirmative Action: Politics, Culture, and Justice in America* (Chicago: University of Chicago Press, 1996).

17. Broadus Butler, "Pillars," *Newsletter on Philosophy and the Black Experience* 95, no. 2 (Spring 1995): 27–29.

11

Alain Locke and Walt Whitman: Manifestos and National Identity

Charles Molesworth

Alain Locke graduated from Harvard in 1907 with a Rhodes scholarship—the first African American to achieve this honor—and embarked for Oxford. While at Oxford he began to examine the complex process of being an American. He wrote an essay entitled "Oxford Contrasts" on assignment for an African American newspaper, the *Independent,* in which he keenly compared English and American traits, with the emphasis squarely on the English side. He found the social reserve of the English unsettling, even for a fastidious elitist such as himself. Locke's experiences of his own national identity were fully analyzed and reflected upon in another essay, one that was the most impressive of his early literary accomplishments. The essay, entitled "The American Temperament," was published in the *North American Review* in August 1911.[1] It enunciated for this intense young intellectual his deepest values, those of racial tolerance, pragmatism, and cultural excellence, and it served as something like a manifesto for the remainder of his career. Locke's publishing this important statement about his country and its culture before he returned to America in 1912 anticipates in some way the appearance of his best-known work, the eponymous "The New Negro," almost fifteen years later. Indeed, the two essays—his two manifestos, so to speak—can be seen as the cultural testament of the first half of Locke's career.

Locke, as the first African American to be named a Rhodes scholar, received national attention. Graduation from Harvard in 1907 and three more years of study at Oxford and the University of Berlin allowed Locke to return to America as perhaps the most deeply and exquisitely educated African American of his generation. His high level of education and elitist temperament often led to his being attacked or mocked by other African American artists and intellectuals. But he remained a committed democrat all his life, and his cultural criticism—ranging over literature, music, and the visual arts—as well as his work as a philosopher strongly justifies our calling him the father of

175

multiculturalism, for he constantly argued for diversity and tolerance as the most important of civic values and the surest antidotes to racism and imperialism. Paradox, as he said, followed him all his days, as he used the benefit of his Rhodes scholarship to train himself as an anti-imperialist, and he argued for an art that honored the experience of common people even as he held to the highest standards of connoisseurship and expertise.

Locke's later reputation comes, of course, from his central role in the Harlem Renaissance as the editor of the anthology called *The New Negro,* published in 1925 as an expanded version of a special issue of *Survey Graphic,* a small liberal magazine of the 1920s and 1930s. His title essay in this anthology served as the manifesto of the movement that embraced artistic self-awareness, urged a modern use of cultural work to raise social consciousness, and advocated a modulated political activism. With a mix of values at once heady and unstable, the movement was the focus of attacks by African Americans from the start, and it dissolved within a few years. Even Locke himself came to reject the movement, lamenting what he called the exhibitionism that was fostered by the more open and advanced views and attitudes of the individuals involved. On a purely personal level, the Harlem Renaissance was the stage for Locke's own coming to maturity as a critic. But the maturation began almost fifteen years earlier, when Locke was still a university student pursuing postgraduate work in philosophy.

The ethos that enveloped the Oxford that Locke attended between 1907 and 1910 was thoroughly Edwardian, and if any American visitor could be seen as all too ready to embrace such an ethos, it was this short and frail African American. Yet Locke was not going to fit in with the English by virtue of his sheer physical presence. Just five feet, two inches tall and with a heart weakened by a childhood bout of rheumatic fever, Locke had been able to satisfy the athletic requirement demanded by the Rhodes scholarship committee only by being the coxswain for the Harvard Rowing Club. But he took to English manners with real verve, buying his morning coat (with a specific style of velvet collar) at a High Street tailor and entertaining, and being entertained by, his classmates at high tea in his rooms.[2] The social polish he acquired at Harvard prepared him for, and vindicated his interest in, the even more rigorously codified gentlemanly identity he was intent on mastering in the English idiom. (Like his classmate Van Wyck Brooks, Locke was one of the students from public schools at Harvard, who made up no more than one-third of the student body.) The fit, so to speak, between Harvard and Oxford was more than just sartorial or social, however; there was a continuity of intellectual interest built around figures like George Santayana and Josiah Royce, who developed Locke's interest in the philosophy of value, an interest he concentrated and refined with various faculty members at Hertford College in Oxford. This seam of awareness, in which England and America were knit together and yet marked as separable, not only shaped his style and his studies but also made him eager to redefine what national categories meant, especially his own.

Philosophical in disposition and training, Locke was nevertheless exceptionally literary in his sensibility. In "The American Temperament" he sets out to define the national character by using the form of the belletristic essay; there are no statistics, no demographics to guide the argument, only reflection and cultural analysis. This is especially apt because one of the essay's chief claims points to the irony that the American temperament "should of all temperaments [be] the least reflective, and for all its self-consciousness, should know itself so ill." Locke even tweaks his fellow Americans by a certain coy use of the passive, impersonal voice, set against their assertiveness, and suggests that "one may point to the need for self-analysis and expression." Coyness matches hardheadedness in the essay, however, as Locke wryly dissects the American character by pretending to see it from the outside even while testifying from a personal point of view as to the truth of what he reveals. The air of knowing dispassion that Locke achieves—so remarkable in a man then less than thirty years of age—is an elaborately constructed artifice, made possible in large measure by the sophistication Locke added to his Harvard education with three years of further study at Oxford.

When, in November 1909, Locke gave a talk to the Rationalist Society at Oxford entitled "The American Temperament," he was probably reading from an earlier version of the essay. The audience included several of Locke's classmates, students from the British colonies who had come to Oxford to learn how to administer the empire.[3] On that occasion, in a passage removed from the printed version, he said that he was faced with "the alternative of either making a composite portrait or drawing an ideal sketch—if forced to choose I should prefer the latter. . . . [I] would rather present you unashamed the bare outlines of pure thought." This choice left him considerable freedom in his approach. Approaching the "ideal" [cosmopolitan in character] would have appealed to Locke, who had recently learned from his classmates, some of whom had developed sharply anti-imperialist attitudes, how national character was an issue of great importance.[4] Added to this was something like an Emersonian commitment to the essay and the manifesto as literary genres—think of the echoes of Emerson's vocabulary in the word "temperament," as well as the emphasis on character in Locke's earlier essay comparing English and American traits. The influence of his Harvard education, under the tutelage of those men who represented the "golden years" of its philosophy department, was blending with the English idealist traditions of what was known as "value philosophy." His "bare outlines of pure thought" signaled a very high-minded approach.

There is even a hint of the reformer in his approach, for he dares to suggest what is most crucially missing from the national psychology during times of crisis: "Historical-mindedness and patience while the natural equilibrium is reestablishing itself are two traits, most lacking and most needed, in the American temperament." Locke certainly harbors no illusion about his own ability to influence these and other traits in any lasting way:

> Public opinion in America asserts itself violently, impulsively, and more often than in any other country perhaps, accomplishes its immediate aims . . . owing to the plastic and tentative nature of our institutions and ideas. But once asserted, it does not maintain itself . . . or does so grudgingly, with a sense of restraint and handicap. This is the price of our amenability to reform.

Since the era of progressive reform was just getting under way, Locke might be alluding at this point to the gentle agitation of Booker T. Washington and the increasingly restrictive ethos of post-Reconstruction America. From the generally positive acceptance of Washington's Atlanta Exposition speech of 1895 to the *Plessy vs. Ferguson* Supreme Court decision condoning segregation of the following year, America's social policy towards its oppressed minority was a subject of confusing and conflicting claims and proscriptions, for which the phrase "does so grudgingly" is very charitable. As for the violent and impulsive expression of public opinion, Locke could well have been thinking of the race riot in Atlanta in 1906. But Locke's personal experiences in the years immediately preceding the essay were of a genteel English and Oxfordian racism of the sort that many Americans found more offensive than that of their fellow citizens. Such experiences produced a mind that seemed at times to indulge in nuance and self-fashioning.

> Much of the readerly delight of this essay comes from Locke's way of characterizing his subject as virtually impossible to define ("plastic," "transitory," etc.), and still proceeding, through recursive loops and rhetorical swerves, to say something illuminating about it. Biographically speaking, the essay is Locke's way of planning his reentry into America, studying paradoxically as a stranger and a native son the internal "contrasts" of the country that he had been outside of for three years. Trying to define the national temperament of the land of his birth would be just the right occasion to apply the insights and methods of the essay on English traits to an even more elusive subject.

Much of what the 1911 essay proposes as a definition or delineation of the national temperament was available to Locke from myriad sources, ranging from Emerson to Tocqueville. But the essay impresses with its own maturity and insight, too. It appeared four years before Van Wyck Brooks's *America's Coming of Age,* fourteen years before William Carlos Williams's *In the Amer-*

ican Grain, and a number of years before the essays and books of Randolph Bourne and Lewis Mumford on the subject. Speculation about the national character, a literary activity since the Republic's earliest days, was rampant in the early years of the century and into the 1920s; Marianne Moore wrote a poem about it (called, ironically, "England," published in 1920), and D. H. Lawrence's *Studies in Classic American Literature* (1919) is obsessed with it. While at college, Locke had reviewed H. G. Wells's book on the subject, *The Future in America.* The atmosphere at Harvard must have been marked at times by discussions of the issue as well, as the efforts of Locke and Brooks (Locke's Harvard classmate and unacknowledged rival) appearing so soon after their graduation would suggest.[5] Santayana also stands as an imposing figure in this context, as his *Character and Opinion in the United States* (1920) makes clear. Many of these efforts centered on the question of American art, and while Locke takes up this aspect of the subject, he is also concerned to say something about American habits and values.

One way to summarize the arguments about American civilization—arguments that can also be seen as the roots of cultural criticism in America—is to contrast two publications that appeared in 1921. Though these were published a decade after Locke's essay, they establish a context for mainstream American thought that Locke was in some ways able to finesse by avoiding the extreme positions for which they argued. The first is Stuart Sherman's essay from the January 1921 issue of the *Atlantic Monthly,* "The National Genius." In it Sherman argues the culturally conservative point of view by attacking the positions of Joel Spingarn and other "younger" men. Sherman praises established community values and insists that the attack on puritanism in the name of aesthetic freedom is misguided. He ends with the somewhat improbable suggestion that artists should not set beauty and puritanism at loggerheads but should instead "make Puritanism beautiful." At the other extreme, in *Civilization in the United States* (1921), a collection of forty essays edited by Harold Stearns, Locke's old classmate Van Wyck Brooks suggests that in America "the creative will . . . is a very weak and sickly plant."[6] Art can flourish here only if it liberates "the spiritual force of the individuals who compose it." The ethos of the crowd versus the freedom of the individual: it is an old American theme, one given to extreme postures, and one that Locke would address in special ways.

Tutelary figures usually stand behind an author, their shadows creating a darkness that often accentuates the light. In the case of Locke's treatment of the American "genius," it is regrettable that some of the later reflections by other writers did not take into account his nuanced presentation, especially given Locke's commitment to pluralism. Of course, many of the authors mentioned above can be heard either by anticipation or as echoes in Locke's essay, but one voice is perhaps most pervasively there—that of Whitman, especially his *Democratic Vistas* (1871). Whitman's essay was written in response to Carlyle's *Shooting Niagara,* and it defends the national character against the aspersions—antidemocratic in both spirit and letter—cast so vividly by the Victorian sage. The defense rests largely on an appeal to culture, which for Whitman has a spiritual, even a religious, dimension.[7] However, Whitman, like Locke, sees flaws in the national character; in this, both men are far from espousing the xenophobic or jingoistic sense of national character that has recently caused the very idea of such terms and explorations to be cast into disfavor. The common practice in the politics of the late 1860s of buying votes with liquor, for example, is a betrayal of Whitman's ideals of democracy that he can neither tolerate nor blink away with false piety. But the most important trait that Locke's essay shares with *Democratic Vistas* is an impulse to turn the analysis into a manifesto, in other words, to transform the sense of failure and deep flaws into a call to higher ideals.

Whitman is in fact the only American author whom Locke explicitly names in his essay. For Locke, Whitman's accomplishments were already viewed as indisputable; the only question is what, exactly, did they signify? Answering that question required another to be posed: could a country as various as America, as experimental, as much a "work in progress," present any clear outlines? In the essay's most celebratory passage, Locke's thoughts turn to the poetics of the democratic vision best exemplified by Whitman. The passage refers to the national temperament, characterized by curiosity and energy, but it casts its description so that it becomes in effect a description of the national poet.

> To such a temperament nothing is really trivial, and the points of contact between things are almost infinite. As soon as one examines this trait on an intellectual plane, one sees what curious laws of association govern the American mind. Its superb eclecticism, its voraciousness, its collector's instinct for facts and details, and its joyous disregard for proportion and an artificial order are still in need of adequate exposition. They impose so many handicaps from an artistic point of view that as yet no literary genius except Whitman has found it possible to accept them all.

Locke here points the way forward, as he was to do so often throughout his career, and sets against the grand ideal a firm but measured condensation of artistic failure: "To instruct pleasantly with the minimum of effort is the debased aim of present-day art." The genteel tradition was swiftly but thoroughly dispensed with, as Locke went on to try to define what American art should be expressing. From this point until the end of his career, Locke would always assert the dual necessity for art to serve as a means of personal expression and as group experience.

If there is a controlling trope in Locke's essay, it is probably the notion that the American temperament is something that is staged, and staged in part because of the evasiveness that is at its center. Locke introduces this figure of speech in the essay's second paragraph, where it is clear that his recent experience as a foreign traveler has highlighted his own Americanness, as well as his perplexity in trying to represent just what this is:

> The histrionic demeanor of Americans abroad, at times so very like the behavior of actors off the stage, exacting calcium-light duty of the sun, is a real due to the national temperament. If only by the reactions of others do we achieve any definite notion of what we ourselves are, it is small wonder that we have cultivated the actor's manner and practice his arts, only it is a strange art for an otherwise inartistic nation, a curious dependence for a free people.

Some of Locke's native Philadelphian sense of propriety is here, as surely there is also a dose of Harvard's strict social expectations. Present here as well is Locke's recognition, central to his *Race Contacts and Interracial Relations,* that any group identity is ultimately known only by its relations with another group; difference defines identity, publicly and individually. To these elements in his background have been added the Oxford experience of the clash of national differences and the English reserve and studied indifference that he felt keenly.

This is the point, perhaps, where Locke and Whitman most diverge. Whitman would applaud such theatricality, even when it was pushed to the level of histrionic self-dramatization. Locke was himself a man of divided temperament; a dandy in dress and speech, he fastidiously concealed his homosexuality. (Whitman, of course, was fastidiously ambiguous on this score.) If Whitman was a constant democrat in his political affections, so, too, was Locke, but he had arrived at his qualified egalitarianism through years of elitist training, from his dearly purchased piano lessons to his arduously pursued philosophical training. Locke refers to America as "an inartistic nation" in large measure because he compares its achievements with the German opera he loved and the French symbolist poetry he read at Oxford. Whitman can refer to the United States as itself the greatest poem because he accepts all the indigenous popular arts as well as the imported "high" traditions. When both men rely on an aesthetic dimension to "fix" the national character most accurately, they are operating in the tradition of the artistic manifesto, a tradition that flourished with the onset of modernist thought.

The question of art is broached more than once in Locke's essay, though there is none of the sustained aesthetic theorizing we find in Whitman, except for the paragraph where Locke seems to be rejecting the genteel tradition that had reigned at Harvard; however, he does not seem prepared to explain exactly what will take its place. He seems wary of the aesthete as a type but is not reluctant to speak about some pressing alternatives:

America is wise, after all, in preferring to remain artless and unenlightened rather than accept contemporary art as a serious expression of itself. Drawn by detached and almost expatriated aesthetes at the commands of the most disinterested class of art patrons ever in existence, it has no real claims except upon the curiosity of the people. To force an art first to digest its civilization in all its crude lumpiness is, after all, a good and sound procedure, and it is safe to prophesy that in America either the result will be representative and unique or that there will emerge no national art at all.

The "lumpiness" mentioned here will figure in many of his discussions about art that follow in the next several decades, as Locke and others wrestle with the widespread dominance of realism and naturalism, with their "low" subject matter and deterministic ideas. Locke at this point had no way of knowing how the "almost expatriated" artists would become physically absent from America in large numbers in the next two decades (but he probably had Henry James much in mind). What remains a key point, though still implicit and undeveloped, is that a purely formalist approach to aesthetic matters will not satisfy Locke, for whom the "reflective and representative arts" will eventually always "make for that sense of institutions, which, beginning in jingo patriotism, ends in sound traditions."

The combination of the "representative" and the "unique" formed the core of Locke's aesthetic for most of his life. Such a conjoining was based in part on Kantian theories of art, especially as they evolved in the German Romantic tradition that Locke had thoroughly absorbed.[8] Emphasis on the representative nature of all good art, however, shows that Locke never neglected the social dimension of aesthetic experience. Furthermore, throughout the 1920s and 1930s the evolution of "jingo patriotism" into "sound traditions" formed for him a problematic central to African American culture. This evolution was the focus of debates between Locke and W. E. B. Du Bois, and Langston Hughes as well, as all three men tried to strike the riveting balance between the social claims of art as propaganda (as the then current phrase had it) and art as the expression of personal insight. For Whitman, the trust in his own muse was so implicit that this problem hardly appeared. He speculated in *Democratic Vistas* about the fate of American culture, and his lack of a sanguine outlook could be traced back to unresolved reflections on how best to produce and appreciate a representative culture. Whitman's great gift, however, was a faith in the power of art not only to express but also to reform and perfect national identity. What might have started as a critique of the national character became in Whitman's large-minded hopefulness a manifesto for historical and spiritual ideals. For

Locke, tempered by his growing awareness of the ravages of British imperialism and straitened by his own experience as a man of color, hope was not so easily lodged in culture.

Locke was saying, in other words, that so far, in the first decade of the new century, the American arts have not sufficiently told us what we need to know about our national character. Such character is best understood as "something more than . . . commercial-mindedness and personal self-assertiveness." Pushing beyond this often cited charge, Locke turns to a description of it as "a mental atmosphere" that is "something spiritual . . . free, accessible, contagious." The temperament takes on a political cast on "festival days" and is often thought of as "corporate prosperity"; the ethos of the robber barons is alluded to here but is not allowed to stand as the highest expression of the nation's striving. At its core the temperament, based on individualism, "is really a very limited and simple system of conventional ideas"; this system is, frankly, "shallow and contentless . . . as an idea," but "the pragmatic verdict will prevail," for it works as a cohesive social force. (This may be the earliest indication of Locke's allegiance, or at least attraction, to the philosophical disposition of pragmatism that, in the person of William James, challenged the genteel tradition at Harvard.)[9] The American's idea of himself is "Protean and even puerile," and his naive individuality is unquestionable, "because it is so plastic it knows no self-contradiction." The Whitmanian embrace of multitudes that cancels all contradictions is here dispassionately presented, as Locke's tone hovers between praise and censure. America's evasiveness is its greatest anomaly, and this quality comes about in part because of the rush of "self-willed energy" and the "modern demand for material progress." Locke even suggests, with some of the wry detachment of a Henry Adams, that the ultimate goal of this energy is the "securing [of] a final and restful mastery over the means of life."

Power and prosperity lie at the root of American patriotism for Locke. But such roots can easily bear strange fruit, especially if history has forces more binding and stronger than men can discern. At one point he indulges in a comparison that would later serve as a common theme for writers such as Robert Lowell and Gore Vidal, likening America to ancient Rome: "A country that worships power, respects the autocrat, and may even come to tolerate the tyrant. Indeed, the analogies between the republican temper of Rome and that of America may well worry those who believe that history repeats itself." He nevertheless sees that the reductive charge of crude materialism misses the point. The temperament, it is true, is made up of "superb eclecticism . . . voraciousness . . . [and a] collector's instinct for facts and details," but somehow "public spiritedness prevails to a marked and unusual degree." In describing "that phenomenon of our civilization, the millionaire philanthropist," he is able to show that

if Americans worship money, they worship it as power, as cornered energy and
not in an intrinsic and miserly way. The time comes when the force he has been
collecting threatens to vanish in latent inertia . . . and the millionaire can only
release it again by giving.

The largess of an Andrew Carnegie, a J. P. Morgan, even a Cecil Rhodes creates an economy of force and scale, as Henry Adams might have put it, that
develops laws of its own. This seemingly neutral description is not meant as an
apologetic for accumulated wealth, and the satiric bite comes in just in time to
suggest that Locke had seen enough of accumulated wealth at Harvard and
Oxford to recognize how insensitive it often makes people. "The process of
accumulation, becoming automatic, discharges him; he takes to his new vocation of giving, but as far as the muscular reactions are concerned there is very
little difference between shoveling in and shoveling out." The passage reveals
some of the resentment of the scholarship student who realizes that the largess
of wealthy benefactors does not always guarantee their commitment to the
highest ideals of those they support. Also audible here is an ironic echo of the
standards of what the period called "muscular Christianity," as well as the
social gospel, with its sanctimonious approval of a "vocation of giving." At the
time this essay was published, Locke was essentially at the end of his limited
financial means and was faced with the prospect of returning to America to
support himself and his mother.

Locke ends the essay by saying, "As long as the American temperament
remains its own excuse for being, one cannot expect it to be humble and
unassertive." To be its own excuse for being was to possess already the
Hegelian spirit of autonomy and self-realization that was promised to each
national group with enough historical purpose and direction to develop a
strong state. Though Locke has worked around and around his subject, balancing one formulation with a qualification or even a paradox, his sense of the
temperament as "its own excuse for being" also suggests something like a final
value. This value can be understood as derived not only from nationalist theories but also from the modernist notion of the autonomy of the self. Such
autonomy also helps to center formalist aesthetics, with its notion of art for
art's sake. The essay rather cannily combines elements of political analysis,
social psychology, a historicizing sensibility, and an aesthetic imagination to
try to represent something "so wholly vital and unique and interesting as the
national character."

Locke's intentions in approaching the national character in this way may be
considered as contributing to the literature of modernism. Alignments between
the self and the nation, and especially the artistic self and the national character, lie at the heart of Whitman's project, and they are part of what makes him,

at the very least, a protomodernist, if not the "first" modern poet. Locke shares Whitman's commitments here and also advances them, as he self-reflexively expresses and criticizes the complexities of identification and distance in ways typical of modernist culture. Provoked in part by his reflections on the English character in his essay about Oxford, Locke may have been trying to balance praise and censure when describing his own national identity. The complexity of the writing and the Whitmanian associative nature of the argument at various points can be put down to the author's need both to embrace his country and to hold it at arm's length. In any case, the essay can also be understood as Locke's first step in recognizing that America's problems, though certainly unique, could not be immune to probing analysis and frank criticism. Both these features would be present in nearly everything he wrote after "The American Temperament."

In a speech to a fraternity at Howard University in 1949, Locke returned to one of his chief themes, the importance of culture.[10] Being then near the end of his career, and only three years from the end of his life, he realized that his constant calls to ideals and high culture were in danger of being further misunderstood. He wanted to set the record straight and have a final say on the subject.

> Culture is nevertheless an essential. In fact, after its achievement, it always has and always will rank first; though I am commonsense [sic] enough to admit readily the basic importance of bread, with or without butter. . . . Real, essential culture is baked into our daily bread or else it *isn't* truly culture. In short, I am willing to stand firmly on the side of the democratic rather than the aristocratic notion of culture and have stood so for many years, without having gotten full credit, however.

Locke goes on to say that culture is worth "the high cost of nurturing it on the upper levels of caste and privilege," but he then adds, "one should not have to pay that exorbitant price for it." He devoted himself to a lifetime as an educator, believing that he was thereby making culture both more advanced and more available. His sense of paradox and nuance in these matters may separate him tonally from Whitman, but the two writers held many of the basic beliefs in common.

To conclude by returning to the biographical context, Locke and his mother, Mary, constantly discussed what prospects he faced upon his return to America after his European sojourn.[11] Here I offer the outline of a crucial moment in Locke's career, one that I think can be seen as highly determinative for all his future efforts. When he returned to Philadelphia after his European studies, there were two directions in which he might turn. To the north was W. E. B. Du Bois, recently named the editor of the *Crisis,* the journal of opinion and cultural criticism published by the National Association for the Advancement of Colored People; Mary Locke had written her son about the appointment in November 1910. Locke and his mother had also earlier exchanged positive remarks about *The Souls of Black Folk,* and clearly Du Bois was on his way to becoming an important spokesperson for his race. To the south was Booker T. Washington, busy advancing the cause through his management of Tuskegee Institute, with its emphasis on practical training.[12] Greatly instructed in the nature of imperialism and racism by his friends at Oxford, Locke was faced with an important choice between taking a direct hands-on approach to educating large numbers of African Americans, and influencing public opinion by writing for an intellectual journal. Of course, in many ways Locke's life was to be a dynamic fusion of both possibilities.

But for the moment he chose to go south; there he met Washington and traveled with him throughout the poor rural communities where most African Americans lived. The experience was exhilarating in many ways, as he saw a landscape and a culture far removed from both the gentility of his native Philadelphia and the cosmopolitanism of London and Berlin. Writing to his mother, he nervously joked about the possibility of being lynched. But he knew he was completing his training to become a "race man" by seeing first-hand the living conditions of the people for whose liberation he was to argue.[13] There was some discussion of Locke's being given a position on Washington's staff, but it did not work out. Locke would never wholly reject the sort of pop-ulist leadership represented by Washington, as his qualified reaction to Marcus Garvey in "The New Negro" demonstrates. But, knowing himself well, he eventually made a stronger commitment to university education and the fullest cultural development, in both personal and public terms.

In the spring of 1911, Mary Locke wrote to her son to express anxiety about his choosing an academic appointment. The administration at Howard Univer-sity, for example, where Locke was under consideration and where he eventu-ally taught for three and a half decades, was excessively puritanical, and it showed little tolerance for any artistic ethos or bohemian way of life. A young drama instructor, Montgomery Gregory, who would later become Locke's friend and colleague, had recently suffered the consequences of the strictness that Mrs. Locke feared: "I do not want you at Howard les[t] they dismiss you in disgrace." Gregory had been seen exiting a saloon by a person whom Mrs. Locke cryptically called the "Official of the lust." She added that the president of the university had given the young instructor just fifteen minutes to write his letter of resignation (14 April 1911). After experiencing considerable personal freedom in Berlin, Locke must have found the the prospect of a return to a repressive environment sobering. He knew, however, that personal freedoms and community standards could both be progressively advanced by education and cultural enrichment. The question would remain, how willing were those in positions of authority and leadership to do the bold thing?

When, in August 1911, Mary Locke saw the copy of the *North American Review* that contained "The American Temperament," Locke was still in Germany, where he had gone to continue his university studies, shortly before his rather abrupt decision to return to America. Mrs. Locke wrote to say that he should "Keep Alain[,] drop that silly old LeRoy—as I see you have." (She herself had given him his middle name, and always referred to him as "Roy," in part so that his initials would spell out "ALL," while he had taken the more literary name to reify his artistic vocation.) Referring to his plans to visit the north of Africa as soon as he could, she added, "Now if you can make Egypt go." The two of them had virtually unbounded trust in his ability to devote his life to culture. Then there was his appearance in a major intellectual journal to seal the identity. He was still fixed on the idea of seeing the world in order to understand its complexities of racial and cultural contacts and relations. His chances for such an education had so far hinged on the beneficence of various well-endowed educational enterprises. Now, however, it was beginning to be an unignorable fact that, although African American leadership in his native land was often limited and overly cautious, he would have to make a living for himself in the service of his race. For that, America seemed the right place.

Notes

1. Alain Locke, "The American Temperament," *North American Review* 19, (August 1911): 262–70. This is reprinted in Jeffrey Stewart, ed., *The Critical Temper of Alain Locke: A Selection of His Essays on Art and Culture* (New York: Garland, 1983). See also Alain Locke, "Oxford Contrasts," Independent 67 (July 1909): 139–42.

2. The sales receipts for Locke's new clothes are in the Locke papers in the Moorland-Spingarn Research Center at Howard University, box 164-160, folder 12. He also wrote home to his mother, Mary Locke, that he was looking for the right flat in which to live: "Good locations have a lot to do with entree into social life." (1 October 1908). All references to letters are from this source, and will be referred to by date; box and folder number will refer to all other material.

3. In a letter home (5 May 1909) Locke spoke of his plans to get a BCL (Bachelor of Civil Law) degree from Oxford, and he said he was interested in "formulating plans for the admission of Asiatic and African peoples into the jurisdiction. of international law." The Rationalist Club was one of several in which Locke participated while at Oxford. Of special importance was the African Union Society, founded in 1908, of which Locke was the honorary secretary, and whose constitution had as its announced purpose the "cultivation of thought and social intercourse between its members as prospective leaders of the African race." (Box 164-160, folder 29) There was also the

Cosmopolitan Club, where Locke worked out some of his ideas about diversity and tolerance. Locke addressed this club on 9 June 1908, beginning with an epigraph from Santayana: "There is a certain plane on which all nations must live in common, that of morals and science" (Box 164-159, folder 8).

4. Locke's use of the concept of cosmopolitanism deserves further study; in addition to serving as a precursor for his notions about cultural pluralism, it can be (at least in part) related to current notions such as civic nationalism. See the articles by Bernard Yack and Nicholas Xenos in *Critical Review* 10 (Spring 1996); and Kwame Anthony Appiah, "Cosmopolitan Patriots," in *Critical Inquiry* 23, no. 3 (Spring 1997): 617–39.

5. Locke's letters to his Harvard classmates after graduation make it clear that there were at least two literary cliques in his class that vied with each other for success. Locke was especially friendly with a Charles Dickerman and a West Indian named J. Arthur Harley, among others; Ned Sheldon (who had a play produced while still an undergraduate) was close to Van Wyck Brooks. John Hall Wheelock may have had relations with both camps. The correspondence with Dickerman is in Box 164-24, folders 36–37, and 164-25, folders 1–4.

6. Stearns also answered Sherman directly, in "America and the Young Intellectuals," *Bookman* 52, no. 1 (March 1921): 42–48. This issue was behind an elaborate and ongoing discussion among many literary intellectuals of the time, though no comprehensive account has yet been written on the subject. The impact of literary nationalism on the development of modernism has recently been explored, but it has not been used as a way of bridging the many gaps that separate discussions of "mainstream" modernist writers from those of African Americans in this period. See, however, the studies by Edward Abrahams, *The Lyrical Left: Randolph Bourne, Alfred Stieglitz, and the Origins of Cultural Radicalism in. America* (Charlottesville: University of Virginia Press, 1986); and Casey Nelson Blake, *Beloved Community: The Cultural Criticism of Randolph Bourne, Van Wyck Brooks, Waldo Frank, and Lewis Mumford* (Chapel Hill: University of North Carolina Press, 1990).

7. I have discussed some of these issues in my "Whitman's Political Vision," *Raritan* 1–2, no. 1 (Summer 1992): 98–112.

8. Locke studied Romantic poetry at Harvard and wrote a long senior thesis on the subject. The aestheticizing idealism that dominated much of his literary and philosophical study in college was drawn in part from Barrett Wendell and George Santayana. His interest in the German notion of *Bildung*, as well as some distinctly Hegelian frameworks for his thought, is apparent in "The New Negro."

9. William James published *Pragmatism: A New Name for Some Old Ways of Thinking* in 1907, Locke's senior year at Harvard. Though James gave his last lecture at Harvard in January of that year, the subject of pragmatism had been the focus of a lecture series he delivered the year before.

10. Alain Locke, "Frontiers of Culture," in *The Philosophy of Alain Locke: Harlem Renaissance and Beyond*, ed. Leonard Harris (Philadelphia: Temple University Press, 1989), 229–37. In a sense, Locke was here returning yet again to his sense of *Bildung* and the great emphasis he put on education as an endless process of self-development.

11. Locke wrote to his mother: "I really long to get back to America and into my

position it will be a stormier and shorter reign than Booker's but so much the better—I want a long arm and the will to use it—heredity has given me both I only need the favorable environment—I have realized definitely and finally at Oxford that I am cast for a practical career . . . every blasted one of the young race-leaders here at Oxford would like to see me secured for his work, his field. . . . I have made up my mind to serve a. great apprenticeship" (5 May 1909). Later, in February 1910, Mary Locke responds to a letter, apparently lost, in which Locke set out his career plans: "I admit I was fairly staggered at first by the 'colossal' scheme—it made my poor head swim." It is clear from references in this letter (in box 164-58, folders 1–7) that Locke planned not only to meet Booker T. Washington but also to travel extensively to Egypt and India.

    12. Houston Baker, in *Modernism and the Harlem Renaissance* (Chicago: University of Chicago Press, 1987), has talked of the contrasting—or dialectical—figures of Du Bois and Washington. I am suggesting here, however, that the two tutelary figures were for Locke immediate presence, and hence could focus his choice of a career.

    13. Sometime in February 1912, Locke wrote his mother from Jacksonville, Florida, that he had "made a bulls-eye with Washington." On the 29th of the same month he was on a Pullman car, traveling to Montgomery, Alabama, to rejoin Washington; writing a letter home, he observed: "As I write this an old confederate opposite sits and glares—I guess it makes him angry that I can write."

12

Alain Locke: Philosophical "Midwife" of the Harlem Renaissance

Verner D. Mitchell

Edited by three British philosophers and published in 1995, the massive, 947-page *Biographical Dictionary of Twentieth-Century Philosophers* chronicles the lives and accomplishments of 1,000 philosophers who lived in some part of the twentieth century.[1] Queried about their selections, the editors acknowledged a "considerable bias towards European philosophers." But even with that bias, they managed to include 175 Americans, for a total of 17.5 percent of the entrants. It is not at all surprising, however, although it is rather disturbing, especially at this late date, that of the 175, not a single one is a black American. As the editors tell it, they refused to bow to the pressures of political correctness.

Absent, then, from their book is the distinguished turn-of-the-century philosopher and educator Anna Julie Cooper, who took her Ph.D. in 1924 from the Sorbonne.[2] Also missing are the many philosophers who grace the pages of Leonard Harris's *Philosophy Born of Struggle: Anthology of Afro-American Philosophy from 1917.*[3] Missing, too, are all contemporary African American philosophy scholars: Angela Davis of the University of California, Santa Cruz; Cornel West of Harvard; Lucius Outlaw of Haverford College; Purdue's Leonard Harris; Howard McGary, Kenneth Taylor, and Jorge Garcia of Rutgers; Syracuse University's Laurence Thomas; and Georgette Sinkler of the University of Chicago, to name only a few. Even more curious is the omission of the twentieth century's American scholar who, after W. E. B. Du Bois, is arguably the most important, Alain Locke.

I want to call attention briefly to Locke's pioneering role as a leader of the artistic movement that would come to be known as the Harlem Renaissance. (I need to stress, however, that I am providing only the smallest of snapshots.) Locke was, in his own words, "philosophical midwife to a generation of younger Negro poets, writers, [and] artists."[4]

Indeed, although he never lived in Harlem until the final year of his life,

191

Locke was at the center of the artistic explosion in the decade following World War I that came to be known as the Harlem Renaissance. Whether in a nightclub, in a literary salon, or on the corner of 135th and 7th Avenues, "Harlem," in Langston Hughes's famous phrase, "was in vogue."[5] Hughes continues:

> The 1920's were the years of Manhattan's black Renaissance. . . . Harlem was like a great magnet for the Negro intellectual, pulling him from everywhere. . . . some Harlemites thought the millennium had come. They thought the race problem had been solved through Art plus Gladys Bentley. They were sure the New Negro would lead a new life from then on in green pastures of tolerance created by Countee Cullen, Ethel Waters, Claude McKay, Duke Ellington, Bojangles, and Alain Locke.[6]

The evening of 21 March 1924 found thirty-eight-year-old Alain Locke at New York City's Civic Club on East 34th Street. One of the few downtown establishments that admitted both blacks and whites to its dining room, the Civic Club was a natural choice for this "coming-out" dinner, staged to celebrate the publication of Jessie Fauset's inaugural novel, *There Is Confusion.*[7] In his role as master of ceremonies, Locke presided over an eclectic gathering of prominent publishers, magazine editors, distinguished white writers, and many of the country's promising young black artists.[8] He was then figuratively and literally center stage at the event many scholars now consider the formal launching of the New Negro Movement, or the Harlem Renaissance.

Renaissance scholar Steven Watson notes that "The Civic Club dinner provided the sort of pageant, played out before a mixed audience of cultural notables, that was necessary to the growth of the young movement."[9] As a direct result of contacts made at the dinner, *Harper's* agreed to publish a number of Countee Cullen's poems, and *Survey Graphic,* which had previously largely ignored writers of color, agreed to devote a full issue to "express the progressive spirit of contemporary Negro life."[10]

As guest editor of this special *Survey Graphic* issue (which appeared in March 1925), Locke brought together a wide array of Harlem's talented, though in most cases heretofore unsung, poets, essayists, illustrators, and fiction writers. So successful was the project that it sold out two printings, on the way to becoming "the most widely read issue in the magazine's history."[11] This dazzling success led, in turn, to Albert and Charles Boni's offer to publish the collection in book form. Elated, but as always discerning and discriminating, Locke decided to expand the magazine version to include such "old-guard" writers as William Stanley Braithwaite, W. E. B. Du Bois, and James Weldon Johnson. He also included a generous sampling of younger artists— Dr. Rudolph Fisher, Jean Toomer, Zora Neale Hurston, Langston Hughes,

Claude McKay, Gwendolyn Bennett, Countee Cullen, and Helene Johnson—to whom he collectively dedicated the book.

The book is divided into two parts. The first, "The Negro Renaissance," features fiction, poetry, drama, music, and criticism, while the second, "The New Negro in a New World," has a sociological bent. Sprinkled throughout are jazzy illustrations and decorative designs by Winold Reiss and Aaron Douglas. Also present are five of Locke's own essays, which, taken together, are richly illustrative of the full range of his intellectual power. Unifying the book is the contributors' collective pointing toward, as the title suggests, a New Negro: one far removed from the old formulas and stereotypes, one who boldly and indeed transgressively celebrates African people's beauty, intellect, and humanity. "The day of 'aunties,' 'uncles' and 'mammies' is equally gone," proclaims Locke in his energetic opening essay. "The popular melodrama has about played itself out, and it is time to scrap the fictions, garret the bogeys and settle down to a realistic facing of facts."[12] In sum, as *The New Negro: An Interpretation,* rolled off the printing press in December 1925, Alain Locke had effectively assembled the movement's seminal text, its manifesto, its bible.

Locke was once more center stage when *Opportunity,* the Urban League's official journal, staged its three literary awards contests, in 1925, 1926, and 1927. Designed to stimulate creative effort among the younger artists, the contests were a stunning success, attracting hundreds of enthusiasts (as had the Civic Club dinner) to New York City from all parts. For the 1925 contest Locke and eight others judged the short stories, and Locke's former student, Zora Neale Hurston, took the second prize for her story "Spunk." In 1926 Locke joined James Weldon Johnson, Vachel Lindsay, Robert Frost, and four others as poetry judge. Finally, indicative of his catholic range, in 1927 he moved to the visual art category, where he awarded first prize to Kansas native Aaron Douglas and honorable mention to twenty-one-year-old Richard Bruce Nugent of Washington, D.C.[13]

Appropriately, Langston Hughes and Zora Neale Hurston, perhaps the most talented of the younger Renaissance writers, were among the many who would occasionally applaud Locke's efforts. Early on, Locke recognized Hughes's poetic gift and decided to include ten of his poems in "Harlem: Mecca of the New Negro," the March 1925 special issue of *Survey Graphic.* Two years later, Locke's anthology *Four Negro Poets* appeared, highlighting the work of Hughes, Countee Cullen, Claude McKay, and Jean Toomer. Writing retrospectively from the vantage point of 1940, Hughes recalled that "Jessie Fauset at the *Crisis,* Charles Johnson at *Opportunity,* and Alain Locke in Washington, were the three people who midwifed the so-called New Negro literature into being. Kind and critical—but not too critical for the young—they nursed us along until our books were born."[14] Three decades later, literary historian Nathan I.

Huggins would echo Hughes's assessment. For him, "Locke's editing of and contribution to this volume [*The New Negro*] and his energetic championing of the intellectual achievement of Negroes in the 1920's made him the father of the . . . Harlem Renaissance."[15]

Zora Neale Hurston and Locke first met in 1918 while he was a professor and she a student at Howard. During her freshman year, she joined the university's literary club, the Stylus, which Locke cosponsored. The second issue of the club magazine featured her poem "O Night" and her short story "John Redding Goes to Sea." Critic Cheryl Wall writes in *Women of the Harlem Renaissance* that "From New York, Charles S. Johnson, editor of *Opportunity*, wrote to congratulate the author of 'John Redding Goes to Sea' and to request more material. Locke had alerted him to Hurston's potential," Wall stresses, "and when her second story, 'Drenched in Light,' arrived, Johnson agreed to publish it."[16] Thus, to his great credit, Locke played a significant role in launching Hurston's career.

Yet for Locke there was also a downside. Born in the prior century, in the shadows of the Civil War, he and Du Bois and others of the old guard quite naturally held views reflective of their time, in particular somewhat Victorian aesthetic views that eventually clashed with the literary tastes of the younger generation. An instance of this generational divide is Du Bois's caustic reaction to Claude McKay's racy 1928 novel, *Home to Harlem*. Jake, McKay's protagonist, goes AWOL from the army, returns home to his beloved Harlem, and promptly falls in love with a prostitute. Disapproving, to put it mildly, of the novel's focus on the seamier side of Negro life, Du Bois famously wrote that the book "for the most part nauseates me, and after the dirtier parts of its filth I feel distinctly like taking a bath."[17]

With the label "Victorian values" I am attempting to suggest a kind of public squeamishness with regard to sexual matters and a cultured, somewhat snobbish gentility. Above all, though, the black elite felt it their duty to set "good" examples for the less fortunate, lower-class masses. Willard B. Gatewood discusses these matters at length in his *Aristocrats of Color: The Black Elite, 1880–1920*.[18] Locke, employing Du Bois's concept of "the Talented Tenth" (which he expounds in his 1903 essay of the same title), envisioned elite artists functioning as "the advance-guard of the African peoples" to rehabilitate "the race in world esteem."[19] "The especially cultural recognition they win," he continues, writing in the "New Negro" essay of 1925, "should in turn prove the key to that revaluation of the Negro which must precede or accompany any considerable further betterment of race relationships."[20] For a number of years Locke would mistakenly continue to believe that art, properly rendered, could join with economics and politics to ameliorate, and in fact eventually wipe out, racism.

Fearful, then, that "low-life" artistic renderings would fuel negative stereo-types, Locke displayed a particular aversion to jazz. In his view, jazz was "a submerged and half-inarticulate motive in Negro doggerel," a "mere trickery of syncopation." The "Jazz school" of Negro poetry was similarly a "vulgar-ization."[21] He sustains and expands this argument in a trenchant 1934 critique:

> Then Langston Hughes came with his revelation of the emotional color of Negro life, and his brilliant discovery of the flow and rhythm of modern and especial-ly the city Negro, substituting this jazz figure and personality of the older plan-tation stereotype. But it was essentially a jazz version of Negro life, and that is to say as much American, or more, as Negro; and though fascinating and true to an epoch this version was surface quality after all.[22]

If the appearance of Hughes's "The Negro Artist and the Racial Mountain" in June of 1926 is any indication, it is apparent that the younger artists were unwilling to suppress either the form or the theme of their work. Hughes, full of youthful defiance, declares:

> We younger Negro artists who create now intend to express our individual dark-skinned selves without fear or shame. If white people are pleased, we are glad. If they are not, it doesn't matter. We know we are beautiful. And ugly too. The tom-tom cries and the tom-tom laughs. If colored people are pleased we are glad. If they are not, their displeasure doesn't matter either. We build our temples for tomorrow, strong as we know how, and we stand on top of the mountain, free within ourselves.[23]

Interestingly, five months later, in November 1926, Hughes and Hurston and five others pooled their resources and organized the avant-garde journal *Fire!!* subtitled *A Quarterly Devoted to the Younger Negro Artists*. Its inau-gural issue featured a number of erotic drawings, Wallace Thurman's vignette of a sixteen-year-old prostitute, "Cordelia the Crude"; Gwendolyn Bennett's "Wedding Day," the story of a former boxer and jazz musician left at the altar by a white prostitute; and Richard Bruce Nugent's "Smoke, Lilies, and Jade," the first African American work openly to explore homosexuality. By chal-lenging forthrightly the Victorian sensibilities of Locke and others in the black literary establishment, the publication of *Fire!!* proved the culminating act in a movement that Arnold Rampersad describes (in something of an over-statement) as the students and younger writers dispensing with their dean, Alain Locke.[24]

While the *Fire!!* conflict was clearly momentous, it is also important to recall that a number of the magazine's writers—Thurman and Nugent, for instance—remained loyal to, and supportive of, Locke. Thurman's dazzling roman à clef, *Infants of the Spring* (1932), which presents Locke as Dr. A. L. Parkes, leaves a compelling account of Locke's contributions. In a pivotal scene, Raymond (Thurman) reads an important letter from Dr. Parkes:

> My dear Raymond:
> I will be in New York on Thursday night. I want you to do me a favor. It seems to me that with the ever-increasing number of younger Negro artists and intellectuals gathering in Harlem, some effort should be made to establish what well might become a distinguished salon. All of you engaged in creative work, should, I believe, welcome the chance to meet together once every fortnight, for the purpose of exchanging ideas and expressing and criticizing individual theories. This might prove to be both stimulating and profitable. And it might also bring into active being a concerted movement that would establish the younger Negro talent once and for all as a vital force. With this in mind, I would appreciate your inviting as many of your colleagues as possible to your studio on Thursday evening. I will be there to preside. I hope you are intrigued by the idea and willing to cooperate. Please wire me your answer. Collect, of course.
>
> Very sincerely yours,
> Dr. A. L. Parkes[25]

By decade's end, the Harlem Renaissance was essentially over, its end precipitated in large part by the stock market crash of October 1929. Nonetheless, Alain Locke had clearly played a pivotal role in encouraging and nurturing the great outpouring of fiction, social discourse, visual art, dance, and poetry that flourished when Harlem "was in vogue." Yet none of these accomplishments was sufficient to shield him from a steady flow of race-based insults and slights, the latest, his exclusion from the *Biographical Dictionary*. It is rather ironic, however, that Locke, cultured and cosmopolitan, concerned through and through with presenting an erudite public image, would be excluded from this group of accepted, erudite philosophers in a "proper" publication. All the same, critic M. Anthony Fitchue is certainly correct in observing in his 1996 essay that "it is difficult not to speak in awed superlatives of Alain LeRoy Locke, America's first—and only until 1962—African-American Rhodes scholar and the man who unwittingly became the cultural impresario of the Harlem Renaissance."[26]

Notes

1. Diane Collinson et al., eds., *Biographical Dictionary of Twentieth-Century Philosophers* (New York: Routledge, 1995).

2 "No Black Americans Included in the Biographical Directory of 1,000 Twentieth Century Philosophers," *Journal of Blacks in Higher Education* 14 (Winter 1996/1997): 144.

3. For a sample of Cooper's philosophical writings, see "The Gain from a Belief," the final chapter of her 1892 work, *A Voice from the South* (repr. New York: Oxford University Press, 1988), 286–304.

4. Leonard Harris, ed., *Philosophy Born of Struggle: Anthology of Afro-American Philosophy from 1917* (Dubuque, Iowa: Kendall/Hunt, 1983). Mark Helbling, "Feeling Universality and Thinking Particularistically: Alain Locke, Franz Boas, Melville Herskovits, and the Harlem Renaissance," *Prospects* 19 (1994): 289–314.

5. Arthur P. Davis, *From the Dark Tower: Afro-American Writers, 1900–1960* (Washington, D.C.: Howard University Press, 1974).

6. Langston Hughes, *The Big Sea* (1940; repr. New York: Hill & Wang, 1963), 223, 228, 240.

7. Jessie Fauset, "There Is Confusion: Twentieth-Century Philosophers," *Journal of Blacks in Higher Education* 13 (Winter 1996/1997): 144.

8. Steven Watson, *The Harlem Renaissance* (New York: Pantheon, 1995), 27.

9. Watson, *Harlem Renaissance,* 28.

10. Watson, *Harlem Renaissance,* 28.

11. Watson, *Harlem Renaissance,* 28.

12. Alain Locke, ed., *The New Negro* (1925; repr. New York: Macmillan, 1992.

13. For the complete list of judges and award winners, see *Opportunity,* May 1925, 142–43; May 1926, 156–57; June 1927, 179.

14. Hughes, *Big Sea,* 218.

15. Nathan I. Huggins, *Harlem Renaissance: Hub of African-American Culture, 1920–1930* (New York: Oxford University Press, 1971), 56–57.

16. Cheryl A. Wall, *Women of the Harlem Renaissance* (Bloomington: Indiana University Press, 1995), 146.

17. W. E. B. Du Bois, "The Novels," *Crisis* 35 (June 1928): 202.

18. Willard B. Gatewood, *Aristocrats of Color: The Black Elite, 1880–1920* (Bloomington: Indiana University Press, 1990).

19. Locke, "The New Negro," in *New Negro,* 14.

20. Locke, "New Negro," 15.

21. Alain Locke, A., "The Negro in American Culture" (1929), in *Black Voices: An Anthology of Afro-American Literature,* ed. Abraham Chapman (New York: Mentor, 1963), 524, 532.

22. Alain Locke, "Sterling Brown: The New Negro Folk-Poet" (1934), in *The Critical Temper of Alain Locke: A Selection of His Essays on Art and Culture,* ed. Jeffrey C. Stewart (New York: Garland, 1983), 53.

23. "The Negro Artist and the Racial Mountain." *Nation* 122 (23 June 1926): 694.

24. Arnold Rampersad, *The Life of Langston Hughes, Vol. 1: 1902–1941* (New York: Oxford University Press, 1986), 135.

25. Wallace Thurman, *Infants of the Spring* (1932; repr. Boston: Northeastern University Press, 1992), 227–28.

26. M. Anthony Fitchue, "Locke and Du Bois: Two Major Black Voices Muzzled by Philanthropic Organizations," *Journal of Blacks in Higher Education* 14 (Winter 1996/1997): 111.

13

Alain Locke: A Sociocultural Conception of Race

Clevis Headley

In their 1994 essay "White Philosophy," Avery Gordon and Christopher Newfield call attention to a certain perspective on race. They maintain that this new thinking reduces the problem of racism to the very concept of race. In describing this new anemic progressivism, they state that "[o]nce the appeal to race is seen analytically, free of the context of racism, the usual causality becomes reversed: racism does not make people talk about race; talk about race sustains racism. [U]ses of race are the same regardless of the race of the user. . . . In short, these analyses replace the race problem with the 'race' problem."[1] This latest development, whether by intention or by coincidence, has recently received some philosophical legitimization.

Anthony Appiah shares this philosophical suspicion about the concept of race; indeed, he seeks to exorcise the curse that race has cast on us, allegedly to counter the evil done by this concept. According to him, "[t]he evil that is done is done by the concept [race], and by easy—yet impossible—assumptions as to its application. Talk of race is particularly distressing for those of us who take culture seriously. For, where race works . . . it works as an attempt at metonymy for culture, and it does so only at the price of biologizing what is culture, ideology."[2] Viewed from a distinctively philosophical perspective, Appiah argues, race is a semantically invalid concept.[3] Race, he maintains, is so cognitively dysfunctional, "such obsolete verbal rubbish," that it warrants immediate rejection from our thinking. Furthermore, in attributing a quasitranscendental status to race, he concludes, all racialist thinking is misleading to the extent that this thinking embraces the notion of race, again, an ontologically degraded category.

I will focus on Alain Locke's conception of race, arguing specifically that this conception escapes Appiah's more radical conclusion. Locke's position, given the recent haste to dismiss concepts as counterfeit if they do not measure up to the sharpness of natural scientific concepts, merits favorable review owing to the fact that Locke deliberates seriously on the significance and cognitive informativeness of theorizing about race even if a philosophical definition of race in terms of biological characteristics is impossible. Furthermore, contrary to Appiah's recent insinuation that many thinkers have been blind to the semantic impotence of race, it is ironic to note that Locke, prior to Appiah, questioned the artificial tidiness of this concept.

Appiah's position is roughly that (1) we lack necessary and sufficient conditions for the application of the concept 'race'; (2) regardless of our criteria and different schemes of classifications of races, there will be many people who do not fit into these classifications; (3) most racial classifications are arbitrary and are not biologically significant; and (4) no racial essences exist in the physical world. These four considerations, from a realist referential analysis, render sentences about races false since races do not exist; that is, no objects actually exist that are designated by these sentences. Hence, the term "race" is referentially opaque.

I turn now to examine Locke's conception of race to correct Appiah's unwarranted and premature ejection of race from what he considers to be the rigorous domain of formal analysis. Locke provides a certain conception of things that transcends Appiah's analytic slaughter of race.

Putting Locke in Context

While at Howard University, Locke confronts the issue of race in a series of public lectures. Anticipating many of Appiah's "nervous" arguments, he, unlike Appiah, seeks an alternative conceptual space in which to locate the concept 'race.' This effort precludes declaring race hopelessly meaningless even if it is impossible to provide a plausible scientific or anthropological definition of race. On a more positive note, Locke anticipates the observations of Omi and Winant that race is "an unstable and 'decentered' complex of social meanings constantly transformed by political struggle."[4] For Locke, talk about the concept of race being a "relic" or "scientifically spurious" betrays a certain "blind progressivism" that should not be allowed to distract critical attention from the sociocultural reality of racial meaning. Indeed, the a priori method favored by philosophers—a method that is evident in Appiah's work and that is firmly committed to the search for necessary and sufficient criteria that should yield global definitions—is antithetical to Locke's more mature pluralistic philosophical sensibilities. His pluralistic philosophical commitments obviously influence his approach to race.[5]

Locke aggressively distances the concept of race from biological entanglements. He never assumes that the concept of race should be innately partial to a biological defense. So instead of viewing race as semantically destined to find a home in biology, he cultivates a conception of race nourished by highly suggestive cultural insights. In treating race as a cultural category, he observes the extent to which race functions, not as a sharply defined concept embedded in a natural scientific theory, but as a conceptual artifact readily malleable to cultural exploitation. Locke clearly considers complacent attempts to treat race as a biological concept—ultimately declaring it scientifically spurious—guilty of committing a category mistake. He correctly identifies race as enjoying a culturally based intellectual function and not one in the service of nature. To this extent, he focuses particularly "on the political [and cultural] implications of the idea that race is given meaning through the agency of human beings in concrete historical and social contexts, and is not a biological or natural category."[6] His lesson is that despite the marvelous analytical skills we competently employ to question the concept of race generally, the idea of race will nevertheless continue to thrive because it seems "reasonably consistent with aspects of people's life experiences."

Locke also considers the issue of race from the perspective of physical anthropology, particularly in his essay "The Problem of Race Classification."[7] Here, Locke anticipates Appiah's eagle-eye attention to the problem of criteria. He construes the issue surrounding the problem of criteria as a dilemma. On his view, if we assume that race requires criteria of usage, then we should either come up with workable criteria for using the concept of race or, as Appiah suggests, simply abandon this concept. Locke frames the issue in the following manner:

> The problem . . . today is not the problem of facts but of proper criteria for the facts; the entire scientific status and future of the consideration of man's group characters rest upon a decisive demonstration of what factors are really indicative of race, retrieving the science from the increasing confusion and cross-classification that the arbitrary selection of such criteria has inevitably brought about. The only other alternative is to abandon as altogether unscientific the conception of . . . physical race . . . as basic . . . and throw the category of race into the discard as another of the many popular misconceptions detrimentally foisted upon sciences.[8]

In the essay mentioned above, Locke reviews a book by Roland Dixon.[9] The significance of this review is that Locke exposes the contradiction at the heart of Dixon's enterprise to provide physical criteria for demarcating races. He points out that Dixon acknowledges the lack of adequate criteria for this identification of races. Dixon, despite this acknowledgment, offers physical criteria for the identification of race, criteria that presuppose that races are ideal types and not empirically real entities. Locke finds Dixon's position quite revealing since it betrays Dixon's contradictory stance on race. Locke writes:

> If we are not seriously mistaken [Dixon's book] will . . . [serve] as a sort of *reductio ad absurdum* test of the purely [physical] approach to the questions of human classification. No book brings us more clearly face to face with the issue between physical and biological anthropology, between the strictly anatomical and the more general morphological approach.[10]

The relevance of mentioning Locke's reaction to Dixon is precisely to underscore the extent to which Locke fully appreciates the more agonizing and frustrating aspects of attempts to provide criteria for the definition and classification of race. According to him:

> The paradox of Professor Dixon's book is that recognizing so clearly that the criteria of race-type which he chooses cannot be expected to conform with descriptive accuracy to the "natural race groups", he nevertheless persists in treating them in his conclusions as historical strains or actual races, with definite cultural traits and heredity, and responsible for characteristic effects and influences throughout human history. There is a flagrant inconsistency involved in treating these abstract race-types as equivalent to actual sub-species or natural and cultural race-groups.[11]

Locke summarily proceeds to quote Dixon confessing to the fact that "If by the term 'race' we mean to describe actually existing groups of people, as I think we should, then our types are certainly not races, since, with few exceptions, there are no groups of men who actually represent them."[12] I mention the last point to establish further that Appiah is not alone in recognizing the logical problems that plague attempts to provide criteria for the identification and definition of races.

Locke displays considerable intellectual bravery when he argues that we should salvage the concept of race even if science or rigorous philosophical thinking cannot offer a viable definition of it for contextually political and functional reasons. In this regard, he refuses to participate in the more complacent denunciations of race.

> [I] have had the courage of a very optimistic and steadfast belief that in the scientific approach to the race question, there was the possibility of a redemption for those false attitudes of mind which have, unfortunately, so complicated the idea and conception of race that there are a great many people who fancy that the best thing that can possibly be done, *if possible at all,* is to throw race out of the categories of human thinking.[13]

But he considers efforts to eliminate race from human thinking premature, even intellectually impotent. Instead of casting the blame on race, Locke certainly would emphasize the frustration experienced by those who subject themselves to the cognitive paralysis engendered by attempts to tame the semantic play of race. As Locke would have it, race is elusive but not necessarily meaningless.

Not intimidated in the least by those who announce the semantic bankruptcy of the concept of race, Locke recognizes race as a very significant category of social thinking in modern culture. He states:

I am fundamentally convinced that the term "race," the thought of race, represents a rather fundamental category in social thinking and that it is an idea that we can ill dispense with. In fact . . . the more thought of the right kind [that] can be centered in it, the more will the term [race] itself be redeemed, in light of its rather unfortunate history. The only way to treat the subject scientifically is to regard it as a center of meaning.[14]

Even while recognizing race as a tremendously compact and highly charged center of meaning, Locke insightfully underscores the fact that race is not an empty category. Indeed, we can correctly state that he did not evade the contestability of the term "race." This interpretation gives to race no finite nor sharp boundaries; race is semantically slippery in that no single determinate underlying principle or set of principles governs its application. This semantic fuzziness is not a defect; it rather testifies to the complexity of sociocultural concepts. Indeed, instead of being a defect, vagueness in the sociocultural realm requires that we study the political constitution of meaning, that is, examine the political, cultural, and social regimes that produce semantic meaning. As Locke writes,

What is race? That is the question which takes us back to the very root of the trouble. Race is not one thing—it is many things. In fact it has so many meanings that even were each meaning scientifically correct . . . there would necessarily arise conflict among such meanings, which would precipitate certain problems.[15]

He settles for a conception of race that is radically incompatible with Appiah's analytical strategy. This fact does not entail that competent critical analysis is useless or, for that matter, necessarily acidic toward social beliefs. What it underscores is that we can effectively unsettle ontologically and metaphysically empty categories through socially and culturally informed philosophical analysis.

Locke's Conception of Race

Locke offers his own accounting of race. Again, not surprisingly, he emphasizes the role that human intentions, practices, interests, and goals play in con-
ferring meaning upon certain concepts. To turn away from this complicated
activity and to launch a piercing attack against such concepts from the seeming
tranquility of disinterested analysis is to engage in a theoretically infertile
endeavor.

Race, according to Locke, is a collective construction. It is a conceptual
artifact burdened with discharging various social and cultural tasks. In another
context he states that "[r]ace . . . is itself a cultural product."[16] It can never succeed in qualifying as designating a physical natural kind. Locke writes:

> [R]eally, when the modern man talks about race . . . he is not talking about the
> anthropological or biological idea at all. [He is really talking about the histori-
> cal record of success or failure of] an ethnic group. As I pointed out, these
> groups, from the point of view of anthropology, are ethnic fictions. This does not
> mean that they do not exist . . . but it can be shown [that these groups do] not
> have as [permanent] designations those very factors upon which they pride
> themselves. They have neither purity of [blood] nor purity of type. They are the
> products of countless interminglings of types . . . and they are the results of infi-
> nite crossings of types. . . . They, however, maintain in name only this fetish of
> biological [purity]. Race as applied to social and ethnic groups has no meaning
> at all beyond that sense of kind, that sense of kith and kin which undoubtedly is
> somewhat of an advantage to any ethnic group that can maintain [it]. And yet,
> useful as it is, it is not to deny its usefulness that we call it an ethnic fiction.[17]

Consistent with his sociocultural conception of race, he admits that race as a
social construction claims no objective ontological status. Ontologically speaking, race takes on an "as if" status. We may talk about race as though it were a
natural kind, but race is actually a social kind or, rather, a cultural kind.[18] However, acknowledging race as either a social or cultural kind does not entail its
rejection. No philosopher can cause race to disappear through magical acts of
analytical wizardry. At the risk of exaggeration, cities are social constructions,
but their being social constructions need not lead us to declare them to be "false
cities." The core of Locke's view is that race is a cultural concept without an
objective empirical referent. The term "race" does not name a thing as the concepts of "tree," "leg," or "stone" do. Race names shifting fields of shared agreements or, put differently, galaxies of shared meanings. Locke continues: "[T]he
biological meaning of race has lapsed and the sociological meaning of race is
growing in significance. But that a group needs to consider itself an ethnic unit
is very different from the view that the group is [literally] an ethnic unit.[19]"

For Locke, the "white" lie about race is not that we believe that, objectively speaking, races exist. Rather the lie about race is the pretense that it is biologically legitimate or that a biological notion is the only plausible one. In making this point, he amplifies, once more, the social regimes that conspire to confer meaning on race. He writes:

> Race is . . . at present then, in a paradoxical stage. It amounts practically to social inheritance . . . and yet it parades itself as biological or anthropological inheritance. It really is either favorable or unfavorable social inheritance, which has been ascribed to anthropological differences. To the extent, therefore, that any man has race, he has inherited either a favorable or an unfavorable social heredity, which unfortunately is (typically) ascribed to factors which have not produced [it].[20]

One central theme in Locke's thinking, a theme articulated within the context of his axiological view and that extends to other areas of inquiry, is the idea that sociocultural concepts need not correspond to an independently existing reality in order to acquire validity within the context of human life. However, they remain legitimate to the extent that they are compatible with our varied interests and desires. Thus, what causes us to put race in question is not doubts about its philosophical and semantic validity but rather the blistering existential doubts generated by its functioning or malfunctioning in the context of our everyday lives. I take it that Locke would agree that for many thinkers, race is a seemingly permanent reality imposed upon them by others. However, we need not mistake its *permanence* for a metaphysical *permanence*.

Conclusion

Contrary to Appiah's call for a more rigorous dismantling of race, Locke brightens the apparent semantic darkness surrounding race by reminding us that "[r]ace is . . . both unreal and a seeming reality. Its demystification cannot be accomplished by even an airtight intellectual case, but only by hard and immensely complicated cultural and political struggle."[21] The virtue of Locke's position over Appiah's is that it allows for the fact that race can be weakened, if events warrant, not by intellectualism or abstraction, but only by contextualizing race within the flux of human life, that is, the world of everyday life. Engaging in formalistic hovering maneuvers above the lifeworld, the world of conflict and struggle, engenders at best a curious glance but not a serious confrontation or engagement with the ready-to-hand sociocultural concepts populating the lifeworld.

It is possible to raise certain critical objections to Locke's position. Let us consider Appiah's claim that all notions of race, even those culturally articulated or ethnically determined, presuppose the biological notion of race.[22] One possible criticism of Locke is that he fatally grounds the ethnic notion of race in the biological reality of race, despite his efforts to distance race from biological contamination. Locke was sensitive to this possible criticism, since he mentions the "unwarranted assumption of race as a determinant of culture."[23] It is not the case that Locke's sociocultural conception of race depends upon a biological notion of race. As previously stated, he understood the term "race" to be functioning as a pragmatic designator and not as rigidly designating groups of individuals based solely on physical characteristics. We can best grasp his position by appreciating his attempt to include ethnic characteristics in understanding race. He claims that if that is done, "[r]ace would have been regarded as primarily a matter of social heredity, and its distinctions due to the selective psychological 'set' of established cultural reactions."[24] His point is that the factors that make it possible to talk about race in the ethnic or sociocultural sense are the collective practice, values, interests, and so on of a group that one generation transfers to another. Here, there is permanence as well as rupture, but, on the whole, isolating certain culturally selected traits suffices for pragmatically isolating one group from another. At the risk of repetition and trying the reader's patience, it would help to amplify Locke's seemingly instructive focus on the sociocultural regime of race and to avoid entanglements with reductionist physical views. Locke, as early as 1923, states that

[t]he best consensus of opinion then seems to be that race is a fact in the social or ethnic sense, that it has been very erroneously associated with race in the physical sense and is therefore not scientifically commensurate with factors or conditions which explain or have produced physical race characters and differentiation, that it has a vital and significant relation to social culture, and that it must be explained in terms of social and historical causes.[25]

It is also instructive to note that Locke does not substitute a stagnant but, rather, a dynamic cultural notion of race for a biological and physical notion. He does not simply embrace an essentialist notion of race built upon an "iron cage" notion of culture. He grafts his notion of race on a fluid notion of cultural and ethnic exchange, continuity, and rupture. To this end, he writes:

[R]ace operates as tradition, as preferred traits and values, and when these things change culturally speaking ethnic remoulding is taking place. Race then ... seems to lie in that peculiar selective preference for certain culture-traits and resistance to certain others which is characteristic of all types and levels of social organization.[26]

Let us also consider a second line of criticism, specifically regarding Locke's attempt to approach race from a sociocultural perspective. K. L. Little refers to the strategy of substituting ethnicity for race to be "almost a species of magical technique based on the idea that something awkward or troublesome can be got rid of by the mere process of calling it by another name."[27] Stanley Garn, a leading American physical anthropologist, unsympathetically refers to these efforts as a form of "lexical surgery."[28] Little and Garn accept the reality of race and bitterly scorn attempts to eliminate the biological or physical notion of race. Obviously, unlike Appiah, they do not believe that the fuzziness of racial boundaries precludes using the concept of race. But at the same time they resist efforts such as Locke's to substitute ethnicity for race.

Their opposition to "lexical surgery" is an approach contrary to Locke's position. Locke does not reject human physical differences. Instead, he argues that human physical differences cannot sustain a coherent biological notion of race. To this extent, he essentially embraces a different style of thinking about race, that is, not viewing race exclusively as a problem about classifying human beings in terms of physical difference, but rather viewing it in terms of values, intentions, shared goals, and agreements. He also insightfully situates talk of race within the context of everyday culture and, in so doing, avoids treating such talk as philosophically equivalent to natural scientific discourse. Race talk, for him, is simply a species of talk about ethnic or cultural groups. We need not construe ethnicities as biological kinds. Once placed within the context of human practices, interests, goals, and values, ethnicities can best be considered "inventions." Locke certainly would agree, given his defense of axiological pluralism, "[t]hat ethnicity is something reinvented and reinterpreted in each generation by each individual, something over which he or she lacks [exclusive] control."[29] He does not seek to purchase philosophical economy at the price of having to declare sociocultural concepts, such as race, to be counterfeit. Finally, his own existence as a person of African descent adequately reinforces for him the everyday reality of social race.

Notes

1. Avery Gordon and Christopher Newfield, "White Philosophy," *Critical Inquiry* 20 (Summer 1994): 739–40.

2. Kwame Anthony Appiah, *In My Father's House: Africa in the Philosophy of Culture* (New York: Oxford University Press, 1992), 45.

3. See Appiah, *In My Father's House.*

4. Michael Omi and Howard Winant, *Racial Formation in the United States from the 1960s to the 1990s* (New York: Routledge, 1986), 68.

5. Leonard Harris's anthology of Locke's writing is the best place to get a grasp on his philosophical thinking. Harris's anthology also contains an excellent critical bibliography on Locke. Of special interest is Harris's essay "Rendering the Subtext: Subterranean Deconstructive Project." Leonard Harris, ed., *The Philosophy of Alain Locke: Harlem Renaissance and Beyond* (Philadelphia: Temple University Press, 1989).

6. David Roediger, *Towards the Abolition of Whiteness* (London: Routledge, 1994), 2.

7. Alain Locke, "The Problem of Racial Classification," in *Philosophy of Alain Locke,* ed. Harris, 165–73.

8 Locke, "Problem of Racial Classification," 164.

9. Roland Dixon, *The Racial History of Man* (New York: Charles Scribner's Sons, 1932).

10. Locke, "Problem of Racial Classification," 165.

11. Locke, "Problem of Racial Classification," 165–66.

12. Dixon, *Racial History of Man,* 502.

13. Alain Locke, *Race Contacts and Interracial Relations,* ed. Jeffrey C. Stewart (Washington, D.C.: Howard University Press, 1992), 1.

14. Locke, *Race Contacts and Interracial Relations,* 1–2.

15. Locke, *Race Contacts and Interracial Relations,* 2.

16. Alain Locke, "The Concept of Race as Applied to Social Culture," in *Philosophy of Alain Locke,* ed. Harris, 193.

17. Locke, *Race Contacts and Interracial Relations,* 11–12.

18. Lucius Outlaw Jr. recently adopted a position similar to Locke's. He refers to races as socionatural kinds. Lucius Outlaw, *On Race and Philosophy* (New York: Routledge, 1996), 7.

19. Locke, *Race Contacts and Interracial Relations,* 12.

20. Locke, *Race Contacts and Interracial Relations,* 12.

21. Roediger, *Towards the Abolition of Whiteness,* 6.

22. Anthony Appiah, "Racisms," in *Anatomy of Racism,* ed. D. T. Goldberg (Minneapolis: University of Minnesota Press, 1990).

23. Locke, "Concept of Race," 188–89.

24. Locke, "Concept of Race," 191.

25. Locke, "Concept of Race," 192.

26. Locke, "Concept of Race," 195.

27. K. L. Little, "UNESCO on Race," *Man,* no. 31 (1951): 17.

28 Stanley Garn, "Race," *Man* 200 (1951): 115.

29. Michael Fischer, "Ethnicity and the Post-Modern Arts of Memory," in *Writing and Culture,* ed. James Clifford and George E. Marcus (Berkeley and Los Angeles: University of California Press, 1986), 195.

14

Instrumental Relativism and Cultivated Pluralism: Alain Locke and Philosophy's Quest for a Common World

Kenneth W. Stikkers

Critics of cultural and philosophical pluralism commonly charge that such a project is but a disguise for vulgar relativism, which abandons philosophy's perennial quest for what is common in human experience, denies all notions of universal truth and goodness (i.e., denies the possibility of a common world, wherein we might all get along, peacefully and justly), and hence succumbs inevitably to partisan power politics of the most vicious sort.[1] Hannah Arendt, for one, well refuted such a criticism of pluralism with her typical eloquence:

> Only where things can be seen by many in a variety of aspects without changing their identity, so that those who are gathered around them know they see sameness in utter diversity, can worldly reality truly and reliably appear.
>
> Under the conditions of a common world, reality is not guaranteed primarily by the "common nature" of all men who constitute it, but rather by the fact that, differences of position and the resulting variety of perspectives notwithstanding, everybody is always concerned with the same object. If the sameness of the object can no longer be discerned, no common nature of men, least of all the unnatural conformism of a mass society, can prevent the destruction of the common world, which is usually preceded by the destruction of the many aspects in which it presents itself to human plurality.[2]

Contrary to its critics, the call for pluralism in philosophy, in terms of race, gender, and class, is a call to seek universality amidst multiplicity honestly and sincerely, rather than merely asserting some privileged perspective as universal.

Critics of philosophical pluralism complain, too, that the demand for diversity is driven by political rather than scholarly motives. I am suspicious of the assumption of a politically neutral philosophy: every philosophical inquiry, it seems, is steered by some set of interests. Such a claim, however, is no threat to philosophical objectivity and universality but only the first step honestly

209

toward it: one still must assess the relative legitimacy of those interests. It is not my intent to argue the point here; rather, I wish to suggest that there are good reasons to privilege, in the name of philosophical rigor, perspectives that historically have been marginalized or outright excluded from philosophy's ongoing conversation and to illustrate the point from African American philosophy. I wish to show, first, that African American philosophy generally and, second, Alain Locke especially, far from abandoning the perennial philosophical quest for universality amidst seeming multiplicity—that is, the quest for a common world—take it far more seriously than has the mainstream of the philosophic profession and, as a result, offer much to deepen our understanding of democracy.

Privileging the Margins: The Case of African American Philosophy

Is "African American philosophy" not legitimate philosophy, but ideology, because, after all, it is steered by a political agenda—to wit, the liberation of an oppressed people? The same is frequently asked (also rhetorically) with respect to "feminist philosophy." African American philosopher William T. Fontaine raised the issue already in 1944:

> [W]hat of [the Black scholar's] knowledge? Does he seek truth disinterestedly or does he have an ax to grind? Is there any correlation between his knowledge and the position occupied by the Negro in the American social order? Is his knowledge "socially determined"? Is it possible that sociopsychological factors such as resentment, aggression, rage, and the desire for equality make the mental set of the Negro scholar one of immediate group defense?[3]

Significantly, it never seemed to occur to Fontaine to ask the same questions of the overwhelmingly white academy. Do not privileged white scholars "have an ax to grind," something to defend?

Numerous scholars, including the American pragmatists, have well challenged the very possibility of a "disinterested truth," and I need not elaborate their critiques. Rather, I wish to note in Fontaine's suggestion the implicit common identification of "disinterested" with "universal." But disinterested knowledge would pertain to no one and not to all and hence is the antithesis, not the equivalent, of universality. We need instead to examine closely the interests represented in particular cases to determine to what extent they genuinely speak for all, but concealing those interests behind claims to disinterested and objective truth severely impedes such examination.

For example, Broadus N. Butler identified how African American philosophers, precisely while promoting their special interests of liberation, have contributed especially to our understanding of what is genuinely universal in the human condition.

In the main, Black American thinkers have contributed profound insights into what America ought to be and, by extension, what the universal condition and quality of existence of humankind ought to be. Their concentration has been upon . . . the achievement of an appropriate humane and democratic quality of life based in the proper universalization of the norms of equality, fraternity, and justice both in law and in the reality of the social contract. They have sought simultaneously a universal normative basis for unity, belonging, and governmental humaneness in the mediate realm and a similar basis for global cultural respect and just peace among the nations and institutions of humankind. This is in contrast to theories and postulations that have as their ultimate effect the support of systems of acquisitiveness, power, and dominance.[4]

Butler illustrates his claim through a detailed analysis of the writings of Frederick Douglass. Moreover, he suggests, such contributions have been made, not in spite of, but precisely because of the very political interests that motivated African American philosophers' inquiry in the first place, namely, full, equal participation in American institutions, which historically appealed to notions of a universal humanity.

Angela Davis, also illustrating her point from the life and writings of Frederick Douglass, makes a similar claim:

Are human beings free or are they not? Ought they be free or ought they not be free? The history of Afro-American literature furnishes an illuminating account of the nature of freedom, its extent and limits. Moreover, we should discover in Black literature an important perspective that is missing in so many of the discussions on the theme of freedom in the history of bourgeois philosophy. Afro-American literature incorporates the consciousness of a people who have continually been denied entrance into the real world of freedom, a people whose struggles and aspirations have exposed the inadequacies not only of the practice of freedom, but also of its very theoretical formulation.[5]

The main point here is that those who have been systematically "denied entrance into the real world of freedom" have a special interest in articulating with maximum clarity those universal human qualities upon which claims to rights and freedom are made. By contrast, those who take such rights and freedom for granted are not so motivated but are more likely to find it in their interests to avoid such clarity so as to conceal and protect their privileged status.

Indeed, both Butler and Davis show that it was precisely Douglass's ability to appeal with extraordinary clarity to the universal humanity that he shared with his slaveholder, in protest against, and resistance to, his enslaved condition that frequently brought down on him the owner's wrath.

A cruel irony of African American history is the many instances in which the yoke of oppression was made more severe precisely because Black Americans sought to hold white America to the rhetoric that it had used for its own liberational purposes. Such was the case, Cornel West shows, with respect to W. E. B. Du Bois. West is correct, I believe, in his judgment that it was Du Bois who first understood the privileged position of the oppressed in bringing humanity to a fuller understanding of the universal conditions for its freedom, dignity, and noblest possibilities: it is the wretched of the earth who have it most deeply within their own interests to guide philosophy in its perennial quest for a common world.

> Du Bois goes beyond them all [viz., all the pragmatists] in the scope and depth of his vision: creative powers reside among the wretched of the earth even in [especially in?] their subjugation, and the fragile structures of democracy in the world depend, in large part, on how these powers are ultimately exercised.[6]

While white America, in the years following Reconstruction, had largely given up on the ideal, nominally expressed in the documents of its founding, of universal freedom and human rights, such an ideal burned brightly in the minds and hearts of Black Americans, and that brightness often brought down on them even more heavily the yoke of oppression. West quotes Du Bois's chilling pronouncement, "Democracy died save in the hearts of Black folk."[7] And it was the tragedy of Du Bois in particular that he was persecuted for believing so wholeheartedly in the claims of universal human dignity, freedom, and rights in the foundational documents of American government, hounded by McCarthyism for daring to take Thomas Jefferson at his word.

What Alain Locke Teaches John Dewey about Democracy

Alain Locke embraced the term "relativism"—unfortunately, I believe—but he quickly and clearly clarified that his was not a final or absolute relativism but a means to a more authentic universalism—that is, a provisional generalization, always open to revision, that is derived inductively from a fair sampling of the rich variety of perspectives cultivated by the numerous cultural traditions inhabiting our globe, and never a universalism arrived at a priori as some particular perspective universally imposed. In other words, to help ensure that any claim about a universal humanity is truly that and not merely some particularism imperialistically imposed as "universal," we must retain as much of the plurality of human experiences as possible, in what I would prefer to call a "cultivated pluralism," rather than "relativism," guided by the principles Locke outlined of equivalence, reciprocity, and limited convertibility. "Equivalence" means the assumption that alien cultures manifest a long history of responses to innumerable difficult circumstances equivalent in structure and value to one's own: underlying the manifold differences in external cultural forms is a striking set of "functional similarities" in those responses.[8] After all, who are we who have not experienced others' history to judge the responses they have made to their own trials and to assume flippantly that our own culture could have done things better? But cultural traditions carry no intrinsic value: they must continually be evaluated in terms of their relevance for dealing with new problematic circumstances. "Reciprocity" means that we must avoid thinking of cultures as monolithic, static structures: they are highly composite and the result of the continuous reciprocal influence of other cultures. Thus, it is foolish to make judgments about cultures—for example, about their "superiority" or "inferiority"—as a whole; rather, specific elements of cultures must be compared, contrasted, and judged. Furthermore, the organic nature of cultural evolution and adaptation places natural limits on one culture's ability to appropriate another. Only selected elements of a culture can be absorbed into the living tissues of another culture; never is there wholesale assimilation.

Locke's instrumental relativism and cultivated pluralism, by contrast to what he described as William James's "anarchic pluralism and relativism," aims, then, not merely to celebrate difference for the sheer aesthetic enjoyment of difference but as a means to create a world in which we can all somehow get along peaceably.[9] Aesthetics is an extremely important element in Locke's understanding of cultural pluralism, but aesthetic values are not the basis for cultivating such pluralism; the evils of bigotry are much too serious to be left to aesthetics. Like John Dewey, Locke embraced democracy as a way of life rather than as merely a political form, as expressive of his universalist ideal, but he rejected Dewey's identification of democracy with experimental science. For Locke, Dewey's notion of experimental science was much too naive, for it assumes some clear and univocal criteria for testing hypotheses. Just as the bulk of traditional Western sciences have frequently been too quick to bestow universal validity upon some particular perspective, so Dewey seems oblivious to the power dynamics whereby the testing of hypotheses is judged successful or not. Rather, as we have suggested above, the "universal validity" of test results, and hence the very notions of "science" and "democracy," already presupposes cultivated pluralism, or the notion that the success of any democratic experiment must be evaluated from a variety of cultural perspectives and according to a multiplicity of norms.

Dewey assumes plurality among both cultures and individuals; differences are taken as a basic fact of social life. Furthermore, following Peirce, the collision of beliefs is a major source of irritation, one large group of problematic situations, that leads to inquiry. Nondemocratic peoples will cling tenaciously to their opinions and seek to resolve differences imperialistically, through sheer force of will and power. By contrast, democratic peoples—those for whom democracy is a habit of living and not merely a political form—will be led by such irritation to examine critically their opinions and to achieve experimentally some peaceful convergence of interests and views. But there is no steady movement toward pure homogeneity; new differences continuously emerge, producing new irritations and problematic situations.

But consensus may be only apparent; the workings of powers that coerce minorities into adopting views of the majority may be hidden. To guard against such camouflaged coercions, plurality cannot be assumed but must be cultivated; difference must be sustained, at least provisionally. Locke's cultivated pluralism, by contrast to Dewey's assumed pluralism, thus serves several very important functions for democracy. First, it helps to ensure that an individual's or group's adoption of another's views, values, or norms is the result of free, deliberative judgment and not of coercion. Second, the intentional sustaining of differences brings into sharper awareness the social character of individual thought. The individual becomes increasingly aware that his or her beliefs have emerged from a definite sociocultural context and hence are strongly shaped by his or her membership in a particular social group—one's socialized opinions cease to be self-evident truths. A critical space is thus created wherein individuals can reflect upon, and better judge the soundness of, their inherited beliefs. Third, cultivated pluralism enhances global culture's ability to respond to new problematic situations by preserving hypotheses that may prove useful in those situations but that may be discarded prematurely if convergence of beliefs comes too quickly. Dewey argued eloquently and forcefully in several places, to be sure, for the need for cultural groups to preserve elements of their heritages.[10] But his statements in this regard appear, within his corpus as a whole, as corrective afterthoughts. The cultivation of cultural pluralism stems more, for Dewey, from the need for cultures to be tolerant of, and to learn from, one another and hence is not as central to his democratic vision as it is to Locke's.

Indeed, it was Josiah Royce's theories of loyalty and community and Locke's experience in the Baha'i faith, rather than Dewey's notion of democracy tied to experimental science, that provided the main intellectual influences on Locke's pluralism. The Baha'i religion provided Locke the concrete experience of unity in diversity, for a central teaching of that faith is that the Word of God is essentially one but is spoken differently through the prophets of the various religions of the world, in ways relative to unique sociohistorical conditions. Locke expressed the Baha'i principle with this metaphor: "think of reality as a central fact and a white light broken up by the prism of human nature into a spectrum of values."[11] For Royce, partisan loyalties must grow into an appreciation of another's loyalties, even when they contradict one's own, lest those loyalties lead to bigotry and xenophobia: I come to recognize the loyalty of my neighbor as "structurally equivalent" to my own—not necessarily equivalent in content—and out of that recognition there may grow a loyalty to an idea of loyalty, which I, my neighbor, and even my enemy might come to share. But loyalty to universal humanity through loyalty to loyalty must be grounded first in some particular loyalty, lest it become too abstract, vague, and hollow: one professes love of humankind while continuing to hate individual persons. One cannot come to love another in his or her loyalty if one has no concrete, particular loyalties of one's own. Thus I might come to love even my enemy in his or her loyalty to his or her own cause, even when that cause is at war with my own. The soldier respects the fact of his enemy's loyalty (e.g., his willingness to die for his cause), and, even while continuing to judge that cause to be wrong, now conceives his enemy as a person capable of loyalties like one's own. Thus, the enemy ceases to appear subhuman. Locke quickly grasped this point in Royce's philosophy that has frequently escaped his readers, and here we see the seed of Locke's own notion of equivalence and the central idea that led him away from ardent assimilationist views and toward becoming one of the chief celebrants of the distinct cultural accomplishments of African Americans in the Harlem Renaissance.[12] Locke came to see that African Americans could not participate meaningfully in the emergent global culture—and, hopefully, global democracy—unless that participation was first grounded in a profound appreciation of, and loyalty to, their own history.

But Locke's relativism, with its notion of structural equivalence, does not end up with all loyalties being equal—the fear of all critics of relativism. The loyalty of the slaveholder to the system of slavery is not, in the end and in substance, equal in value to the loyalty of the slave to his freedom. One can, and ought to, condemn the institution of slavery to which the slaveholder is loyal, while still valuing the slaveholder as a human being who, like oneself, is capable of forming loyalties of his or her own, however misguided we might judge the objects of those loyalties to be. Royce's principle of loyalty to loyalty provides a powerful conceptual tool for enabling us to love the sinner while condemning the sin. Valuative judgment is both possible and necessary, but it must never be the judgment of one community, with its own loyalties, of another culture, with its own loyalties, for then justice will be but as Thrasymachus described it long ago, "the interest of the strongest," and might will forever make right. Rather, valuative judgment must be the radically inclusive judgment of all communities, out of the plurality of their own loyalties. When all the human communities are gathered round to view the matter "in [their] utter diversity," to borrow Arendt's phrase from the quotation with which we opened, and all the voices heard, then, and only then, can objective "worldly reality truly and reliably appear."

Notes

1. See, e.g., Gary Hull, "Multiculturalism and the Assault on Objectivity" (paper presented at meeting of the Ayn Rand Society, in conjunction with the American Philosophical Association, Eastern Division, Boston, 29 December 1994).

2. Hannah Arendt, *The Human Condition: A Study of the Central Dilemmas Facing Modern Man* (Garden City, N.Y.: Doubleday, 1958), 52–53. Johnny Washington rightfully has noted striking similarities between Arendt and Locke in this regard. See Johnny Washington, *Alain Locke and Philosophy: A Quest for Cultural Pluralism,* Contributions in Afro-American and African Studies no. 94 (New York: Greenwood Press, 1986), 39 ff.

3. William T. Fontaine, "'Social Determination' in the Writings of Negro Scholars" (1944), in *Philosophy Born of Struggle: Anthology of Afro-American Philosophy from 1917,* ed. Leonard Harris (Dubuque, Iowa: Kendall/Hunt, 1983), 90.

4. Broadus N. Butler, "Frederick Douglass: The Black Philosopher in the United States: A Commentary," in *Philosophy Born of Struggle,* ed. Harris, 2.

5. Angela Davis, "Unfinished Lecture on Liberation–2," in *Philosophy Born of Struggle,* ed. Harris, 130.

6. Cornel West, *The American Evasion of Philosophy: A Genealogy of Pragmatism* (Madison: University of Wisconsin Press, 1989), 148.

7. W. E. B. Du Bois, *Black Reconstruction: An Essay toward a History of the Part Which Black Folk Played in the Attempt to Reconstruct Democracy in America, 1860–1877* (New York: Russell & Russell, 1935), 30, quoted in West, *American Evasion of Philosophy,* 147.

8. Leonard Harris, ed., *The Philosophy of Alain Locke: Harlem Renaissance and Beyond* (Philadelphia: Temple University Press, 1989), 73.

9. Alain Locke, "Pluralism and Intellectual Democracy," in *Philosophy of Alain Locke,* ed. Harris, 55.

10. See, e.g., John Dewey, "Nationalizing Education," in *The Middle Works, 1899–1924,* ed. Jo Ann Boydston (Carbondale: Southern Illinois University Press, 1976), 10: 205.

11. Alain Locke, "Values and Imperatives," in *Philosophy of Alain Locke,* ed. Harris, 47.

12. George Hutchinson, *The Harlem Renaissance in Black and White* (Cambridge: Harvard University Press, 1995), 81.

PART IV

EDIFICATION AND EDUCATION

15

Adult Education and Democratic Values: Alain Locke on the Nature and Purpose of Adult Education for African Americans

Talmadge C. Guy

In the several decades from the turn of the century to the civil rights movement of the 1950s and 1960s, African American educators and activists debated the goals and purpose of education for African Americans in the United States. The primary focus of this debate was the education of children. While much has been written about this (e.g., the Booker T. Washington–W. E. B. Du Bois debate of the early twentieth century), little is actually known about the efforts of African American educators and activists to build an adult education movement to meet the educational needs of African American adults. This chapter addresses Alain Locke's quest to develop a rationale and a model for African American adult education. This discussion is important since the question of the aim and purpose of education for African Americans continues to be discussed by activists and educators, although with little direct focus on adult educational needs of the African American community.[1]

In examining Locke's views about African American adult education in American society, I will refer to the period of the late 1930s and early 1940s, during which interest grew in the nascent African American adult education movement. I want to use some of the discussions during the series of conferences on adult education and the Negro that took place from 1938 to 1941 along with the publication of syllabi on African American issues and culture to illuminate the issues related to African American adult education and how cultural and political influences helped to shape Locke's philosophy of adult education for African Americans. Key in this discussion will be a review of Locke's thinking as it emerged during the 1940s in the context of world war and the emergence of the nuclear age. I will conclude with some comments about the continuing relevance of the issues Locke examined as he sought to situate African American adult education within the larger political and cultural context of American society.

The Paradox of Negro Adult Education

In the 1920s and 1930s, at the time of the growth of the organized adult education movement in the United States, education for African Americans was generally segregated in most parts of the country. In the South, Jim Crow laws prevented Blacks from using the same public accommodations as whites including public schools, libraries, and colleges and universities. In the North and West, de facto segregation was the rule, as segregated housing led to segregated education.[2] In this climate of segregation, white leaders of the adult education movement asked whether adult education, with its nonformal and voluntary character, could serve Negro needs.[3] The liberal establishment of the American Association of Adult Education (AAAE) and its philanthropic benefactor, the Carnegie Corporation, became interested in expanding opportunities for adult education throughout the United States, including adult education among African Americans.

While serving on the executive board of the AAAE, Alain Locke advocated cultural education as the basis for adult education among African Americans— indeed for all Americans. Locke had served as the primary liaison between two pilot projects in African American adult education in Harlem and Atlanta and the AAAE, which was responsible for overseeing the projects. During his service as liaison with, and evaluator of, the projects, Locke made clear his ideas about the importance of race-based, culturally oriented curricula to extend "such programs to every considerable Negro community in the country."[4] Despite its support of adult education among racial and ethnic minorities, the AAAE board and executive leadership eschewed race-based or culturally grounded adult education programs as having too narrow a basis and focusing too much on popular rather than higher culture.

Similar but Not Same: A Rationale for a Separate Program of African American Adult Education

What rationale did Locke develop for a national program of adult education? In a 1938 keynote speech before the First Conference on Adult Education and the Negro at Hampton Institute in Virginia, Locke stated: "The movement for adult education among any disadvantaged group must have a dynamic and enthusiasm-compelling drive. Beyond the mere literacy level, enlarging horizons and broadening human values must dominate it or the movement will stall."[5] Speaking before an interracial audience, Locke opposed the view of Negro adult education needs as somehow different from, or irrelevant to, the adult education needs of white America. He complained that "educational meat for one racial group must [not be seen as] educational poison or anathema to another," and he worried that this idea had infiltrated the adult education movement to "frustrate the general application" of adult education to the learning needs of adults from all backgrounds.[6] In the end, the adult educational needs of African Americans were no different in kind from those of white Americans.

Locke believed, in his philosophy of cultural adult education for African Americans, that African American adult education was not to be swallowed up into an American educational melting pot.[7] Consistent with his progressive adult education philosophy, Locke's goal was much more subtle. On a human level, African American adult learners had needs and concerns similar to those of European Americans. But because of racism, Negro needs were different in degree, which made all the difference in terms of adult education. Locke argued that African Americans, like whites, wanted to lead fulfilling lives and to be respected as contributing members of society. As victims of racism, African Americans faced dire problems of poverty and discrimination that produced low morale and lack of self-confidence and group solidarity. These circumstances called for special educational measures.

Locke argued that self-knowledge through cultural studies was essential to African American race progress in America. Absent a reconstructed sense of self and community, African Americans were doomed to be passive recipients of white America's racist image of them. Locke's views about ethnic and cultural diversity were similar to those of other cultural pluralists who argued that European ethnic groups should be allowed the opportunity to retain their ethnic heritage while being fully American.[8]

Elaborating on the idea of a similar but separate adult education for Negroes, Ira D. A. Reid asserted a need for a "different type of adult education for Negroes"—a race-based program of adult education relating directly to the problems faced by African Americans in their daily lives.[9] In other words, the discrepancy between the American democratic ideal and the American white supremacist reality was the basis for establishing a unique program of adult education to meet the particular needs of Negroes. After all, who else was in a position to "advise about the Negro's economic [social, or cultural] plight . . . if not the Negro?"[10]

Locke agreed with Reid and went even further, arguing that the cultural and psychological dimensions of the African American existence should be a central focus of adult education. African American culture should serve as a basis for culturally relevant adult education that would address the fundamental issues of self-definition, self-determination, identity, and community faced by African Americans. Locke's emphasis upon culture as the basis for African American adult education was undoubtedly influenced by the Harlem

Renaissance, in which he played an important background role as commentator and critic. Several factors fueled the possibility of establishing a program of cultural education. Among these was the growing recognition of African American cultural production spawned in part by the writers, artists, and musicians of the Harlem Renaissance. In addition, several important studies were published that identified Africanisms evident in African American culture that had survived the slave experience.[11]

Prior to the Harlem Renaissance and the idea of the New Negro, cultural education had not been a major element in the debate over African American education.[12] With the recognition of a viable African American cultural heritage, Locke's proposal for African American adult education took advantage of the newly identified elements of African American culture and coupled them with the focus on contemporary problems that was part and parcel of the progressive adult education movement.[13] African American education could refocus on the nature of the cultural heritage of African Americans as an answer to the double-consciousness dilemma articulated by Du Bois.[14]

Locke's ideas about cultural adult education for African Americans were largely outside African American educational discourse. This discourse had been framed by the Washington–Du Bois debate over practical versus liberal education. Locke's vision of adult education was influenced by the conceptual development within the adult education movement itself. Falling clearly within the tradition that saw adult education as contributing to social change, Locke was loosely aligned with other adult educators, such as Eduard Lindeman, who argued that adult education should contribute something to the individual or group development of adult learners but should also contribute to the growth and development of the larger society.[15]

Author of *The Meaning of Adult Education*, Lindeman had produced a classic statement for adult educators influenced by the philosophical school of progressivism. Progressivism embraced a modernist optimism—the possibility of broad social change in the future coupled with a belief in the ability of individuals to create change in the short term. Central to Lindeman's vision of adult education was the idea of social change, that is, that progress could be made given the right focus of adult learners' energies and the application of a sound process based on rational definition of problems and consideration of appropriate solutions.[16] This view of adult education, absent its more activist strains, was at the heart of the vision of adult education of the Carnegie Corporation and the AAAE, which saw the aim of adult education as helping adults live more productively and participate more fully in American democracy.

It was just such a notion of adult education and social change that animated Locke's view of cultural adult education. Using adult education to provide a revitalized self-image, African American adult learners would develop a positive sense of self and be motivated to address their problems in a "constructive and non-partisan way."[17] Locke saw, as Lindeman did, that adult education is a process in which problems and situations confronting adults "could be analyzed and actions planned and in which adults could discover the meaning of their experiences."[18] Locke was concerned about the demoralizing effect of racism and segregation upon the African American mind and spirit, which subverted the possibility for constructive social action.

Given that adult education provided a process, what, then, was to be the content of African American cultural adult education? The cultural explosion among the Harlem Renaissance literati and the discoveries regarding continuities in African culture to the New World provided a basis for curriculum development. In fact, Locke's work with the adult education experiments in Negro adult education during the early 1930s, especially the adult education program in Harlem, depended heavily on the availability of materials and artifacts in the collection of Arthur Schomburg.[19]

The emergence of cultural adult education, then, was partly related to the new attitudes toward African American culture and the discovery of Africanisms in African American culture and language. However, adult educators faced a significant obstacle created by the lack of suitable curriculum materials related to racial and cultural topics. In an effort to fill some of the gaps, Locke had served as general editor of a series of sourcebooks, the Bronze Booklets, to be used in African American adult education groups. The series was published beginning in 1936 by the Associates in Negro Folk Education. The anticipated titles suggest the cultural and social themes that Locke saw as central to the development of cultural adult education and also provide a glimpse into the African cultural elements that carried over to African American culture and language: *World Aspects of the Race Problem, The Economic Side of the Race Question, The Negro and His Music, The Negro in American Drama, Social Reconstruction and the Negro, the Art of the Negro Past and Present, The Negro in American Fiction and Poetry, An Outline of Negro History*, and *Experiments in Negro Adult Education.*

The Critical Turn: The Experience and Status of African Americans in American Social Structure

The beginning of the 1940s marked a significant turn in national interests.[20] The 1930s had been marked by economic crisis. At the turn of the decade, it was increasingly clear that the United States would be drawn into the war in Europe as well as a possible conflict with Japan in Asia. Among African American leaders, the possibility of war called attention to the position of African

Americans in the so-called defense of democracy. Where the earlier conferences on adult education and the Negro had concentrated on the economic needs of African Americans, the 1940 conference focused on the preparation for America's entry into the war and national defense.

This refocusing of attention highlighted the problem that African Americans faced in trying to determine their support for the war against racism in Europe. Speaking to the conference participants, Rayford Logan said: "I am quite disturbed by the emphasis that is given in the United States to religious persecution in Germany. . . . The emphasis is on religion rather than upon race . . . because careful students of public opinion in the United States know that *religious* freedom is the better issue on which to gain support than racial equality."[21] White America's desire to keep African Americans in a subordinate position was sufficient cause to question the role that African Americans should play in the defense of liberty, a liberty denied to them.

It is no surprise, then, that at the 1940 conference Locke asserted the need for more than a cultural emphasis blended with attention to practical concerns. He suggested that adult education for African Americans look at the broader problem of American society and African Americans' place in that society as a racial minority. "The first stepping stone of constructive social effort is to know where you are and to know what socio-economic situations are back of it."[22] This statement marked a turning point in Locke's thinking about education, culture, and social change. In his earlier speeches and writings, Locke had emphasized the importance of education and cultural knowledge for the "morale" of the Negro in hopes of providing hope and vision for change. Locke's interest in this earlier phase was to reconstruct the African American self-image as a first step to constructive social change. Learning about African American and African culture and history, the discussion of pressing social problems, the identification of resources to address those problems, and the development of a sense of community based on a sense of ethnic identity rather than common oppression were the aims to which Locke aspired in developing a rationale for African American adult education prior to 1940.

A significant dimension of black-white relations in America is the sociopolitical problem of majority-minority relations. African Americans continued to be marginal and oppressed people with little political or economic power to change their circumstances. Gunnar Myrdal's study of the American Negro, *An American Dilemma,* portrayed the race problem as a unique problem of American democracy—one that presented a dilemma for Americans in the sense that the core American values of freedom and justice were only partly realized. The dilemma rested in the American belief in freedom and democracy while many white Americans were reluctant to recognize African Americans as equals.

The caste condition of African Americans was difficult to justify in a society founded on democratic values and the principle of freedom. Locke's attention to the peculiar problems of the American democracy and race meant the rethinking of fundamental cultural pluralist principles. With his typical penchant for directness and clarity, Locke drew the question into immediate focus. How could the subservient status of African Americans be transformed into one of equality and respect in American society? The answer to this question depended on two factors: the ability of African Americans to transform their own reality, and the willingness of white Americans to be open to, if not entirely accepting of, African Americans. The melting pot metaphor would be dispensed with and, in its place, a kind of cosmopolitan multicultural stew would be substituted. Locke's cosmopolitanism rested on the idea that assimilation was not a feasible alternative for African Americans and separatism was equally unfeasible if not unwise. The only practical choice was "merger without fusion."[23]

For example, for those persons able to acquire the education and mannerisms of middle-class American society, assimilation could allow them to participate in the larger society while retaining a clear cultural identity. Locke himself attempted to bridge the two worlds of color. As an intellectual, he obtained a first-rate education and was intellectually capable of participating in the life of the Anglo-American intelligentsia. His involvement with the AAAE and the fledgling African American adult education movement made it clear that no matter how capable or talented the African American leadership, a person of color was subordinate to white leadership.

However, the societal transformation that Locke envisioned did not relegate African Americans to a place of permanent minority status. In fact, he specifically condemned the notion of "minority" as a consequence of numerical insufficiency. Locke observed that minority status was essentially a political status: "Minority does not mean numbers it means status."[24] Lack of political or economic power relegated African Americans to a minor place in American society. The implication is that the very use of the term "minority" suggests its mode of creation—cultural domination.

The Choices of Cultural Minorities: Assimilation, Separation, or "Merger without Fusion"

Living as a minority group within a hostile larger society, African Americans faced a central question: to integrate—that is, to merge—or to remain separate. The political consequence of remaining separate was to remain isolated and marginal. The political consequence of merging with the larger society was to gain some measure of influence for individuals at the loss of group identity and cohesion. While African American leadership was not united in its ideology, it was certainly aware of the loss of political power resulting from assimilation.

Many ethnic groups had arrived in America only to be more or less assimilated into Anglo-American cultural values and living patterns. Yet, some groups—African Americans chief among them—could not assimilate satisfactorily without risking loss of identity and esteem within their own community or without suffering alienation and subtle discrimination from whites. For middle-class, educated African Americans, this situation seemed most acute. Nevertheless, adopting the style, dress, manners, and education necessary to compete within white society still left this group with a problem of the color line.

In an article entitled "The Negro Group" (1944) Locke observed a third option for African Americans: protest. "We have made more substantial gains in the militant phases [of our history] than in others."[25] But protest should be based on ideals that transcend particular group interests.

Adult Education and Democratic Process: Particularism and Universalism

Locke argued that the success of America depended in large measure on the universal acceptance of the principles of equality expressed in the Constitution. American democracy required the uncritical acceptance of faith in constitutional values. Therefore, the acceptance of African Americans as full citizens and participants in American society represented only part of a larger problem. All groups that were perceived as being different represented threats to social cohesion. To embrace American democratic constitutional values meant conformity to a single standard of belief and conduct, particularly in times of crisis. Any form of protest or dissent from a minority group was likely to be regarded as treason and would not be tolerated. Lyman Bryson alerted representatives to the 1940 conference on the Negro and adult education to this very situation, commenting that "the vast majority of the people are getting more intolerant of minority opinions, more angry with those who disagree with them and less patient with the slow deliberations of democracy."[26]

Locke perceived this as a paradox of democratic living. Valuing and advancing one's own culture, especially a minority culture, led to the risk of being different and, therefore, viewed as antidemocratic. The dynamic process of interacting with members of other cultural groups on the basis of fairness and equity while retaining one's own cultural identity was an ideal that cultural pluralists had advanced. However, shared, democratic, communal life on the basis of openness and acceptance of the culturally different remained an elusive goal. In this formulation, particularism and universalism must live side-by-side and not as antithetical aspects of the assimilation/separation assumptions of America the melting pot. In this regard, particularism and universalism become aspects of the dynamic tension involved in social relations based on a cosmopolitan conception of American society. The values of democracy and liberty are transformed, inasmuch as one of the criteria of effective liberty is the quality of the relationships among social groups that are culturally constituted.

For Locke, then, culturally relevant and socially effective adult education in such a context must strive to inculcate the values that drive such a conception of democracy, not just the explicit values of freedom, justice, and equality but also, and just as important, the educational concomitants of democratic values, such as lifelong learning, dialogue, and reflection. Learning understood simply as the acquisition of skills or the formation of moral habits falls short of the requirements for a society democratically constituted on pluralistic cultural values.

Adult Education as a Method of Resolving Racial Conflict

In a very important essay on education written in 1950, "The Need for a New Organon in Education," Locke challenged the then conventional education wisdom of emphasizing the development of critical thinking skills as a means to successful living. Locke believed that the crisis of contemporary education depended on two points: "the discovery of integrating elements for knowledge and the search for focalizing approaches in education."[27] Locke believed that specialized scientific knowledge was increasingly separated from the routine of everyday life. The cultural knowledge of African Americans and other ethnic groups became secondary to the regulation of scientifically derived knowledge. Local experience was devalued in favor of universal scientific knowledge, effectively disadvantaging adult learners whose lived experience belied the existence of universal values such as truth, human progress, justice, and equality.

What Locke called for was not continued refinement of curricula or instructional methods but a fundamental rethinking of educational direction and purposes. The reason for this was what he termed the "cultural crisis," by which he meant the increasing distance between the requirements of daily life and the formal demands of education and credentialed learning as a requirement for successful economic and political life. Acknowledging that some curricular reform was desirable from time to time, Locke called for the use of pedagogical processes that ensured the "development of new ways of thinking *about* [education's] newly reorganized content"—a critical pedagogy, if you will, that would bring to light the disjunctures between articulated social values on the one hand and actual lived experiences and the realities of social structure within American society on the other.[28]

Rather than emphasizing modes of thinking that derive from positivist conceptions of knowledge, Locke saw as an essential the development of new, more global modes of thinking. Patently antitechnicist in his conception of this process, Locke advocated that educators should develop in their learners a "capacity for evaluative criticism" as opposed to a detached critical capacity that only served to undermine the goals of cross-cultural understanding.[29] Furthermore, adult education must combat the disadvantages of parochial thinking and anticipate that cross-cultural learning situations produce conflict. Educators must not shy away from this conflict but rather trace the history of its development to bring to light objective features of the current social conflict and inequality. In all of this, adult educators must hold to an ideological position to act against oppression and to support the disadvantaged.

Locke placed faith in the capacity of humankind, properly developed, to resolve the conflict among peoples of varying cultural, ethnic, racial, and ideological backgrounds. Social life, constituted in an understanding of culture in which values are central, must become a real touch point in the educational process to adequately prepare people to live in a pluralistic society.

But in the same article Locke also called for curricular reform that is more culturally and ethnically inclusive. Recalling that during the AAAE experiments in Negro education, he had argued that the racially oriented material of African American adult education should also be used in white adult education groups, Locke expanded this idea to include a reformulation and broadening of traditional liberal arts curricula to be more inclusive of the world's cultures.

> With very few exceptions, the general education curriculum centers around the history of civilization. This seems a general recognition of the prime importance today of a fuller and more comprehending knowledge of man. This generally conceded goal of an "integrated" education is, of course, the old humanist ideal and objective of the best possible human and self-understanding. But it recurs in our age in a radically new context, and as something only realizable in an essentially scientific way. Instead of being based as before on the universal, common character of man, abstractly and rationalistically conceived, it rests on the concrete study of man in all his infinite variety. If it is to yield any effective integration, that must be derived from an objective appraisal and understanding of the particularities of difference, both cultural and ideological.[30]

Citing cultural anthropology as a paradigm of such a curricular approach,

Locke argued for what he terms a "historical-comparative approach" in which cross-cultural learning and understanding would be developed on the basis of an attitude of nonjudgmental openness, while not forsaking one's own cultural or ideological background.

Calling his approach "critical relativism," Locke identifies six potential goals:

1. implement an objective interpretation of values by referring them realistically to their social and cultural backgrounds,

2. interpret values concretely as functional adaptations to these backgrounds, and thus make clear their historical and functional relativity. An objective criterion of functional sufficiency and insufficiency would thereby be set up as a pragmatic test of value adequacy or inadequacy,

3. claim or impute no validity for values beyond this relativistic framework, and so counteract value dogmatism based on regarding them as universals good and true for all times and all places,

4. confine its consideration of ideology to the prime function and real status of being the adjunct rationalization of values and value interests,

5. trace value development and change as a dynamic process instead of in terms of unrealistic analytic categories, and so eliminating the traditional illusions produced by generalized value terms—*viz.*, static values and fixed value concepts and 'ideals,'

6. reinforce current semantic criticism of academic value controversy by stressing this realistic value dynamics as a substitute for traditional value analytics, with its unrealistic symbols and overgeneralized concepts.

Although Locke began this paper with a modest defense of his views, no less than a complete reformulation of the educational process was his objective. At the end, he charged education with the purpose of fulfilling the aims of cultural pluralism.[31]

Adult Education: Cultural Interaction and Race Contact

While Locke's critical relativism was broad in its outline and general in its statement of pedagogy, he offered it as a basis for a revitalized system of education.[32] It thereby becomes a tool to reconceptualize adult education as a medium of intercultural contact. Adult education, however, should not make the mistake of seeing the solution to intergroup conflict as resting in the changed attitudes of individuals within specific interactional situations. Locke argued that one of the drawbacks of approaches like intercultural education or the intergroup method that became popular during the 1940s was their emphasis on changing individual attitudes. This focus on individual attitudes and behaviors shifted attention away from the more fundamental issue of how attitudes and behaviors are shaped by social structure. "[The] chief error in the moralistic approach is the treatment of the individual as a source and center of group attitudes rather than society itself."[33] Even when traditional intercultural education is successful at changing individual attitudes, according to Locke, its results are spotty and insufficient. It is society that must be indicted, not the individuals who make it up.

The importance of analyzing the societal sources for intercultural conflict is a theme that Locke developed throughout the 1940s. African Americans, he claimed, should come to a greater understanding that their subordinate condition is a consequence of societal factors, not of deficits among African Americans. As if to reflect critically on his own experience, Locke asserted that "One has only to call to mind such frequently observable majority phenomena as those persons sentimentally friendly and philanthropically inclined toward one particular minority group while rabidly prejudiced toward some other minority. In some cases it almost seems as though prejudice was intensified through being focused upon a narrower social area."[34] Surely, his own experience provided a critical point of reevaluation of these issues, because Locke had been in close communication with white philanthropists who supported the Harlem Renaissance.

During the AAAE experiments in African American education, Locke's service as consultant and go-between for the Harlem and Atlanta experiments, as well as his experience editing the Bronze Booklets, led him to a clearer understanding of the relationship between the white, well-meaning friend of African American progress and the real limitations imposed by such a relationship. The well-intentioned majority person is still subject to limitations that might undermine his or her stated intentions. The supported minority person must be aware of the risks involved in accepting assistance.

Another problem arising from a wider contact among racial groups is the problem faced by disempowered minority groups who must now interact with confidence and self-assurance with the majority group. Constant vigilance must be given to the reactions of minority groups to intercultural contact because of the legacy of oppression and separation: "one need only call to mind such flagrant inconsistencies as anti-Semitism among negroes [*sic*] and Negrophobia among Jews and foreign immigrants."[35] The internalization of racism and ethnocentrism among minority groups was a serious problem that manifested itself in minority conflict and bigotry. The development of such attitudes and behaviors not only was inconsistent with empowering persons through education but also undermined the practice of democracy. Adult educators must challenge such negative attitudes and beliefs among ethnic and racial minorities.

The process of addressing intergroup conflict and misunderstanding must take the form of dialectically objectifying or mediating two opposing positions. Here Locke points out the need to assure the incorporation of the minority group viewpoint, since so often it is only the majority view that holds sway. If intergroup conflict is truly to be resolved, a situation analysis that includes the perspectives of both sides must be conducted. The process of mediating the two views is threefold: "[F]irst, transcending the limitations of the orthodox majority viewpoint, second, taking into careful but unsentimental consideration minority attitudes and reaction, [and] third, striking an objective mean between these positions."[36] Locke certainly did not mean, however, that egregious wrongs by one group against another could be resolved by striking some compromise.

It is not the extreme case of obvious violence and injustice at which Locke aims. Rather, it is the incidental but explosive contact among groups in everyday life that needs correction. He asserts the need for both majority and minority group attitudes to change. Meaningful social change is total and is accomplished by a transformation of the relationships and corresponding attitudes of all groups, not by holding one group solely accountable for producing social change while the other sits and awaits the benefits of the change.

Summary

If adult education is to be seen as a means of social change, the source of the inequality or injustice must be satisfactorily specified. During the war and postwar periods, Locke came to appreciate the fact that no matter how complete or sincere the change in individual attitudes of members of one group towards members of another group, that change in attitude is largely superfluous if not also accompanied by a broader change in group relations. As long as one group remains dominant—in terms of status and power rather than numbers—the fundamental social situation will not change.

During the 1940s Locke appeared to shift his attention from more discretely cultural matters to an exploration of the political and social ramifications of cultural pluralism. Throughout his writings and speeches during that period, and especially in his statements on education, he paid increasing attention to a critical view of society based on his conception of cultural pluralism. It was during this period that the implications of his emphasis on group culture became clearer in the field of education.

Adult education, in Locke's view, must challenge the conceptions of communal life both within and among cultural groups. Both the content and the pedagogy of adult education, and all education, must be reconceptualized to overcome the culture crisis to which Locke alluded. Traditional processes of education, based on positivist assumptions about knowledge and values, must be eschewed in favor of an educational process imbued with value relativism and cross-cultural content.

In contemporary discourse on race relations, it is frequently observed that African Americans have made great progress toward equity in the past half century.[37] There are more African American leaders in government, business, and education than ever before. Many white Americans, and a few African Americans, are opposed to what they perceive as preferential treatment for blacks in employment through race-preference policies such as affirmative action. Yet, the facts continue to show that there are significant historically grounded differences between blacks and whites.[38] These conditions are similar to the social conditions of the 1930s and 1940s in which African Americans were making economic and political gains but which also left the majority of them living in poverty and in isolation from the larger white community. It was precisely this set of circumstances to which Locke directed attention in promoting a similar but separate program of adult education for African Americans. Because circumstances are similar, the conclusion is easily reached that a separate focus for African American programs of adult education is required at the beginning of the twenty-first century. And the focus of such programs should be precisely the one that Locke articulated a half century ago: the cultural, social, and political circumstances of African Americans.

Notes

1. See, e.g., James D. Anderson, *The Education of Blacks in the South, 1860–1935* (Chapel Hill: University of North Carolina Press, 1988); Henry Louis Gates, "Parable of the Talents," in *The Future of the Race,* ed. Henry Louis Gates Jr. and Cornel West (New York: Vintage, 1996), 1–52; Beverly Gordon, "Curriculum, Policy, and African American Cultural Knowledge: Challenges and Possibilities for the Year 2000 and Beyond," *Educational Policy* 11, no. 2: 227–42; Randall Kennedy, "My Race Problem—and Ours," *Atlantic Monthly,* May 1997, 55–66; Marable Manning, *Beyond Black and White: Transforming African American Politics* (London: Verso, 1995); Shelby Steele, "The New Sovereignty: Grievance Groups Have Become Nations unto Themselves," *Focus* 4, no. 2: 26–31; and Cornel West, "Black Strivings in a Twilight Civilization," in *Future of the Race,* ed. Gates, 53–112.

2. St. Clair Drake and Horace Cayton, *Black Metropolis: A Study of Negro Life in a Northern City,* vol. 1 (New York: Harcourt, Brace & World, 1945); and Gunnar Myrdal, *An American Dilemma* (New York: McGraw Hill, 1962).

3. Morse A. Cartwright, "Annual Report of the Director," *Journal of Adult Education* 3 (1931): 380.

4. Alain Locke, "Report on Negro Adult Education Projects," dated 15 March

1934. Writings by Locke file, Moorland-Spingarn Research Center, Howard University, p. 1.

5. Locke, "Report on Education Projects," 6.

6. Alain Locke, "Negro Needs as Adult Education Opportunities: Keynote Speech," in "Findings of the First Annual Conference on Adult Education and the Negro" *(*Hampton Institute, American Association for Adult Education and Associates in Negro Folk Education, 1938, mimeographed), 5–10.

7. Talmadge C. Guy, "Prophecy from the Periphery: Alain Locke's Philosophy of Cultural Pluralism," *Adult Education Quarterly* 46, no. 4 (1996): 209–23.

8. Horace Kallen, "Democracy and the Melting Pot: A Study of American Nationality," *Nation* 100 (1915): 190–94, 216–20.

9. Ira D. A. Reid, *Adult Education among Negroes* (Washington, D.C.: Associates in Negro Folk Education, 1936).

10. Alain Locke, *The Negro and His Music* (Washington, D.C.: Associates in Negro Folk Education, 1936).

11. See esp. Carter G. Woodson, *The African Background Outlined* (1936; repr. New York: Negro Universities Press, 1968); Newbell Puckett, *Folk Beliefs of the Southern Negro* (1926; repr. New York: Dover, 1968); W. E. B. Du Bois, *Souls of Black Folk* (1903; repr. New York: Basic Books, 1970).

12. Alain Locke, ed., *The New Negro* (New York: Atheneum, 1992).

13. Eduard Lindeman, *The Meaning of Adult Education* (New York: Republic, 1926).

14. Du Bois, *Souls of Black Folk.*

15. See Lindeman, *Meaning of Adult Education.*

16. Tom Heaney, *Adult Education for Social Change: From Center Stage to the Wings and Back Again,* Information Series no. 365 (Washington, D.C.: Office of Educational Research and Improvement, Department of Education, 1996), ERIC doc. 396190.

17. See Locke, "Report on Education."

18. See Lindeman, *Meaning of Adult Education,* 115.

19. See Guy, "Prophecy from the Periphery."

20. Harold Stubblefield and Harvey Keane, *Adult Education in the American Experience: From the Colonial Period to the Present* (San Francisco: Jossey Bass, 1994).

21. Rayford Logan, "Minority Needs in the National Crisis," in *Proceedings of the First Annual Conference on Adult Education and the Negro,* Schomburg Collection of African American History and Culture, New York Public Library, 1940, 49. Mimeograph. (Hereafter *Proceedings* 1940).

22. Alain Locke, "Minority Group Strategy." Unpublished seminar presentation,17 February 1941. Alain Locke papers, Writings by Locke file. Moorland-Spingarn Research Center, Howard University, Washington D.C.

23. Everett Helmut Akam, "Pluralism and the Search for Community: The Social Thought of American Cultural Pluralists" (Ph.D. diss., University of Rochester, 1990).

24. See Locke, "Minority Group Strategy."

25. Alain Locke, "The Negro Group," in *Group Relations and Group Antagonisms,* ed. R. M. McIver and Alain Locke (New York: Harper Brothers. 1944), 46–51.

26. See Lyman Bryson in *Proceedings* 1940, 53.

27. Alain Locke, "The Need for a New Organon in Education: Goals for American Education," in *Proceedings of the Ninth Symposium Conference on Science, Philosophy, and Religion* (New York: Conference on Science, Philosophy, and Religion, 1950), 201–12.

28. Locke, "New Organon," 203.

29. Locke, "New Organon," 205.

30. Locke, "New Organon," 210.

31. Locke, "New Organon," 210.

32. Alain Locke, "The Minority Side of Intercultural Education," *Education for Cultural Unity* 17 (1945): 60–64.

33. Locke, "Intercultural Education."

34. Locke, "Intercultural Education," 1.

35. Locke, "Intercultural Education," 2.

36. Locke, "Intercultural Education," 2.

37. Stephen Thernstrom and Abigail Thernstrom, *America in Black and White: One Nation, Indivisible* (New York : Simon & Schuster, 1997).

38. Andrew Hacker, *Two Nations: Black and White, Separate, Hostile, Unequal* (New York: Ballantine Books, 1995).

16

Alain Locke and His Contributions to Black Studies

LaVerne Gyant

Black studies as a discipline focused on the peoples of sub-Saharan Africa, should begin with the study of the African past and the present experiences, characteristics, achievements, issues, and problems of Africa and the diaspora. The emergence of Black studies as an academic discipline began around the late nineteenth century in many Black colleges and universities. Martin Delany, Frederick Douglass, W. E. B. Du Bois, E. Franklin Frazier, Marcus Garvey, Charles S. Johnson, Phyllis Wheatley, and Carter G. Woodson are only a few of the scholar-activists who were fundamental in the study and research of the Black experience and the origin and development of Black studies. Many of these scholar-activists were self-taught, while others were educated at some of the most prestigious colleges and universities. Yet, they all received minimal incentive to study the culture and history of people of African descent. It was missing pieces of the puzzle that led them to study and research their culture and history and to encourage African Americans to learn about and recognize their connection to Africa and the African Diaspora. It was these missing pieces that led them to lay the foundation for Black studies.

Alain LeRoy Locke is one of the scholar-activists who helped to lay the social theory and ideological bases for Black studies. Yet he is better known as the father of the New Negro Movement than for his contributions to Black studies. Anderson and Linnemann, however, state that he was one of the major contributors to the theoretical and cultural foundation of Black studies.[1]

Locke's interest in Black studies was centered on his identity as a Black man living in America. This was evident in his writings, which were "derived from the social contradiction rooted in the racism which he tried to understand"[2] and represented the depth and complexities of the race problem.

> The American side of his identity was . . . [the] external, objective aspect of his identity, which called for little discussion or clarification. . . . But the Black side

of the Black man's identity was not so easily defined. This was a subjective . . . dimension of his identity which was in the process of formation.[3]

Locke believed that Black studies would help African Americans understand their double consciousness. The failure to recognize and acknowledge their duality made it impossible for African Americans to uplift the race, build racial consciousness and unity, and help develop an internal healthy life. Black studies would help artists, educators, writers, and leaders to understand their role in society. Locke saw this role as a cultural one:

> It is obvious . . . that the main line of Negro development must necessarily be artistic, cultural, moral, and spiritual . . . in contrast with the predominantly practical, and scientific trend of the nation. . . . Although he must qualify in all the branches of American life and activity, the Negro can be of more general good in supplementing Nordic civilization than through merely competitively imitating or extending it along lines in which it is at present successful and preeminent.[4]

This role was based on the effect of enslavement:

> Just as slavery may now in perspective be viewed as having first threatened our democratic institutions and then forced them to more consistent maturity, the artistic and cultural impact of the Negro must be credited with producing unforeseen constructive pressures and generating unexpected creative ferment in the literary and artistic culture in America. In cutting the Negro loose from his ancestral culture, slavery set up a unique and unprecedented situation between Anglo-Saxon majority and the Negro minority. . . . The peculiar conditions of American slavery so scrambled Africans from the diverse regions and cultures of our entire continent that was the original background culture . . . [that] with neither a minority language nor an ancestral tradition . . . [t]he American Negro was left no alternative but to share the language and tradition of the majority culture.[5]

Black studies offered African Americans the opportunity to be grounded in their history and culture and to understand their cultural role in society. This foundation would assist them in acquiring recognition and racial solidarity; give them dignity and pride and allow them to take their rightful place in society as active and productive citizens; and inspire them to acquire more knowledge. This foundation was not just about "feeling good being Black"; it was about celebrating and appreciating their experiences, developing an African worldview, reconstructing history and myths, and adding the missing pieces to the puzzle. These were the messages that came through as I read Locke's writings and lectures.

Locke's work is interdisciplinary. His works included some, if not all, of the seven subject areas defined by Karenga: history, social organizations, creative production, religion, psychology, economics, and politics.[6] Locke's work also meets four of the five objectives of Black studies: (1) to teach the Black experience by examining the history and contributions of Blacks; (2) to assemble and create a body of knowledge for intellectual and political emancipation; (3) to create Black intellectuals dedicated to community service and conscious, capable, and committed to the uplift of the community; and (4) to cultivate, maintain, and expand relationships between higher education institutions and the community. The fifth objective, to establish Black studies as a legitimate respected, and permanent discipline, is contingent on the first four. These objectives will serve as a guide for examining Alain Locke's contributions to Black studies.

To Teach the Black Experience by Examining the History and Contributions of Blacks

For Locke, teaching the Black experience meant that every effort should be made to educate the Black community about the history and culture of people of African descent. The knowledge they gained by learning about their history and culture would heighten racial consciousness, dignity, and pride and open doors to a new world. In studying the culture and history of Africa, we are reminded of our emotional connection to Africa—a connection that, when combined with our experiences in the United States, created a new culture and history. The combination of our African connection and our experiences here help explain our role.

> What we have thought primitive in the American Negro—his naivete, his sentimentalism, his exuberance, and his improvising are then neither characteristically African nor to be explained as an ancestral heritage. They are the results of his peculiar experience in America and the emotional upheaval of its traits and ordeals.[7]

While encouraging African Americans to study their culture and history, he reminded us that when we are presented with information, we still tend to look at it from a European perspective. This tendency allows us neither to appreciate the positive and negative aspects of our experiences nor to challenge the myths and stereotypes about people of African descent. By looking at culture and history from an African perspective, we are able to see both sides, reconstruct the myths and stereotypes, and better understand our role and contributions to American society.

In exploring the contributions and history of people of African descent, we begin to acknowledge that our history and social life are rooted in Black culture, which also is the root of American history and social life: "separate as it may be in color and substance, the culture of the Negro is of a pattern integral with the times and with its cultural settings."[8] This is evident when we look at spirituals and jazz. The foundation of spirituals is very much African, but the genre also includes compositions from various religious sources. Southern noted that spirituals have a folksong style, are rough and irregular, refer to scriptural concepts and everyday experiences, and include verses from other songs. "Steal Away," "Go Down Moses," "My Lord What a Morning," "Somebody's Calling My Name," "I Found the Answer" are only a few of the spirituals that are unique and representative of our experiences in the United States.

In *The Negro and His Music,* Locke noted how the Fisk Jubilee Singers introduced spirituals at a concert at Oberlin College that brought not only fame and funding for Fisk University but also recognition to spirituals and Black folk music.[9] He also recognized that spirituals, or "sorrow songs," as he called them, are

> a priceless heritage from the racial past. They are promising material for the Negro music of the future. And they are the common possession of all, part of the cultural currency of the land, as their popularity and universal appeal only too clearly proves.[10]

Joel A. Rogers (1925), historian and social critic, found these same characteristics in jazz, noting that "jazz . . . is one part American and three parts American Negro, and was originally the nobody's child of the levee and the city slum." He continued:

> With its cowbells, auto horns, calliopes, rattles, dinner gongs, kitchen utensils, cymbals, screams, crashes, clankings, and monotonous rhythm it bears all the marks of a nerve-strung, strident, mechanized civilization. It is a thing of the jungles—modern-man jungles. . . . Jazz proper, however, is in idiom—rhythmic, musical, and pantomimic—thoroughly American Negro; it is his spiritual picture on that lighter comedy side, just as spirituals are the pictures on the tragedy side. The two are poles apart, but the former is by no means to be despised and it is just characteristically the product of the peculiar and unique experience of the Negro in this country. . . . Once achieved, it is common property, and jazz has absorbed the national spirit.[11]

Locke and Rogers agreed that spirituals, blues, and jazz were here to stay. Jazz has proved to be the foundation for music to come—rhythm and blues, hard rock, rap, gospel, and classical.

In examining the history of people of African descent living in the United States, we must begin in Africa and continue by looking at enslavement. In "The Negro Digs Up His Past," Arthur A. Schomburg wrote:

> The American Negro must remake his past in order to make his future. Though it is orthodox to think of America as the one country where it is unnecessary to have a past, what is a luxury for the nation as a whole becomes a prime social necessity for the Negro . . . a group tradition must supply compensation for persecution, and pride of race the antidote for prejudice. History must restore what slavery took away, for it is the social damage of slavery that the present generation must repair and offset.[12]

Thus, history for African Americans must be documented to show that they have been active collaborators and often pioneers in their struggle for advancement and freedom. Likewise, history offers a record of group achievement and shows that African Americans are of interest because of their bearing on the beginning and early development of human culture. The history of people of African descent has arguably been documented since the beginning of time, via art, music, literature (fiction and nonfiction), fashion, cooking, and religion.

"The Negro Digs Up His Past" and Locke's *The Negro in America* highlighted the contributions and achievements of people of African descent in the United States, the African Diaspora, and Europe.[13] Also there were Jupiter Hammon's "Address to the Negroes of the State of New York" (1787), John Marrant's St. John's Day eulogy to the "Brothers of African Lodge No. 459" (1789), and Peter Williams of St. Phillip's speech on the abolition of the slave trade (1808). In these works we are also introduced to Gustavus Vassa's autobiography and Julien Raymond's Paris exposé of the disabilities of the free people of color in Hayti (Haiti); we meet Juan Latino, author of *Poems* (1573) and a book on the Escurial (1576), and John Baptist Phillips, African graduate of Edinburgh, who wrote on the capitulation guaranteeing freedom to Blacks from Trinidad. These works were based on sound scholarship and research. They educate the mind and introduce us to men and women who stood "shoulder to shoulder in courage and zeal, and often on a parity of intelligence and talent."[14]

By studying the contributions, achievements, and history of people of African descent, I believe we begin to identify and subscribe to various African traditional concepts—sense of community and cooperation, sense of family, respect for elders and the ancestors, notion of communal property, and respect for nature. These concepts have played a key role in shaping the Black experience and our everyday life.

To Assemble and Create a Body of Knowledge
for Intellectual and Political Emancipation

In promoting and providing information about the Black experience, Locke urged educators, artists, writers, and leaders to make learning dynamic and creative. The information should have intellectual value that would urge Blacks to acquire more knowledge. It should appeal to the imagination, touch the senses, and be dynamic and enthusiastic.

One way Locke met this objective was to join E. Kincke Jones, executive director of the National Urban League, in organizing the Associates in Negro Folk Education (ANFE), which was supported by the American Association for Adult Education (AAAE), the Carnegie Corporation, and the Rosenwald Foundation. The goal of the ANFE was to develop and publish material on the history and contributions of Blacks. Specifically, the ANFE sought to

1. prepare and publish study materials on the life and culture of African Americans

2. publish syllabi, outlines, and booklets for use in educational programs for African Americans

3. influence a constructive program and policy in adult education[15]

The ANFE developed a series of national conferences along with several other activities to link the community, higher education, and various social and civic organizations. The ANFE also published Bronze Booklets, a series of readers that highlighted the history, problems, and contributions of people of African descent. The goal of the series was to provide African Americans with "knowledge of and respect for African culture."[16] The booklets were designed to be used either individually or in study groups in libraries, high schools, churches, YMCAs and YWCAs, and meeting halls. Each booklet contained study outlines, reading lists, and suggestions for further study.[17] They were examples of an African-centered and interdisciplinary curriculum designed for both high school students and adults. As editor of the series, Locke urged the authors to use "a colloquial style . . . preferable to an academic one. . . an Anglo Saxon style away from a Latin one . . . so that the series could make a real contribution to the technique of simple, readable but mature discussions and exposition of subject matter."[18]

The series, which was published from 1936 to 1941, included works such as *Adult Education among Negroes* (Ira D. A. Reid), *World View of Race* (Ralphe Bunche), *The Negro in American Fiction* and *Negro Poetry and Drama* (Sterling A. Brown), *The Negro and Economic Reconstruction* (Timothy A. Hill), and *The Negro and the Caribbean* (Eric E. Williams). Locke's contributions to the series included *The Negro and His Music* and *Negro Art: Past and Present.* Each of these booklets exposed readers to new aspects of history and achievements of people of African descent. They opened with a discussion of the culture or history of Africa and moved forward to discuss its relationship with, and effect on, life in the United States, the African Diaspora, and Europe. For example, in the first chapter of *Negro Art: Past and Present,* Locke wrote about the greatness and sophistication of African art.

> The Western world had yet to learn, to its amazement, that primitive civilization not only had artists but had produced a great art, and that of the many types of primitive arts now known but then yet to be discovered, that of the Negro in Africa was by all odds the greatest and the most sophisticated . . . believe it or not, the most sophisticated; at least it is the most sophisticated modern artists and critics of our present generation say so. And even should they be wrong as to the quality of African art, the fact still remains that there is an artistic tradition and skill in all the major crafts art running back for generations and centuries, among the principal African tribes . . . of the West Coast and Equatorial Africa from which Afro-Americans descended.[19]

This discussion provided readers with a basis to understand the history of African art and its contribution to society.

The Bronze Booklets have been considered one of Locke's greatest contributions. For Locke, "the real criteria of the worth of the approach through racial interest will be, first, whether emotional spot interest can be raised to a sustained interest and, second, whether a special interest can develop into a vital general interest in the problems of contemporary life."[20] They have also become a must-read for students who are studying the history and culture of people of African descent.

Based on our peculiar experiences, African Americans are beginning to recognize their traits of spontaneity, openness, gregariousness, and other forms of behavior.[20] Our experiences and traits have served as the foundation and background for the scholarship, literature, and music that have been produced over the years. This is seen in the works of Langston Hughes, Jean Toomer, Nella Larsen, Jessie Fauset, Zora Neale Hurston, W. E. B. Du Bois, Marcus A. Garvey, Joel A. Rogers, and others.

The New Negro (1925) has been recognized as the literary and artistic symbol of the Harlem Renaissance. It focused on the will and accomplishments of African Americans, documented their social and cultural contribution, and served as a protest against racist assumptions about Blacks.[21] It was also an example of the combination of our experiences. These elements come through in the writings by Albert C. Barnes ("Negro Art and America"), Countee Cullen ("Heritage"), Arthur A. Schomburg ("The Negro Digs Up His Past"), W. A. Domingo ("Gift of the Black Tropics"), along with other pieces in *The New Negro*. It should be considered mandatory reading for students in Black studies, especially when we as a people are defining ourselves and moving toward a more African worldview.

The theater was another dimension that Locke felt would contribute to the body of knowledge on the Black experience. Via the theater, race issues could be presented dramatically and artistically, while helping to develop Black playwrights, for it was only Black playwrights who could understand and gain access to the Black community and portray Blacks and their experiences more truthfully.[22] Locke urged Black educational institutions to establish drama departments or theater organizations so that works by Black playwrights could be produced and viewed by the community. The theater, in Locke's opinion, served as an educational and social outlet that was open to all regardless of economic background.

The March 1925 issue of *Survey Graphic*, *The Negro in America* (1933), and his yearly reviews of literature were only a few of Locke's works that provided the community and society with information on the Black experience.

To Create Black Intellectuals Dedicated to Community Service and Conscious, Capable, and Committed to the Uplift of the Community

Recognizing the need for better educational opportunities for African Americans, Locke wrote of

> the need for more positive and favorable conditions for the expression and cultivation of the developing race spirit. . . . Negro education . . . ought to be free to develop its own racial interests and special aims for both positive and compensatory reasons. . . . [R]acial separation presents . . . a negative and irritating challenge or disparagement instead of a welcome and inspiring challenge.[23]

This was his challenge to Black colleges and universities: to educate African Americans for leadership roles and provide them with skills necessary to transform and uplift the race. Both he and Du Bois encouraged Black institutions to educate "the Talented Tenth" and the masses. Locke also challenged African Americans to gain control of their institutions. To him the current policies and practices of these institutions were based on missionary ideologies that prevented them from encouraging the development of strong leadership, racial pride, self-help, social reform, racial spirituality, and autonomy.[24] This system "constantly reminds Negro youth . . . of the unpleasant side of the race problem, instead of utilizing it as a positive factor in his education."[25] Many students joined Locke in urging Black educational institutions to meet these challenges.

By administering their own policies and practices, Black educational institutions would, first, develop a racially inspired and devoted professional class, the Talented Tenth. Second, they would promote positive attitudes, racial dignity, and pride. Third, the curriculum would emphasize Black culture and history via the classroom and research. Finally, students would become self-directed. These changes would "provide for more positive and favorable conditions for the expression and cultivation of the developing race spirit."[26]

Along with these changes, a new type of education for African Americans would help them participate in the political and economic areas of society. For Locke, African Americans' equal participation in society helped them to have a fuller life. It also helped them to develop their intellectual, political, and economic interests. "On their various levels and in their local environments Negroes are for the most part terribly American. . . . they have abundant curiosity but very little knowledge . . . plenty of interest but few of them [are] intellectuals."[27]

While Locke encouraged the development of the Talented Tenth, he acknowledged the fact that African Americans had produced intellectual and artistic scholar-activists. W. E. B. Du Bois, William S. Braithwaite, Arthur Schomburg, Paul Robeson, Jessie Fauset, and Ralph Bunche are only a few of the many among the Talented Tenth. Recognizing these scholar-activists, Locke rejected any notion that Blacks were intellectually or creatively inferior to whites.[28] He reminded whites that if they continued to reject the Talented Tenth, some would leave the country, while some would be diverted to controversy and agitation, and still others would break through the barrier.[29] For Locke, these scholar-activists were achievers who made it despite the oppressive conditions under which they lived.

It was the Talented Tenth who, Locke believed, should be admitted to society and who would be the key to desegregation.

By recognizing the talent and the representative types among Negroes, an easing and vindicating satisfaction can be carried down to the masses, as well as the most quickening and stimulating sort of inspiration that could be given them.

Their elite would then become symbols in advance of expected justice and of a peaceful solution.[30]

To Cultivate, Maintain, and Expand Relationships between Higher Education Institutions and the Community

Under the aegis of the ANFE, eight conferences were held between 1938 and 1949 at various Black colleges and universities—Fisk, Howard, Tuskegee, South Carolina State. The conferences, which centered on providing adult education for African Americans, were attended by educators, community and religious leaders, and members of various organizations and foundations. Recommendations from the conferences urged adult education providers to sponsor community-based forums, integrate information on the Black experience into all phases of adult education programs, use visual aids in classes, and inform educators about the characteristics and culture of African Americans.[31] Locke felt that adult education programs, especially if sponsored by Black institutions and organizations, would provide the Black community with an opportunity to obtain new knowledge and skills and develop leadership skills while learning about their culture and history. These conferences served as a bridge between higher education institutions and the community. Like the Moveable Schools and the Tuskegee Negro Conferences, these eight conferences sought ways to bring education to the community.[32] At the same time, these conferences continued the work that was begun by Black conferences during the late eighteenth century. That is, they shared sessions on health, politics, economics, music, and other topics that met the needs and concerns of the community.

Along with the eight conferences, ANFE also sponsored the Harlem and Atlanta library projects, which were cosponsored by the AAAE, local libraries, social and religious organizations, and higher education institutions. Again, these institutions and organizations worked together to bridge the gap. Harlem was selected because of its strong sense of community and the cross section of professional and working-class people living there, and the library was a strong educational center.[33] In Atlanta, the education department at Atlanta University worked with the library in supporting the literacy programs. Each project focused on the particular needs and concerns of the local people.

The programs of the library projects included creative and recreational activities, informative forums and panels, social case work, and special library services. These programs emphasized African and African American customs, values, traditions, and history. Included were discussions on social education, economic thought, artistic expression, and race solidarity.[34] In a letter to Locke, Miss Ernestine Rose, executive director of the 135th Street Library (Schomburg Library), informed him about the series of historical and sociological discussions: "The subject of the first course . . . will be 'The Social History of the Negro as Reflected Through His Leaders.' These four lectures will be on Nat Turner and Frederick Douglass, Du Bois, Booker T. Washington, and Marcus Garvey."[35] A study group of Atlanta public school teachers discussed issues concerning international affairs and education. These are only two examples of the several programs offered by the Harlem and Atlanta library projects.

These adult education programs in the Black community had a strong Black studies foundation. In his evaluation of the Harlem and Atlanta projects, Locke wrote that they

demonstrated unmistakably the need for and desirability of special programs in adult education for Negro groups. . . . Such programs should ultimately be extended to every considerable Negro community in the country, but should always be regarded as supplemental to a general program and to whatever general community plan exists in the locality and should aim ultimately at being incorporated in such a program under local municipal community support.[36]

Diversity and Multiculturalism

Locke was known not only for his contributions to the New Negro Movement and Black studies but also as one of the earlier supporters of diversity. He urged other groups, not just Blacks, to study their own culture and history as well as those of others. He did not believe in racial exclusiveness, for he saw himself as an example of the situation and problems of humans who were being oppressed and discriminated against because of their differences.[37]

In teaching diverse populations, Locke believed, educators should have an open attitude and an appreciation for the differences of others. Educators should help to dispel myths and attitudes of inferiority and superiority among races or ethnic groups and to provide an integrated curriculum that included information on various groups. A diverse education would broaden students' vision via global thinking and process understanding, developing their capacity for critical thinking and evaluation, and change the way they think.[38]

If modernized contemporary education is to deal with attitudes, it must . . . grapple realistically with values and value judgements; if it is to build constructive mind-sets, or even fashion efficient critical ones, it must somehow restore the normative elements in education.[39]

Through the cultural and historical approach, students learn cultural and historical values, comparisons, contrasts, and conflicts. Locke described this approach as the only "way of understanding values, including . . . those of one's own culture and way of life . . . [and learning] to view values relativistically . . . to comprehend value change and development, and . . . to see [values] in comparative perspective, so as to understand and appreciate . . . diversity.[40]

Locke believed in the oneness of humanity—that is, that in humanity there was a uniqueness of personality and that recognition of this uniqueness was predicated upon a democratic ethos that included personal experiences, physical and moral stance, and the continuing development of one's inner personality and freedom.[41] Thus, Locke worked with scholars and students from various races, cultures, and nations.

Locke's views and ideas on diversity and multiculturalism or cultural pluralism can be found in *When Peoples Meet: A Study of Race and Culture Contacts,* which was coedited by B. Stern.[42] The book included essays by a variety of anthropologists, economists, educators, psychologists, sociologists, humanists, and other distinguished scholar-activists. Its focus was on race, religion, culture, and their interaction with each other. His other works on diversity or cultural pluralism include "Understanding World Cultures" (1944) and "The Concept of Race as Applied to Social Culture" (1924).[41]

Conclusion

Locke believed that Black studies played a major role in the social, political, and economic development of people of African descent. As long as we remained outsiders, society remained at a standstill, the road to advancement was slow, and the conflicts between the races continued. This has been evident throughout various stages of our history. When we were making progress during Reconstruction, the economy was good and tension was minimal. Once jealousy and fear enraged the white community, the economy had a setback, unemployment increased, and tension was on the rise. We have seen the same thing after soldiers returned from the various wars, during the late 1980s, and again today. While there was jealousy and fear when people of African descent became insiders, there was a stronger sense of fear when we moved in the other direction, toward racial consciousness and racial solidarity. Again, this has been evident throughout history, beginning with the abolitionist movement, Black History Month, and Kwanza, and moving up to the Million Man

March, the Million Woman March, and the observance by some of October 16 (the Day of Atonement).

It was, and is, within the context of Black studies that the quality, beauty, truth, and political implication of the Black experience unfold. This was evident in Locke's work and in his support for scholar-activists of all ages, especially for the younger generation. It was also evident in his recognition and appreciation of works by Frederick Douglass, Du Bois's scientific approach to history, Woodson's pioneer work in the history of enslavement and the Negro past, and Washington's work in the area of vocational education.[42] Via Black studies, African Americans can accept their role in the economic and political development of America. They can also assist in reclaiming the lost history and culture of Africa.

Locke's knowledge of history and culture of people of African descent gave him the ability to reevaluate history, its effect on the scholar-activists, and the development of racial consciousness. His work in Black studies helped lay the foundation for the theoretical and philosophical aspect of the field; opened the door for both scholarly and fictional works; recognized Africa's contribution to art, literature, music, and dance; extolled the richness, beauty, and variety of people of African descent; cultivated goodwill; and improved human relations. More important, Locke's works developed a sense of racial pride and dignity among people of African descent.

Locke's contribution to Black studies should be given more attention. His contribution has had an effect on some of the work and dialogue now occurring in the field. Students, researchers, and scholar-activists are encouraged to include—and to further—Locke's contribution to the field of Black studies.

Notes

1. T. Anderson, *Introduction to African American Studies* (Dubuque, Iowa: Kendall/Hunt, 1993); R. J. Linnemann, *Alain Locke: Reflections on a Modern Renaissance Man* (Baton Rouge: Louisiana State University Press, 1982).

2. Johnny Washington, *Alain Locke and Philosophy: A Quest for Cultural Pluralism* (New York: Greenwood Press, 1986).

3. W. D. Wright, "The Cultural Thought and Leadership of Alain Locke," *Freedomways* 14 (1974): 35–50.

4. Alain Locke, "Negro Contributions to America," *World Tomorrow* 12 (June 1929): 255–57.

5. Alain Locke, "The Negro in American Literature," *New World Writing* 1 (1952): 18–33.

6. M. Karenga, *Introduction to Black Studies* (Los Angeles: Kawaida, 1983).

7. Alain Locke, ed., *The New Negro* (New York: Boni, 1925); Alain Locke, "Negro

Education Bids for Par," *Survey Graphic* 54 (September 1925): 567–70; Alain Locke, *Survey Graphic*, special issue, March 1925.

8. Locke, *New Negro*, xvi.

9. See Eileen Southern, *The Music of Black Americans: A History* (New York: W. W. Norton, 1971).

10. Alain Locke, *The Negro and His Music* (Washington, D.C.: Associates in Negro Folk Education, 1936), 25.

11. Joel A. Rogers, "Jazz at Home," in *New Negro*, 218–20.

12. A. A. Schomburg, "The Negro Digs Up His Past," in *New Negro*, 231–38.

13. Alain Locke, *The Negro in America* (Chicago: American Library Association, 1933).

14. Schomburg, "Negro Digs Up His Past," 233.

15. V. J. Harris, "The Brownies' Book: Challenge to the Selective Tradition in Children's Literature" (Ph.D. diss., University of Georgia, Athens), 1986.

16. E. A. Days, "Alain Leroy Locke (1886–1954): Pioneer in Adult Education and Catalyst in the Adult Education Movement for Black Americans" (Ed.D. diss., North Carolina University at Raleigh, 1965).

17. Eugene C. Holmes, "Alain L. Locke and the Adult Education Movement," *Journal of Negro Education* 34, no. 1 (1965): 5–10. See also Eugene C. Holmes, "The Legacy of Alain Locke," *Freedomways* 3 (Summer 1963): 293–306; Eugene C. Holmes, "Alain L. Locke: A Sketch," *Phylon* 20 (1959): 82–89.

18. Alain Locke, *Negro Art: Past and Present* (Washington, D.C.: Associates in Negro Folk Education, 1936).

19. Alain Locke, "The Intellectual Interests of Negroes," *Journal of Adult Education* 8, no. 3 (1935–36): 352.

20. See W. D. Wright, "The Cultural Thought and Leadership of Alain Locke," *Freedomways* 14 (1974): 35–50.

21. Arnold Rampersad, introduction to *The New Negro*, ed. Alain Locke (1925; repr. New York: Atheneum, 1992), ix–xxiii.

22. Wright, "Cultural Thought and Leadership," 35–50.

23. Locke, *New Negro*, 569.

24. See Wright, *Alain Locke and Philosophy*.

25. Locke, *New Negro*, 570.

26. Locke, *New Negro*, 568.

27. Locke, "Intellectual Interests of Negroes," 352.

28. Alain Locke, *Messenger* 5, no. 5 (May 1923): 711, 720.

29. Alain Locke, "Should the Negro Be Encouraged to Cultural Equality?" *Forum* 78 (December 1927): 500–510.

30. Locke, "Cultural Equality," 509.

31. "Findings of the First Annual Conference on Adult Education and the Negro" (Hampton Institute, Associates in Negro Folk Education, and American Association for Adult Education, 1938, mimeographed).

32. Basil J. Matthews, *Booker T. Washington: Educator and Inter-Racial Interpreter* (London: SCM, 1949).

33. Talmadge C. Guy, "The American Association of Adult Education and the

Experiments in African American Education," in *Freedom Road: Adult Education of African Americans,* ed. Elizabeth A. Peterson (Malabar, Fla.: Krieger Publishing, 1996), 89–108.

34. See Guy, "Experiments in African American Education," 89–108.

35. Holmes, "Locke and Adult Education," 8.

36. Alain Locke, "Reciprocity Instead of Regimentation: Lessons of Negro Adult Education," *Journal of Adult Education* 6 (1934): 418–20.

37. Holmes, "Locke and Adult Education," 5–10.

38. Washington,"Locke and Philosophy."

39. Alain Locke, "The Need for a New Organon in Education," *Goals for American Education, Ninth Symposium, Conference on Science, Philosophy, and Religion,* (New York: Conference on Science, Philosphy and Religion, 1950), 201–12.

40. Locke, "New Organon," 209.

41. Holmes, "Locke and Adult Education," 5–10.

42. Alain Locke and Bernard J. Stern, eds., *When Peoples Meet: A Study of Race and Culture Contacts* (New York: Committee on Workshops, Progressive Education Association, 1942).

43. Alain Locke, "The Concept of Race as Applied to Social Culture," *Howard Review* 1 (1924): 290–99.

44. Holmes, "Locke and Adult Education," 5–10.

17

Andragogy and the Education of African American Adults

Rudolph A. Cain

> Let us, then, take the Negro case merely as a special instance of a general problem requiring special attention and effort, perhaps, because of its acute degree but in its significance and bearing on educational problems and methods considered generally diagnostic and universally applicable.
>
> —Alain Locke, "Negro Needs as Adult Education Opportunities"

The concept of andragogy presupposes a set of assumptions about how adults learn as opposed to pedagogy, which focuses on how youth learn. The pivotal principle is that learning for adults becomes a collaborative process, yet one that recognizes the importance of self-directedness in the instructional process. Critical to the formulation of an andragogical approach are methods and techniques for teaching. The andragogue would argue that techniques and, certainly, material resources for learning must of necessity be different for adults than for children. In this context, Dr. Alain Locke was truly an andragogue. For instance, his discourse on the culture approach as preferable to the conventional literacy approach to adult education was indeed a recognition that adults learn differently from children and thus require alternative instructional materials such as popular literature and audio and visual tools. In this respect Locke noted that "the core of the problem of our field today is . . . the development of the most effective techniques of mass education, bold and pioneering experimentation with the new mass media of communication and enlightenment to make them serve constructively the social and cultural needs of even larger segments of the people."[1] Furthermore, Locke emphasized the need for a more uniquely conceived approach to teaching and learning for adults when he noted:

> We can too early make a fetish of literacy and [conformity] and deceive ourselves as to the scope and value of our gains. We can also waste too much effort,

time, and money in what is after all a conventional pedagogic from the regular school curriculum.[2]

This criticism by Locke is somewhat reminiscent of the more contemporary arguments about phonics versus the use of whole language in teaching basic adult literacy. The phonics approach would be symbolic of the more conventional literacy pedagogy; the whole language, more representative of an unconventional, andragogic approach.

In his most recent work, *Applying Modern Principles of Adult Education,* Malcolm Knowles considers his early struggle to label appropriately the new and evolving art and science of teaching adults. In the following scenario, he provides a historical context for the appearance of the term "andragogy" in the literature of adult education:

> I found the solution in the summer of 1967, when a Yugoslavian adult educator, Dusan Savicevic, attended my summer session course on adult learning and at the end of it exclaimed, "Malcolm, you are preaching and practicing andragogy. I responded, "Whatagogy?" because I had never heard the term before. He explained that European adult educators had coined the term as a parallel to pedagogy, to supply a label for the growing body of knowledge and technology in regard to adult learning, and that it was being defined as "the art and science of helping adults learn." It made sense to me to have a differentiating label, and I started using the term in 1968, in articles describing my theoretical framework for thinking about adult learning.[3]

Knowles posits two underlying assumptions that serve as a broad context for explicating andragogy.[4] They constitute: (1) a set of assumptions about adults as learners, and (2) a series of recommendations for the planning, management, and evaluation of adult learning. Knowles further underscores two major propositions: (1) intrinsic to adulthood is a sense of self-directedness; and (2) in congruence with this self-directedness, andragogical practice is a collaborative venture that involves the learner in most or all institutional functions. The issue of self-directedness is a rather "ticklish" one, as Pratt observes.[5] Even for some adults, a function of self-directedness might involve relinquishing independent decision making in deference to the authority of the institution. The implication is that andragogy should encompass and acknowledge both self-directedness and dependency.

In "When Adults Want to Learn," Locke outlined the need for adult education among African Americans.[6] Three reasons were particularly noted: (1) education in youth was insufficient and not sustaining for adulthood, (2) recurrent education was necessary to keep pace with changing world conditions, and (3) the demands of an increasingly technological society require adaptation of new strategies for living. Essentially, the reasons reinforced and restated Hope and Howes's observation that "adult education is necessary because the world is changing so rapidly that however well one may be educated, unless he keeps up and continues to make adjustments, he finds himself behind the procession."[7] As an example, one need only consider the rapid escalation of computer technology and cybernetics in the 1990s, which is sure to continue into the twenty-first century. Recurrent education has significantly focused on the acquisition or honing of computer skills. Unfortunately, the jury is out in terms of the long-term impact on the character of the workplace. For instance, interpersonal skills may very well be sacrificed in favor of e-mail, and in Lockean terms (i.e., conjecturally), that could adversely affect the way that individuals and groups relate to one another.

Locke places the need for a transformation of the purpose and mission of adult education in a larger context by first noting:

> Adult education efforts today have no core program and little, if any, common denominator objectives. Can they and should they? That seems the critical question. Certainly no adequate answer can be expected from the present semi-vocational, semi-cultural or semi-recreational objectives which between them, seem to motivate so regrettably large an amount of adult education activity. Not that these are bad in themselves, but even they would function better as a marginal fringe to a more seriously conceived and professionally directed core program expressing a common consensus as to what in common the average adult needed in his continuing informal education.[8]

Then, he continues with an assessment of prior efforts, by observing:

> Historically, two such generally accepted core objectives have galvanized and documented adult educative effort, the "illiteracy crusade" and the "Americanization program" [designed for European immigrants, not formerly enslaved African Americans]. Unfortunately, both were at the subnormal level, but in spite of these limitations were constructively useful and gained wide public support and respect for adult education in general.[9]

He goes on to suggest the nature of the core philosophy and curriculum for adult education, thus capturing the essence of his recommendations.

> My hunch as to the proper answer stems from the unprecedented reception—the promotion of social maturity for all and at all levels, without regard to age, race, sex, class, formal training—and in a perspective of true democratic scope, that is to say, some tolerant and understanding citizenship of the community, the nation and the world?

After all in this reorientation of values and attitude, it is the changed mind, the emancipated social attitudes which currently count.[10]

Locke next explores the challenge for professionals to formulate curricula that reflect a meaningful purpose, noting:

> So that with a deliberate and enthusiastic consensus of opinion on this point of view and approach, all sorts and varieties of educative content could be focused, unified and cooperatively coordinated. The main core content, however, would have to be worked out by competent professionals and in addition to giving more authority and coherence, this necessary step would restore the central guidance of adult education where it properly belongs, to the field of the professional rather than the amateur educator.[11]

Locke underscores the problems when he notes that "in the early days, adult education for or by Negroes was conducted only by such organizations as the Church, the YMCA, the YWCA, parent-teacher associations, federated women's clubs, and the various branches of the National Urban League," noting that "there was little or no coordination and integration of programs." Reid supported these observations and needs when he observed:

> In addition to these basic reasonings, it was stated that: First, there was a large group of illiterates among Negroes, which is a drag on the whole race. Second, that nearly three-fourths of all Negro children never get beyond the fourth grade, Third, the education which has been received has been below standard in terms of teacher preparation, equipment, curriculum, and administrative procedures. For this reason, it was felt that Negroes were in greater need of adult education of all kinds than perhaps any group in the United States.[12]

This observation made by Reid over sixty years ago seems to mirror some of the criticisms of public education made by Jonathan Kozol in his 1995 book, *Savage Inequalities*. Locke would be terribly demoralized at the apparent slow pace of change. As a matter of fact, Locke would have expected that at this juncture in the social history of America, there would be no need to discuss the woes of African American education in a vacuum but rather that we would have achieved an integrated society that focused on the collective good. Locke's proposal is compelling when he notes, "Beyond the mere literacy level, enlarging horizons and broadening human values must dominate [adult education]."[13]

Locke was clearly perceptive in suggesting that the United States, in terms of social and economic stability, should have a vested interest in adult education, particularly the education of African American adults. Certainly, this observation has noteworthy contemporary implications, as many states, including New York, grapple with changing demographics (e.g, significant increases in Black and Hispanic populations) in relationship to potential work-force needs and the available pool of trained workers. Consequently, the role of adult education in its broader sense seems as relevant in the 1990s as in the 1930s. Therefore, the issues of need and of how to respond using andragogy continue to be compelling.

The basic approach that Alain Locke advocated for teaching African American adults clearly embraced methodologies that infused cultural and historical appreciation. However, the larger and more pointed question is how Locke incorporated dimensions of his philosophy of values generally, and his philosophical perspectives on African American adult education specifically, in the formulation of andragogical models.

Addressing numerous audiences, Locke challenged the applicability of methods and techniques of conventional literacy teaching normally used for teaching youth. In a speech delivered at the annual meeting of the American Association of Adult Education (AAAE) in 1934 he took the organization to task for its adherence to, and propagation of, a "conventional pedagogic objective borrowed uncritically from the regular school curriculum." In that same presentation, he said:

> I am not enough of a specialist to suggest in specific detail the best procedures and techniques, but I do throw forward the suggestion that visual and oral aids be effectively and decisively mobilized in our type of education and used with an eye to mass scale and effect. Certainly with regard to the Negro or any such disadvantaged group, of whom there are millions more than the illiterate and semi-illiterate Negroes, I can sense the futility of the homeopathic pill dosage that are too often an imitation of the elementary school procedure and materials inevitably involved. They [African American adults] must be deluged with enlightenment, through change is already seasoned and open, and made assimilable in terms of practical common sense and practical life situations.[14]

Locke's observation calls to mind the subsequent thinking and philosophy of Paulo Freire, who addresses the dichotomy between banking and purposive education: the former suggests that teachers feed information to students and they simply regurgitate the information; the latter implies educating learners with a variety of thematic purposes in mind. Freire believed, as did Locke, that people must not be educated simply for "education's sake" but that education must be a catalyst for changing aspects of the human condition.[15] Though their methods and approaches differed, both Freire and Locke saw education generally, and the education of the adult masses specifically, as a conduit for enlightenment and consciousness about social, political, and economic realities. The ultimate goal of this praxis for both Locke and Freire was the full participation of the masses in the social, political, and economic systems that affected their lives. Literacy (both social and cultural) played a key role in the readiness of the masses to empower themselves.

Locke's educational philosophy was well reflected in his ultimate pleas to those assembled at the 1934 AAAE meeting to acknowledge the needs of African Americans in education. However, he cautioned:

> Adult education particularly in this field of Negro African American need, is too orthodox in its techniques and too conservative in its objectives. The general results even of widening effort and increasing public response are still too superficial for really vital and satisfactory results. A change of techniques and tactics is therefore rather imperative, whether that involves a shift from the main established agencies of service in force at present or not;—extension [of] public school agencies and the public welfare educational services. Competing for the Negro African American mass audience for the moment come the relatively new agencies of the labor union and volunteer racial organizations, interested in mass education largely in its civic and cultural aspects.[16]

Then, he continues with a critique of new and evolving programs, noting:

> These new programs are making considerable appeal although yet neither is well organized or planned.
>
>   Their popularity arise[s] mainly from their immediate touch with the practical problems of the man [woman] in the street, and the morale technique which stimulates unequal zeal and interest on the part of even the most apathetic groups when once they become convinced of the lack of formality and condescension too characteristic in much of the older varieties of adult education.[17]

Thus, Locke recommended in "The Role of the Talented Tenth" that

> Instead of a narrow, specialized, scientific education, of which the dawn of the twentieth century offered us a mirage, there now stands out clearly before us the more distant, but more real prospect of an education broadly cultural, deeply humanistic, thoroughly socialized, justified now for the first time by practical reasons and democratic motives. Education of the cultural type has thus in our judgement been given a new lease of life; in fact, has become our lease on the life itself.[18]

For Locke, mass education "must have a dynamic and enthusiasm-compelling drive."[19]

Throughout his career, Alain Locke strongly advocated a new pedagogy, or andragogy, that focused on inculcating democratic values through intercultural education.[20] In "More than Blasting Brick and Mortar" he notes: "It's not enough to raze ghettos. We must throw open men's minds. Democracy is a living language of social behavior. The charge of American education is to teach it."[21]

Alain Locke was quite innovative in his approach to methods and materials for teaching adults generally, and African American adults specifically. He countered potential criticism of the use of visual aids and other innovative techniques. In "Trends in Adult Education for Negroes" he says:

This plea for education through visual channels, demonstrations and group activity programs does not minimize the medium of the book and pamphlet in adult education. Particularly for the Negro masses the inaccessibility of the printed materials, especially modern and progressive materials, is pathetic and alarming. Even communities with reasonably extensive adult education work have such poor library facilities that the sparks of literacy kindled may be expected to die out for want of intellectual fuel. The cheap and adequately illustrated pamphlet, the circulating and mobile library are the only modern solution[s] of this problem; [efforts that do not offer] formal instruction may just as well be written off as wasted.[22]

Clearly, Locke was a visionary in emphasizing the need for new and innovative technologies and methods for educating adults. Interestingly, current and continuing developments in the design of innovative systems for delivery of educational services have been greatly enhanced by telecommunications, computer hardware and software, satellite dishes, and a variety of systems that extend the realm of teaching and learning.

Locke further warned, in "Negro Needs as Adult Education Opportunity," that

As a mere extension of traditional methods and values [adult education] ceases to be worthy of its name; which is my reason for a final warning that adult education for Negroes, or for that matter any group, cannot possibly be second-hand, traditional or conservatively directed, To the extent that we can influence it, we must see that it becomes increasingly progressive and experimental. If it is to serve minority group interests, this becomes more than desirable; it becomes imperative.[23]

The critical role of popularized literature as an organ for educating the masses, both European and African American, was strongly advocated by Locke, and his view was shared by others, including James Atkins, Special

Assistant for Negro Affairs in the Office of Education at the time of the Second Annual Conference on Adult Education and the Negro, held at the Tuskegee Institute in 1940. Atkins challenged adult education teachers, both white and African American, to teach African American adults how to make use of the "vital stuff of Negro Life."[24] At the same conference, Locke suggested that popularized literature could serve "to better inform the white constituency with respect to the Negro and may be even more important to have the Negro constituents well informed about themselves."[25] The importance of information dissemination was underscored at the Third Annual Conference on Adult Education and the Negro, held at Howard University in 1941. Alain Locke was reelected president of the annual conference. A press release on the conference, written by Otto McClarrin, of Howard University's press service, noted:

> Adult education in the current American crisis was seen necessary to help the Negro masses to maintain morale and understand the workings of a democracy. Adult Education will play an important role in assisting the Negro in discriminating between propaganda, truth and subversive information and influences. A program of information for the average Negro and arranged to meet and serve his wants, was seen as a major need in the current crisis. Community organizations to provide informational services to Negro groups was encouraged.[26]

As an andragogue, more in practice than in name, Locke held early ideals on the appropriate approach to teaching adults in an atmosphere of mass education that bordered on an egalitarian and strongly African-American-centered philosophical perspective. For instance, he advocated, on one hand, in a rather idealistic manner, the democratization of adult education, implying equal opportunity of access to the same services; yet, on the other, he acknowledged that the needs of African American adult learners were different.

However, it would seem that Locke, who as a philosopher objected to absolutism and thus was critical of parochialism in adult education, was often torn between his philosophical perspectives and the realistic practice of adult education. He may have experienced a series of conflicts in this regard. Absolutism posed a series of problems for Locke, who was concerned with the diabolical social predicaments of African Americans and the resulting insidiousness of their plight in American society. Thus, he argued that although the goals of adult education should be the same for all groups, the experiences of African Americans required alternative approaches and strategies. Consequently, for Locke, as Burgett observes, "social and cultural reciprocity, on an equal basis, among cultures of varying ideologies, all existing within an essentially monistic framework is a contradiction."[27] Therefore, absolutism was clearly anathema to

Locke's vision of a world that respected and tolerated the plethora of cultural entities and perspectives, a community that would value the imperatives of different groups. Also, though he agreed that adult education should be the same for all, he argued for programs that acknowledged differences, advocating a "special needs" approach to adult education, for instance, for African Americans. While Locke advocated strongly and vehemently for what might be prospectively viewed as an African-centered approach to African American adult education, in some respects he might have been perceived as an accommodationist and cultural assimilationist. In his paper "Areas of Extension" he separates the immediate need from the long-term goal:

> Whatever warrantable special emphases there may be can be justified only as special remedial and corrective procedures to overcome particular results of neglect, isolation or disparagement, and they may be regarded as temporary and transitional until the minority situation is brought up to educational par and put into a democratically integrated alignment.
>
> Ultimately, if we envisage a democratic national situation at all, we must hope to see all such special and separate programs absorbed as speedily as possible into general programs of mass education, such as community projects, worker's education, basic programs of publicly supported adult education.[28]

Locke seems to be saying that until there is parity in education, which can only be achieved through cultural remediation, there will be no realization of a democratization of education. Thus, there seems to be some tension between Locke's assimilationist posture, his objection to the notion of a "melting pot," and his optimism about the integration of race-based programs into the larger mosaic of the adult education program.

The reader should bear in mind that Locke's larger frame of reference was the ultimate realization of a culturally pluralist global society, in which differences become *non sine gravitas*. The short-term goals to be reached include remediation and parity.

In his presentation at the First Annual Conference on Adult Education and the Negro, held at Hampton Institute, Hampton, Virginia, 20–22 October 1938, under the auspices of the AAAE, the Associates in Negro Folk Education, and the extension department of Hampton Institute, Locke noted:

> Let us, then, take the Negro case merely as a special instance of a general problem, requiring special attention and effort perhaps because of its acute degree, but in its significance and bearing upon educational problems and methods considered generally diagnostic and universally applicable. The condition of the Negro and its educational implications will fit and parallel any similar circumstanced

group, and in addition, like many another acute situation, will point the lesson of new and generally applicable techniques.[29]

As he consistently advocated for mass social education, Locke concurrently challenged the legitimacy and viability of "rugged individualization," ingrained in the American ethos. He notes the following:

> We Americans, traditional individualists that we are, do not seem to like either the term or the idea of mass education, believing—erroneously I think—that the educating of individuals cumulatively adds up to the same thing and automatically leads to mass rationality and social enlightenment. But call it what you will, mass education or folk education—I confess to liking the latter term—we cannot be at odds over the eventual, commonly accepted objectives of adult education. This is a democratic widening of all sorts of educative opportunities and experiences for more and more people over greater areas not only of knowledge and understanding.[30]

Locke emphasized the critical importance of relevant cultural and historical materials for teaching African Americans. He further cautioned:

> Adult education seems to me to misdirect its own deepest aims in not immediately embarking on a strenuous program of health, civic and social education at least as an auxiliary approach, and perhaps as a main approach. What is crucially important is an awakened, galvanized individual in place of the stagnant, conservative person who is the crude toddler of our process.[31]

This observation by Locke is somewhat akin to Paulo Freire's call for a kind of praxis that would transform the "culture of silence" to an energized mass movement directed at purposeful change.

The ideal of absolutism and the imposition of "standards" are social bedfellows. Alain Locke would argue that standards are necessary to maintain some degree of balance, order, and sanity in a democracy. On the other hand, he would strongly object to ill-conceived standards that are arbitrarily and capriciously applied and that serve only to subjugate, oppress, and inflict psychological damage on the powerless in society. To suggest that there is only one standard way of doing or thinking would be appalling and absurd to Locke. A case in point is the recurrent issue of IQ, which has elements of absolutism, as opposed to new and emerging research that is grounded in a more relativistic perspective, underscoring the existence of not one intelligence but "multiple intelligences." Thus, the ways in which individuals and groups negotiate what Johnny Washington calls "destinicity" may be quite fluid and varied and not conditional on absolutism, which has no place in adult education, if for no other reason than the realization that the life experiences of individuals and groups vary.[32]

Notes

1. Alain Locke, "The Coming of Age," *Journal of Adult Education* 6 (1947): 3.

2. Alain Locke, "Trends in Adult Education for Negroes" (speech delivered at the annual meeting of the American Association for Adult Education, 22 May 1940), 12., box 108; see also "Report on Negro Adult Education Projects," 15 March 1934, Box 164-126, folder 1, Moorland-Spingarn Research Center, Howard University, Washington, D.C.

3. Malcolm Knowles, *Applying Modern Principles of Adult Learning* (San Francisco: Malcolm S. Knowles Associates, 1984), 6.

4. Malcolm Knowles, *The Modern Practice of Adult Education: From Pedagogy to Adragogy*, rev. ed. (Chicago: Association Press, 1980).

5. Daniel D. Pratt, "Andragogy as a Relational Construct," *Adult Education Quarterly* 38, no. 3 (Spring 1988): 160.

6. Alain Locke, "When Adults Want to Learn," Locke papers, Moorland-Spingarn Research Center.

7. John Hope and Mae Howes, "Need for Adult Education," in *Fundamentals in the Education of Negroes*, by Ambrose Caliver (Washington, D.C.: U.S. Department of Interior, Office of Education, 1935), 67. John Hope was president of Atlanta University, and Mae Howes was director of the Adult Education Experiment in Atlanta.

8. Alain Locke, untitled speech, twenty-fifth Anniversary of AAAE, 1–2. Locke papers, Moorland-Spingarn Research Center.

9. Locke, AAAE anniversary speech, 1–2.

10. Locke, AAAE anniversary speech, 2–3.

11. Locke, AAAE anniversary speech, 2–3.

12. Ira D. A. Reid, "The Development of Adult Education for Negroes in the United States," *Journal of Adult Education* 14 (Summer 1945): 304..

13. Alain Locke, "Negro Needs as Adult Education Opportunities," in *"Findings of the First Annual Conference on Adult Education and the Negro"* (Hampton Institute, Associates in Negro Folk Education, and American Association for Adult Education, 1938, mimeographed), 7.

14. Locke, "Trends in Adult Education," 2.

15. Paulo Freire, *Pedagogy of the Oppressed* (New York: Continuum, 1970); and Paulo Freire, *Educating for Critical Consciousness* (New York: Continuum, 1973).

16. Locke, "Trends in Adult Education," 6–7.

17. Locke, "Trends in Adult Education," 6–7.

18, Alain Locke, "The Role of the Talented Tenth," *Howard University Record* 12 (1918): 15–18.

19, Locke, "Negro Needs," 7. See also Leonard Harris, ed., *The Philosophy of Alain*

262 *Rudolph A. Cain*

Locke: Harlem Renaissance and Beyond (Philadelphia: Temple University Press, 1984), 253–62.

20. Locke, "Negro Needs," 7.

21. Alain Locke, "More than Blasting Brick and Mortar," Moorland-Spingarn Research Center. See also *Survey Graphic,* January 1947, 87–89.

22. Locke, "Trends in Adult Education," 5.

23. Locke, "Negro Needs," 8.

24. J. A. Atkins. "Special Training Needed by Adult Education and the Negro, " in "Findings of the Second Annual Conference on Adult Education and the Negro" (Tuskegee Institute, Associates in Negro Folk Education, and American Association of Adult Education, 1940, mimeographed), 29–36.

25. Alain Locke. "Popularized Literature," in *Findings of the Second Annual Conference on Adult Education and the Negro,* 48–50.

26. Locke papers, Moorland-Spingarn Research Center.

27. David Joseph Burgett, "Vindication as a Thematic Principle in Alain Locke's Writings on the Music of African-Americans," in *The Harlem Renaissance: Revaluation,* ed. Amiritif Singh, William S. Shriver, and Stanley Brodwin (New York: Garland Publishing, 1989), 140–41.

28. Alain Locke, "Areas of Extension and Improvement of Adult Education among Negroes," *Journal of Negro Education* 25 (Summer 1945): 455.

29. Alain Locke, "Education for Adulthood," *Adult Education Journal* 6 (July 1947): 104.

30. Locke, "Negro Needs," 255.

31. Alain Locke, "Trends in Adult Education," 2–3.

32. See Johnny Washington, *A Journey into the Philosophy of Alain Locke* (Westport, Conn.: Greenwood Press, 1994). Washington's term "destinicity" is taken from *destiny,* which he defines as relatively enduring ideals toward which a people strives in successive generations. I would think the ideal of destinicity/destiny could apply very well to an individual's quest for guiding and sustaining ideals over the life course.

18

Alain Locke: A Paradigm for Transformative Education— Addressing the Relationship of Knowledge to Social Concerns

Blanche Radford Curry

Transformative Education

What is the purpose of education? What are the relations between education, the individual, culture, and society? Too many of us within and outside of academe view public and private education as significantly lacking, nontransformative in regard to each of these questions. From methodology to curricula, there are too many examples, past and present, of education as nontransformative. There is, as Alain Locke advocated, a "need for a new organon in education."[1]

Transformative education integrates cognitive thinking processes with our normative life experiences. It addresses the current need to integrate knowledge and social-cultural problems like race-, class-, and gender-based injustices as a means for more effectively achieving justice, fairness, and quality of life for all. As such, education is understood not only as cognitive thinking processes but also as critical thinking about values that rejects dogmatic ideology. Locke's essay "The Need for a New Organon in Education" offers us a compelling paradigm for transformative education.

In 1950 Locke argued for a need to reform the abstract, neutral, and contentless critical thinking that was the paradigm for reasoning methodologies and logical techniques. Locke's critique of education reflected an intense dispute over a major objective of educational policies to reform dogmatic and fallacious cognitive thinking processes—logic and contentless critical thinking as the fundamental "integrating elements for knowledge." This paradigm of education lacked any valuable application to social concerns, and it overlooked any meaningful examination of values in relation to social concerns. Moreover, the problems of dogmatic and fallacious cognitive thinking processes it rendered promoted and perpetuated racism.

Locke's view of education during the 1950s echoes a 1990s approach. In

263

her 1990 essay "Diversity and Democracy: Multicultural Education in America," Diane Ravitch asserts that "The history of American public education contains numerous examples of racial, religious, and ethnic conflict. The curriculum of the schools is often seen by parents, policy makers, and interest groups as a means to shape the minds and values of the generation." The prevailing American view of education does not see cultural differences positively. It is a paradigm of education that generally represents the thinking of America's "dominant culture," namely, white America, and allows the exploitation of nondominant groups.[3] It advocates knowledge that oppresses and forsakes greater progress towards the democratic ideal. Too many of our educational institutions—elementary, secondary, postsecondary, and graduate—were cited in 1992 by myself and others as exhibiting "institutional inertia to achieving diversity" and as being in need of "transforming resistance into celebration."[4]

The serious problems presented by each of these paradigms are eliminated by Locke's approach to education. Under Locke's paradigm of education, the examination of values does not lead to a neutral and impartial stance that fails to account adequately for different values; instead, it provides for a meaningful examination of values. Similarly, under Locke's paradigm, it is not possible to assert that the values of one culture are universal or to maintain that commonalities of values reflect people more realistically than the particularities of different values.

Locke's essay addresses three problems of contemporary learning: questionable historical solutions to these problems, the need for education to address the normative dimension, and critical relativism as a viable theory and application of the normative dimension. In this chapter I examine the importance of the normative dimension of education and Locke's critical relativism methodology as a viable theory and application of the normative dimension.

For Locke, there needs to be a coordination between philosophy and education in the quest to address common objectives of integrating elements for knowledge and to provide consistent approaches in education. He states that philosophers and educators agree on three points:

> first, that contemporary learning suffers from a serious and immobilizing lack of any vital and effective integration, both as a body of knowledge and as a taught curriculum (excepting, of course, the pragmatic vocational clusters in the various professional fields); second, that this "ineffectiveness" is not so much an internal fault as it is an external dislocation in the relationship of knowledge to the problems of the social culture; and third, that unless some revitalizing integration is soon attained, not only the social impotence of our knowledge must be conceded in spite of its technological effectiveness, but a breakdown of the culture itself may be anticipated.[5]

These points, according to Locke, reflect the pragmatic pressures of a culture crisis and concerns for the systematization of knowledge, along with our special contemporary need for "unified knowledge," which has resulted in a problem of great significance and urgency. Locke explains that, historically, orientation courses, general education, and the core curriculum were proposed as the solution; and today I would add multicultural courses and special studies courses. Such curricula, he acknowledges, have merit as educational directives, linking "academic learning with the practical issues of living, and thus developing critical acumen and trained aptitudes leading to responsible and intelligent action."[6]

Locke embraced these educational directives and their objectives with his instrumental role in making Howard University the first university to require general education and principles of reasoning for graduation,[7] but he persisted in thinking that more was needed than curriculum extension or revision. Equally important, he argued, is a fundamental methodological revision both in the ways we teach and in the ways we think, "if we are to achieve the objectives of reorientation and integration in education."[8] Assuming that a change in our *scope* of thinking will change our *way* of thinking is a patent fallacy for Locke. If parochial thinking is to be transformed into global thinking, it is necessary to address issues of conflict; to account realistically for their differences by examining the history of their development; and, from a process-logic of this development, to assert bravely a normative stand. To continue traditional neutral scholarship about values in the name of impartial objectivity—the old academic balancing of pros and cons—no matter how wide the scope of the curriculum, will likely produce, in the end, a student who is more widely informed "but with the same old mind-sets, and more entrenched in the conceit of knowing more."[9]

The acuteness of the cultural crisis, according to Locke, calls for a fundamental methodological revision, in particular for a radical methodology as the solution to educational reconstruction. This methodology has specific correctives for traditional ways of thinking. Second, it "treat[s] materials . . . with critical and normative regard for values, but without becoming didactic or dogmatic."[10] It ensures pedagogic attention to students' ways of thinking, thereby improving "global thinking," "process understanding," and the capacity for "evaluative criticism." It develops students' "capacity for thinking objectively but critically about situations and problems involving social and cultural values."[11] Locke refers to this radical methodology as "critical relativism." It is, for Locke, the essence of addressing the normative sense of education, both critically and objectively.

Locke's objection to the cognitive sense of education and, in particular, his emphasis on the normative sense of education shape the core of his ideas about the nature of education. The normative features of education address the application of our lived experiences, effectively integrating knowledge and social concerns. Normative education for Locke involves developing attitudes, dispositions, values, and value judgments that lead to thinking and actions about ourselves and others that reject dogmatic ideology. Dogmatic dispositions and values are learned habits. Transforming these kinds of attitudes, dispositions, values, and value judgments into thinking and actions about ourselves and others that lessen racial, religious, ethnic, gender, class, age, and economic conflict is possible through Locke's paradigm for transformative education. For education to endeavor to achieve such results suggests a worthy purpose and a meaningful reason to pursue it. Accordingly, we understand that there is an intrinsic link between education, the individual, culture, and society. Thus, education is related to resolving social-cultural problems. We learn to rethink economic problems, implementing innovative strategies that address limited resources in conjunction with individuals' needs and reject the use of race, gender, class, age, and the physically challenged as frequent scapegoats for economic problems.

Values and Education

For a fuller sense of normative education, an understanding of the nature of values is essential. Our behavior, thoughts, perceptions, values, goals, morals, and cognitive processes count as knowledge that is derived from our culture. Locke wrote extensively on the nature of values. His analysis of values includes their psychological, social, and historical aspects; their impact on our social problems; the relation between values, culture, and education; and the complexity of examining values objectively and critically. Locke thinks that "values are rooted in attitudes, not in reality and pertain to ourselves, not to the world."[13] Locke explains that it is from our culture, which evolves and changes constantly, that we learn valuations about ourselves and others. Our cultures are the bonds of thoughts and values between people that bind them as a given group. When we reflect upon our values and determine them to be inadequate, the result is new valuations, which Locke refers to as "transvaluations." Values for Locke affect our relations with others and our effective resolution of many social-cultural problems.

Locke's analysis of the psychological, social, and historical phenomena of values reveals that the values we derive from our culture consist of particular parameters that are experience-based "functional adaptations" that have an interpretive, perspectival character. These parameters determine the choices we make in life and often prevent us from valuing the choices of others and from acknowledging the shortcomings of our own choices. For instance, white Americans and Asian cultures view eye contact very differently. Lack of sustained eye contact for white Americans in some situations suggests poor command of conversation and communication skills, while for Asian cultures it suggests respect and honor in many situations. Locke explains that it is from our culture, which evolves and changes constantly, that we learn valuations of others and ourselves. We should understand that others may not share our values, beliefs, perceptions, thoughts, morals, goals, and cognitive processes; realize the arbitrary basis of our own choices; and be willing to reexamine our choices in relation to choices made by others. We should learn to "view values relativistically in time perspective, so as to comprehend value change and development, and likewise, to see them in comparative perspective, so as to understand and appreciate value diversity."[14] Locke's paradigm for transformative education challenges us to examine our valuations in ways that are inclusive rather than exclusive and dogmatic.

Like Ralph Barton Perry, Locke thought that "one of the most important functions of value theory is to provide a rational ground for the comparison of values, particularly those ultimate values by which [people] estimate their civilization, their progress, and the salvation of their existence. The problem of values constitutes the very core of human life."[15] In Locke's review of Perry's *Realms of Value* (1954), he maintains that value is one of most significant and complex areas of philosophy.[16] It provides an initial "point of contact between thought and actual living" that is usually not addressed by "professional or lay thinking." One of the reasons for this is "our chronic inclination to take values for granted." Locke asserts of Perry's work that

> It is both a notable and welcome exception to encounter an analysis of value that, without loss of scholarly depth, examines values in the vital context of their actual functioning, and as in the case of *Realms of Value,* yields cumulative insight into the role of values in motivating and in providing sanctions—rational and rationalized—for our civilization.[17]

Insofar as values are learned, Locke says that adult education, in particular, is more than mere literacy, it is enlarging horizons and broadening human values, with the latter being more important.[18] Education is a means to cultural self-knowledge and knowledge of one's race and others through cultural studies, expanding beyond one's individual ethnic group to multicultural Americanness and global humanity. Education should address cultural values and their relation to social problems. An effective curriculum connects social problems and education. Whether in the arts, the social sciences, or the natural sciences, the curriculum examines social concerns and provides knowledge of the causes of human action. Locke explains that adult education must address the person "farthest down" and put him or her on equal footing with the rest of America.[19] An important result of the education experience is the encouragement of collaboration, consultation, and coalition building between African Americans, whites, and others.

Education provides us with an ongoing reorganization of our social and personal experience. As an ongoing transforming process of our individual, cultural, and social selves, education can enable us to reshape our superiorist or inferiorist ideology of attitudes, dispositions, values, and value judgments. This reshaping of experience produces critical informed thinking that strengthens the quality of our personal, cultural, and social lives.

Of further importance to Locke's discussion of values and education is the philosophical framework of cultural pluralism. Locke's friend and collaborator Horace Kallen explains that cultural pluralism

> is intended to signify [an] endeavor toward friendship by people who are different from each other but who, as different, hold themselves equal to each other. By "equal" we commonly mean "similar" or "identical." Cultural Pluralism, however, intends by "equal" also parity of the unequal, equality of the unlike, not only of the like or the same. It postulates that individuality is indefeasible, that differences are primary, and that consequently human beings have an indefeasible right to their differences and should not be penalized for their differences, however they may be constituted, whatever they may consist in: color, faith, sex, occupation, possession, or what have you. On the record, nevertheless, human beings continually penalize one another for their differences.[20]

Cultural pluralism for Locke, according to Kallen, is "a way of life, the projection of value judgment into the milieu of contemporary problems" and "a practical model through which congenial relations between conflicting groups could be achieved."[21] Locke thinks of it as a model of action in which each individual is an active participant; it provides people with self-respect, self-pride, and self-esteem.[22] Cultural pluralism provides a philosophical framework for overcoming the barriers of segregation and racism that have afflicted general education since Reconstruction.[23] It means an inclusiveness of all American ethnic groups, including the American Negro.

For contemporary education to deal with attitudes, Locke explains, it must perforce grapple realistically with values and value judgments; to develop constructive mind-sets and efficient critical ones, the normative element must be a part of education. Adequate thinking on social issues must involve critical evaluation rather than stop short at descriptive neutrality. We must aim to deal with values as objectively as we deal with facts; further, it is important to be able to significantly and realistically correlate the factual and the value aspects in the social science fields. The proper study of people is a comprehensive, comparative study with a realistic regard for difference instead of a rationalistic study with a zeal for commonalities and conformity. The result is a scientific humanism with a critical and relativistic basis.[24]

Locke cites Karl Deutsch regarding what such training could accomplish: "It might aid [students] to achieve a better understanding of the nature of values and a greater openness to the values of other peoples and other cultures without weakening their understanding and attachment to their own."[25] Such training helps to "pivot the center," in the words of Bettina Aptheker. Elsa Barkley Brown explains that "all people can learn to center in another experience, validate it, and judge it by its own standards without need of comparison or need to adopt that framework as their own. Thus, one has no need to 'decenter' anyone in order to center someone else; one has only to constantly, appropriately, 'pivot the center.'"[26] This approach also understands that we truly know ourselves only when we know ourselves in relation to others; similarly, we can appropriately appropriate one another's experiences. For Locke, self-knowledge and knowledge of one's race through cultural studies are an important part of the Negro's progress in America. His view reflected that of Kallen and other cultural pluralists who asserted that European ethnic groups should be able to acknowledge their ethnic heritage and be fully American at the same time.[27]

It is also understanding that we truly know ourselves when we know ourselves in relation to others. Similarly, it is learning too that we can appropriately "appropriate" one another's experiences. Appropriate appropriations of others' experiences involves acknowledging various experiences as belonging to others in real and significant ways that cannot be claimed by you. While it is inappropriate for white women to appropriate some senses of being a slave that are appropriate for African American women, there are other senses that are appropriate and meaningful to developing further understanding, cooperation, and appreciation of one another.

Race for Locke is a social, not a biological, phenomenon. He criticizes racism in several ways, pointing out biological fallacies, fallacies of groups, and the erroneous belief in the permanency of race types. In *Race Contacts and Interracial Relations,* Locke argues that racial temperaments are regularly traceable to historical economic and social causes.[28] He believes that while racial identity is important in a racial world, cosmopolitan citizenship identity is also important. As individuals, we are part of a community. We express our individuality through community, and our individual ideas are carried on through various communities. The self is community *and* individual, not either/or, but both, and not mutually exclusive but different perspectives of interconnection between individual and community.

Locke contends that the value humans place on race is fictitious and that "the real value of things, that which gives meaning and substance, lies in their possibility of providing the human with a healthy emotional state. . . . The real value of race, the positive value . . . [is] the great contribution it could make to the diversity as well as the unity of the human race."[29] Locke explains that differences reflect power bases and power relationships that have structured our values. White Americans should acknowledge some of the presumptions of powerful people. Similarly, helping people to appreciate what is valuable in other people's cultures and understanding of human values is important to learning the worth and strength of diversity. Much of history reflects a sense of power as hierarchy, which distorts and minimizes a sense of shared power that is more inclusive and diverse, resulting in more valuable and greater strength.

Critical Relativism

In 1950, Alain Locke advocated a new system of principles in education in his essay "The Need for a New Organon in Education." Locke's new system provides a significant theoretical and pragmatic vision of a paradigm for transforming education into a multicultural, collaborative approach that values unity within diversity. He refers to his new methodological approach to education as "critical relativism." It includes six important principles:

1. implement an objective interpretation of values by referring them realistically to their social and cultural backgrounds,

2. interpret values concretely as functional adaptations to these backgrounds, and thus make clear their historical and functional relativity. An objective criterion of functional sufficiency and insufficiency would thereby be set up as a pragmatic test of value adequacy or inadequacy,

3. claim or impute no validity for values beyond this relativistic framework, and so counteract value dogmatism based on regarding them as universals good and true for all times and all places,

4. confine its consideration of ideology to the prime function and real status of being the adjunct rationalization of values and value interests,

5. trace value development and change as a dynamic process instead of in terms of unrealistic analytic categories, and so eliminating the traditional illusions produced by generalized value terms—*viz.*, static values and fixed value concepts and 'ideals,'

6. reinforce current semantic criticism of academic value controversy by stressing this realistic value dynamics as a substitute for traditional value analytics, with its unrealistic symbols and overgeneralized concepts.[30]

For Locke, critical relativism provides a systematic process of value analysis in response to Karl W. Deutsch's call for formal training about values. From Locke's view, critical relativism is a corrective discipline that undermines "dogma-forming attitudes in thinking and the elimination of the partisan hundred percentist mentality at its very psychological roots." Critical relativism is a process grounding "some normative principle or criterion of objective validity for values without resort to dogmatism and absolutism."[31] It addresses the historical, social, and cultural perspectives of values.

Ernest Mason notes that Locke's critical relativism is "ethical insofar as it demands that we treat people different from ourselves with respect, with concern, and above all with understanding and tolerance."[32] Crucial to this goal, Mason explains, is overcoming "the belief that before people of different races and cultures can live together they must adhere to the same principles and values."[33] Locke strongly objects to this view on the principle of unity in diversity, on which he elaborates in "Unity through Diversity: A Baha'i Principle."[34] Locke's critical relativism rejects any superiorist ideology, whether espoused by whites, African Americans, or another group. It encourages open dialogue, coalition building, and peaceful coexistence among diverse groups during a time of social crisis.

Locke's use of the term "relativism" does not mean that he is a [subjectivist] relativist about value judgments or the value of human pursuits. His critical relativism provides objective standards for the evaluation of values while avoiding absolutism and dogmatism, and it is not to be confused with "value pluralism" or "value subjectivism."[35] Locke explains it as the middle ground between subjectivism and objectivism, representing the natural distinction of values.[36] It is like Kant's regulatory principle, constantly moving between two extremes, resulting in an appreciation for value diversity. This quality of critical relativism is possible for Locke through reflection. If relativism is to work properly, it is important that we continuously reflect on our values as they influence our thoughts and practices and introduce necessary changes leading to what Locke called "transvaluation." With self-reflection and self-scrutiny, we better position ourselves to realize, in the words of Mason, "that genuine coexistence for which Alain Locke so passionately, thoughtfully, and humanely lived."[37]

Conclusion

How can we manifest Locke's paradigm for transformative education today? How do we change our traditional narrow, exclusive, and disconnected paradigms of education? We know from Locke that changing the scope of thinking—

adding orientation courses, general education, a core curriculum, multicultural courses, or special studies courses—is not adequate for closing the gap between education and social-cultural problems. In addition to these curriculum offerings, we need to transform both the ways we teach and the ways we think. Locke's theory of critical relativism provides us with a methodological framework applicable to any curriculum. When we utilize it, the curriculum focus is enhanced as we critically notice the exclusiveness of ideas and concepts along with their cultural absolutism and subjectivism, thus transforming the ways we teach, which results in transforming the ways we think, thereby enriching the value of education for resolving our social-cultural problems.

It is necessary that we teach students the importance of culture; in so doing, the contributions of others are acknowledged, and critical analysis of our own position is encouraged. We are reminded by Mark Cohen that while we have improved in our understanding, too many still think that there are only three races—Caucasian, Negroid, and Mongoloid. Similarly, too many think that there is only one desirable pattern of human cognition, perception, and formation of categories, which leads to other false beliefs like the idea that standardized IQ tests are equally valid for assessing individuals from different cultural backgrounds, or that the use of analogy problems to test students' skills in logic reveals an innate, genetically driven intelligence, when the categories that are utilized are cultural and not universal.

With Locke's paradigm of transformative education, we champion education as fundamental to resolving many of our social-cultural problems. Given our contemporary multidimensional social crisis, the quality of life for all—including that of the dominant white American culture—is threatened by the reality of our not being able to live together and the possibility of destroying each other. This bleak scenario may reawaken our conscience and force us into action for transformative change. Who are the agents of change for this endeavor? If we in education, philosophers in particular, are not responsible for taking the lead in transforming it, then who? Yet, we know that many of us are still in need of understanding and acknowledging the value of transformative education in order to become agents of change for this endeavor. Locke's philosophy represents bridging theory and praxis, examining and living philosophy. In an interview with Locke, Cedric Parker said of Locke that he "is a member of that school of philosophers who believe in connecting classroom philosophy with current issues and the practical problems of everyday living."[38] Philosophy for Locke is not a leisure activity reserved for the elite. Rather, it is a guide and a tool that can enrich life for all people. Not to acknowledge Locke's paradigm for transformative education is to ignore our potential to better resolve our contemporary social-cultural problems.

Notes

I am indebted to Johnny Washington, Beth Singer, and Judith Green for their helpful comments on earlier drafts of this paper.

1. See Alain Locke, "The Need for a New Organon in Education" (1950), in *The Philosophy of Alain Locke: Harlem Renaissance and Beyond*, ed. Leonard Harris (Philadelphia: Temple University Press, 1989).

2. Leonard Harris, ed., *The Philosophy of Alain Locke: Harlem Renaissance and Beyond* (Philadelphia: Temple University Press, 1989), 263.

3. See Diane Ravitch, "Diversity and Democracy: Multicultural Education in America," *American Educator* (Spring 1990): 407.

4. See Nancy P. Greenman et al., "Institutional Inertia to Achieving Diversity: Transforming Resistance into Celebration," *Educational Foundations* 6, no. 2 (Spring 1992).

5. Locke, "New Organon," 265.

6. Locke, "New Organon," 266.

7. See LaVerne Gyant, "Alain Leroy Locke: More Than an Adult Educator," in *Freedom Road: Adult Education of African Americans*, ed. Elizabeth A. Peterson (Malabar, Fla.: Krieger Publishing, 1996).

8. Locke, "New Organon," 266.

9. Locke, "New Organon," 268.

10. Locke, "New Organon," 269.

11. Locke, "New Organon," 270.

12. Locke, "New Organon," 272.

13. Alain Locke, "Values and Imperatives," in *American Philosophy Today and Tomorrow*, ed. Horace M. Kallen and Sidney Hook (New York: Lee Furman, 1935), 328.

14. Locke, "New Organon," 273.

15. Ernest D. Mason, "Alain Locke's Philosophy of Value," in *Alain Locke: Reflections on a Modern Renaissance Man*, ed. Russell J. Linnemann (Baton Rouge: Louisiana State University Press, 1982), 3.

16. Alain Locke, "Values That Matter," *Key Reporter* 19 (3 May 1954): 4.

17. Locke, "Values That Matter," 4.

18. See Alain Locke, "Negro Needs as Adult Education Opportunities" (1938), in *Philosophy of Alain Locke*, ed. Harris, 253–62.

19. Alain Locke, "Negro Education Bids for Par" (1925), in *Philosophy of Alain Locke*, ed. Harris, 239–52.

20. Horace Kallen, "Alain Locke and Cultural Pluralism," *Journal of Philosophy* 54 (February 1957): 120.

21. Kallen, "Locke and Cultural Pluralism," 120.

22. Gyant, "Alain Leroy Locke," 71.

23. See Gyant, "Alain Leroy Locke."

24. See Talmadge C. Guy, "The American Association of Adult Education and the Experiments in African American Education," in *Freedom Road,* ed. Peterson, 89–108.

25. Locke, "New Organon," 272.

26. Elsa Barkley Brown, "African American Women's Quilting: A Framework for Conceptualizing and Teaching African American Women's History," in *Black Women in America: Social Science Perspective* (Chicago: University of Chicago Press, 1990), 415.

27. See Horace Kallen, "Democracy and the Melting Pot: A Study of American Nationality," *Nation* 100 (1915).

28. See Alain Locke, "Race Contact and Interracial Relations: A Study in the Theory and Practice of Race" (1916), in *The Critical Temper of Alain Locke: A Selection of His Essays on Art and Culture,* ed. Jeffrey C. Stewart (New York: Garland Publishing, 1983).

29. Gyant, "Alain Leroy Locke," 71.

30. Locke, "New Organon," 273–74.

31. Locke, "Values and Imperatives," 319.

32. Mason, "Locke's Philosophy of Value," 12

33. Mason, "Locke's Philosophy of Value," 12.

34. Alain Locke, "Unity through Diversity: A Baha'i Principle," in *Philosophy of Alain Locke,* ed. Harris, 133–37.

35. Mason, "Locke's Philosophy of Value," 7.

36. Locke, "Values and Imperatives," 319.

37. Mason, "Locke's Philosophy of Value," 16.

38. Alain Locke, *Madison (Wis.) Capital Times,* 2 January 1946.

Part V

Paradoxes, Dilemmas, and Critiques

19

Values, Imperatives, and the Imperative of Democratic Values

Segun Gbadegesin

The first paragraph of "Values and Imperatives" betrays, most pointedly, Locke's sense of philosophy.[1] For him, philosophy is a subjective activity with a view towards some objective reality. All philosophies, he insists, "are in ultimate derivation philosophies of life" (34). They are not "abstract disembodied objective reality"; they are "products of time, place and situation." They may just be "the lineaments of a personality, its temperaments and dispositional attitude" (34). This is the subjective aspect, and as we shall see, it borders on relativism. On the other hand, however personal a philosophy may be, it cannot avoid the question of ultimates. The quest for certainty is an essential element of any philosophical endeavor, including one focused on values. For as Locke puts it, a thorough-going relativistic or subjectivist philosophy will not only abandon a discredited absolutism, it will also endanger the growth of axiology "with its promising analysis of norms" (34). The objective, then, is to stay a middle course: "In dethroning our absolutes, we must take care not to exile our imperatives for after all, we live by them" (34). It follows, of course, that imperatives are not necessarily absolutes. Locke argues that values create imperatives as well as the more formally superimposed absolutes. What is required is an analysis of values, imperatives, and absolutes to see what light, if any, they throw on the question of democratic values.

In what follows, I first present an interpretation of Locke's account of values as imperatives. I raise some issues regarding his defense of relativism. Then I present an account of what he identifies as the value of pluralism. Finally, I argue that rather than encourage cultural pluralism per se, we must insist on openness in the discussion and evaluation of our plural values, which may otherwise be mutually antagonistic.

The Philosophical Imperatives of Values

Can philosophy abandon interest in values and normative principles? The question arises for Locke in the light of what he considered to be the tendency toward "philosophical nihilism" in the early part of the twentieth century. He argues for the relevance of values and the need for value analysis. For "without some account of normative principles, no philosophical system can differentiate itself from descriptive science or present a functional interpretive version of human experience" (34). Values are so central to life that human beings cannot avoid them. The world is not value free, and therefore philosophy cannot be value neutral. Of course, Locke seems to concede that objective reality of value is not independent of the process of valuation. And since this implies a backhanded denial of the reality of value without human valuation, Locke has to develop a complex argument for his brand of "critical relativism."

So we cannot avoid value ultimates. At the same time, however, we cannot afford dogmatism and absolutism. The problem is to reconcile the need for value ultimates with the need for value tolerance. It is posed as a philosophical problem, and Locke frames it thus:

> The greatest problem of contemporary philosophy is how to ground some normative principle or criterion of objective validity of values without resort to dogmatism and absolutism on the intellectual plane, and without falling into their corollaries on the plane of social behavior and action, of intolerance and mass coercion. (36)

In other words, how can values be granted objective validity without resort to absolutism and intolerance? The solution, for Locke, is to develop "a functional analysis of value norms and search for normative principles in the immediate context of valuation" (36). By a functional analysis of value norms, Locke means one that is focused on the analysis of value norms as functional instruments; and by normative principles, he means those principles that guide and validate action. In the context of valuation (*x* is good; *y* is beautiful), we make use of our subjective experience to declare the object of that experience as good or beautiful.

In "A Functional View of Value Ultimates" Locke defines a functionalist approach as one that places emphasis on the interrelationship among values and the functional relation of a value—say, goodness—to its reference in the value situation that it depicts.[2] From a functional approach, two sets of problems may be identified: theoretical, regarding the formal definition of the generic character of value ultimates; practical, regarding the conflicts of values and their bearing on the question of value ultimacy. These two problems are correlated by a functional approach; they are not separated, because the theoretical is not separable from the practical. More important, the functional approach does not see the definitional problem as prior to the practical. Indeed, it appears that for this approach, the practical is at least as important as the theoretical. This is why Locke suggests that the immediate context of valuation should serve as basis for developing normative principles. This should be possible if the fundamental value modes (ethical, aesthetic, logical, religious) can set up automatically or dispositionally their end values prior to evaluative judgments. That is, is it the case that an ethical value (good) proceeds from a feeling attitude towards an object and independent of, and prior to, the evaluative judgment of the object? This appears to be Locke's view: value modes have a way of setting up their end values prior to evaluative judgments. It also appears that they do this through the medium of feeling attitude. This is why Locke thinks that the primary normative character (of value ultimates) "reside[s] in their functional role as stereotypes of feeling-attitudes and dispositional imperatives of action-choices, with this character reenforced only secondarily by reason and judgment about them as absolutes."[3]

This approach can ease our practical understanding of the mechanism of valuation, and the basis for agreements and conflicts over values. This is what makes it functional, and it is in furtherance of the aim of Brentano, to whom Locke refers as the father of modern value theory, to

> derive a functional theory of value from a descriptive and empirical psychology of valuation and to discover in value-experience itself the source of those normative and categorical elements construed for centuries so arbitrarily and so artificially in the realm of rational absolutes. (36)

This aim cannot be achieved by looking at values from outside the process of valuation, and this is why Locke suggests that the real nature of values can only be discovered when we adopt a functional approach.

The Nature of Value Judgment

Do values have an objective validity independent of the valuer and the valuation process? Locke seeks a middle ground between subjectivism and objectivism, between what he calls "the atomistic relativism of a pleasure-pain scale and the colorless uniformitarian criterion of logic" (38). For him, though values may not be as universal or objective as logical truths, they have their own relative objectivity and universality. But there are no realms of values out there grounding categorization of values; there are only modes or kinds of valuing, and it is only from these that we derive our qualitative category of values. If so, as Locke argues, it follows that "the primary judgments of value are emotional judgments, and the initial reference for value-predication (e.g. 'good' in 'that is good') is based on a form-quality revealed in feeling and efficacious in valuation through feeling" (39). In other words, Locke is here suggesting that the various values are known and recognized in our qualitative apprehension of phenomena: beauty, goodness, truth (as approval), righteousness are all known in immediate quality apprehension no matter how we then choose to validate them. When we see an object that is good or beautiful, we know it immediately.

Pursuing the argument further, Locke claims that "the generic types of value are basic and fundamental feeling-modes each with its own characteristic form criterion in value perception" (39). But what does this mean? The generic types of value, I think, are the examples he had given (goodness, beauty, truth, holiness). He says that these are "basic and fundamental feeling modes," meaning that we have them when we have these feeling modes. We do not need any other criterion save the feeling mode that signifies goodness. But does this mean that this feeling mode varies from person to person with respect to one single occurrence? If I have a feeling mode of goodness vis-à-vis an object, can my friend have a feeling mode of badness? Is this where Locke's critical relativism makes sense?

Locke anticipates and tries to respond to this problem by suggesting that each of the fundamental feeling modes has its own characteristic form criterion in value perception. That is, if I perceive *x* as good, there is a goodness form criterion that helps me to identify *x* as good. But this could mean that the criterion is outside of human influence. This is not Locke's meaning. For it is in value perception (not outside or independent of it) that the form criterion operates. Locke then suggests that common sense discriminates accurately between the fundamental kinds of value: moral/ethical, aesthetic, logical and religious. The point, here, I think, is that although it is possible to have formal defining criteria as to the distinctiveness of the various values, it is more useful to discriminate in terms of feeling and attitude and their "affective-volitional dimensions and factors" (39).

In other words, when we apprehend a value, it conveys its mode (kind). We apprehend it as "good" in the moral sense or in the aesthetic sense. We may wonder about its place in the value series, about its validation, and so on. But we are certain about what kind (mode) it is. Therefore, it is better, according to Locke, to think of value quality in terms of feeling or attitude and not as a predicate of judgment. Locke emphasizes that if the value type is given in our immediate apprehension of the value (as he thinks it is), then some qualitative universal is given. Thus, this is what he means when he declares that "in the feeling-reference to some value-mode, some value ulti-mate becomes the birthmark of the value" (39). And further: "if values are thus normatively stamped by form-qualities of feeling in the original value experience, then the evaluative judgment merely renders explicit what was implicit in the original value sensing at least as far as the modal quality of the value is concerned" (39).

Locke suggests two assumptions either of which may make the foregoing true: (a) some abstract feeling character functions dispositionally as a substi-tute for formal judgment (of the value); or (b) the feeling attitude itself molded the value-mode and reflected sympathetically its own pattern. "If the latter be the case, a value-type or category is a feeling mode carved out dispositionally by a fundamental attitude" (39).

In anticipation of the objection to the idea of a feeling reference constitut-ing the essential identity and unity of a value mode (especially objections from those who are scientifically minded and would therefore demand demonstra-tion of such a claim), Locke argues that "there is nothing scientifically impos-sible or bizarre in assuming a form-quality felt along with the specific value context and constituting its modal value-quality and reference" (40).

For instance, if we investigate carefully, according to Locke, we will dis-cover that values have no fixed content and no permanent group identity as such. Some value genre can break out of its definition or "through its logical barrier to include content not usually associated with it" (40). An awe-inspir-ing scene becomes "holy"; the logical proof becomes "beautiful," etc. New predicates are created following new attitudes, and the attitude succeeds in canceling out the old predicates. Locke then concludes that "the feeling-quali-ty irrespective of content, makes a value of a given kind, and that a transfor-mation of the attitude effects a change of type in the value situation" (40).

Each situation, through the feeling form (attitude) it generates, creates its own value category, which cannot be universalized. Thus an artist, who nor-mally operates under the category of aesthetic values, may feel a moral oblig-ation to finish a work. This feeling form dictates a value (moral) distinct from aesthetics. This new dimension is what Locke terms "a functional categorical factor." This way of accounting for values starts from feeling: what is the feel-ing attitude that gave rise to the value? The traditional way of accounting for various values, however, starts from evaluation, and leans too heavily upon logical definition. By emphasizing feeling attitude as the basis for classifying values, Locke is putting a premium on psychological as opposed to logical definition, on the genetic origin of value groups in the psyche as opposed to their generic grouping.

Using this criterion of classification, Locke identifies four value modes and corresponding feeling modes:

Value: religious   moral   logical   aesthetic
Feeling mode: exaltation   tension   acceptance repose or equilibrium

On this schema, Locke concludes that "there is a form-feeling (exaltation, tension etc.) or form quality characteristic of each fundamental value type (religious, moral etc.) and that values are discriminated in terms of such feeling factors in the primary processes of valuation" (42). The constitution of values is therefore not on the basis of logical judgment. This is how Locke explains such phrases as a "beautiful proof" or a "pretty demonstration." They make sense, not in the light of or by appeal to change of judgments in a process of valuation, but rather as a result of the quality of feeling. The predicates are appropriate and reflect the actual attitude in the valuation. "They are in direct functional relation and agreement" (42).

Locke explains the conflict of values as value groups from the same principle. The preference over any other for beauty, truth, and goodness in our value scheme is due to our feeling preferences and temperament. He sees these "grand ultimates" as doomed to perpetual logical opposition because their basic value attitudes are psychologically incompatible.

Besides conflicts between value-types (religious, scientific, moral, aesthetic) Locke also identifies conflicts within each value type (e.g., between the mystic and the reformer in religion) due to division between people in their orientation to their common values. Locke thinks that certain directional drives are responsible for these differences and are the "root of civil feuds within the several value provinces" (45). It is the setting of attitudes and their rationalizations that lead to the value loyalties that divide humanity. He argues that what comes down to us as justified or true and valid ways of life are, really, "merely the projections of predominant value tendencies and attitudes" (46).

Locke suggests that we should understand this process of valuation stemming from feeling and attitudes so that we may also, through understanding find the principle of control from the mechanisms of valuation themselves: "The effective antidote to value absolutism lies in a systematic and realistic demonstration that values are rooted in attitudes, not in reality, and pertain to ourselves, not to the world" (46). The suggestion here is that an adequate recognition of the pluralism of values is essential for the elimination of value bigotry.

What about value anarchism resulting from this type of value pluralism? Locke denies that pluralism can lead to this. He thinks that value pluralism is not based on the distinctions provided by factual reality (e.g., pleasure-pain or end-means distinctions). The presence of facts does not neutralize the force of values. We cannot banish imperatives from our lives; therefore, we must find some principle for keeping them within bounds. What Locke thought of is to see values as functional instruments. Seeing that norms are functional and native to the process of experience does not justify arbitrary absolutes. These types of norms would then be "functional constants and practical sustaining imperatives of their correlated modes of experience" (47).

The "ends" that are reflected in one value experience, for Locke, just "totalize merely an aspect of human experience and stand only for a subsistent order of reality" (47). They should not be taken as the whole of reality, nor should they attempt to mask other values reflected by that aspect of human experience that they totalize. Even with this otherwise relativistic approach, Locke still insists that fact and values should not be seen as antagonistic orders; "rather should we think of reality as a central fact and a white light broken up by the prism of human nature into a spectrum of values" (47).

Defense of Functionalism

Locke defends the functional approach. He argues that it is able to deal with a critique of values, especially during periods of value conflicts and social stress. A formalist analysis shies away from such a critique. But suppose a value realist objects that the functional approach is a temptation to subjectivism and relativism. Locke's response is twofold: First, this is not true, because the functionalist is not a rabid relativist; rather the object of the functionalist is "to give a consistent account of the relative permanencies of value-modes."[4] Second, Locke challenges the value realist to account for the "numerous observable cases of value transposition" (85), that is, cases in which an aesthetic value norm is referenced in an otherwise epistemological or logic situation. For instance, we see "a beautiful logical proof." These cases cannot be dismissed as mere metaphors or analogies; this, for Locke, is the basic error of the value realists who "regard the formal value as the cause of valuation or as an essence of the value object rather than the system value of the mode of valuing, which is sometimes the symbol, sometimes its rationale, but in practice an implementation of the value as apprehended" (86).

In support of his position, Locke chooses examples from each of the major value genres: moral, logical, aesthetic, and so on. His most cogent case is that of the conflict, brought by exposure to other cultures, in the value system of the Eskimos regarding the morality of parricide. Locke illustrates with the play by Soviet dramatist Korneichuk in which the hero, a young Eskimo man, has been exposed to the Soviet code of morality while training in the USSR. This young man refuses to throw his aged father into the sea as required by tradition. The father, shocked by the son's reluctance, walks into the sea by himself, without the dignity of a last ceremony. Locke's point is that we must not see this event as just a case of conflict of good versus bad value systems. Rather, we have to see each as "right" on its own level—the old value is right in the mind of the father and the relatives, just as the new value is right in the mind of the son. Each of the value systems has its own "truth," its own "rightness." The case, for him, is "an exemplary instance of functional normativity, and one calculated to disprove the value formalist's charge of the non-normative character of the functionalist value interpretation" (88).

There is no doubt, then, that the functional approach is a relativist approach, and that Locke's argument is for relativism in value theory. He hopes that the trend will be toward "a relativistic but not anarchic ethics, world view and religion which will be more functionally related with the actualities of life and conduct and more effectively normative without rigidly imposed and dictatorial authority" (93).

Understanding Locke

What sense does one make of Locke's functional approach to value analysis and its relativistic implications for democratic values? It is significant that Locke identifies the functional approach with critical relativism, which he takes as the answer to absolutism in thought and totalitarianism in practice.

Locke's theory can be understood on two levels. First, there is a need to avoid a formalistic distinction between the value modes. Locke advocates the need to understand that individuals confer on particular value scenes their own feeling modes. Thus, what evokes in me a sense of exaltation becomes a religious value for me, whereas someone else has a feeling of tension or conflict towards it—in which case it is endowed with a moral value. Yet someone else, or I at some other time, may feel that it is beautiful in the aesthetic sense. The suggestion here is that the various kinds of values are interchangeable. This is why we cannot have a strict formal distinction and why Locke insists on a functional account of value ultimates.

The second level is within different value modes. Consider for instance, an ethical value, such as "good." A situation that A describes as "good" may appear to B as "bad." Since feeling mode suggests our attitudes and impression of a situation, this is hardly contestable. Thus, Locke suggests that "rightness" may be seen from different angles and any one situation may have its own "rightness" and appear differently to different individuals, depending on their unique feeling modes.

Locke appears to identify his point of view regarding values with the subjectivist position that what A describes as good is good for A. This denies any objective standard that cuts across persons, independent of their desires and feelings. So value judgments have no objective basis other than the personal attitudes and feelings of persons. When Locke argues that "values are rooted in attitudes, not in reality and pertain to ourselves, not the world," he may be taken as expressing this viewpoint—of subjectivism.[5] Yet, as Mason rightly noted, Locke does not accept subjectivism. Indeed, he argues against what he calls "Protagorean relativism," which he interprets as the doctrine of "each man the measure and the gauge of value."[6]

Yet Locke is also against what he refers to as the "uniformitarian criterion of logic"; and he thinks that the positivist reaction against metaphysics has led it to an uncongenial commitment to "scientific objectivism."[7] If he claims that values are rooted in attitude, not in reality, how can he be antisubjectivist? And if he thinks less of scientific objectivism, how can he not be a Protagorean relativist? This, perhaps more than the record of his life to which Harris refers in his introductory remarks to *The Philosophy of Alain Locke,* appears to me to represent the enigma of Locke.

Still, it appears that Locke has a handle on something remarkable. Extreme subjectivism, which may lead to anarchy, is not an attractive doctrine. On the other hand, extreme objectivism, which may lead to absolutism, is also not an attractive doctrine. There is a middle ground, and it is the destination of Locke. This is especially so in the context of the political implications of the epistemological theory.

This is what value relativism and value pluralism are meant to accomplish. This is why Locke says, "the effective antidote to value absolutism lies in a systematic and realistic demonstration that values are rooted in attitudes, not in reality and pertain to ourselves, not to the world" (36). Through "value pluralism," we may have value loyalty without "value bigotry."

In "The Need for a New Organon in Education," Locke, with an eye on the practical aspect of the problem, argues for the "historical-comparative approach" as "the only proper . . . way of understanding values, including particularly those of one's own culture and way of life."[8] Continuing, he thinks that it would be "educationally mandatory to view values relativistically in time perspective so as to comprehend value change and development, and likewise to see them in comparative perspective, so as to understand and appreciate value diversity" (273).

This is, obviously, an educational objective aimed at attacking absolutism at its source and thus preventing the totalitarian end product from coming to fruition. This is what Locke refers to as the method of critical relativism that, carried through as "a consistent methodological approach," would:

1. implement an objective interpretation of values by referring them realistically to their social and cultural backgrounds,

2. interpret values concretely as functional adaptations to these backgrounds, and thus make clear their historical and functional relativity. An objective criterion of functional sufficiency and insufficiency would thereby be set up as a pragmatic test of value adequacy or inadequacy,

3. claim or impute no validity for values beyond this relativistic framework, and so counteract value dogmatism based on regarding them as universals good and true for all times and all places,

4. confine its consideration of ideology to the prime function and real status of being the adjunct rationalization of values and value interests,

5. trace value development and change as a dynamic process instead of in terms of unrealistic analytic categories, and so eliminating the traditional illusions produced by generalized value terms—*viz.*, static values and fixed value concepts and 'ideals,'

6. reinforce current semantic criticism of academic value controversy by stressing this realistic value dynamics as a substitute for traditional value analytics, with its unrealistic symbols and overgeneralized concepts. (273–74)

This approach has two goals: (1) theoretically, to keep value analysis and discussion on a plane of realism and the maximum attainable degree of scientific objectivity; and (2) practically, to train students to attack the psychological roots of dogmatism. It should be noted that scientific objectivity here, for Locke, does not mean evaluation independent of context. Rather, for him, to be objective is to refer values realistically to their social and cultural backgrounds. This means that critical relativism is just another name for the functional approach, and in spite of the effort to keep scientific objectivity alive through the theoretical goal, it appears that it does not survive the first blow, and the apparent attraction of the practical goal, in view of the danger of dogmatism, assures the victory of the latter. A functional view of value ultimates assures the ultimate value of critical relativism.

The Imperative of Democratic Values

Locke's case for value relativism and value pluralism extends beyond the typical values such as the good, the bad, the true, and the beautiful. For him, even the values that the West has come to cherish and adore may, after all, be relative. "The value disciplines" must, Locke argues, "dethrone their absolutes—as arbitrary universals," for example, as "perfect forms of the state or society."[9] Locke is here making a demand for value pluralism and relativism in all fields, including politics. The advantage he sees out of this is a Pax Romana of values. Democracy of values entails value tolerance, and Locke seems to suggest that if democracy is such a worthy good, then there must also be a democracy of values.

It seems that for Locke, value pluralism as an approach has two contributions to make, first, toward a realistic understanding of values, and, second, toward a more practical and consistent way of holding and advocating values. On the latter, fundamentalism is outlawed, while tolerance is entertained. Thus adherence to values must be critical, selective, and tentative, not final: Value assertion would thus be a tolerant assertion of preference, not an intolerant insistence on agreement or finality (57).

There is a basic paradox of values and valuation, which Locke is trying to resolve: "We cannot, soundly and safely at least, preach liberalism and at the same time abet and condone bigotry, condemn uniformitarianism and placate orthodoxy, promote tolerance and harbor the seeds of intolerance" (57).

He then suggests that "our duty to democracy on the plane of ideas, especially in time of crisis, is the analysis of just this problem and some consideration of its possible solution" (57). But what problem? Promoting tolerance while harboring the seeds of intolerance? But how could this be? Obviously, it could occur when democracy meets dictatorship. Does Locke then mean that the intolerant condemnation of dictatorial regimes by committed democrats is wrong? Was Ronald Reagan guilty of this sin when he referred to the Soviet Union as the "evil empire"? Or do we belong to the same class when we condemn the ill-fated Abacha regime in Nigeria? Are we to condone repression in the name of value pluralism and value relativism? If we do, and if this is the meaning of Locke's relativism, are we not condemning ourselves to eternal suffering? And are we not condoning double standards? Perhaps this is not how Locke wants us to understand his point. We should make an attempt at an adequate understanding. Locke's observations include:

1. We are for the most part unaware of the latent absolutism at the core of many of our traditional loyalties.

2. This absolutism may very well condition current concepts and sanctions of democracy.

3. Instances of absolutist loyalty of the secular dogma "my country, right or wrong" confront us with the paradox of democratic loyalties absolutistically conceived, dogmatically sanctioned, and undemocratically practiced.

4. Too much of our present democratic creed and practice is cast in the mold of blind loyalty and en bloc rationalization with too many citizens the best of democrats for the worst reasons—mere conformity.

5. Uncritical democratic tolerance, because propagated on a too emotional and too abstract basis, easily leads to intolerance and bigotry.

It should be clear that, taken together, these five observations constitute our key to understanding Locke's argument. The object is not to denounce democracy. He is not suggesting that we abandon democratic norms. He is not even suggesting that dictatorship might be a better option. Rather, he is concerned with process rather than content. He is concerned about the process of inculcating democratic values and ideals. He thinks democracy is more professed than practiced. While tolerance, reciprocity, and loyalty have been "promulgated" by democracy, it has not succeeded in implementing them. To do that requires that they be presented as realistically connected with one's own values and interests, and, Locke says, rarely have they been so connected.

Locke argues that idealistic liberalism and goodwill humanitarianism have nursed the Western democratic tradition; that democratic liberalism, with a limited viewpoint and close affiliation with doctrinal religious and philosophical traditions, has modeled its rationale for democracy too closely on authoritarian patterns. It has compromised with too much dogmatism and orthodoxy and is the refuge for too much intolerance and prejudice. Therefore, democracy needs a new rationale, liberal but scientific and realistic. Pluralism is Locke's candidate.

How, if at all, does liberalism differ from pluralism? Liberalism's emphasis is freedom; freedom is its battle cry. But there are other values, including justice (recall Mill's attempt at reconciliation) and community. Liberalism's focus on freedom may therefore reject values that are allegedly opposed to it. Thus liberalism may lead to intolerance if not based on a strong and critical intellectual foundation. Thus far, Locke's position appears unassailable. But we must now ask, what values does pluralism rule in and out? Can it discriminate and still remain plural?

The Value of Pluralism

Locke argues that no single tradition, specific value, or particular institution has a justification for identifying itself en bloc with an ideal like democracy. Why not? Is this because democracy is only an unrealizable ideal? But how about certain institutional structures that are identified with democracy: free association, free press, open elections, separation of powers? Can a society or tradition that has none of these claim to be democratic? There are degrees of conformity to democratic values and it would appear that a minimum set of conditions can be identified without presenting one tradition as a perfect set of "articulated specification[s] for the concept" (59).

What does relativism contribute to this? Locke suggests that it is capable of freeing our minds "from [their] provincial limitations and dogmatic bias" by revealing "our values in proper objective perspective with other sets of values."

But how? In the case of a democracy, consider the value of, say, free press vis-à-vis press censorship. There are justifications on both sides, on the basis of the ultimate value a society espouses. But there must also be ways of evaluating these ultimate values independently of one's own tradition. If Locke's point is that we need to go beyond mere conformity generated by "love of country" to an intellectual justification of the values we espouse, this may certainly be justified on rational grounds beyond relativism. If, on the other hand, Locke's point is that there can be no final rational determination of which value is superior—free or censored press—and if this is the "basic unity—of values" that he espouses, then we have to see what support there is for it. It is easy to suggest that "value pluralism has a point of view able to lift us out of egocentric and ethnocentric predicaments," provided that we recognize that some values are so mutually antagonistic that they cannot coexist even in a plural universe of values.

We may approach the matter from another angle and ask, "What is it to be intolerant?" It is, among other things, to despise and disrespect other people's opinions and values. This attitude is obviously more at home with dictatorships than with democracies. To the extent that a democratic regime is intolerant of, say, press freedom, it bears traces of dictatorship. Therefore Locke's argument may have missed its real target. Of course, individuals in a democracy may turn out to be intolerant of the views of others, but this cannot be attributed to the system, and it is the system that must have the responsibility to correct and reform.

Now, the issue of the conflict of values between the two systems (democracy and dictatorship) is not easily resolved. We cannot condemn a democracy for insisting on freedom. And it may also be argued that a dictatorship cannot be condemned for insisting on community and development as prior to freedom. In this regard, the question must then be raised, which value is most inclusive and which has the probability of realizing itself as well as other values? Can development that denies freedom achieve its purpose? Can community that denies individual freedom achieve its purpose? Or can freedom enhance development and community? A critical analysis of questions such as these can resolve the issues and provide an intellectual basis for the acceptance of democracy without being unnecessarily intolerant or dogmatic. It would appear to me, then, that it is not cultural pluralism per se that must be encouraged, because mutually antagonistic values would eventually cancel themselves out. Rather, we must insist on openness in the discussion and evaluation of our plural values. Such openness, coupled with a readiness to give up values that are inimical to our ultimate values, not only ensures peaceful coexistence but also becomes what Locke refers to as our "intellectual weapon against the totalitarian challenge" (64). That challenge is as real today as it was in 1942.

The challenge cuts across nations, big and small. A relative concept of democracy is dangerous for marginalized peoples, because it only supports dictators who define democracy in their own way and for their own interests while hiding behind cultural differences. It turns out, always, that in the matter of political norms, cultural difference is a refuge for the oppressor. Dictators must be engaged and confronted frontally, and the obligation is on every decent human being, presidents and citizens, parliamentarians and constituents, to stand up for the freedom of human beings and against injustice of any kind wherever it may occur. Yes, there are traditional forms of governance that may fall short of the requirements of Western democracy. But it must be realized that Western democracies did not start as exemplars of human freedom. They went through periods of oppressive monarchical structures and military adventurism. That they have attained some measure of stability and enhanced freedom is due to the struggles of their people. The problem is that whereas those battles were not obstructed by interests from outside, in the case of peoples and nations currently struggling against dictatorships, the stakes are terribly high. For when it suits its interest, the West would support a dictatorship, no matter how much suffering its citizens endure. This accounted for the Mobutus and Abachas of this world. It currently accounts for Abubakar and the warming of the West to him. Cultural pluralism does not justify turning a deaf ear to the cry of the oppressed. It calls for intellectual openness and political will.

Notes

1. Alain Locke, "Values and Imperatives," first published in A*merican Philosophy Today and Tomorrow,* ed. Horace Kallen and Sidney Hook (New York: Lee Furman, 1935), now available in *The Philosophy of Alain Locke: Harlem Renaissance and Beyond,* ed. Leonard Harris (Temple University Press, 1989), 34–50. References in this chapter are to Harris's book.

2. Alain Locke, "A Functional View of Value Ultimates," in *Philosophy of Alain Locke,* ed. Harris, 81–93.

3. Locke, "Values and Imperatives," 36.

4. Locke, "Value Ultimates," 83.

5. Ernest D. Mason, "Alain Locke's Philosophy of Value," in *Alain Locke: Reflections on a Modern Renaissance Man,* ed. Russell J. Linnemann (Baton Rouge: Louisiana State University Press, 1982), 5.

6. Mason, "Locke's Philosophy of Value," 8.

7. Locke, "Values and Imperatives," 36.

8. Alain Locke, "The Need for a New Organon in Education," in *Philosophy of Alain Locke,* ed. Harris,272.

9. Locke, "Pluralism and Intellectual Democracy," in *Philosophy of Alain Locke,* ed. Harris, 55.

20

Meaning in an Epistemic System

Stephen Lester Thompson

Meaning often slips through the grasp of speakers, believers, and valuers, despite their best intentions. What is meant might not be what is said, what is believed might not be expressed, and what is felt and valued might be another thing altogether. What follows from this slippery character of meaning for what meaning itself is like—or, for that matter, what the content of a belief or a value is like? Do slips like these obviate talk of "meaning itself," as if there were no sense to speaking of meaning apart from slippery talk, value, or belief? There is no consensus among (Alain) Lockeans about meaning, though some notions now in the literature on his thought suggest what I consider unpromising leads. In this chapter I will say why I think they are so unpromising; after all, getting clear on the epistemological geography of Locke's thought is necessary for seeing in what ways it is cogent.

It is in the context of an argument about culture that Locke took this slip—this semantic gap—to show that meaning curiously has both a loose and a tight relationship to what we know and what we value. Cultural practices trade on semantic gaps, partly accounting for the richness of their associated symbols. Whatever we should finally say about meaning itself, we ought to begin at the gap, as does the relativism for which Locke is known. That relativism consists equally in a suspicion about absolutes and an earnestness to avoid anything-goes relativism. The Lockean middle ground restrains absolutist approaches to value and knowledge, even as relativist views respect the normative power that claims to value and know imply. His most complete treatment of this middle position appears in "Values and Imperatives,"[1] though subsequent essays extend his analysis through a range of symbolically rich contexts, especially "Pluralism and Intellectual Democracy."[2] The work of symbols and their gaps does much to make the middle position plausible.

His middle-position relativism has been variously interpreted by philosophers in the style of deconstruction, emphasizing the contingency and indeterminacy of knowledge and meaning.[3] I do not think this reading of Locke can be maintained alongside his view of symbols, though, and to the degree that that view undergirds his epistemology, the interpretations of deconstructivists fail to do him justice. Yet, the work is trickier since Locke was a complex thinker who (unfortunately) wrote no extended systematic work that might otherwise help settle some of these questions. (In that regard he is like Peirce, and the emerging literature on Locke's philosophy resembles the early Peircian secondary literature that came out as his papers were published in the 1930s.) I will only attempt in this paper the modest task of saying what Locke's semantic gap is supposed to be, showing it to be central to his epistemology; hence its value as a benchmark for Lockeans. The incompatibilities between Locke and the deconstructive readings (in my view) thus become obvious.

I begin with Locke's gappy symbols.

Gappy Symbols

Locke referred a number of times to a semantic gap in symbols and always at the point in his argument when he sought an epistemological justification for his relativism.[4] But his clearest reference appears in the 1942 paper on pluralist democracy. In it he claimed that his relativism

> breaks down the worship of the form—that dangerous identification of the symbol with the value, which is the prime psychological root of the fallacies and errors we have been discussing. We might pose it as the acid test for an enlightened value loyalty that it is able to distinguish between the *symbol* and *form* of its loyalty and the *essence* and *objective* of that loyalty. Such critical insight, for example, would recognize a real basic similarity or functional equivalence in other values, even when cloaked in considerable superficial difference.[5]

This is worth dwelling on. Although symbols hug the values they stand for, valuers ought to remain a bit suspicious of them. Not only ought valuers to be in contact with feelings—which, Locke argued in "Values and Imperatives," causally underwrite valuing acts—valuers ought also to understand them in some favored "enlightened" way.

It is helpful to call the myriad pathways among feelings and their interpretations *epistemic liaisons* since that makes it obvious that, when these liaisons systematically interact with each other, an *epistemic system* is at work. (Neither term occurs in Locke's writing, but the concepts they express very closely approximate concepts that he in fact used.) Interpretations of all sorts obviously inform value-based practices, and Locke has just told us one fact about them: they are distinct from what is essential in values, from what gives value commitments (following Royce, Locke called these "loyalties") their practical point. Perhaps it is right to say, then, that value commitments have one set of epistemic liaisons, while interpretations of them have another. In any case it is right to say that both sets of liaisons have a rightful place in some system and that that system is itself rightly associated with some value-based practice.

Locke's claim about symbols captures this intersection. Value loyalties are causally anchored in feelings, while how we interpret and represent them has some distinct epistemic profile—not so distinct as to make the interpretations irrelevant, of course, but distinct enough to sort them semantically from the values in question. Let me express Locke's symbol claim as [S1].

[S1] What a symbol means when it stands for a value loyalty is distinct from the essence or objective of that loyalty.

Notice that on [S1] Locke's symbol function has three argument places. A symbol *means something,* it *stands for* some value loyalty, and that loyalty has some *essence* or *objective* distinct from either *meaning* or *standing-for.*

My explication seems to add something, but is it something Locke did not intend? After all, the quoted passage does not explicitly refer to what a symbol means as does [S1]. In fact, [S1]'s three argument places are not apparent in Locke's own syntax. Besides, his distinction seems to be chasing a slightly different aspect of the semantic gap between what is valued and how it is represented. He wants to loosen what valuers are committed to, practically speaking—that is, what they are prepared to do—from what they believe about it, cognitively speaking—that is, how they interpret what they do in a larger, symbolically rich context.

While this may feel truer, notice that it also contains three arguments: what a valuer is *prepared to do* and how she or he *interprets* that, both relative to some symbolic *context.* Though Locke's syntax seems to suggest a two-place function, I do not think it can be faithfully expressed without introducing a third place after all. I even suspect that context will be ineliminable in any sound symbol function, a resonance with Peirce. I will thus formalize the symbol function as S or (equivalently) as $S(x,y,z)$ to make its three-place character obvious; [S1] therefore explicates S. Much of the controversy among Lockeans in fact will consist in specifying the proper domain of $S(x,y,z)$ as well as the range of values it assigns.

An example makes this clearer. In the midst of the 1996 American League pennant race, Baltimore Oriole Roberto Alomar protested to home-plate umpire John Hirschbeck about a called third strike. During that notorious exchange, Alomar spat in Hirschbeck's face. He was later to say to the media that Hirschbeck was unwilling to reverse what Alomar considered a bad call because he had become "bitter" about the tragic death of his young son three years earlier. How should we hear Alomar's bitter-umpire comment, presumably issued to repair his good name? Is it some kind of poor-taste insult, or else a clumsy attempt at sympathetic explanation, or what?

Something is going on in Alomar's psychobiography for starters. That includes his values and feelings (what Locke calls "emotional attitudes"). He interprets and represents germane slices of his psychobiography in the shared, symbolically rich context of the (otherwise useless) sports interview. To read Alomar's comment, then, we need some robust notion of how meanings, values, and beliefs—such as those he had and used in uttering the comment—fit together. How does what goes on in the head land on talk?

This will not be simple. Like ordinary talk, Alomar's comment turns on a good deal of subtlety. It is ambiguous, for instance, since his intentions are not easily ascertained even though his comment is put into play within a highly structured linguistic context. That is, x, y, and z—the stand-alone meaning of his expression, his contextual interpretation of his value, and what he values straight out—are related in certain predictable ways, but some gappiness will keep the semantic accounting interesting. Speaking to the media about talk on the baseball field is as sophisticated a language game as any.

But the gap is ineliminable in a normative sense as well. Even Alomar himself ought to take some distance on the symbolic interpretations—the utterances—he puts into play, as should we hearers. To go felicitously (as Austin might say), culturally inflected communication needs to be loose this way. Speakers and hearers need to retain the option—indefinitely—to modify, retract, or extend what they have introduced into the symbolic context. That Alomar's comment was itself retracted via an apology testifies to this. Symbols are wonderful as social lubricants precisely because they can go out like wolves but come back like sheep.

One problem with [S1], though, is that value-sensitive notions like the essence of loyalty are too opaque to be very useful in a discussion about their associated symbols. And since I want to focus on the symbol function, I would like to isolate ethical notions, if only for clarity's sake. Trying to say how Alomar's beliefs relate to what his comment means will certainly have something to do with what he values, but we cannot keep both questions in play at once and hope to illuminate either. Thesis [S2] is a first attempt at this.

> [S2] What a symbol means when it interprets how a valuer interprets what he/she is prepared to do is distinct from what he/she is prepared to do.

Though I have sacrificed some elegance, [S2] isolates the value-sensitive aspects of the claim with a single idiom, translating Locke's *value loyalty* by my *what [a valuer is] prepared to do.*

Thesis [S2] makes obvious several things that remain obscure in [S1]. Consider how it translates *loyalty,* for instance. The two occurrences of the phrase *what he is prepared to do* differ from each other. Only the second occurrence in the explication is value loyalty as such—that which a person is prepared to do. (Locke's familiar 1935 notion of an emotional attitude in a valuing act goes here, as I show elsewhere.)[6] However, on its first occurrence it is not loyalty as such that is at issue—not simple preparedness, commitment, or feeling—but preparedness as an object of interpretation. What we feel when we value is what it is, though it can jump up a story to play in the lives of our choices, judgments, and interpretations. (Again, how Locke took emotional attitudes to engage the epistemic liaisons of imperatives in valuing acts goes here.) Alomar felt what he felt, was moved to do what he was prepared to do, but in engaging it at the level of imperatives—that is, to fit it in with the world of social norms—he put into play a particular interpretation of it. And it is his interpretation that mediates how we interpret his act and the values with which it is linked. We respond one way to his spitting if he takes it to be caused by a lapse in his own judgment (his apology) and another if he takes it to be caused by a lapse in Hirschbeck's (his original comment).

The other key feature of *S* that [S2] makes obvious—as does the Alomar example—is that a second function operates in tandem with *S* in symbolically rich cultural contexts. The phrase *it interprets how a valuer interprets* captures a nest of interpretations. Not only is some object—what a valuer is prepared to do—put into play as an object of interpretation, but that interpretation is *itself* put into play in the life of the symbols associated with it.

For clarity, then, let *I(x,y)* be an interpretive function, one of whose arguments is satisfiable by our emotional attitudes (what we are prepared to do, as I have been saying) and the other by our interpretations of them. (One ought to suspect that our interpretations are themselves determined functionally for Locke as well. See figure 20.1.) Explicating *I* is beyond this discussion; it is enough to note that for Locke it docks with *S*. More specifically, the argument place in the symbol function for interpretation—*y* in *S(x,y,z)*—will be a value in the range of *I(x,y)*.

One final comment before I consider deconstructive readings and their relation to *S*. I have already said that context—the use of symbols—is ineliminable in *S*. However, [S2] does not mark the contribution of context any more than by the word *when* in *what a symbol means when....* This leaves the explication less clear than it could be. To clear this up is really to say how symbols behave —*I* and all—context-sensitively, as distinct from what they are like apart from

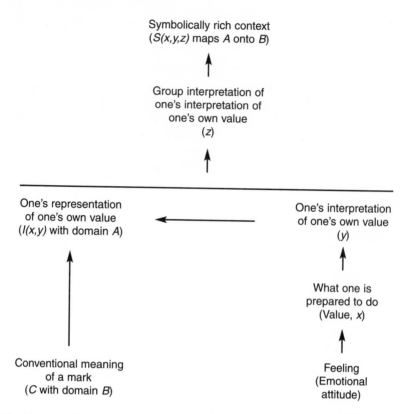

Fig. 20.1. The symbol function *S* showing its tandem functions and emotional component. Any of the arrows could be double-headed to suggest the gappy character of symbols.

context. A better explication would sort context-sensitive meaning from stand-alone meaning, however those ought ultimately to be understood. Thesis [S3] captures this by translating symbol meaning as what a symbol conveys in itself, even if—as deconstructivists might like—that turns out to be either unsatisfiable or inert.

> [S3] What a symbol conveys in itself when it interprets how a valuer interprets what he/she is prepared to do is distinct from what he/she is prepared to do.

(Notice that *when* continues to oppose stand-alone meaning—conceptually, of course—to contextual meaning.)

So now, as explicated in [S3], we may say that part of the domain of S is not just contextual meaning but also stand-alone meaning. More precisely, if A is the domain of I, and B is the domain of some conventional semantic function assigning stand-alone meanings to presymbolic marks—call this function C to indicate its conventional character—then S maps A onto B. That is, S maps values from I onto marks with stand-alone meanings. Informally, what we feel and value epistemically is linked with how we interpret them in valuing acts (Locke's 1935 arguments). Those nested interpretations guide our use of symbols by landing on them in virtue of a semantic gap function (Locke's 1942 arguments), which is sensitive to both context and conventional meaning. The docking of the messy and the clean alike constitutes the epistemic system that underwrites what members of cultures know and value.

So much for breaking ground; on to controversies. What is the contribution of stand-alone meaning to S?

I take Ernest Mason and Leonard Harris, two important philosophical commentators on Locke, to imply a revision of [S3] that neutralizes the contribution of stand-alone meaning to S. Neither philosopher explicitly discusses any version of S as such, but both treat meaning and interpretation in Locke's relativist philosophy with a deconstructive qualification. Let me state the impact of their views for S as [S4].

[S4] What a symbol conveys in itself when it interprets how a valuer interprets what he/she is prepared to do is distinct from what he/she is prepared to do, though it is semantically inert.

By the phrase *semantically inert* I am suggesting—as do Mason's and Harris's arguments—that if symbol meaning has any stand-alone character, that character is either irrelevant to correct semantic interpretations of symbols, or else it is relevant only in an ironic or subversive sense. What justifies adding the qualification?

One deconstructive argument to [S4] is based on knowledge, but I begin with a deconstructive argument based on value.

Value

The value argument implies [S4] in two steps. The first step defends the claim that theory always reflects the values of theorists. Theory is thus only as epistemologically stable as values. The second step completes the inference to [S4] by seeing values as determined by feelings. In other words, theory is as opaque and resistant to convention as are a theorist's feelings. To the extent this generalizes in language, any utterance or symbol will be similarly unconventional. Conventional stand-alone meaning becomes semantically inert; hence [S4].

Harris, for instance, observes:

> Discourse about general conceptions divorced from normative commitments, as if general conceptions were justified in a value-free fashion or were themselves free of normative implications, was not a human power because all forms of thought were necessarily entwined to some degree with pre-reflective preferences.[7]

This claim about prereflective preferences is of course the view that theory construction is always value-laden. It implies that no theoretical explanation is value-free. Hence, no explanation is detachable from the context in which it is produced.

Mason gets to the value-laden claim by looking at value types. Despite the proliferation of values throughout human experience, no type can be universal. That Locke gave an epistemological argument to this conclusion is beyond question; it is prominent in his 1935 paper. But Mason takes it to follow from Locke's view of metaphysics. That view was not intended to radically undermine the "metaphysical enterprise itself," though he did attempt to deconstruct (what Locke referred to as value) absolutism using an analytical strategy Mason calls the method of reversal. This amounts to "demonstrating how [absolutism] breeds precisely what it seeks to suppress, namely, schisms, disunity, and antagonisms," which it does inevitably.[8] Out of absolutist dogma, wrote Locke, "come those inevitable schisms which disrupt the parent dogmatism and deny it in the name of a new orthodoxy."[9] Locke thought absolutism confused part and whole (he called it "totalizing"), claiming that "[t]his totalizing character is purely functional in valuation, and it is a mockery of fact either to raise it to the level of transcendental worship or to endow it with objective universality."[10] He concludes that relativism provides a "safer and saner approach" to social cooperation.

According to Mason, this illustrates Locke's deconstructive turn, endorsing relativistic parity in the face of the proliferation of values. If there is a need to reconcile competing value types it must be that no single value type has the universe of action as its jurisdiction. It is not just the scope of value types—whether the logical, the ethical, the scientific, whatever—but also the ironic character of absolutism that Mason takes to be deconstructive.

Mason's gloss has a number of ramifications for *S*. Given Locke's emphasis on knowledge's "affective dimension," as well as the importance of context and the rejection of absolutism, Mason argues that knowledge is subject to the contingent standards we use to assess data. Data are never simply observed.

But even observations have standards and norms by which we make them. And standards and norms are not idle things. They have properties that distinguish them from things like Harris's preferences. Mason seems to appreciate this.

> The simplest discrimination ("This means that"), simplest report ("This is that"), or simplest valuation ("This should be thus") is no mere discovery of fact but a judgment, affectively conditioned and arrived at by comparing some object or event with some standard which has become accepted as the appropriate norm.[11]

Mason's relativist Locke rejects absolutism about values but keeps theory alive in the norm-regulated observation of data.

But then Mason's faith in these norms falters. Locke's relativism, argues Mason, implies that norms are culture-sensitive—true enough—but then he takes that to imply that what is said and known is "open-ended, multiple, and elusive [in] character" in the style of deconstruction. Surely this is too strong. Culture sensitivity does not imply that norms cannot be normative or that standards do not standardize. If the Yankees prefer to use home-run hitters to win baseball games while the Mets prefer batters who hit singles and doubles, what counts as good hitting remains unaffected. Good hitting is that which advances runners safely to put them in scoring positions, ultimately delivering runs. The goals of the game of baseball still set whatever standards constrain its actual play. The team sensitivity of hitting strategy does not change this fact.

I am no deconstructivist, so I confess confusion about its character in Mason's argument. If deconstruction is not inimical to norms and values, then what sort of character does it have? What distinguishes it from the metaphysics it criticizes? Mason must certainly be helping himself to too much here. He argues that deconstruction explains how we should read Locke's value pluralism, though it seems to imply anything-goes nihilism. Nihilism, though (he argues), does not *really* follow, provided we read deconstruction value-pluralistically in the style of Locke. Derrida explains Locke, but Derridean deconstructive puzzles are explained by Locke. This is circular if anything is.

Another objection ought to be raised here as well. Lockeans ought to take Locke's commitment to, and optimism about, objective, systematic science seriously enough to try to reconcile it with his suspicion of absolutes. That is difficult but necessary to making sense of him. But if the deconstructive spin on Locke is a fair interpretation of his thought, it seems to imply that symbolic phenomena (value-based practices of all sorts that play in the theory ballpark) are anomalous or at least irregular *in principle*. How then could a science of values—or any social science for that matter—be possible? That would be an odd view for a thinker who took himself to be putting the social sciences on solid philosophical footing to hold. The problem seems not to be whether conventions and norms were attractive to Locke—they clearly were—but how they contribute to an emotion-rich value epistemology. Zeroing out conventional meaning in *S* will thus be inherently troubled.

Before addressing Harris's move directly, I want to look at step 2 in the argument; some of what I say about it applies to Harris as well.

Locke took values—what we are prepared to do—to be driven by emotional attitudes. One way to interpret this is radically deflationary. If values are simply emotions promoted to the rank of loyalty, then there are no epistemological questions left to ask of them other than the causal ones. What feelings did Alomar have, in other words, that were manifest as loyalties in actions and words? This completes the inference to [S4] since, if theory is epistemologically no better off than value, and value is no better off than feeling, then theory goes the way of feeling—which is presumably as convention independent as anything is.

Mason emphasizes the emotional component of valuing acts in Locke; they are that to which epistemology deflates. And they are essentially affective, implying that claims to know can be only parasitically symbol determining; that is, the meanings of symbols can be determined only in deference to one's emotional attitudes. The semantic cannot be autonomous, and stand-alone symbol meaning is inert or even empty. If we could get the right perspective on Alomar's emotional psychobiography, we could, by tracking every one of his value commitments according to Locke, determine the meaning of his utterance. But the deconstructive theorist's caveat should already be obvious. What perspective will give us these crucial data? None we outsiders can hope to occupy. The semantic, once again, is inextricably attached to the emotional, which cannot sustain third-person perspectives. Stand-alone meaning closes down.

So, both Harris and Mason imply [S4] by claiming or implying that nested interpretations are determined by the value commitments of valuers, neutralizing symbol stand-alone meaning.

But there is a difference between Locke's concern about *how we make value judgments* and a concern with *what justifies them.* He does not claim that justification is impossible or empty—that would be anything-goes nihilism, which he self-consciously avoided—but that judgment is emotionally driven. That we judge in response to those aspects of our psychobiographies that urge us does not imply that the content of our judgments is unruly.

Even if Locke's argument did go to justification, there is another problem. Mason seems to be presuming that the normative (justificatory) aspects of value are isomorphic to the normative (epistemological) aspects of symbol meaning. How else could deflating value imply deflating meaning? Why, though, should we take Locke's rejection of absolutism and its dogmatic character to imply that all judgments are open ended, multiple, and elusive? Of course there is *some* link between value and meaning. I have been presuming that values can be represented, for instance, and that representing implies an interpreting step. But this is much weaker than isomorphism.

Mason's isomorphic view takes the deflation of justification and the rejection of absolutes to model how symbols get loaded with meaning. To show one is to show the other. But this depends on what is controversial at best, and likely unsound. What rules out the idea (for example) that we come to hold the values we hold but that we capture those values in some distinct way once we have given them entrance into our thought lives? In fact, is that not what we do when we load a symbol with a representational task? If all representing did was to put values into play *directly*—without gain, loss, or any semantically interesting shifts—would not the study of symbols look like the study of emotions? Surely symbols have a cognitive richness and fineness that emotions lack. Some symbols do not easily map onto emotions—artwork, novels, music, and movies vary emotionally for this reason, and two artists could represent some feeling in widely divergent ways. We need some argument to see why these divergences occur despite isomorphism's truth if it is true. On the face of it, though, isomorphism seems to fall apart around symbols precisely because, if it were true, symbols would become either unnecessary or boringly predictable.

This ramifies back to the value-laden view of theory, the first step in the value argument for [S4]. Isomorphism is too strong to follow from it alone, if it is supposed to. The most that value-ladenness could show (for present purposes) is that the same content may be shared by descriptions of fact (the objects of theory) and values (the feelings and preferences of theorists) alike. We would need additional argument for thinking they thus share all the interesting semantics. Compare, for instance, the *description of the fact* that

[1] Earth revolves around the Sun

with the *belief* that [1]. To get to be a factual description, an expression has to meet such referential criteria as "accurately describing some state of affairs." But for an expression to become a belief, the referential-semantic demands are considerably weaker. As is commonplace, the intentional need only be represented in the belief box in the trunk of someone's mind to reach the status of a belief. It does not need to be true. The same content—the subordinate clause [1]—may diverge semantically given the ways it enters our psychobiographies and hence (of course) epistemologically. If factual descriptions can diverge this much from beliefs, how much more play comes between theory and value?

And even if we accept value-ladenness, there is no need to infer deflationary isomorphism. Take Harris's earlier claim about prereflective preferences and reconsider the factual description whose content is [1]. What sort of preference is present there? Is there some implicit value in the observation that Earth revolves as it does? How fat could the buried value be, if there is one? The most I can imagine is a value like Occam's razor. Facts as bits of reality ought not introduce any extravagant ontological entities, as opposed to (say) a factual description whose content is [2]:

[2] Earth revolves around the Sun through the galactic ether.

If *that* is the sort of preference or value that value-ladenness implies, fine. But it is not fat enough to sort beliefs from factual descriptions any differently than I already have. Of course, the sorting is itself in Occam's shaving kit. If that is the problem, I see no way to register the value-laden complaint *and* maintain scientific integrity. The baby of science, if the deconstructivists have not already thrown it out, is drowning in its bathwater.

In any case, if discourse about facts of the matter stands apart from other parts of our psychobiographies (such as our values), then I see no reason to suppose stand-alone meaning to be empty. That is, [S4] remains unmotivated.

Knowledge

The second argument deconstructivists offer that implies [S4] is based on knowledge.

Mason takes Locke's emphasis on the contingency of what we know to be a key argument against the autonomy of symbol meaning. While what Locke called "normative fictions"—statements taken as true, though in the qualified (pragmatist) sense that they nonetheless remain amenable to revision—are structural features of epistemic processes, they are nonetheless constrained by functional demands. Indeed, Locke's aim was to demonstrate the functional value of such fictions. "Locke interprets logical thought as an activity which fulfills the biological and social function of assisting man in accommodating to his physical and social environment."[12] Mason regards Locke's suspicion of unqualified truths and knowledge claims to amount to a kind of instrumental agnosticism, played out in a struggle of values. He argues that Locke took values to be "means of control, domination, and power . . . allowing us to impose a system of ends which imprint our preferred choices and imperatives."[13] Knowledge thus serves, on Mason's interpretation, as a façade for a power struggle among value preferences.

This view, if it is in fact faithful to Locke's own, has far-reaching consequences for knowledge and meaning. Not only are knowledge claims *not* pegged to a determinate reality (giving the view its agnostic spin), but also they serve simply as surrogates for competing value claims, which respond to our functional needs (giving the view its instrumentalist spin, with perhaps a dose of cynicism). So, Mason implies that our epistemic uptake of what may be believed and known is limited, either in virtue of the uptake itself or else in how what is understood relates to the world it ostensibly represents. We may not know what we think we know, and in any case it may not be true.

That knowledge claims are always revisable implies [S4] if, by being agnostic about either the content or the object of knowledge claims, semantic concepts like meaning and truth are not autonomous from the domain of feeling-based value. Symbolic meaning is determined by the affective attitudes that make up value commitments. At best, interpretations by valuers themselves set up symbol meaning, making the latter a species of contextual interpretation—the contribution of I to S approaches 1, while C's contribution approaches 0.

This generalizes as follows. Semantic properties attach to the utterances to which they attach in virtue of the propositional features of such utterances. What an utterance means will be a function (at least partly) of what proposition it expresses. Hence, if propositions are epistemically inaccessible, then meaning can never communicatively succeed, since determinations of meaning cannot be issued. Meaning enjoys no secure and independent jurisdiction. It is subject to the wide, socially normative uses of the utterance in question— what value attaches to it rather than what it means per se. On these arguments, agnosticism delivers [S4].

The state of affairs undergirding baseball-field talk (complete with its constitutive epistemic systems) is less at issue on this view than is the set of values held by those systems' members—Hirschbeck, Alomar, and so on. There is room for widely divergent interpretations of fact (was Hirschbeck actually bitter? was the pitch in question actually a strike?) in determining what the world is like. Those of us who are not part of the system(s) in question cannot independently reconstruct those events so as to determine their truth.

This view depends on a broad skepticism about beliefs and the grounds for their truth. Propositional features impede knowledge at a deep level, and that in principle. Relating this point to meaning, Mason calls Locke's account indeterminate, claiming that "multiple interpretations and perspectives" are always possible, rendering meaning provisional at best.[14] The emptiness (or at least semantic inertness) of stand-alone meaning thus follows for Mason from agnosticism.

Does [S4] in fact follow? Not really. Mason seems to be confusing two kinds of problems, those about what we know and those about whether something is real. Either we are unable to know something that may nonetheless be the case (we cannot say what Alomar was really thinking, though surely he was really thinking) or else something is not real and therefore cannot be the basis of knowledge claims (we cannot say the Devil made Alomar do it since the Devil does not really exist). The arguments supporting each of these spins will, accordingly, diverge. Is Mason saying that meaning is inaccessible or that it is illusory? I do not know.

Besides, it seems that "multiple interpretations" cannot be as wide as he suggests. Why should we suppose that facts of the matter contained in utterances and meaningful actions, though imbued with speaker and actor values, are untraceable? This is like the Earth/Sun example. Can we not check the facts?

It seems there is a holist presumption at the heart of Mason's argument. To know what any representational bit of knowledge is about, whether the content of a thought, a phrase, or symbols generally, we need to know what "wide" semantic features it has. We need to settle what its semantic neighbors are doing before we can justifiably claim to know what it itself means. Like Wittgenstein's familiar view of meaning, to say what something means is to say what role it plays in a language game. Or else, on a Quinean spin, the holist says that to know what something means is to know what position it occupies relative to a whole body of beliefs.

Given Locke's foundationalism about emotional attitudes in a relativist view of knowledge, it is tempting to presume holism in reading him. The Lockean holist might like to claim that feelings shape the content of values in some important sense, and so one needs to have fat access to feelings (since feelings have so much lifeworld character, so to speak) in order to have reliable access to their values. And if values shape how symbols play semantically in cultural contexts, it seems to follow that that same foundational fat access is necessary for semantically evaluating the cultural symbols in question. The symmetry with Wittgenstein and Quine is strengthened further if we take their metaphors—webs of belief, forms of life—to occur in Locke's thought under the cover of his term *culture,* which is probably not an unfair reading.

The major difficulty with holism, though, is that primary fat access needs to be *too* fat for any knowledge of meaning to be possible. If to know what a symbol means an evaluator needs to know what contribution a semantic neighbor makes, how can the neighbor's contribution be evaluated without knowing the contributions of *its* neighbors, and so on? Is there any nonarbitrary way of saying that knowledge of meaning starts at some spot in the web, without presupposing knowledge of meaningful neighboring terms?

So to evaluate Alomar's bitter-umpire comment, the Lockean holist needs to know the meanings of words like *Hirschbeck* and *bitter* and *bad call*. But to know what *bad call* means, the holist says that we need to know what *call* means, and all its proximal semantic notions. Those include, I guess, *umpire, strike,* and *pitch,* but not *telephone* or *bird,* since the latter are not (or should not be) proximal. But does that imply that *call* in Alomar's utterance counts *not-telephone* and *not-bird* in its semantic neighborhood? You cannot have the belief

[3] Hirschbeck's bad call was really not a strike

without also implying in your conceptual web of belief the belief that

[4] Hirschbeck's bad call was really not a telephone call.

But if [4] is semantically proximal, relevant to semantically settling [3], then how is *any* meaning in Alomar's semantic web distal as opposed to proximal? How can the holist sort telephone-beliefs from umpire-beliefs?

Even if we want to be holist and say something about the broad public and social character of meaning (an unclear notion if ever there was one), certainly we do not want to render our explanatory tools ineffective. If holism is true, we lose our distinction between what is relevant and what is irrelevant in our analysis of epistemic systems, a disastrous consequence for any theory that takes meaningful communication as seriously as Locke's does.

Part of the difficulty in the epistemic accounting of these sorts of systems is the sheer thickness of the lifeworld issues that any system with an Alomar in it faces. Certainly deconstructive readings are wrestling with this. If Lockeans ought to reject holism, as I am urging, what is it that makes possible the liaisons we have been discussing? What are the meaning-determining features of (nonholist) Lockean epistemic systems?

A full answer is beyond this paper, though it seems to me that any discussion of epistemic systems in Locke has to account for the layered nature of epistemic contact that a knower has with other nested knowers and valuers in symbolically rich contexts. Alomar's place in the nesting illustrates this, but so does an early epistemological metaphor of Locke's, that of the "New Negro."[15] Locke wrote of a New Negro concept that could serve as a prism through which Americans generally and blacks in particular could see the rich texture of black life, complete with optimism about future prospects as well as a sober sense of responsibility for their collective destiny. As a standpoint device it is epistemologically live. It negotiates the complex ways black life is to be interpreted, suggesting the layering effect I have in mind. (I develop this point in a paper called "Pragmatism and the New Negro.") The New Negro is a lens that consists of a set of epistemic protocols for translating the terms of knowledge in the system more generally into terms for particular knowers. (Du Bois invokes a similar notion in his familiar account of double consciousness.)

So, while I see no way to maintain holism, even the nonholist Lockean needs a sufficiently subtle analysis to capture this layering effect to which deconstructivists are sensitive. Thesis [S3] seems capable of this. And in any case, [S4] comes up short once again, since we still lack motivation to deny autonomy to the semantic.

Harris's knowledge argument begins metatheoretically. Though a pragmatist himself, Locke took issue with what he took to be that movement's failure to question its own operating assumptions, including (for instance) its science bias. Harris uses Locke's dissatisfaction on this point to launch his own argument about knowledge and belief to deconstruction, in turn (on my reading) implying [S4]. Harris argues that pragmatism shipwrecks on a "problem of enunciation," the difficulty being to "escape the limitations of one's own language and its canons of rationality."[16] How does one state some claim or articulate some belief without already presuming a systematic vocabulary? One cannot inspect that part of the rock on which one's foot is resting. And if what a speaker presumes cannot be bracketed for questioning, then any analysis— no matter how cogent it seems—will be incomplete in principle. The implication Harris intends is that even pragmatism presupposes, and so imports into its analyses, some preconceived (and hence unexamined) notions—an unpragmatist approach if any is.

This is a little ambiguous. Is Harris indicating a problem for *language users,* namely, that nothing can be known apart from a language, whose epistemic liaisons put certain beliefs beyond question? Or, is Harris indicating a problem for *theory builders,* namely, that one needs already to have some theory—with all its unchallenged axiomatic scaffolding—before one can evaluate any theory at all? He seems to shuttle between these two distinct problems. The issue is not insignificant, since Locke seems indeed to point out the theory problem, though we would be hard-pressed to find any discussion of this sort of language-use problem. However, Harris infers (what amounts to) [S4] from Locke's discussions, and, while it is an open question whether the language-use problem implies that, it seems that the inertness of stand-alone meaning is much too strong to follow from the theory problem alone. (I owe this point to a conversation with Ligia Römer.)

Putting aside this ambiguity, Harris goes on to say that Locke's "discursive act" was one of extreme deformation, in his "deforming a master code of symbols to fit a reformed agenda." This bold rendering of contextualism is even stronger than Mason's agnosticism argument. The claim is that Locke strategically used the "master code" of pragmatism to subvert that very philosophy. To decode—interpret—the content of Locke's positive theory of knowledge, his readers need to interpret *past* that content, so to speak, since the straight interpretation of his claims is subverted by deformed meanings. And this (at least on Harris's gloss) has the consequence of introducing previously marginal concerns and perspectives into the philosophical mainstream as follows.

> The worlds of African people, however, represented a counter-standpoint to Western cultural biases for Locke. That standpoint was used to both see and be seen; to critique without the presumption of having escaped the inescapable limitations of cultural context.... Locke's cultural strategy involved continual reconstitution of the nature of public dialogue by and about African people for the negation of forms of domination.[17]

The problem of enunciation is thus taken to support [S4], albeit with the caveat that interpretations of valuers are subversive, with all the connotations that follow. They are opaque to those who do not have reliable "insider" access to them, for example.

Harris presents an even stronger version of the argument in his ensuing discussion.

> Locke's metaphysical pluralism is deconstructive in character, in part, because on Locke's account axiology always entails a normative dimension and metaphysics entails pre-reflective hierarchies. Locke exposes the way uniformitarian universals lead to or condition pluralities. Moreover, Locke requires that we continually revalue our conceptions of reality because they are always subject to our fallibility.[18]

In this stronger version, deconstruction in Locke goes beyond mere self-conscious theorizing to recognizing prereflective hierarchies, an analog to the pre-reflective preferences discussed earlier. This development does not clear things up much, though, since it will be subject to the same criticisms.

If Locke is deforming the meaning of pragmatism's master code, is he not flouting some maxim for theorists to argue sincerely, subverting that argument in the process? If he was doing that, then his positive theory—perhaps *any* positive theory—cannot be reliably interpreted. Is that not an undesirable consequence? And how do we insiders know we are reading him correctly? How do we even know we are insiders? How would we?

Harris goes on to cast Locke's project in terms of the metaphor of a "subterranean deconstruction" that ties into his master-code analysis, but I am not sure it dissipates my objection.

Locke [speaks] in the code of value theory, particularly value relativism and cultural pluralism, as his master code of deconstruction. His views consistently rejected the hierarchical constitution of metaphysics, the possibility of a meta-metalanguage or presuppositionless valuation, and what William James termed the "block universe" picture of reality. But that code was itself not the magic. . . . The magic was the subterranean message conveyed in a subterranean world for which the deconstructive code was itself a master form that also served, in [Houston] Baker's terms, deformatively. . . . [Locke's] views were expressed in a subterranean world.[19]

Like any metaphor, this one invites interpretation. As far as I can tell, the pertinent sense of "subterranean" philosophy consists of two additional arguments: an argument from cognitive privacy and the appeal to value-ladenness. I have already discussed the theory/value distinction. Let me say something about cognitive privacy.

On Locke's account, Harris maintains that no one's "belief system is totally available to them or others," making cognitive processes at least partially "hidden."[20] If the world of cognition is hidden, our knowledge is limited in some important ways. Cognition—the mental life—is hidden since one's belief system is not fully available. And perhaps hidden cognition is the subterranean element in theory and meaning.

Cognitive privacy motivates the inertness (and lends some support to the subversiveness) of stand-alone meaning given the unavailability of one's belief system to others. If what one believes cannot be accessed by others, then perhaps the important sort of meaning fails apart from context, which in this case is radically internal to the psychobiography of the valuer/knower in question. On these lines we might see Alomar's bitter-umpire comment as epistemologically opaque. We outsiders have no hope of tracking its meaning and hence cannot assess knowledge claims that it might be enlisted to support. Perhaps even Hirschbeck stands in that relation to Alomar. I suppose this would account for the ensuing hijinks and misunderstandings.

The term *belief system* in Harris's argument is ambiguous, though. Either it designates an individual's set of beliefs and their entailments, or else it refers to the set of beliefs and entailments held in a shared way by members of some culture. The precise meaning matters somewhat since it seems contradictory for the belief system of a cultural group to be unavailable to the members of that very culture. Whatever else such a system is, it has to be shared—hence, available by definition. After all, is that not the force of Harris's provocative and interesting claim about African insider/outsider standpoints? From the standpoint of an individual mental life, it is unclear what it would be for an individual's belief system to be unavailable to that very individual, but at least it need not be self-contradictory. Self-deception, bad faith, and delusion make this point. But this is not very satisfying. Certainly such irregular cognitive conditions as these should not serve as epistemic benchmarks. Is there a way to construe the notion of a standard belief system for an individual that can in some sense be unavailable? And if this reflects some Freudian insights about the subconscious and/or subdoxastic, that is fine. Is not the point of psychotherapy that one can bring to consciousness that which is repressed through fear, fantasy, or habit? If that is an impossible task, a lot of depressed people are wasting their money, a hundred dollars an hour.

If this is the right way to read Harris's claim, it still would not imply deconstruction. If the hidden cognitive life *may* be recovered, albeit with pain and difficulty, then that implies that epistemic liaisons are available. Beliefs only imply deconstruction—and [S4]—if those liaisons are in principle unavailable to knowers. The expense and difficulty involved with that task do not establish principled unavailability.

And even if we settle this ambiguity, certainly cognitive privacy as such does not imply anything like the strong deconstructive conclusion Harris draws. Even if we cast privacy in its strongest terms, we are no longer on Freudian epistemological territory but on that of Cartesian skepticism. The idea that Descartes endorsed that the mental life is radically private puts cognition in the hidden territory of subjective consciousness. But Cartesian epistemology is a companion view that I cannot imagine deconstructivists embracing. Whether Cartesian or Freudian theories of meaning are attractive or cogent is not the point. It is enough to see that neither is (on the face of it) deconstructive. Thesis [S4] remains unmotivated.

So what is the contribution of stand-alone meaning to Locke's symbol function? I see no reason to think it is not positive.

Notes

1. Alain Locke, "Values and Imperatives" (1935), in *The Philosophy of Alain Locke: Harlem Renaissance and Beyond,* ed. Leonard Harris (Philadelphia: Temple University Press, 1989), 34–50.

2. Alain Locke, "Pluralism and Intellectual Democracy" (1942), in *Philosophy of Alain Locke,* ed. Harris, 53–66. See also Alain Locke, "Cultural Relativism and Ideological Peace" (1944), in *Philosophy of Alain Locke,* ed. Harris, 69–78; Alain Locke, "Pluralism and Ideological Peace" (1947) in *Philosophy of Alain Locke,* ed. Harris, 96–102; Alain Locke, "A Functional View of Value Ultimates" (1945), in *Philosophy of Alain Locke,* ed. Harris, 81–93; Alain Locke, "Value" (between 1935 and 1947?), in *Philosophy of Alain Locke,* ed. Harris, 111–26.

3. Ernest D. Mason, "Deconstruction in the Philosophy of Alain Locke," *Transactions of the Charles S. Peirce Society* 24 (1988): 88–106; Leonard Harris, ed., *The*

Philosophy of Alain Locke: Harlem Renaissance and Beyond (Philadelphia: Temple University Press, 1989), 3–27, 279–89.

4. See, e.g., Locke, "Cultural Relativism and Ideological Peace"; Locke, "Functional View of Value Ultimates," 85; and Locke, "Value," 125.

5. Locke, "Pluralism and Intellectual Democracy," 60. Emphasis added.

6. Stephen Lester Thompson, "Feeling—and Thinking about Feeling," in *Key Figures in African-American Thought*, ed. Lewis Gordon (Oxford: Basil Blackwell, forthcoming).

7. Harris, *Philosophy of Alain Locke*, 280.

8. Mason, "Deconstruction in Locke," 87–88.

9. Locke, "Pluralism and Ideological Peace," 101.

10. Locke, "Values and Imperatives," 47.

11. Mason, "Deconstruction in Locke," 94.

12. Mason, "Deconstruction in Locke," 97.

13. Mason, "Deconstruction in Locke," 97.

14. Mason, "Deconstruction in Locke," 91.

15. Alain Locke, "The New Negro," in *The New Negro: Voices of the Harlem Renaissance,* ed. Alain Locke (1925; repr. New York: Atheneum, 1992), 3–16.

16. Harris, *Philosophy of Alain Locke*, 18.

17. Harris, *Philosophy of Alain Locke*, 19.

18. Harris, *Philosophy of Alain Locke*, 19–20.

19. Harris, *Philosophy of Alain Locke*, 279–80.

20. Harris, *Philosophy of Alain Locke*, 280.

21

Alain Locke, Critical Relativism, and Multicultural Education

Paul Weithman

In the introduction to his book *How the Irish Became White,* Noel Ignatiev writes that when immigrants from Ireland moved to American cities, they commonly found themselves thrown together with free Negroes. Irish and African Americans fought each other and the police, socialized and occasionally intermarried, and developed a common culture of the lowly. They also both suffered the scorn of those better situated. Along with Jim Crow and Jim Dandy, the drunken, belligerent, and foolish Pat and Bridget were stock characters on the early stage. In antebellum America it was speculated that if racial amalgamation were ever to take place, it would begin between those two groups.

As we know, things turned out otherwise. The outcome was not the inevitable consequence of blind historic forces, still less of biology, but the result of choices made, by the Irish and by others, from among available alternatives. To enter the white race was a strategy to secure an advantage in a competitive society.[1]

In the course of exploring how Irish Americans pursued that strategy, Ignatiev traces the divergence of two peoples who once shared what he calls a "culture of the lowly." He thus documents the historical processes in virtue of which inviting an Irish American Catholic to contribute to a volume on the thought of Alain Locke is an exercise in multiculturalism.[2] Indeed it is an exercise, not just in multiculturalism, but also in multicultural education, an education of which I am a student and beneficiary. That it is so shows how varied are the phenomena that fall under the rubrics of multiculturalism and multicultural education.

That multicultural education can and should assume diverse forms for different purposes is a point central to this chapter. There is one form of multicultural education that currently receives a great deal of attention, a form associated with what I shall call "aesthetic multiculturalism." This is, I shall argue, a very important form of multicultural education, and it is one for which Alain

Locke was a powerful advocate. Locke argues that this form of multicultural education depends upon students' employing a methodology that he labeled "critical relativism." This methodology presupposes an attitude, or family of attitudes, toward the cultures being studied. In the first section of this chapter, I raise questions about critical relativism by posing objections to the conception of culture that seems to underwrite it. I conclude that what is essential to Locke's views about aesthetic multiculturalism can be preserved even if his commitment to critical relativism is revised or abandoned.

Aesthetic multiculturalsm is associated with only one form of multicultural education. There is another form of multicultural education that receives a good deal less explicit attention in contemporary debates and to which Alain Locke devoted relatively little attention. The importance of this form of multicultural education can be brought out by returning briefly to Ignatiev's book. *How the Irish Became White* does far more than trace the movement of the Irish into white society and away from a status they shared with African Americans. The book also attempts to explain the concurrent emergence of Irish racism. In doing so, Ignatiev begins with a premise that Locke would also endorse: race is not a meaningful biological category but a cultural construction that is constantly being rebuilt.[3] It is the instability of racial lines that allowed the Irish to "become" white. And it is because considerations of economics and class help to determine where on the blueprint those racial lines are drawn that it was economically and socially attractive to the Irish to do so. Thus their race was, Ignatiev claims, adopted as a "strategy to secure an advantage in a competitive society."[4] Their *racism*—their antipathy toward African Americans—was a concomitant of their attitudes toward the economic and social status of the race from which they sought to distinguish themselves. Ignatiev therefore argues that to understand the genesis of Irish American racism, it is necessary to understand why Irish Americans came to associate skin color with status and to make judgments of race on grounds of class. Part of what makes *How the Irish Became White* so interesting a book is the way it attempts to do just that.

What is true of the racism that Ignatiev studies is true of racism generally: its roots are entangled with those of class-based prejudices. This fact was not lost on Locke, as he made clear in the third of his lectures in the series "Race Contacts and Interracial Relations."[5] Uprooting racism therefore requires a form of education that attacks class-based ignorance and prejudice as well. In particular, it requires a sustained attempt to address preconceptions and misconceptions about economic status, its causes, and its consequences. Such an education should give a central place to studying what has been called the "culture of poverty."

I employ the term "culture of poverty" guardedly, knowing that it has been abused and that its abuse has drawn criticism from scholars who reject the notion. On the other hand, the notion of a culture of poverty has been pressed into service in ways that these critics should find unexceptionable; I hope that mine is one of them.[6] An education that gives some attention to the culture of poverty can be appropriately described as a form of multicultural education, one associated with what I shall call "the multiculturalism of class." Such an education is an essential supplement to the sort of multicultural education that I discuss in the next paragraph. Locke did not go far enough, I think, in exploring the possibilities of a multicultural education of this sort. In this he has something in common with those contemporary champions of multicultural education who concentrate exclusively, or almost exclusively, on aesthetic multiculturalism. Yet a curriculum that attaches importance to both aesthetic multiculturalism and the multiculturalism of class is essential to achieving one of the most important aims Locke himself set for education: bridging this country's racial divides. I begin with aesthetic multiculturalism and the implications of Locke's work for it.

The form of multicultural education with which I begin is one that attempts to introduce students to the history and development, the values, attitudes, and ways of life of groups ignored by what we might call the "traditional curriculum." It lays special emphasis on exposing students to the accomplishments of these groups, particularly their contributions to intellectual inquiry and to folk and high culture. Multicultural education of this sort attempts to foster aesthetic multiculturalism: the family of capacities and attitudes needed to appreciate and enjoy the artistic, humanistic, and scientific achievements of a number of cultures, including but not exclusively one's own. Recent attempts to construct curricula that foster aesthetic multiculturalism have received a great deal of attention in academic and public debate. This is because the ability to appreciate the achievements of one's own and other cultures, while regarded by its proponents as intrinsically valuable, is also thought worth cultivating for other reasons. Among these reasons is that it in acquiring it, students are led to critical reflection on the construction of knowledge and value that dominant cultures have traditionally privileged.

What is important for present purposes is that Locke both favored an education that fostered aesthetic multiculturalism and believed that it required radical educational reform. He did not think that simply expanding the curriculum to include works of literature, art, and music that had previously been excluded would suffice, for simple expansion of the curriculum beyond the traditional would not, he claimed, "exorcise parochial thinking and correct traditional culture bias."[7] A culturally diverse education does not by itself engender the attitudes necessary for appreciating cultural diversity. Rather, Locke maintained, they would be engendered only if students acquire a set of attitudes with which to approach the works they are taught. Multicultural education requires, Locke concluded, that students be taught a method of studying culture that he called "critical relativism."

It is worth taking a moment to explore what Locke meant by talking of relativism in this connection. He did not endorse relativism about any and all value judgments. He would, I assume, deny the truth of the Benthamite assertion that "Pushpin is as good as poetry." Nor was he a relativist about the value of human pursuits, thinking that endeavors are on a par if they yield equal amounts of subjective satisfaction. He therefore has room to deny that the activity of pushpin is as valuable as that of poetry, the utility produced in the player and the poet notwithstanding. More seriously, I believe that his account of relativism, properly interpreted, leaves him room to deny that footbinding and female genital mutilation are practices that must be presented as acceptable in the name of multiculturalism and that the works of Robert Ludlum must be taught alongside those of Shakespeare. Locke should be interpreted as advocating, at least in the first instance, relativism about *cultures as wholes.*

How are we to understand this sort of relativism? Let us say that cultures are coherent and reflective systems of thought and practice, prominently including the practice of making value judgments of various kinds that inform the lives of a population separable from other groups for analytical purposes. By saying that cultures are reflective, I mean that those whose lives they inform assess the adequacy of their practices and value judgments and consequently introduce such changes as seem to be called for. This is the process Locke called "transvaluation."[8] By saying that cultures are systematic, I mean that as a result of reflection and transvaluation, the bearers of culture continually develop and revise criteria for the adequacy of the value judgments they make. They also develop and revise loosely ordered hierarchies of value and activity. These hierarchies should, Locke thought, accord privileged places to artistic endeavor and accomplishment, and to personal cultivation.[9] When Locke endorses relativism, he means that the set of valuations, hierarchies, and practices that together make up one culture are neither inferior nor superior to those that make up another.

Locke's critical relativism has three important implications that I mention in passing.

1. Because he recognizes that cultures include hierarchies of practice, he is not committed to the view that every practice associated with one culture is to be judged the equal of every other practice associated with the same or other cultures.

2. Because cultures as wholes are equal, students should not approach other cultures clinging dogmatically to the beliefs and values of their own. As Locke says "Cultural Relativism would . . . claim or impute no validity for values beyond this relativistic framework, and so counteract value dogmatism."[10]

3. Because artistic endeavor is among the most valuable elements of culture, those who study other peoples should be exposed to their artistic accomplishments. Students who approach other cultures free of dogmatic attachment to their own should come away with a genuine appreciation of the higher achievements, particularly the artistic achievements, of the peoples and civilizations they study.

But what, exactly, did Locke think was wrong with judgments of cultural inferiority and superiority? Why are the usual judgments of cultural inferiority and superiority mistaken?[11] The answer, I conjecture, lies in the family of ideas Locke designated by the terms "common denominators," "basic equivalences," and "pragmatic similarities" of culture.[12] In teasing out what Locke has in mind here, his attraction to the Baha'i faith proves instructive. Every religion, it might be thought, faces the task of rendering significant and sacred certain fundamental events and experiences of human life: procreation and birth; the vicissitudes of fortune; the tragedies of pain, loss, and death; the experiences of guilt and atonement, forgiveness and redemption. Different religions do this in different ways; all too often their adherents insist that their way is the only true one. But according to the Baha'i faith, other faiths were valid responses to the exigencies facing a particular people under a certain set of historical conditions. The revelations of the Baha'i faith are addressed to all peoples in the modern world; they incorporate certain elements of Christianity, for example, while supplementing them in light of modern conditions. Baha'i teaches that Christianity and other ancient religions should not be seen as false, for they were appropriate responses to the time and place of their propagation. They need supplementation and integration rather than wholesale replacement.

Perhaps Locke thought, similarly, that all populations must cope with certain exigencies and experiences of life. The diverse cultures of the world might be thought different, highly complex responses to those exigencies that enable the populations whose lives they inform to cope with them. Locke thought that under modern conditions of increasing cultural contact, what is needed is not the replacement of traditional cultures but their supplementation and integration. Thus he favored development of a "joint civilization" characterized by the mutual borrowing and enjoyment of diverse peoples' cultural achievements.[13] The constituent cultures of this joint civilization, he might argue, are not to be ranked as better and worse. Rather he would claim that if two cultures are equal in what he calls their "effective adaptation"[14]—if they contribute equally well to the ability of their bearers to cope over time with the human condition—then neither of those cultures is superior to the other. And so, he might conclude, the usual judgments to the contrary are false.[15] This is an intriguing line of thought. There are, however, some problems with it that show themselves on closer inspection.

One is that the notion of adaptational effectiveness, and the associated notion of coping effectively with the human condition, would be very difficult to spell out with the necessary precision. But without this elaboration, how are we to tell, given any two cultures, whether they are equivalent in their effective adaptation? Of course this may tell as much in favor of Locke's point as against it. If standards of adaptational effectiveness are unclear and if they provide the criteria by which cultures are to be compared, then the dogmatist's judgment of superiority will be every bit as questionable as the relativist's judgment of parity.

More problematic is the idea that it is possible to isolate common exigencies and experiences that make up the human condition and to which the various practices that comprise cultures are evolved responses. Characterization of those exigencies and cross-cultural recognition of certain practices as responses to them are themselves practices that presuppose value judgments of a quite sophisticated kind. Students who receive a multicultural education are initiated into those practices and therefore depend upon the value judgments the practice requires. Multicultural education therefore presupposes that those value judgments are true and cannot be called into question without calling into question the conclusions of that education itself. This implies that at the heart of multicultural education is a certain amount of the dogmatism Locke thought it necessary to avoid if such an education was to be possible at all.

To see this, let us look at one plausible candidate for an "exigency" of human life. Every society needs to transmit information and mores to the next generation. But why does it need to do so? What is the best description of the exigency to which diverse educational practices are responses? Consider the Great Books program as it developed in the United States in the middle part of the twentieth century. This is a program to which Locke makes passing reference and which some proponents of multicultural education would like to displace.[16] Did that program respond to the need of a pluralistic society to identify, publish, and hand on a common intellectual patrimony? or to the need of a society confronting Nazism to assure itself and its children that democracy rather than fascism was the political form most faithful to its heritage?[17] or to the need of a male, WASP elite to solidify its hold on those it regarded as the best and the brightest of the ascendant generation? Or would the best explanation appeal to all three of these possibilities and more besides?

My purpose in raising these questions is not to set the stage for an answer that I hope to defend. It is instead to show that which answer or answers seem most plausible will depend upon a range of value judgments.[18] Among those value judgments are judgments about the works that constituted the curriculum of the Great Books program and about the likely consequences of an education that gives them a privileged place. The Great Books program is only an example, and my argument could be repeated for any educational practice whether traditional or revisionary. Indeed it could be repeated, mutatis mutandis, for multicultural education itself. My point is therefore that the educational practices that are partially constitutive of a culture cannot be responses to human or societal needs that can be conceptualized without making value judgments. What value judgments one makes about how best to describe the needs to which education responds will depend in part upon the culture or subculture to which one belongs. It follows, then, that it is impossible consistently to regard diverse cultures as diverse adaptive responses to a common set of needs and exigencies that can be characterized by an observer independent of her culture and its valuations.

This shows a difficulty with another view that I have imputed to Locke: the view that we should apply the method of critical relativism to cultures considered as wholes, even as we criticize one or another of a culture's constituent practices. One's opinion of an educational practice like the Great Books program depends upon which of the foregoing descriptions one thinks accurately describes the need it fills. If one thinks that the Great Books program is best described as a means for illegitimately reinforcing the values of an elite, it will be very difficult for her to remain neutral toward a culture that attaches very great importance to passing them on. Thus the central role of value judgments in conceptualizing the exigencies to which educational practices are a response shows the difficulty of sustaining the attitudes that Locke enjoined in endorsing critical relativism.

I have assumed for the sake of argument that it is possible to isolate educational practices. I realize, however, that the assumption is not unproblematic. What practices we recognize as instances of education depends upon the paradigms of educational practice with which we begin, and different observers who begin with different paradigms may reach different conclusions about whether a given practice is an instance of education. Education is, as Alasdair MacIntyre has argued, an "essentially contested concept"; MacIntyre also argues that identifying paradigms of essentially contested concepts depends upon value judgments. If MacIntyre is correct, then it follows that an observer's classification of practices depends upon her prior judgments of value. If this is so and if those value judgments depend upon her initiation into a set of practices associated with her home culture, then social practices can be classified only from within one or another culture. But then it is hard to see how the practices of another culture could be identified, still less studied, without some degree of dogmatic adherence to the value judgments of one's own culture.

Here it might be replied on Locke's behalf that my example depends upon taking the debate between multiculturalists and advocates of the Great Books program as a confrontation of two cultures. This, it might be said, is a confusion. Multiculturalists and traditionalists are, it might be said, bearers of the same culture who disagree about the requirements of its transmission. This defense raises an important question. Many cultures are riven by internal struggles. At some point, the severity or persistence of the struggle raises the question of whether the contending parties should any longer be regarded as bearers of the same culture. Thus the problem with this defense is that it raises the further question of how cultures are to be individuated.

The question of how cultures are to be individuated is one whose import for multicultural education is not merely theoretical. This is clear from the controversy over whether to recognize Ebonics as a second language. For how one thinks that controversy should be resolved depends upon whether one thinks that the large number of Americans who speak Ebonics are, and deserve to be, legally recognized as bearers of a distinct culture. How one answers that question depends in part upon whether one thinks that to recognize Ebonics is to stigmatize its speakers or whether one thinks it a laudable attempt to encourage the development of new pedagogics for the benefit of the Oakland schoolchildren who speak it. This, in turn, makes clear how the individuation of cultures, like the description of the needs to which they respond, depends crucially upon judgments of value. Those judgments, too, depend in part upon the culture or subculture of those making them. So to individuate cultures, to recognize a culture as such, one has to assume that some of the judgments of one's own culture are true. Therefore, culture cannot be a family of adaptive responses to the human condition, a condition that can be characterized, as it were, in the view from cultural nowhere.

Finally, there are serious problems with the claim that cultures that are equal in their "adaptational effectiveness" should be judged equal. Quite apart from the problem of saying exactly what cultures are adaptations to, there is the difficulty of determining when two cultures have been equally effective. The criteria of effectiveness would have to be formulated so that a culture that depends upon slavery, like that of the antebellum South, is not judged equal to a culture that does not, despite the fact that the former may have helped slave-owners cope with the exigencies of human life. More generally, the problem of formulating criteria of effectiveness will be complicated by the need to take into account the various forms of oppression and marginalization found in diverse cultures. This, in turn, entails relying on judgments of value drawn from the home culture of the agent formulating and employing those criteria— judgments about, for example, whether what Westerners regard as the oppression of women counts against the adaptational effectiveness of certain traditional Islamic cultures.

Perhaps critical relativism can be defended against these objections. Or perhaps there are alternatives that will accomplish what Locke wanted critical relativism to do. Recall that Locke introduced critical relativism as a method that students must apply to other cultures if they are to learn the right lessons from multicultural education. Part of what they should take away from such an education, Locke thought, was a sense of what he called "culture-citizenship." By this Locke meant that human beings should regard one another as members of a joint civilization to which all races and cultures can make artistic and intellectual contributions of intrinsic merit.[19] Locke's promotion of the Harlem Renaissance should, I believe, be seen as his attempt to show that Africans and African Americans have made just such contributions.[20] Thus Locke favored an education that fostered what I earlier called "aesthetic multiculturalism." It is not clear, however, that aesthetic multiculturalism requires critical relativism. If some other attitude or set of attitudes than those presupposed by critical relativism will do, then difficulties with the conception of culture that underlies critical relativism do not affect Locke's notions of cultural-citizenship and joint civilization. Nor do they undercut his hopes for aesthetic multiculturalism.

What are those hopes? The title of one of Locke's most important essays on education provides a promising clue. In that essay, "The Need for a New Organon in Education," Locke argued for a multicultural curriculum rightly presented. Francis Bacon famously argued that a new form of intellectual inquiry was necessary if humanity was to break the hold of the "idols" that had enthralled it until his own time, idols he described in his *New Organon*.[21] I believe that Locke, who self-consciously borrowed the title of his essay from Bacon, thought the educational program of *his* "New Organon" necessary to break the hold of the idol he identified in *Race Contacts and Interracial Relations*. There Locke wrote that

> One of the earliest attempts to study social instincts unfortunately came long before the development of modern sociological methods. It was Bacon's remarkable anticipation of this phase in his famous study of the idols. The Baconian "idol" is, after all, just this kind of social instinct, *of which racial antipathy is one of the most potent*.[22]

In the remarks that follow this one, Locke compares racial antipathy to

Bacon's "idola theatri." Locke's employment of Baconian imagery thus suggests that he thought that aesthetic multiculturalism, a consequence of multicultural education rightly presented, could break the hold of racial antipathy. This is confirmed by the concluding passages of *Race Contacts*, where Locke lays out his notion of culture-citizenship. Commenting on the Europe of his day, Locke said:

> The Celtic and the Pan-Slavic movements in arts and letters—movements by which the submerged classes are coming to their expression in art—*seem to be the forerunners of that kind of recognition which they are ultimately striving for, namely, recognition of an economic, a civic and a social sort;* and these movements are the gateways through which culture-citizenship can be finally reached.[23]

Thus Locke thought that the artistic and literary achievements of the Irish and the Slavs had to be recognized if those groups were to attain the "recognition they are ultimately striving for": recognition as full participants in the economic, civic, and social life of Europe. More generally, I believe that Locke thought that the artistic and literary achievements of any race or people must be recognized if they are to be accorded recognition as full participants in economic, civic, and social life. He thought this especially true of oppressed races and peoples.[24] And so Locke would conclude that aesthetic multiculturalism was necessary if American racism was to be overcome and if African Americans were to be accorded recognition as full participants in American life.

I do not deny that education that aims at fostering aesthetic multiculturalism is important. The informed enjoyment of the intellectual achievements and of the folk and high cultures of other peoples is a source of both education and pleasure. It broadens the perspective on one's own culture. It reinforces a sense of the humanity, and sometimes the profundity, of others, even of those far removed in time or place. Cultivating the capacities and sentiments necessary for such enjoyment can therefore be morally improving, and such cultivation ought to be one of the aims of education. Aesthetic multiculturalism may be especially important in the United States, where the treatment of African Americans has been rationalized by views about their cognitive and cultural inferiority. It is, however, worth asking how much this sort of multicultural education can do to bridge this country's racial divides and overcome prejudices.

My own opinion is that racial prejudice is tied in complex ways to class stereotypes and to value judgments about economic and social class. Prejudice against African Americans depends in large part, though not entirely, upon widespread opinions about their economic and social class and stereotypes about their initiative, ability, and behavior. We will make little headway in extirpating the prejudice unless we correct the opinions and stereotypes. Thus, learning that some African Americans are and have been intellectuals and artists of the first rank does little, I conjecture, to alter widely held opinions about what "most" African Americans are like. Examples of artistic or intellectual excellence, like examples of professional, commercial, or even athletic accomplishment, may only tempt some to ask why other African Americans have not also worked hard enough to excel. Indeed, conspicuous examples of success, as judged by the standards of the dominant culture, may tempt some to ask why African Americans do not choose the strategy Ignatiev says the Irish adopted. One answer to these questions is, of course, that not everyone wants or should want to "become white." This is, I believe, a perfectly valid response, but one I shall not pursue, for another valid answer is that doing so is impossible. Among the tasks of contemporary higher education should be that of showing the youngest cohort of citizens and voters that the reasons this is so are not only the obvious ones. African Americans cannot become white as the Irish did because there are structural barriers to their social and economic mobility. We will make little headway in ending the prejudice unless we remove the systematic disadvantages African Americans face. Therefore, while an education aimed at teaching aesthetic multiculturalism is valuable for many reasons, Locke's hopes and aims will be realized only if that form of education is supplemented by other forms of multicultural education aimed at heightening awareness of the roots of class differences and of the culture, or better, the cultures, of poverty.

By "cultures of poverty" I mean the reflective and systematic sets of values and practices, tastes, attitudes, and aspirations that inform the lives of those who are poor. Some social scientists appeal to a culture of poverty as an explanation of poverty, particularly of intergenerational poverty. It is important to understand that my use of the phrase carries no such implication. My usage is compatible with the view that the genesis, revision, and transmission of cultures of poverty are themselves phenomena that require explanation. The explanations put forward will be extremely complicated. The best explanation, I believe, will show cultures of poverty to be, in large part, adaptive responses to the conditions under which poor Americans live. When I discussed Locke's critical relativism, I argued that it is a mistake to see cultures as responses to conditions and needs that can be conceptualized without recourse to judgments of value. It follows from this that cultures of poverty ought not to be seen as a response to conditions that can be so described. Instead, the best explanation of cultures of poverty will show them to be, in large part, responses to the persistence of social and economic conditions that are *unjust*.

Some might maintain that the persistence of poverty can be explained in large part by "pathological" or self-destructive elements in one or another culture of poverty; we need not, they might continue, appeal to the justice or injustice of the larger society to understand it. But suppose for the sake of argument that a culture does contain such elements. Once we recognize that the origin and transmission of culture are themselves in need of explanation and that they are responses to conditions whose descriptions depend upon judgments of value, then questions about the justice of the larger society immediately arise. And it surely tells against the justice of a society that it engenders among its most vulnerable members cultures that are ex hypothesi self-destructive.

An education that acquaints students with the cultures of poverty will therefore have as one of its aims to teach them to recognize and reason about unjust social conditions. It will be, to that extent, a moral education.

What might such an education be like? It should be a philosophical education, one that equips students to think systematically about the justice and injustice of social conditions. At religious colleges and universities like the one at which I teach, students should be exposed to theological resources for thinking about economic justice. But many students enter and leave college knowing relatively little about what sustains the cultures of poverty, about what the lives of their bearers are like, about who is poor, about the racial and ethnic composition of the American poor, and about what economic, social, political, and cultural factors work to keep some people that way. This makes it easier, not only to sustain prejudices and stereotypes, but also to overestimate what can be accomplished by individuals acting on their goodwill. At some point in their higher education, students should be exposed to empirical work on poverty and economics; on the lives of the poor, including the white and working poor; on race and the history of American race relations since the Civil War. Some of this literature is accessible to beginning undergraduates. Among the books that might be assigned are Michael Harrington's *The Other America,* Robert Coles's *Children of Crisis,* Nicholas Lemann's *The Promised Land: The Great Black Migration and How It Changed America,* Alex Kotlowitz's *There Are No Children Here: The Story of Two Boys Growing Up in the Other America,* William Julius Wilson's *When Work Disappears,* and John Rawls's *A Theory of Justice.*[27] Education about class differences, their roots, and their injustices is education to which Locke gave little heed, as other readers of his work have noted.[28] In this, at least, it is important to supplement his suggestions and construct forms of multicultural education that stress economics, sociology, and philosophy, as well as literature, art, and poetry.

Notes

1. Noel Ignatiev, *How the Irish Became White* (New York: Routledge, 1995), 24.

2. This essay was written as a commentary on Blanche Radford Curry's essay "Alain Locke: A Provocative Analysis of Multicultural Education." Professor Curry's paper and my comment were presented at a session of the Alain Locke Society on 30 December 1996. That session, organized by Leonard Harris, was held in conjunction with the American Philosophical Association's Eastern Division meeting. I am grateful to Professors Curry and Harris for the opportunity to participate, and to Jorge Garcia, Leonard Harris, and Martha Nussbaum for helpful comments on an earlier draft.

3. For Ignatiev, see *How the Irish Became White*, xi.; for Locke, see Alain Locke, *Race Contacts and Interracial Relations*, ed. Jeffrey Stewart (Washington, D.C.: Howard University Press, 1992), 11, 85 ff.

4. See Ignatiev, *How the Irish Became White*, 179 n. 4 and accompanying text.

5. See Locke, *Race Contacts*, 41 ff.

6. For criticism, see Eleanor Burke Leacock, introduction to *The Culture of Poverty: A Critique*, ed. Eleanor Burke Leacock (New York: Simon & Schuster, 1971). For an unexceptionable use, see Michael Harrington, *The Other America* (New York: Macmillan, 1962), 15 and *passim*.

7. Leonard Harris, ed., *The Philosophy of Alain Locke: Harlem Renaissance and Beyond* (Philadelphia: Temple University Press, 1989), 268.

8. Harris, *Philosophy of Alain Locke*, 124.

9. Harris, *Philosophy of Alain Locke*, 179–85.

10. Harris, *Philosophy of Alain Locke*, 274.

11. The word "usual" is an important qualifier, for Locke did think that some comparative evaluation of culture was possible. He thought such comparative judgments should be made on a "scientific" basis and that comparative judgments usually made do not have such a basis. See Harris, *Philosophy of Alain Locke*, 74.

12. Harris, *Philosophy of Alain Locke*, 76.

13. Locke, *Race Contacts*, 100; a fuller discussion of "joint civilization" would, I believe, have to draw on the crucial discussion of reciprocity at Harris, *Philosophy of Alain Locke*, 135–37.

14. Harris, *Philosophy of Alain Locke*, 74.

15. In this and the preceding paragraph, I have drawn on Horace Holley, *Religion for Mankind* (Wilmette, Ill.: Baha'i Publishing Trust, 1956) 16–28. I claim no expertise on the Baha'i faith and introduce it here primarily to suggest that the relationship between Locke's philosophical views and the tenets of his religious faith merits further exploration.

16. Harris, *Philosophy of Alain Locke*, 266.

17. For this suggestion, see Judith Shklar, "A Life of Learning," Occasional Paper no. 9, American Council of Learned Societies (Washington, D.C.: American Council of Learned Societies, 1989), 6.

18. Alasdair MacIntyre, "The Essential Contestability of Some Social Concepts," *Ethics* 84 (1973): 1–9.

19. Here I draw on Locke, *Race Contacts,* 99–100; see also note 13.

20. On Locke's promotion of African and African American culture, see Harris, *Philosophy of Alain Locke,* 5–8.

21. The essay can be found at Harris, *Philosophy of Alain Locke,* 265–76.

22. Locke, *Race Contacts,* 66; emphasis added.

23. Locke, *Race Contacts,* 100; emphasis added.

24. On the reasons for this, see the perceptive remarks by Stewart in his introduction to Locke, *Race Contacts,* xxxi ff.

25. I am grateful to Martha Nussbaum for this point.

26. See note 6.

27. See note 6.

28. See Robert Coles, *Children of Crisis* (Boston: Little, Brown, 1964); Nicholas Lemann, *Promised Land: The Great Black Migration and How It Changed America* (New York: Alfred A. Knopf, 1991); Alex Kotlowitz, *There Are No Children Here: The Story of Two Boys Growing Up in the Other America* (New York: Doubleday, 1991); William Julius Wilson, *When Work Disappears* (New York: Alfred A. Knopf, 1996); John Rawls, *A Theory of Justice* (Cambridge: Harvard University Press, 1971); Johnny Washington, "Alain L. Locke's 'Values and Imperatives': An Interpretation," in *Philosophy Born of Struggle,* ed. Leonard Harris (Dubuque, Iowa: Kendall/Hunt, 1983), 148–58.

PART VI

POSTSCRIPT

22

Alain Locke Remembered

Beth J. Singer

On 2 January 1946, articles in the *Madison (Wis.) Capital Times* and the *Wisconsin State Journal* announced that Professor Alain L. Locke, whose photograph was in both papers, would be a philosophy teacher at the University of Wisconsin. The subhead of the *Capital Times* article read: "Noted Negro Educator, Philosopher, to Teach Here in 2d Semester." The *Milwaukee Journal,* on 3 January, also announced, "Negro Scholar Named Visiting U.W. Teacher." This was not the only time Dr. Locke was to be featured in the news, but more of this later. Regarding his appointment, the *Wisconsin State Journal* article said that "Dr. Locke's principal course will be 'The Philosophy of the Arts' and he will also conduct a seminar on 'Value' and give one of the regular philosophy department logic courses." The *Journal* and the *Capital Times* both noted that Professor Locke was born in Philadelphia on 13 September 1886 and was graduated from the Philadelphia School of Pedagogy and Harvard University, following which he was selected, in 1907, as Rhodes scholar from Pennsylvania. After studying for three years at Oxford University, he did additional graduate work at the University of Berlin in 1910 and 1911 and returned to Harvard, where he received his Ph.D. in 1918. All in the far distant past in the eyes of a young undergraduate, which I was at the time. But the papers also mentioned that Locke had served as Inter-American Exchange Professor to Haiti as recently as 1943. And in addition to mentioning his membership in Phi Beta Kappa and two fraternities, they noted that he was on the faculty of Howard University, "famed Negro institution of higher learning" (*Wisconsin State Journal*) and that he had "written extensively on Negro art and race relations in America," listing among his books *Race Contacts and Interracial Relations, The New Negro, The Negro in America, The Negro and his Music, Negro Art: Past and Present, Frederick Douglass: A Biography of Antislavery,* and *A Study in Race and Culture Contact.* According to his University of Wisconsin faculty employment form, this unusually distinguished person, Alain LeRoy

Locke, was appointed visiting professor of philosophy, at the munificent salary of $2,500 for the semester. (This will not seem such a small amount in comparison with undergraduate tuition at that time, which was $48 per semester for in-state students and $148 for those who came from out of state—all inclusive: no registration fee, and complete health care provided, including hospital stays if necessary.)

I was fortunate enough (I will not say wise enough) to enroll in Locke's course, Philosophy 53, Philosophy of the Arts. As I remember it, this was a lecture course, and the class was quite large but inordinately attentive. Locke was a quiet, extremely scholarly, and well-organized lecturer; I do not recall his speaking from notes. The primary text that he used is not a surprising choice for a former Rhodes scholar, but it is somewhat unexpected for an authority on Negro art. He had published *Negro Art: Past and Present* in 1936 and an important paper, "A Note on African Art," in 1924.[1] Since *Negro Art* was apparently designed to be a textbook, with discussion questions and a list of additional references at the end of each chapter, that it was not assigned is doubly surprising, although it may have been allowed to go out of print by 1946. But the reading assignments, as I remember, were in the British philosopher R. G. Collingwood's *Principles of Art*.[2] However, one connection between Collingwood's book and Locke's work on Negro and African art is the fact that, in the very first chapter, Collingwood discusses the relation between art and craft (he refuses to reduce art to either craft or technique) and rejects the concept of "fine art," along with the supposed inherent connection between art and beauty.

In class, and in the final chapter of *Negro Art,* entitled "The Future of African Negro Art," Locke took up the issue of so-called primitive art. I clearly remember his stressing, in class, that the latter is truly art and, reviewing what he took to be the distinguishing traits of art, showing that what at least at that time was termed "primitive" art possesses them all. I only wish I could find my class notes, but, alas, they have disappeared. But in the chapter of *Negro Art* entitled "African or Primitive Negro Art," discussing the development of art among the peoples of Africa, Locke uses somewhat different terminology. He points out that not only at the time these peoples were discovered by the Europeans but still when he was writing, there remained some artisans in virtually every African society who were carrying on traditional crafts. However, he says: "Most African art . . . is by no means a primitive art. . . . For only a peasant art or primary craft art is a primitive art" (95). And, he points out, "The peak of almost every well-known strain of African art is definitely associated with the heyday of some feudal African dynasty" (94). "So really," he states, "speaking of African art is like speaking of European art, when we should and in our own case, really do speak of French art, German art, Italian art," despite the fact that there are certain "common characteristics among them" (94).

What strikes me today in reading this book, which is only 122 pages long, is the tremendous amount of information and interpretation that is packed into such a small work. Most impressive is Locke's enormous erudition regarding virtually the entire history of art worldwide. Well aware of the influence that African art came to have on "modern" European and American art, for instance, in discussing the background of this movement, Locke shows himself to be a thorough historian, analyst, and critic of both Western and African art and to know Russian art as well as he knows American Negro art and American art in general. We students had enormous respect for Dr. Locke, but I must admit that, in my case at least, this respect, great as it was, did not do justice to his scholarly achievement in this field.

Part of the respect, though, was a response to his quiet dignity and personal restraint. The general atmosphere in the department was very informal, but as I recall, Dr. Locke seemed to us to stand somewhat apart. There was another factor that may help to account for this. Many philosophy students, myself included, became friendly with other faculty members, partly through a departmental organization called Vanguard, subtitled "An Experiment in Naturalistic Religion." Its program and goals, which grew out of John Dewey's *Common Faith,* were those of Max Otto's humanism—Otto was chairman of the department—and not consonant with Locke's religious orientation [3] (One of the newspaper articles mistakenly identified him as an Episcopalian, but Locke was a member of the Baha'i faith.) But, in addition to this, Dr. Locke seemed somehow aloof, and my friends and I were pretty much in awe of him. Many years later, I used to see him on 125th Street in Harlem, standing in front of the Apollo Theater, elegantly dressed as usual and with his walking stick in front of him, just as dignified as I remembered him being. I would greet him and mention that I had studied with him at Wisconsin, and whether he recognized me or not, he would return my "Good evening" in the quiet but still cordial manner to which I had become accustomed.

Despite his quiet demeanor, Locke had strong convictions and was a militant fighter for democracy, and he did more in Madison than teach—or, I should say, he did not limit his teaching to the classroom, and he reached a broader audience than the university community. Madison was the capital of a very liberal state in which a well-known progressive family, the LaFollettes, had played a significant role, and the newspapers there followed Locke's public addresses faithfully. In one article, headlined "Dr. Locke Pleads for World Culture," he is reported to have said in a public address that "we are fast approaching a stage in which culture will have to be international." The article goes on to quote him: "This culture must have courtesy and reciprocity and must be aided by religious tolerance. . . . And, in order to have tolerance, we must have every person intelligently aware of the common denominators of basic ideas and basic moral issues. That is necessary for basic unity." Continuing, the author of the column writes, "The philosophy instructor, on leave from Howard University, Washington, D.C., said that religious conviction and zealous faith have often been conducive to intolerant attitudes and warned that these attitudes will have less of a place in the future world than they had in the world of the past." And, in the final paragraph, "Dr. Locke closed his address on 'Comparative Cultures' by quoting several axioms that would solve religious conflicts—'In accommodating others you accommodate yourself;' 'Blame yourself as you would others,' and 'Good for good.'"[4]

On 20 March 1946, the *State Journal* reported another talk, this time to about two hundred teachers in the Madison schools and members of the city's board of education. His topic, particularly relevant today during the wars over "multiculturalism," was "Intercultural Education in America," which he took necessarily to mean teaching democracy. He was concerned that this ideal was being abandoned because of the growing tendency of neighborhoods to be based on economic or class distinctions. "Some schools are not now democratic because of this. Therefore we must campaign for democracy now." Several other points he made are significant. One is that the teaching must be done by individuals: "It is a question of an alert, socially minded teacher who has some convictions about democracy." He went on to say, "If democracy can not be taught, it can at least be communicated," and "When democracy is gotten across in the formative years, it sticks." But his final conclusion, at least partly unexpected, I am sure, was that "Teachers must help to fortify democracy nationally and internationally and help to justify the expenditure of public money."

Some of the most important things Locke said in Madison were expressed in an interview conducted by Cedric Parker for the *Madison Capital Times* and reported on 26 January 1946. It should be remembered that World War II was not long over. Parker's report opens as follows:

> To complete the building of democracy in America, there is another war to be won. . . . It is the struggle within the United States to establish all races and minorities as Americans, with equal rights, privileges, and obligations. . . . Unless this war for fuller democracy is won, fascism will always be a home-front threat, and America will not have made her proper contribution to lasting peace in the world. . . .
>
> In these three sentences is summed up the day-by-day, practical, working, and living philosophy of Dr. Alain L. Locke, American philosopher and Negro educator who last week became the first person of his race to join the University of Wisconsin faculty with full professorial rank.

Parker takes pains to note that "Dr. Locke is a member of that school of philosophers who believe in connecting classroom philosophy with current issues and the practical problems of everyday living." This is the school of philosophy exemplified at that time by the Madison department under the leadership of Max Otto. In the interview, Locke said, "Wisconsin is pioneering in a trend which I believe will grow—a trend which must spread widely if we are to realize full democracy in American education." Six years later, paying tribute to Otto on the occasion of the presentation to him of the volume of essays entitled *The Cleavage in Our Culture* and subtitled *Studies in Scientific Humanism in Honor of Max Otto,* after noting the ancient roots of humanism, Locke asserted that "it can truthfully be said that Max Otto has made a creative contribution to contemporary humanism by construing it more progressively and developing it more democratically."[5] He might have been describing his own position when he said of Otto, "He urges that with due respect for individual differences, we work toward an ever-expanding harmony of common agreement, uncoerced and flexible. He rightly insists that only by tolerating others can we come fully and sanely to understand ourselves."

To return to Parker's interview and the topic with which it opened, the interviewer makes a point of saying that "in warning that fascism threatens any nation which harbors white supremacy, anti-Semitism, Ku Klux Klanism, or any other form of racism, Dr. Locke does not use the word 'fascism' loosely. He is no alarmist, but one who sees America's racial cleavage as part of a broad world problem." Locke acknowledged that some progress was made toward full democracy during World War II and noted that it came about "as a necessary part of the war effort." Like women, Blacks were suddenly welcomed as workers in factories producing war materiel, even if they were still segregated in the armed forces. But even this welcome did not happen automatically. "Under the duress of war," Parker quotes Locke as saying, "there was a large volume of minority protest against the exclusion of the Negro from upgrading and full employment in our national industry. The outcome of that was a presidential order, the famous FEPC [Fair Employment Practices Committee] order, which tried in the interests of national efficiency to remove some of these handicaps." And Locke went on to note that "When the cases were prepared for the first hearing under the FEPC in New York, the board was surprised to discover that although the law was set up primarily as a measure to protect the Negro minority, a considerable proportion of the cases involved discrimination against Jews, and some involved women." "The big lesson" from this, Locke concluded, is "that the protection of minority rights becomes an instrument for guaranteeing, safeguarding, and enlarging common rights." And in the interview he made a comparable point about public education, drawing attention to the negative consequences for the common welfare of the fact that many southern states spent less on the education of Negro children than on that of whites. As a result, they spent less on education in general, which had to have consequences for the average level of educational achievement. As Locke put it, "there is a definite connection there, because the level of the Negro is part of the whole situation and either raises or decreases it." According to Parker, Locke's firm conviction concerning public education was that "[t]here can be no fundamental improvement if the minority is treated in isolation." And applying this to each state or region as a whole, Locke cited the dangers of taking different minority group situations as isolated problems. "Enlightened communities," he is quoted as saying, "now realize that if a minority problem is serious anywhere, it is, by implication and in terms of democracy, a matter of serious concern for them."

Locke's optimism regarding this realization was probably greater than many of us would hold to be justified. But his statement at the conclusion of the interview, while it fails to remark on the deep-seated prejudices that characterized elements in our society, and continue to do so to this day, at the same time states the problem that it still remains for us to solve:

> I should like to express my gratification that intelligent Americans are today considering that our democracy is not a finished thing, and that the problems of postwar reconstruction and reconversion involve full democracy so vitally that we really have another war—a domestic war to win.

Some intelligent Americans did understand Locke's point and not only agreed with it but also made it clear that they already knew of Locke and his support for democracy and equal rights. In a letter dated 20 March 1946, Professor Harold R. Cole of Dakota Wesleyan University in Winchell, South Dakota, wrote to President Edwin B. Fred of the University of Wisconsin–Madison:

> Dear sir:
>
> I have noted in the Educational section of "Headlines," a weekly magazine, that Dr. Locke has been appointed a full professor in philosophy. I want to take this opportunity to congratulate you and the administration of the University and to praise you for your wisdom and courage. This step will without a doubt help, more than can be realized at the present time, in the attainment of social and economic peace in the world which we are now facing.
>
> The equality of races and mankind must be established beyond a doubt and we, of the white race who are socially conscious of our responsibilities to fellowman, are the ones who must push forward and light the way for others to follow.[6]

Notes

1. Alain Locke, *Negro Art: Past and Present,* Bronze Booklet no. 3 (Washington, D.C.: Associates in Negro Folk Education, 1936); Alain Locke, "A Note on African Art," *Opportunity,* May 1924.

2. R. G. Collingwood, *The Principles of Art* (Oxford: Clarendon Press, 1938).

3. John Dewey, *A Common Faith* (New Haven: Yale University Press, 1934).

4. *Wisconsin State Journal,* 15 February 1946.

5. Frederick H. Burkhardt, ed., *The Cleavage in Our Culture: Studies in Scientific Humanism in Honor of Max Otto* (Boston: Beacon Press, 1952).

6. I am grateful to the University of Wisconsin Archives for supplying me with this and other documentation I used in preparing this paper. [See also Moorland-Spingarn Research Center, Alain Locke Collection, University of Wisconsin–1946, Lecture Notes, "Philosophy of Arts," Box 164-164, Folder 5.]

Select Bibliography

Aaron, Daniel, ed. *America in Crisis*. New York: Alfred Knopf, 1952.

Abrahams, Edward. *The Lyrical Left: Randolph Bourne, Alfred Stieglitz, and the Origins of Cultural Radicalism in America*. Charlottesville: University of Virginia, 1986.

Africa: The Art of a Continent. New York: Guggenheim Museum Publishers, 1996.

Akam, Everett Helmut. "Pluralism and the Search for Community: The Social Thought of American Cultural Pluralists." Ph.D. diss., University of Rochester, 1990.

Anderson, James D. *The Education of Blacks in the South, 1860–1935*. Chapel Hill: University of North Carolina Press, 1990.

Anderson, Talmadge. *Introduction to African American Studies*. Dubuque, Iowa: Kendall/Hunt, 1993.

Anzaldúa, Gloria. *Borderlands: The New Mestiza–La Frontera*. San Francisco: Spinsters/Aunt Lute, 1987.

Appiah, Kwame Anthony. *In My Father's House: Africa in the Philosophy of Culture*. New York: Oxford University Press, 1992.

Arendt, Hannah. *The Human Condition: A Study of the Central Dilemmas Facing Modern Man*. Garden City, N.Y.: Doubleday, 1958.

Baker, Houston. *Modernism and the Harlem Renaissance*. Chicago: University of Chicago Press, 1987.

Baraka, Amiri. *Blues People: Negro Music in White America*. New York: Morrow Quill, 1963.

Barnes, Albert C. *The Art of Painting*. New York: Harcourt Brace, 1925.

Bell, Clive. *Art*. New York: Frederick Stokes, 1913.

Bernstein, Richard. *Beyond Objectivism and Relativism: Science, Hermeneutics, and Praxis*. Philadelphia: University of Pennsylvania Press, 1983.

———. *The New Constellation: The Ethical-Political Horizons of Modernity/Postmodernity*. Cambridge: MIT Press, 1991.

Binder, Wolfgang, ed. *Ethnic Cultures in the 1920s in North America*. Frankfurt am Main: Peter Lang, 1993.

Blake, Casey N. *Beloved Community: The Cultural Criticism of Randolph Bourne, Van Wyck Brooks, Waldo Frank, and Lewis Mumford*. Chapel Hill: University of North Carolina Press, 1990.

Boas, Franz. *Primitive Art*. New York: Dover, 1955.

Bone, Robert. *Down Home*. New York: G. P. Putnam's Sons, 1975.

Bontemps, Arna, ed. *The Harlem Renaissance Remembered*. New York: Dodd, Mead, 1972.

335

Bourne, Randolph S. *The Radical Will: Randolph Bourne—Selected Writings, 1911–1918.* Edited by Olaf Hansen. New York: Urizen, 1977.

Brawley, Benjamin. *The Negro in Literature and Art in the United States.* 3d ed. New York: Duffield, 1929.

Brooks, Van Wyck. *America's Coming-of-Age.* New York: B. W. Huebsch, 1915.

Brown, Sterling Allen. *The Negro in American Fiction.* 1937. Reprint. New York: Arno Press, 1969.

———. *Negro Poetry and Drama.* Washington, D.C.: Associates in Negro Folk Education, 1936.

Bunche, Ralph. *World View of Race.* Washington, D.C.: Associates in Negro Folk Education, 1936.

Burkhardt, Frederick, ed. *The Cleavage in Our Culture: Studies in Scientific Humanism in Honor of Max Otto.* Boston: Beacon Press, 1952.

Caliver, Ambrose. Fundamentals in the Education of Negroes. Washington, D.C.: U.S. Department of Interior, Office of Education, 1935.

Carmichael, Stokely [Kwame Ture], and Charles V. Hamilton. Black Power. 1967. Reprint. New York: Vintage, 1992.

Chapman, Abraham, ed. *Black Voices: An Anthology of Afro-American Literature.* New York: Mentor, 1968.

Clifford, James, and George Marcus, eds., *Writing and Culture.* Berkeley and Los Angeles: University of California Press, 1986.

Coleman, Leon D., *The Contribution of Carl Van Vechten to the Negro Renaissance: 1920–1930.* Ann Arbor: University of Michigan Press, 1969.

Coles, Robert. *Children of Crisis.* Boston: Little, Brown, 1964.

Collingwood, R. G. *The Principles of Art.* 1938. Reprint. Oxford: Oxford University Press, 1972.

Collins, Patricia Hill. *Black Feminist Thought: Knowledge, Consciousness, and the Politics of Empowerment.* New York: Routledge, 1991.

Collinson, Diane, et al., eds. *Biographical Dictionary of Twentieth-Century Philosophers.* New York: Routledge, 1995.

Cooper, Alice. *A Voice from the South.* New York: Oxford University Press, 1988.

Cox, Oliver Cromwell. *Caste, Class, and Race.* New York: Monthly Review Press, 1970.

Cruse, Harold. *The Crisis of the Negro Intellectual.* New York: William Morris, 1967.

Davidson, Donald. *Inquiries into Truth and Interpretation.* New York: Oxford University Press, 1984.

Davis, Arthur P. *From the Dark Tower: Afro-American Writers, 1900–1960.* Washington, D.C.: Howard University Press, 1974.

Days, E. A. "Alain Leroy Locke, 1886–1954: Pioneer in Adult Education and Catalyst in the Adult Education Movement for Black Americans." Ed.D. diss., North Carolina University at Raleigh, 1965.

de Zayas, Marius. *African Negro Art: Its Influence on Modern Art.* New York: Modern Gallery, 1916.

Dewey, John. *Art as Experience.* Carbondale: Southern Illinois University Press, 1987.

———. *A Common Faith.* New Haven: Yale University Press, 1934.

———. *The Middle Works, 1899–1924,* vol. 10, ed. Jo Ann Boylston Carbondale: Southern Illinois University Press, 1976.

———. *The Public and Its Problems.* New York: Henry Holt, 1927.

Diop, Cheikh Anta. *Civilization or Barbarism: An Authentic Anthropology.* Translated by Yaa-Lengi Meema Ngemi. Edited by Harold J. Salemson and Marjolin de Jager. Brooklyn: Lawrence Hill Books, 1991.

Dixon, Ronald. *The Racial History of Man.* New York: Charles Scribner's Sons, 1932.

Dixon, Thomas, Jr. *The Clansman: A Romance of the Ku Klux Klan.* New York: Grosset & Dunlap, 1905.

———. *The Leopard's Spots: A Romance of the White Man's Burden.* New York: Doubleday, Page, 1902.

Drake, St. Clair, and Horace Clayton. *Black Metropolis: A Study of Negro Life in a Northern City.* New York: Harcourt, Brace & World, 1945.

Drewal, Margaret Thompson. *Yoruba Ritual: Performers, Play, Agency.* Indianapolis: Indiana University Press, 1992.

Du Bois. W. E. B. *Black Folk: Then and Now; An Essay in the History and Sociology of the Negro Race.* New York: Octagon Books, 1970.

———. *Black Reconstruction: An Essay toward a History of the Part Which Black Folk Played in the Attempt to Reconstruct Democracy in America, 1860–1877.* New York: Russell & Russell, 1935.

———. *The Correspondence of W. E. B. Du Bois.* Amherst: University of Massachusetts Press, 1973.

———. *Dark Princess.* Millwood, N.Y.: Kraus-Thomson, 1974.

———. *The Quest of the Silver Fleece.* Chicago: A. C. McClurg, 1911.

———. *Souls of Black Folk.* 1903. Reprint. New York: Basic Books, 1968.

———. *W. E. B. Du Bois Speaks: Speeches and Addresses, 1890–1919.* Edited by Philip S. Foner. New York: Pathfinder Press, 1970.

———. *Writings by W. E. B. Du Bois in Periodicals Edited by Others.* Edited by Herbert Aptheker. Millwood, N.Y.: Kraus-Thomson, 1982.

Dummett, Michael. *Truth and Other Enigmas.* Cambridge: Harvard University Press, 1978.

Einstein, Carl. *Negerplastik.* Leipzig: Verlag der Weissen Bucher, 1915.

Evnine, Simon. *Donald Davidson.* Stanford, Calif.: Stanford University Press, 1991.

Faulkner, William. *Light in August.* New York: Random House, 1932.

"Findings of the First Annual Conference on Adult Education and the Negro." Hampton Institute, Associates in Negro Folk Education, American Association for Adult Education, 1938. Mimeographed.

"Findings of the Second Annual Conference on Adult Education and the Negro." Tuskegee Institute, Associates in Negro Folk Education, American Association for Adult Education, 1940. Mimeographed.

Fine, Elsa Honig. *The Afro- American Artist: A Search for Identity.* New York: Holt, Rinehart & Winston, 1973.

Fisher, Philip, ed. *The New American Studies: Essays from Representations.* Berkeley and Los Angeles: University of California Press, 1991.

Fraser, Nancy. *Justice Interruptus: Critical Reflections on the "Postsocialist" Condition.* New York: Routledge, 1997.

Freire, Paulo. *Pedagogy of the Oppressed.* New York: Continuum, 1970.

Garrisson, J.,ed. *The New Dewey Scholarship.* Dordrecht: Kluwe Academic, 1995.

Garry, Ann, and Marilyn Pearsall, eds. *Women, Knowledge, and Reality.* Boston: Unwin Hyman, 1989.

Gates, Henry Louis, Jr., and Cornel West. *The Future of the Race.* New York: Vintage Books, 1996.

Gates, Henry Louis, Jr., ed. *Race, Writing, and Difference.* Chicago: University of Chicago Press, 1986.

Gatewood, Willard B. *Aristocrats of Color: The Black Elite, 1880–1920.* Bloomington: Indiana University Press, 1990.

Gayle, Addison. *The Black Aesthetic.* New York: Doubleday, 1972.

Goldberg, David T., ed. *Anatomy of Racism.* Minneapolis: University of Minnesota Press, 1990.

Goldwater, Robert. *Primitivism in Modern Art.* 1938. Reprint. Cambridge: Harvard University Press, Belknap Press, 1986.

Gross, Seymour L., and John E. Hardy, eds., *Images of the Negro in American Literature.* Chicago: University of Chicago Press, 1966.

Hacker, Andrew. *Two Nations: Black and White, Separate, Hostile, Unequal.* New York: Ballantine Books, 1995.

Harrington, Michael. *The Other America.* New York: Macmillan, 1962.

Harris, Leonard, ed. *Philosophy Born of Struggle: Anthology of Afro-American Philosophy from 1917.* Dubuque, Iowa: Kendall/Hunt, 1983.

———. *The Philosophy of Alain Locke: Harlem Renaissance and Beyond.* Philadelphia: Temple University Press, 1989.

Harris, V. J. *The Brownies' Book: Challenge to the Selective Tradition in Children's Literature.* Ph.D. diss. University of Georgia, Athens, 1986.

Heaney, Tom. *Adult Education for Social Change: From Center Stage to the Wings and Back Again.* Information Series no. 365. Washington, D.C.: Office of Educational Research and Improvement, Department of Education, 1996. ERIC doc. 396190.

Hegel, G. W. F. *The Phenomenology of Mind.* Translated by J. B. Baillie. New York: Harper & Row, 1967.

Herrnstein, Richard J., and Charles Murray. *The Bell Curve: Intelligence and Class Structure in American Life.* New York: Free Press, 1994.

Herskovits, Melville J. *The Myth of the Negro Past.* Boston: Beacon Press, 1941.

Hill, Timothy Arnold. *The Negro and Economic Reconstruction.* Washington, D.C.: Associates in Negro Folk Education, 1937.

Hiller, Susan. *The Myth of Primitivism.* New York: Routledge, 1991.

Holley, Horace. *Religion for Mankind.* Wilmette: Baha'i Publishing Trust, 1956.

Hollis, Martin, and Steven Lukes, eds. *Rationality and Relativism.* Cambridge: MIT Press, 1989.

Hountondji, Paulin. *African Philosophy: Myth and Reality.* London: Hutchinson, 1983.

Huggins, Nathan. *Harlem Renaissance.* New York: Oxford University Press, 1971.

Hughes, Langston. *The Big Sea: An Autobiography.* 1940. Reprint. New York: Thunder's Mouth Press, 1986.

Hutchinson, George. *The Harlem Renaissance in Black and White.* Cambridge: Harvard University Press, 1995.

Ignatiev, Noel. *How the Irish Became White.* New York: Routledge, 1995.

James, William. *Pragmatism: A New Name for Some Old Ways of Thinking.* New York: Longmans, Green, 1907.

Jahn, Janhheinz. *Muntu: African Culture and the Western World.* Translated by Marjorie Greene. Rev. ed. New York: Grove Weidenfeld, 1990.

Joplin, Scott. *Collected Works of Scott Joplin.* New York: New York Public Library, 1971.

Kallen, Horace M. *Culture and Democracy in the United States: Studies in the Group Psychology of the American Peoples.* New York: Boni & Liveright, 1924.

Kallen, Horace M., and Sidney Hook, eds. *American Philosophy Today and Tomorrow.* New York: L. Furman, 1935.

Karenga, Maulana. *Introduction to Black Studies.* Los Angeles: Kawaida, 1983.

Kellner, Bruce, ed. *The Harlem Renaissance: A Historical Dictionary for the Era.* Westport, Conn.: Greenwood Press, 1984.

———. *Selected Writings of Carl Van Vechten about Black Art and Letters.* Westport, Conn.: Greenwood Press, 1979.

King, Martin Luther, Jr. *Where Do We Go from Here: Chaos or Community?* New York: Harper & Row, 1967.

Kirsche, Amy Helene. *Aaron Douglas: Art, Race, and the Harlem Renaissance.* Jackson: University Press of Mississippi, 1995.

Knowles, Malcolm S. *Applying Modern Principles of Adult Learning.* New York: Association Press, 1970.

Knowles Associates, 1984. *The Modern Practice of Adult Education: From Pedagogy to Andragogy.* Rev. ed. Chicago: Association Press, 1980.

Konvitz, Milton R., and Sidney Hook. *Freedom and Experience.* Ithaca, N.Y.: Cornell University Press, 1947.

Kotlowitz, Alex. *There Are No Children Here: The Story of Two Boys Growing Up in the Other America.* New York: Doubleday, 1991.

Kousser, J. M., and J. M. McPherson. *Region, Race, and Reconstruction: Essays in Honor of C. Vann Woodward.* Oxford: Oxford University Press, 1982.

Kuper, Adam. *The Invention of Primitive Society.* New York: Routledge, 1988.

Leacock, Eleanor Burke, ed. *The Culture of Poverty: A Critique.* New York: Simon & Schuster, 1971.

Lemann, Nicholas. *The Promised Land: The Great Black Migration and How It Changed America.* New York: Alfred A. Knopf, 1991.

Levine, George, ed. *Aesthetics and Ideology.* New Brunswick, N.J.: Rutgers University Press, 1994.

Lindeman, Eduard. *The Meaning of Adult Education.* New York: Republic, 1926.

Linnemann, Russell J., ed. *Alain Locke: Reflections on a Modern Renaissance Man.* Baton Rouge: Louisiana State University Press, 1982.

Lippmann, Walter. *Public Opinion.* New York: Free Press, 1965.

Locke, Alain. *The Negro and His Music.* Washington, D.C.: Associates in Negro Folk Education, 1936.

———. *Negro Art: Past and Present.* Washington, D.C.: Associates in Negro Folk Education, 1936.

———. *The Negro in America.* Chicago: American Library Association, 1933.

———. *The Negro in Art.* Washington, D.C.: Associates in Negro Folk Education, 1940.

———. *Race Contacts and Interracial Relations.* Ed. Jeffrey C. Stewart. Washington, D.C.: Howard University Press, 1992.

———. "Report on Negro Adult Education Projects." 15 March 1934. Writings by Locke file, Moorland-Spingarn Manuscript Collection, Howard University.

Locke, Alain, ed. *Four Negro Poets.* New York: Simon & Schuster, 1927.

———. *The New Negro.* 1925. Reprint. New York: Atheneum, 1992.

Locke, Alain, and Montgomery Gregory, eds. *Plays of Negro Life: A Source-Book of Native American Drama.* New York: Harper, 1927.

Locke, Alain, and R. M. McIver, eds. *Group Relations and Group Antagonisms.* New York: Harper Brothers, 1944.

Locke, Alain, and Bernard J. Stern, eds. *When Peoples Meet: A Study in Race and Culture Contacts.* New York: Hinds, Hayden & Eldredge, 1946.

Lodge, David, ed. *Modern Criticism and Theory: A Reader.* London: Longmans, 1988.

Lycan, William G. *Logical Form in Natural Language.* Cambridge: MIT Press, 1986.

Major, Clarence. *All-Night Visitors.* New York: Olympia, 1969.

———. *Emergency Exit.* New York: Harper & Row, 1968.

———. *My Amputations.* New York: Fiction Collective, 1986.

———. *Such Was the Season.* San Francisco: Mercury, 1987.

Manning, Marable. *Beyond Black and White: Transforming African American Politics.* London: Verso, 1995.

Matthew, Basil J., *Booker T. Washington: Educator and Inter-Racial Interpreter.* London: SCM, 1949.

McCullers, Carson. *The Heart Is a Lonely Hunter.* Boston: Houghton Mufflin, 1940.

McNeillie, Andrew, ed. *The Common Reader.* New York: Harcourt Brace Jovanovich, 1984.

Morrison, Toni. *The Bluest Eye.* New York: Alfred A. Knopf, 1995.

———. *Sula.* New York: Plume/Penguin, 1982.

———. *Tar Baby.* New York: Plume/Penguin, 1981.

Moses, Wilson J. *Alexander Crummell: A Study of Civilization and Discontent.* New York: Oxford University Press, 1989.

Mudimbe, V. Y. *The Idea of Africa.* Bloomington: Indiana University Press, 1994.

Myrdal, Gunnar. *An American Dilemma.* New York: McGraw Hill, 1962.

Nelson, Lynn Hankinson. *Who Knows: From Quine to a Feminist Empiricism.* Philadelphia: Temple University Press, 1990.

Nicholson, Linda, ed. *Feminism/Postmodernism.* New York: Routledge, 1990.

North, Michael. *The Dialect of Modernism: Race, Language and Twentieth-Century Literature*. New York: Oxford University Press, 1994.

Omi, Michael, and Howard Winant. *Racial Formations in the United States: From the 1960s to the 1990s*. New York: Routledge, 1986.

O'Neill, Eugene. The Emperor Jones. New York: Boni & Liveright, 1925.

Outlaw, Lucius. *On Race and Philosophy*. New York: Routledge, 1996.

Palmer, Robert. *Deep Blues*. New York: Penguin, 1981.

Peterson, Elizabeth A., ed. *Freedom Road: Adult Education of African Americans*. Malabar, Fla.: Krieger Publishing, 1996.

Pound, Ezra. *Make It New*. London: Faber & Faber, 1934.

Puckett, Newbell. *Folk Beliefs of the Southern Negro*. New York: Dover, 1969.

Quine, Willard Van Orman. *Theories and Things*. Cambridge: Harvard University Press, 1981.

———. *Word and Object*. Cambridge: MIT Press, 1960.

Rampersad, Arnold. *The Life of Langston Hughes: 1902–1941*. New York: Oxford University Press, 1986.

Rawls, John. *A Theory of Justice*. Cambridge: Harvard University Press, 1971.

Reid, Ira D. A. *Adult Education among Negroes*. Washington, D.C.: Associates in Negro Folk Education, 1936.

Roediger, David. *Towards the Abolition of Whiteness*. London: Routledge, 1994.

Royce, Josiah. *The Spirit of Modern Philosophy*. New York: Houghton, Mifflin, 1982.

Salzman, Jack, ed. *Bridges and Boundaries: African Americans and American Jews*. New York: George Braziller and The Jewish Museum, 1992.

Scott, Bonnie Kime, ed. *The Gender of Modernism*. Bloomington: Indiana University Press, 1990.

Segy, Ladislas. *Masks of Black Africa*. New York: Dover, 1976.

Sellers, M. N. S., ed. An Ethical Education: Community and Morality in the Multicultural University. Providence, R.I.: Berg, 1994.

Shapiro, Norman R., ed. and trans. *Negritude: Black Poetry from Africa and the Caribbean*. New York: October House, 1970.

Shusterman, Richard. *Practicing Philosophy: Pragmatism and the Philosophical Life*. New York: Routledge, 1997.

———. *Pragmatist Aesthetics: Living Beauty, Rethinking Art*. Oxford: Blackwell, 1992.

Singh, Amiritif, William S. Shriver, and Stanley Brodwin, eds. *The Harlem Renaissance: Revaluation*. New York: Garland Publishing, 1989.

Skrentny, John David. *The Ironies of Affirmative Action: Politics, Culture, and Justice in America*. Chicago: University of Chicago Press, 1996.

Slote, Michael. *Common-Sense Morality and Consequentialism*. London: Routledge & Kegan Paul, 1985.

Sollors, Werner. *Beyond Ethnicity: Consent and Descent in American Culture*. Oxford: Oxford University Press, 1986.

Sollors, Werner, and Maria Diedrich, eds. *The Black Columbiad: Defining Moments in*

African American Literature and Culture. Harvard English Studies no. 19. Cambridge: Harvard University Press, 1994.

Southern, Eileen. *The Music of Black Americans: A History.* New York: W. W. Norton, 1971.

Soyinka, Wole. *Myth, Literature, and the African World.* 1976. Reprint, Cambridge: Cambridge University Press, 1992.

Spalding, Frances. *Roger Fry: Art and Life.* Berkeley and Los Angeles: University of California Press, 1980.

Stewart, Jeffrey, ed. *The Critical Temper of Alain Locke: A Selection of His Essays on Art and Culture.* New York: Garland Publishing, 1983.

Stocking, George. *Objects and Others: Essays on Museums and Material Culture.* Vol. 3 of *History of Anthropology.* Madison: University of Wisconsin Press, 1985.

Stonequist, Everett V., *The Marginal Man: A Study in Personality and Culture Conflict.* New York: Russell & Russell, 1961.

Stubblefield, Harold, and Harvey Keane. *Adult Education in the American Experience: From the Colonial Period to the Present.* San Francisco: Jossey Bass, 1994.

Sundquist, Eric. *To Wake the Nations: Race in the Making of American Literature.* Cambridge: Harvard University Press, Belknap Press, 1993.

Taylor, Charles, and Amy Gutmann, eds. *Multiculturalism: Examining the Politics of Recognition.* Princeton, N.J.: Princeton University Press, 1994.

Thernstrom, Stephen, and Abigail Thernstrom. *America in Black and White: One Nation, Indivisible.* New York: Simon & Schuster, 1997.

Thurman, Wallace. *Infants of the Spring.* 1932. Reprint. Boston: Northeastern University Press, 1992.

Torgovnick, Marianna. *Gone Primitive: Savage Intellects, Modern Lives.* Chicago: University of Chicago Press, 1990.

Turner, Lorenzo. *Africanisms in the Gullah Dialect.* New York: Arno Press, 1968.

Twitchell, Beverly H. *Cézanne and Formalism in Bloomsbury.* Ann Arbor: University of Michigan Research Press, 1987.

Vasconcelos, José. *La Raza Cósmica.* Los Angeles: Centro de Publicaciones CSULA, 1979.

Wall, Cheryl A. *Women of the Harlem Renaissance.* Bloomington: Indiana University Press, 1995.

Washington, James Melvin, ed. *A Testament of Hope: The Essential Writings of Martin Luther King Jr.* San Francisco: Harper & Row, 1986.

Washington, Johnny. *A Journey into the Philosophy of Alain Locke.* Westport, Conn.: Greenwood Press, 1994.

Watson, Steven. *The Harlem Renaissance: Hub of African-American Culture, 1920–1930.* New York: Pantheon, 1995.

Welsh-Asante, Kariamu. *The African Aesthetic: Keeper of the Traditions.* Westport, Conn.: Greenwood Press, 1993.

Wertheim, Arthur F., *The New York Little Renaissance: Iconoclasm, Modernism, and Nationalism in American Culture, 1908–1917.* New York: New York University Press, 1976.

West, Cornel. *The American Evasion of Philosophy.* Madison: University of Wisconsin Press, 1989.

———. *Prophesy Deliverance: An Afro-American Revolutionary Christianity.* Philadelphia: Westminster, 1982.

———. *Race Matters.* Boston: Beacon, 1993.

Westbrook, Robert B. *John Dewey and American Democracy.* Ithaca, N.Y.: Cornell University Press, 1991.

Whitman, Walt. *Democratic Vistas.* 1871. Reprint. New York: Liberal Arts Press, 1949.

———. *Leaves of Grass.* 1855. Reprint, New York: Penguin Books, 1986.

Wiggins, David. *Needs, Value, Truth.* New York: Blackwell, 1987.

Williams, Eric E. The Negro in the Caribbean. Washington, D.C.: Associates in Negro Folk Education, 1942.

Williams, Julius Wilson. *When Work Disappears.* New York: Alfred A. Knopf, 1996.

Williams, Patricia. *The Alchemy of Race and Rights.* Cambridge: Harvard University Press, 1991.

Williams, William Carlos. *In the American Grain.* New York: New Directions, 1956.

Wistrich, Robert. *Antisemitism: The Longest Hatred.* New York: Pantheon, 1992.

Woodson, Carter G. *The African Background Outlined: Handbook for the Study of the Negro.* New York: Negro Universities Press, 1968.

Young, Iris Marion. *Justice and the Politics of Difference.* Princeton, N.J.: Princeton University Press, 1990.

Index

About the Contributors

RUDOLPH A. CAIN is professor of human services and education at Empire State College and is the author of *Alain LeRoy Locke: Race, Culture, and the Education of African American Adults.* He has been active in the Philosophy Born of Struggle conference series in New York.

BLANCHE RADFORD CURRY is an associate professor of philosophy at Fayetteville State University. Her teaching and research areas include oral and social value inquiry, African American philosophy, feminist theory, African American studies, and contemporary Black philosophy. She is an assistant editor of the American Philosophical Association's *Newsletter on Philosophy and the Black Experience,* serves on the board of *Hypatia: Journal of Feminist Philosophy,* and is a former Fulbright-Hayes Japan Fellow.

JANE DURAN is a fellow in the Department of Philosophy and lecturer in the humanities at the University of California at Santa Barbara. She received her Ph.D. from Rutgers University in 1982 and is the author of numerous works on feminist theory, philosophy of science, and the concept of the Black aesthetic.

ASTRID FRANKE is a graduate of the Frei Universität, Berlin, and is an assistant professor of American studies at the Johann Wolfgang von Goethe Universität in Frankfurt. She has recently finished a study on stereotypes in the modern American novel and is currently working on public voices in American poetry.

NANCY FRASER is professor of political science at the Graduate Faculty of the New School for Social Research and coeditor of the journal *Constellations.* Her books include *Justice Interruptus: Critical Reflections on the "Postsocialist" Condition* and *Unruly Practices: Power, Discourse, and Gender in Contemporary Social Theory.* She is also the coauthor of *Feminist Contentions: A Philosophical Exchange* and coeditor of *Revaluing French Feminism: Critical Essays on Difference, Agency, and Culture.* Two new books will be published in 1999, *Adding Insult to Injury: Social Justice and the Politics of Recognition* (edited by Kevin Olson and introduced by Richard Rorty), and *Redistribution* *or Recognition? A Political Philosophical Exchange,* coauthored with Axel Honneth.

SEGUN GBADEGESIN is professor and chairman of the Department of Philosophy at Howard University. He formerly was head of the philosophy department at Obafemi Awolowo University, Ile-Ife, Nigeria, and taught at the University of Wisconsin–Madison and Colgate University. He has written extensively on Africana philosophy and is the author of *African Philosophy: Traditional Yoruba Philosophy* and *Contemporary African Realities.*

JUDITH M. GREEN is an assistant professor in the Department of Philosophy and Religion at Fordham University and is the author of *Deep Democracy: Community, Diversity, and Transformation* (1999). She has taught courses in American philosophy, African American philosophy, and feminism, as well as Native American philosophy. She is a noted pragmatist; author of works on multiculturalism, ethics, and American philosophy; and a board member of the Alain Locke Society.

TALMADGE C. GUY is assistant professor of adult education in the Department of Adult Education at the University of Georgia. He holds a doctor of education degree from Northern Illinois University. His interests include history and philosophy of African American adult education, multicultural education, and culturally relevant adult education. He has published articles and conducted numerous workshops on African American adult education, diversity, and multicultural education.

LAVERNE GYANT is director of the Center for Black Studies and assistant professor in continuing adult education at Northern Illinois University. She is a graduate of Cheyney State University. Her research interests are in African American women and the contributions and participation of African Americans in adult education. Her publications include *All That and More: A Genealogy of African American Women Educators; Educating Head, Hand, and Heart: Anna Cooper and Nannie Burroughs; Passing the Torch: African American Women and the Civil Rights Movement; Henrietta V. Davis and Amy J. Garvey: Women of the UNIA;* and *The Problems and Promises of Diversity in the Professions.* She is president of the African Heritage Studies Association and is currently conducting research on women from 1900 to 1940.

LEONARD HARRIS is professor of philosophy at Purdue University. He is the editor of *Philosophy Born of Struggle: Anthology of African American Philosophy from 1917* and *Children in Chaos: A Philosophy for Children Experi-*

ence, coeditor of *Exploitation and Exclusion,* and editor of *The Philosophy of Alain Locke* and *The Concept of Racism.* He is a former Portia-Washington Pittman Fellow and Fulbright Scholar at Addis Ababa University, Ethiopia, and a graduate of Cornell University. He is a founding member of the Philosophy Born of Struggle Association and the Alain Locke Society.

CLEVIS HEADLEY is an associate professor of philosophy at Florida Atlantic University. He is a graduate in philosophy of the University of Miami (Ohio). He attended the 1992 Summer Seminar, National Endowment for the Humanities, and is currently working on "Post-Modernism and the Question of the Black Subject."

MARK HELBLING is associate professor of American studies at the University of Hawaii. He holds a Ph.D. in American studies from the University of Minnesota. He has also taught at Karimjee Secondary School, Tanga, Tanzania; the Faculté des Lettres, Tunis, Tunisia; the National University of Abidjan, Ivory Coast; and the Johann Wolfgang von Goethe Universität, Frankfurt. He is currently working on a study of Alain Locke and the concept of personality. His book, *The Harlem Renaissance: The One and the Many,* will be published in 1999.

RICHARD KEAVENY holds a master's degree in African American history from the University of Western Ontario, where he completed his thesis on the Harlem Renaissance and African American identity. He continues to work on issues of cultural identity.

VERNER D. MITCHELL is an associate professor of English at the U.S. Air Force Academy. He is a graduate of Rutgers University and is currently working on a study of Harlem Renaissance poet Helene Johnson.

CHARLES MOLESWORTH, professor of English at Queens College, New York, is the author of *Donald Barthelme's Fiction, Fierce Embrace, Gary Snyder's Vision,* and *Marianne Moore: A Literary Life.* He is currently working on a biography of Alain Locke and literary criticism.

GREG MOSES is assistant professor of philosophy at Marist College and author of *Revolution of Conscience: Martin Luther King Jr. and the Philosophy of Nonviolence.* He has published articles about Kingian approaches to the ethics of affirmative action and is editor of the Web-based *Texas Civil Rights Review.*

SALLY J. SCHOLZ received her Ph.D. in philosophy from Purdue University and is currently an assistant professor of philosophy at Villanova University. She has written articles on social philosophy and feminist theory and is currently working on a study of solidarity ethics.

RICHARD SHUSTERMAN is a professor of philosophy and chairman of the Department of Philosophy at Temple University; a member of the Graduate Faculty, New School for Social Research; and Directeur de programme at the Collège International de Philosophie, Paris. He is the author of *The Object of Literary Criticism; T. S. Eliot and the Philosophy of Criticism; Analytic Aesthetics; Pragmatic Aesthetics: Living Beauty, Rethinking Art;* and *Practicing Philosophy.* He is coeditor of *Sources for the Study of Philosophy in High School* and *The Interpretive Turn: Philosophy, Science, Culture.* He is especially noted for his work on popular culture and internationalism in art and philosophy.

BETH J. SINGER, professor emerita of Brooklyn College, is a graduate of Columbia University and author of *Rational Society, Ordinal Naturalism, and Operative Rights* and editor (with Tom Rockmore) of *Antifoundationalism Old and New.* She is one of the world's most noted pragmatists, a founding member of the Alain Locke Society, and a former student of Alain Locke at the University of Wisconsin, Madison.

EARL L. STEWART is a professor in the Department of Black Studies at the University of California at Santa Barbara. He is the author of works on music, aesthetics, and the Black experience.

KENNETH W. STIKKERS is chair and professor of philosophy at Southern Illinois University. He is editor of *Max Scheler, Problems of the Sociology of Knowledge.* He received his Ph.D. from DePaul University and has published in the areas of philosophy of economics, contemporary continental philosophy, and American philosophy. He is a board member of the Society for the Advancement of American Philosophy and the Alain Locke Society.

STEPHEN LESTER THOMPSON is an assistant professor of philosophy at Howard University. He took his Ph.D. in philosophy at the City University of New York Graduate Center in 1994. He is author of *Grammars and Negroes: Alain Locke on the Epistemology of Symbols* and *Pronoun Trouble: Peirce on Language and Logic.* He has been president of the Society for the Study of Africana Philosophy and is a charter member of the Alain Locke Philosophical Society.

RUDOLPH V. VANTERPOOL is professor and chair of the Department of Philosophy of California State University, Dominguez Hills. He is also a faculty associate in the department of Africana Studies. He earned his Ph.D. in philosophy from Southern Illinois University. His areas of expertise are ethics and philosophy of law, and his publications have centered generally on those thematic areas. His recent research has focused on the interrelated areas of aesthetics and African philosophy/philosophy in the African Diaspora.

PAUL WEITHMAN is an assistant professor of philosophy at Notre Dame University and a graudate of Harvard's Department of Philosophy. He is currently working on issues of religion and democratic theory.